CULTURE AND LIBERATION

THE AFRICA LIST

CULTURE AND LIBERATION
Exile Writings, 1966–1985

ALEX LA GUMA

EDITED AND INTRODUCED BY
CHRISTOPHER J. LEE

FOREWORD BY ALBIE SACHS
AFTERWORD BY BILL NASSON

LONDON NEW YORK CALCUTTA

THE AFRICA LIST
Series Editor: Rosalind C. Morris

Seagull Books, 2022

Culture and Liberation: *Exile Writings, 1966–1985*
by Alex La Guma

© Blanche La Guma, 2022

'Distant Writing: African Literature
and Its Cold War Itineraries' © Christopher J. Lee, 2022

Foreword © Albie Sachs, 2022

Afterword © Bill Nasson, 2022

ISBN 978 0 8574 2 789 2

British Library Cataloguing-in-Publication Data
A catalogue record for this book is available from the British Library.

Typeset by Seagull Books, Calcutta, India
Printed and bound in the USA by Integrated Books International

CONTENTS

Foreword by Albie Sachs
1

Acknowledgements
11

A Note on Editing and Selection
13

INTRODUCTION
Distant Writing: African Literature and
Its Cold War Itineraries
Christopher J. Lee
15

PART I
Political Worlds

CHAPTER ONE
Great Power Conspiracy: Review
55

CHAPTER TWO
The Time Has Come: New Forms of Struggle Face the South
African Coloured Community
58

CHAPTER THREE
The Time Has Come: S. A. Coloured People's Social and
Economic Deterioration
64

CHAPTER FOUR
The Time Has Come
69

CHAPTER FIVE
The Time Has Come: The Coloured People Must Prepare to Bear Arms for Liberation
75

CHAPTER SIX
The Coloured Cadets Bill
80

CHAPTER SEVEN
The Coloured People of South Africa
85

CHAPTER EIGHT
Pumpkins and Dark Skins
97

CHAPTER NINE
On the Coloured People
102

CHAPTER TEN
The Immorality Act: South Africa's Sex Law
106

CHAPTER ELEVEN
Dialogue 'A Gross Betrayal'
117

CHAPTER TWELVE
Apartheid and the Coloured People of South Africa
123

CHAPTER THIRTEEN
Vietnam: A People's Victory
165

CHAPTER FOURTEEN
Whither South Africa?
171

CHAPTER FIFTEEN
Apartheid Coloured Council Flounders
185

CHAPTER SIXTEEN
Africa and the USSR: A Friendly Handshake
192

CHAPTER SEVENTEEN
Apartheid Is Not Just a Regional Problem
199

CHAPTER EIGHTEEN
Caribbean Against Apartheid
202

CHAPTER NINETEEN
'This Is Our Vanguard, a Vanguard of Communists'
206

CHAPTER TWENTY
Caribbean—Nobody's Backyard
222

CHAPTER TWENTY-ONE
Israel and South Africa—Where the Vultures Perch
230

CHAPTER TWENTY-TWO
Message to the People and the Government of the Socialist Republic of Vietnam
235

CHAPTER TWENTY-THREE
Israel-South Africa: The Unholy Alliance
238

CHAPTER TWENTY-FOUR
Cuba and Africa
244

CHAPTER TWENTY-FIVE
Tribute to Indira Gandhi
252

PART II
Cultural Scenes and Arguments

CHAPTER ONE
The Third Afro-Asian Writers' Conference
255

CHAPTER TWO
Culture and Apartheid in South Africa
257

CHAPTER THREE
Culture and Revolution
266

CHAPTER FOUR
African Culture and National Liberation
270

CHAPTER FIVE
Paul Robeson and Africa
273

CHAPTER SIX
The Condition of Culture in South Africa
281

CHAPTER SEVEN
GDR Opera Supports Liberation Struggle
293

CHAPTER EIGHT
Culture and Liberation
295

CHAPTER NINE
Has Art Failed South Africa?
312

CHAPTER TEN
To Alternate Member of the Politbureau, CPSU CC,
First Secretary of the Communist Party of Uzbekistan,
Comrade Sharaf R. Rashidov
319

CHAPTER ELEVEN
Report of the Acting Secretary General
321

CHAPTER TWELVE
Final Speech, Secretary General of the
Afro-Asian Writers Association
333

CHAPTER THIRTEEN
'Walk Among the Multitudes'
336

CHAPTER FOURTEEN
To Yuri Andropov, General Secretary of the CPSU CC,
President of the USSR Supreme Soviet
341

CHAPTER FIFTEEN
Is There a South African National Culture?
343

PART III
Literary Criticism and the Writing Life

CHAPTER ONE
Literature and Life
353

CHAPTER TWO
Address by Lotus Award Winner
359

CHAPTER THREE
A Poet Is Born
364

CHAPTER FOUR
On Short Stories
368

CHAPTER FIVE
In Memory of Hutch: Alfred Hutchinson
372

CHAPTER SIX
Lust without Passion
374

CHAPTER SEVEN
Alexander Solzhenitsyn: 'Life through a Crooked Eye'
377

CHAPTER EIGHT
Hello or Goodbye, Athol Fugard?
389

CHAPTER NINE
Against Literary Apartheid
397

CHAPTER TEN
Sounds of a Cowhide Drum by Oswald Joseph Mtshali
408

CHAPTER ELEVEN
I Came Here to Sing: A Tribute to Pablo Neruda
419

CHAPTER TWELVE
South African Freedom Poetry
423

CHAPTER THIRTEEN
South African Writing under Apartheid
425

CHAPTER FOURTEEN
What I Learned from Maxim Gorky
440

PART IV
Five Stories and One Play

CHAPTER ONE
Come Back to Tashkent
451

CHAPTER TWO
The Man in the Tree
455

CHAPTER THREE
The Exile
469

CHAPTER FOUR
Late Edition
479

CHAPTER FIVE
Thang's Bicycle
489

CHAPTER SIX
Blankets
499

PART V
Interviews and Memoir

CHAPTER ONE
Alex La Guma, South African Author
Recently Settled in London: Interview with Robert Serumaga
509

CHAPTER TWO
A Home Away from Home
513

CHAPTER THREE
Why I Joined the Communist Party
517

CHAPTER FOUR
Answers to Our Questionnaire
523

CHAPTER FIVE
Why I Joined the Communist Party: Doing Something Useful
526

CHAPTER SIX
Two Letters from *Sechaba*
530

CHAPTER SEVEN
'My Books Have Gone Back Home'
534

CHAPTER EIGHT
Report of the Secretary General to the Seventh General
(Twenty-Fifth Anniversary) Conference, Tashkent, Uzbekistan,
September–October, 1983
540

Afterword by Bill Nasson
558

Bibliography
565

Index
574

Foreword

ALBIE SACHS

It was easy, perhaps too easy, to pigeonhole Alex La Guma. The problem was that he fitted comfortably into not one but two pigeonholes that usually were quite opposed: one was for the writer, slightly bohemian; the other for the political activist, loyalist to the core.

Alex, the writer, didn't dedicate his words to London publishers or a white audience. Nor for that matter was he writing for a black audience with a range of shared codes and points of experiential reference. He certainly wasn't writing for a South African publisher, as he was banned in the early 1960s by the then Minister of Justice, Balthazar Johannes Vorster, and it was a criminal offence for anyone in the country to possess literature produced by him. Literary agents were virtually unknown in South Africa, and publishers were interested in school books and books on travel or about animals. The biggest seller then was on how to get a driving licence. Alex was just writing about the world he knew for whoever was willing to read. Perhaps that's why now, over three decades after his death, his fiction is still so alive and gaining new readers.

Alex La Guma, the political activist, seemed to be a different person altogether. He and his wife, Blanche, worked in a deeply committed way for the banned Communist Party. He was part of the core clandestine leadership in Cape Town that struggled for the overthrow of apartheid. Blanche was a midwife who worked in the most impoverished areas of the city, driving her little car through the puddles to deliver babies in shacks in Windermere and other windswept and waterlogged neighbourhoods across the Cape Flats. The joke was that she didn't just deliver babies—she also delivered pamphlets.

Alex, the writer, was quirky, ambiguous, lyrical, delving into the intimacy of the soul. Alex, the political activist, was sombre, straight down the line, rigorous, disciplined in word and deed. And only occasionally did there seem to be an overlap of these two personae. When he was one of the 156 people placed on trial for treason after the Freedom Charter had been adopted at Kliptown in 1955, he sent hilarious weekly reports—from the dock, as one of the accused—to the left-wing newspaper *New Age*.

He also produced a cartoon column about the adventures of 'Liberation Chabalala' under the title *Little Libby*. Little Libby, an audacious young teenager from a poor township family, was always in trouble with the police, but invariably found ingenious ways to wriggle out of their clutches. Everyday politics were conveyed in a sardonic and irreverent manner. *Liberation Chabalala: The World of Alex La Guma* (1992), a collection of his writings before the appearance of his powerful first novel *A Walk in the Night* (1962), sketches a rich portrait of Cape Town life and politics as the repressive Sixties arrived. Edited by André Odendaal and Roger Field, it appeared in the Mayibuye History and Literature Series of the 1990s.

Alex's irreverence followed through even into the underground meetings where he and other comrades and I would get together to continue the resistance. In the first place, our 'underground' meeting spot was not in the traditional dingy basement but above ground, up on the mountainside. We would meet secretly in Newlands Forest, on the slopes of Table Mountain, mainly on Sunday mornings. Our comrade Fred Carneson would say as we sheltered under a big oak tree, sometimes with the rain falling down: 'Welcome to the boardroom.'

I was amused to discover that three of us in the Communist Party had something unusual in common—our fathers had all been expelled from the Party. Sidney, the father of Brian Bunting, and Solly, my dad, for right-wing deviationism, and Jimmy La Guma for deviationism of the left-wing kind. Thankfully, under the leadership of Moses Kotane, for whom my mother, Ray Sachs, had worked as a typist, the Party had become far less sectarian, with the focus on destroying apartheid rather than each other.

One by one our numbers were reduced as repression intensified, and one by one individuals left Cape Town to take up the struggle from abroad. The first to go were Chris Hani and Archie Sibeko, who faced prison sentences. We hid them in a student's cottage before enabling them to get to Johannesburg and then across the border. Reggie September was called away to do special work in Swaziland. Brian Bunting left to carry on editorial functions from London. Ray Alexander—who, despite being banned, had continued to give covert leadership to the Food and Canning Workers' Union—went with her husband, Professor Jack Simons, to Lusaka. 'Achmat' Osman was held for long weeks in solitary confinement. I was to find myself in a cell with his name scratched on the wall when I, too, was detained. Two years later, I was to be held for several months before going into exile in London. During this period, Fred Carneson had been captured, made to stand on bricks for five days and eventually sent to Pretoria Central Prison for five years.

Meanwhile, Alex had been placed under house arrest, restricted to their small home in Athlone for five years. It was there in fact that Alex the writer and Alex the activist became fully fused. The only way he could survive was through writing. It was there that he produced what I regard as his masterpiece, *The Stone Country* (1967), set in the Roeland Street Prison where, on different occasions, both he and I had been locked up in solitary confinement.

But what made the book so interesting was that the hero who had been locked up for his political activity was not at the centre of the action. Rather, he was an observer of the teeming and intense activity of his fellow prisoners drawn from what we then called the 'lumpen proletariat'. This was a double decentering. First, the gaze of the readers was deflected from the heroic figure of the activist. It was disturbing to be confronted by savage killers who would stealthily stab fellow inmates with specially sharpened wire while in other instances expressing extreme compassion and intense humanity. His second literary disruption was to give voice and personality to working-class people in the Coloured and African community. He was breaking a literary silence. His prose was the complete Other of Alan Paton's *Cry, the Beloved Country* (1948), which was written in biblical-style prose, presenting black–white relationships in tragic terms. Alex's writing was richly idiosyncratic and accented, using words as they were actually spoken on the street, in the gambling den or in the prison cell.

Alex and Blanche took life as it came. Defined as 'Coloured persons' under the Population Registration Act of 1950, they were compelled under the Group Areas Act to live in a racial ghetto on the Cape Flats. Then, in terms of a banning order under the Suppression of Communism Act, Alex was further confined for 24 hours a day within the small perimeter of their working-class home. Yet their destiny was to travel across all continents to the furthest corners of the world. They went into exile in the mid-1960s and based themselves in London where they lived as part of a large but dispersed South African exile community.

Alex was to become a prominent figure in the Afro-Asian writers' movement. The year after he went into exile in 1966, he attended the Third Afro-Asian Writers Conference in Beirut as part of a delegation that also included anti-apartheid activist and scholar Ruth First and poet Mazisi Kunene. This started his involvement with the Afro-Asian Writers Association that was based in Cairo and received major support from writers in India and the Asian republics of the Soviet Union. Having been presented in 1969 with the Association's distinguished Lotus Award, which he received at a ceremony hosted by Indira Gandhi in New Delhi in 1970, Alex later attended its Fifth Congress in Alma-Ata (Kazakhstan) and went on to become its secretary general in 1979.

This was the time of the Cold War. People from what came to be known as the 'Third World' were expressing themselves with a new voice that was overtly anti-imperialist and anti-colonialist. Alex was sent to be the African National Congress (ANC) representative in Cuba where he connected with the 'Tricontinental' movement, which brought revolutionary Latin America into the equation. Cuba regarded itself as part of the socialist camp, but had its own distinctive dynamic. It was in Havana that I was to see him for the last time.

It was fun to be with him and Blanche. They combined a deep, spontaneous loyalty to the Cuban Revolution with a strong sense of irreverence in relation to the contradictory elements of daily life. In appearance and manner, they easily passed as Cubans. Yet Blanche was truly indignant when, mistaken for a Cuban, she was refused admission to some important social event and then only allowed in with effusive apologies when the gatekeepers discovered she was the spouse of a diplomat. Her anger wasn't that she had been blocked from going in, but that she had been let in because of a privilege ordinary Cubans couldn't enjoy.

* * *

This collection contributes some vital insights for contemporary debates on decolonization in South Africa and beyond. To the extent that writing in and about Africa had been dominated by writers and publishers working within a strong white and Western cultural matrix, the lived experience of black people had not been given the opportunity to appear on the page. In particular, the experience of the poor and dispossessed had either been completely ignored or else represented by writers from a totally different milieu.

It is worthwhile bearing in mind that the articles and essays published here were not written primarily for literary or academic journals; they appeared to a large extent in struggle publications, which were read mainly by political activists. *Sechaba,* the journal of the ANC, was produced in London and published in East Germany. Along with *The African Communist*, a serious political and sociocultural journal in which contentious issues were debated at the height of the struggle, it was circulated clandestinely in South Africa. I'm sure that a third of the copies of each would have been bought by the CIA or similar institutions. Alex wrote under his own name for *Sechaba* and under his pseudonym, Gala, for *The African Communist.* The content of these publications was primarily political, with some attention given to culture and literature. *Lotus* was different. Published out of Cairo and Beirut by the Afro-Asian Writers Association from the late 1960s until the early 1990s, this trilingual periodical in English, French and Arabic was primarily literary with an infusion of politics. Its contributors were mutually concerned with articulating a vision of a world free of imperialism and creating an artistic solidarity born out of their shared histories of fighting colonialism.

Alex was in constant robust dialogue with fellow African writers like Es'kia Mphahlele and Ngũgĩ wa Thiong'o. There was no dispute about the urgency of resisting the colonial stranglehold on the production, circulation and reception of literary works, both domestically and internationally. But philosophically Alex bore closer affinity to Mphahlele, who rejected the idea of a distinct African literary canon arising out of 'Negritude' as a definitive ideological position. Alex wanted South African writers to do what great writers had been doing in other countries across history—to enrich world literature with a challenging and emancipatory voice rooted in and reflecting the timbre of the specific conditions of the world as they experienced them.

Today the notion of universalism has come under attack for different reasons from both left- and the right-wing critics. When I speak of universalism, I distinguish it from globalization. Globalization is something hegemonic that starts at a centre and spreads its control to engulf the whole world. In doing so, it paradoxically produces global opposition to itself and its reach. Universalism, on the other hand, does not spread from one centre; it picks up on the commonalities in diverse human experiences throughout the world, whether of oppression, resistance or achievement, and distils and transmits these shared experiences across time and place.

I remember being told in Mozambique that socialism wasn't a tree in one part of the world from which you took seeds to plant somewhere else. It was a single tree fed by roots of struggle in all parts of the world, producing a multiplicity of flowers and fruits. It would be the same with literature. The universal tree of literature should be nourished by roots that lay deep in the sufferings, struggles and aspirations of many people.

Alex wrote a particularly interesting piece in response to Nadine Gordimer's investigation of modern African fiction in English. His position is conveyed in the title 'Against Literary Apartheid'. Writing under the pseudonym Gala, he challenges the very concept of African literature as a special category that was somehow different and apart from world literature. Nadine's position was that new African voices were emerging, writing about African experiences with a distinctive thematic and style of their own. While welcoming the thoughts of a writer who is 'at least permanently on the scene', Alex points out that Gordimer herself is an African writer and should not separate herself out in the way she does. He takes issue with Gordimer's reading of modern African writing as having emerged out of the 'Negritude' movement, which 'came across seas and language barriers' arising out of the Caribbean's search for its lost African identity. He rejects this notion of contemporary African writing having been transplanted from afar as if 'divorced from old or traditional literature'. Instead, he argues that the shift to 'modern' literature was more culturally endemic—an intrinsic response to 'the development of Africa itself from old to new' and a reaction to the emergence of new social, economic and social structures at the beginning of the twentieth century. He rejects Gordimer's comparative analysis of the central themes and content of the European novel with those of the new African literature as somewhat 'superficial' and 'cursory', arguing for a deeper analysis of the 'epicentre of events' in relation to which each writer has determined his/her place and voice. Instead of focusing on difference, divergence and exceptionalism, as Gordimer does, Alex argues for an analysis that foregrounds commonality across 'all examples of good literature', irrespective of language, country or 'the level of development of the society in which they originate'. Otherwise, he says, we would have to accept a sort of 'separate development' or apartheid of literature.

Alex prefers to see writers in Africa as being an indivisible part of a wider universal literary movement seeking to observe and understand the events and ideological conditions of life as they experience it. 'While the creative work is an individual act, the sum total of these acts is the artistic chronicle,' he writes, 'We are witnessing how the cultural heritage of Africa is transformed into the modern, socially and politically oriented literatures and arts. This is one of the most important tasks of the cultural revolution and a stirring event in modern and progressive world culture.'

To Alex, modernity was directly linked to the political. Alex was a revolutionary and an internationalist. I do not know the extent of his engagement with Frantz Fanon, who died in 1961, though at the time was an emerging revolutionary figure in the Francophone literary and political worlds. Fanon's eyes, too, were focused on transforming the present and the future rather than reclaiming a forgotten African past presented in idyllic, communal terms without class formation and struggle. As Fanon wrote: 'I do not want to sing the past to the detriment of my present and my future.'

The universalism of experience is brought out in a beautiful essay by Alex on the impact that reading Maxim Gorky had on him as a young boy. He describes how he would use his ten cents pocket money each week to buy novels, which he would then summarize to spellbound schoolmates, telling the stories of the heroes in Robert Louis Stevenson or Alexander Dumas. And then one day he found a story by Gorky, which changed his literary imagination entirely. Writing about life in Russia before the 1917 revolution, Gorky gave prominence to child beggars in St Petersburg tugging at the sleeves of his central figure. Alex realized that there were child beggars in Cape Town who pleaded with him for money. The revelation was not that they existed, but that they, too, could feature in books. Gorky's books did not have the happy sentimental ending of *Oliver Twist*. The grittiness, the harshness of life for the downtrodden, remained unrelieved. What Alex found in Gorky was a passion for resistance and change, which came through powerfully in his own writing.

Even though Alex established himself as a highly regarded writer in Africa, Asia and Latin America, his writings were banned and virtually unknown within South Africa until the late 1980s. Because the literary force of his fiction centred largely on his vivid descriptions of characters locked into the peculiarities of place, his work could easily be received simply as a chronicle of the oppressive and abject conditions of life under apartheid. Without a doubt, his fiction did give vivid idiomatic voice to the downtrodden, the dispossessed and the outcasts who populated the streets, prisons, factories and shebeens of polyglot Cape Town. But the lyrical poignancy of his stories transcends the milieu from which they sprang.

This book helps us to reframe and further understand Alex's voice. He travelled the world, and his imagination and pen travelled with him, absorbing the simultaneously familiar and otherworldly landscapes of Beirut, Algiers, Cairo, Havana, New Delhi, Moscow and Tashkent. Christopher Lee has seized the moment in assembling this collection of Alex's exile writing, giving contemporary readers rare access to the universal political vision that informed the gritty contradictions of his fiction. Redolent with the passions of the political, cultural and literary struggles of those decades, this collection ensures that the voice of this pioneering South African writer will take its rightful place in current debates over decolonization and readings of emancipatory literature.

Acknowledgements

Culture and Liberation is a sequel to a preceding project that resulted in the publication of a critical annotated edition of Alex La Guma's travel memoir *A Soviet Journey* (2017[1978]). Many who helped with that project also contributed to this one. For this book, I would like to thank in particular Louise Bethlehem, Isabel Hofmeyr, Constantin Katsakioris, Sarah Duff, Tiferet Bassel, Gül Han, Uhuru Phalafala, Susan Pennybacker, Ian Morse, André Odendaal, Jerry Buttrey, Lindsay Ceballos and Jennifer Furlong for their help and support. Versions of the introduction were delivered at New York University, Bayreuth University, the University of the Witwatersrand, the Wolf Humanities Center at the University of Pennsylvania, Penn State University, the 2017 meeting of the Modernist Studies Association in Amsterdam, and the 2018 American Comparative Literature Association Annual Meeting at UCLA. I want to thank the organizers and participants at these events, especially Magalí Armillas-Tiseyra, Neilesh Bose, Eleni Coundouriotis, Rossen Djagalov, James English, Huda Fakhreddine, Hala Halim, Stefan Helgesson, Rosemary Jolly, Laurie Lambert, Sierra Lomuto, Projit Mukharji, Kathy Peiss, Brian Russell Roberts, Mark Sanders, Fatemeh Shams, Edgar Taylor, Salamishah Tillet, Jini Kim Watson, Colin Williamson, Emily Wilson and Duncan Yoon. Anne Garland Mahler provided crucial help with the journal *Tricontinental*. Monica Popescu, Peter Kalliney, Andrew van der Vlies, and Dorian Bell provided excellent feedback on drafts of the introduction.

Library and archival staff at Lafayette College, Harvard University, the Schomburg Center of the New York Public Library, the Nettie Lee Benson Latin American Collection at the University of Texas at Austin, and the Mayibuye Centre at the University of the Western Cape provided indispensable assistance in finding and securing documents. This project has been supported by funding from Lafayette College, a Mercator fellowship from the German Research Foundation, two fellowships at the Bayreuth Academy of Advanced African Studies, and the Department of Higher Education of the South African government. A regional faculty fellowship at the Wolf Humanities Center at the University of Pennsylvania sustained a late stage of writing and editing, as did a residential fellowship at the Stellenbosch Institute for Advanced Study. I completed this book while a resident fellow at the Munich Centre for Global History, Ludwig Maximilian University.

My greatest debts are to those involved in the production of this book. I owe much to Rosalind Morris, Bishan Samaddar and Naveen Kishore for taking on this project as part of the Africa List at Seagull Books—a beautiful and prestigious series. Sayoni Ghosh provided excellent editorial assistance. Albie Sachs and Bill Nasson responded to my queries with enthusiasm and contributed insights into Alex La Guma's *oeuvre* as only they could. J. M. Coetzee, Zoë Wicomb and Mandla Langa have been equally generous with their endorsements. It has been a rare privilege to work with them all. Finally, this book would not have been possible without the support of Blanche La Guma. More than anyone, she sustained Alex's writing while he was alive by taking on work to maintain their family financially and raise their sons when he was away. She has continued to promote his work since his passing, and I hope this book is read against this personal backdrop. This collection of essays, stories and other pieces reflects not solely an individual life in exile but also a family, a marriage and a partnership that was mutually committed to a future democratic South Africa.

A Note on Editing and Selection

This volume consists of previously uncollected writing by Alex La Guma published between 1966 and 1985 while he was in exile. Three exceptions are 'Paul Robeson and Africa' (1971), 'Culture and Liberation' (1976) and 'Has Art Failed South Africa?' (1977), all of which appeared in *Memories of Home: The Writings of Alex La Guma* (1991) edited by Cecil Abrahams. I have included them in this collection due to their importance. Otherwise I have not included pieces that have appeared in preceding books. Reprints of his work published before 1966 have also not been included, with the exception of the short story 'Blankets' which first appeared in *Black Orpheus* (1964) and was later reprinted in *A Walk in the Night and Other Stories* (1968). It was republished once more in *Lotus: Afro-Asian Writings* in 1978, and I have decided to include it here to give an example of how La Guma at times repurposed and recirculated his past work for new audiences.

I have made small corrections of spelling, grammar and formatting when necessary given the likelihood that La Guma may not have had the opportunity to copy-edit his work. Furthermore, I have conformed his writing to the style of Seagull Books. I have kept annotations to a minimum, due to the length of this book and its intention to reach a popular audience. All notes and citations are from the original texts unless otherwise mentioned. I have also tried to provide as much information as possible regarding months and years of publication, though this information has not always been complete, either due to the formatting style of periodicals or limited information from archives at the time of research.

Finally, given the wide range of international journals and periodicals in which La Guma published, this book does not claim to be comprehensive, accounting for all his uncollected work. Translations into Russian, German, Spanish and other languages also raise the possibility of new work to be discovered—material for a later project. For the sake of reference to assist other scholars, I have included in the bibliography a brief list of publications in Spanish from the Cuban journal *Tricontinental*, which appear to be original and not translations of his work published elsewhere.

Blanche La Guma, the executor of Alex La Guma's estate, has granted permission for the republication of these writings. The title of this book draws from the title of La Guma's 1976 essay cited previously. I believe it captures the theme of this book—and his life—as a whole.

INTRODUCTION

Distant Writing

African Literature and Its Cold War Itineraries

CHRISTOPHER J. LEE

What does it mean to edit the work of the dead? What ethical considerations must be undertaken when collecting, revising and republishing the writing of those who have passed away and are unable to oversee and finish such tasks themselves? Similarly, how does the intimate labour of transcribing and editing the voice of someone else impact the editor? What lessons, emotions and consciousness are imparted through restoring the words of someone else? In sum, to what literary, historical and interpersonal ends should writing from the past be reinstated for the present? What audience remains? What afterlife is possible?

These questions capture the parameters, dilemmas and opportunities that reside at the centre of *Culture and Liberation*. The exile writings of Alex La Guma (1925–1985) present an occasion not only for revisiting the author and activist himself but also for addressing matters of life and death within the context of literature, confronting the role of the political past in the political present and re-examining patterns of experience that defined South African life and letters during the twentieth century. These artistic, political and historical contexts encompassed La Guma's career. And yet for reasons of political contingency, geographic location and personal identity, La Guma was not always a part of these worlds either. In different ways, he retained the qualities of an outsider—at times by choice, at times by force. His political departure from South Africa in 1966, which ended with his premature death in Havana, Cuba, at the age of sixty, had the effect of exiling him from both the country of his birth and post-apartheid discussions of South African literature. His orthodox Marxism, based on his membership in the South African Communist Party (SACP), has further contributed to the gradual marginalization of his *oeuvre*—a reflection of the sidelining of socialist politics in South Africa more generally since the end of apartheid in 1994. Finally, his 'Coloured' identity—being of racially 'mixed' origins—has also often provincialized his writing to Cape Town and its vicinity, his work seen as neither representative of South Africa's black majority and its future concerns nor expressive of the country's white minority and its existential anxieties. Like other South African writers, he faced the challenge of depicting the nation as a whole.

Culture and Liberation resists these perceptions. For those already familiar with his writing, it aims to broaden existing understandings of his work and its intentions. But for those who know him only by name or not at all, this book seeks to re-establish La Guma within South African literature, as well as South Africa's political and intellectual history. It intends, simply, to bring him home. In doing so, this collection confronts current working assumptions and definitions of these fields—specifically, the role that exile during the apartheid period had in shaping South Africa's literary, political and intellectual life. This experience that La Guma shared with many during the anti-apartheid struggle is unexceptional—thousands went abroad either temporarily or permanently—yet it remains incompletely examined. Scholarship by Stephen Ellis, Hugh Macmillan and Thula Simpson, for example, has focused primarily on party organization, diplomatic efforts and life among lower-level recruits within the Frontline States and elsewhere.¹ Though committed to this broader effort, La Guma's writing casts a different light on the complexity of this condition for individuals—the constant vulnerabilities of being a political émigré, the strength derived from common cause with other activists, and the day-to-day intellectual labour involved in building a transnational movement. Exile was a time of both political uncertainty and personal freedom, a liminal status of being forced to become an outsider while still retaining the commitments of an insider. It is a situation of tension and paradox that could suppress the imagination but also unleash new forms of creativity. As Edward Said has written, exile is both a terrible fate and an ideal vantage point for the intellectual.² The pieces in this book—published between 1966, when he, his wife Blanche, and his two sons, Eugene and Bartholomew (Barto), left Cape Town for exile in London, and 1985 when he died of a heart attack while serving as the diplomatic representative for the African National Congress (ANC) in Havana—provide a unique window onto these themes and the international dimensions of South Africa's liberation struggle. They offer a direct perspective on the condition of exile.

Culture and Liberation is the second book by La Guma I have edited, the first being his political travelogue, *A Soviet Journey* (2017[1978]), originally released by Progress Publishers in Moscow. Republished a century after the Bolshevik Revolution, *A Soviet Journey* is significant for being the longest account of the USSR by an African writer.³ It is a reminder of the deep history of communist

---

1 Stephen Ellis, *External Mission: The ANC in Exile, 1960–1990* (New York: Oxford University press, 2013); Hugh Macmillan, *The Lusaka Years: The ANC in Exile in Zambia, 1963–1994* (Johannesburg: Jacana, 2013); Thula Simpson, *Umkhonto we Sizwe: The ANC's Armed Struggle* (Johannesburg: Penguin Random House South Africa, 2016).

2 Edward W. Said, *Representations of the Intellectual* (New York: Vintage, 1996).

3 A technical exception to this claim is an account by the controversial and widely discredited white South African writer Laurens van der Post. See Laurens van der Post, *Journey into Russia* (London: Hogarth, 1964).

politics in South Africa and the longstanding connections between both countries during the twentieth century. This new collection shares a similar set of intentions as its predecessor by restoring an oft-neglected dimension of La Guma's writing life: his non-fiction. But, in doing so, this book also illuminates a wider transnational landscape of an incipient Third World, which shaped his career as it did South African politics. Both volumes should be read in dialogue with each other. Over the course of two decades, La Guma wrote a number of literary essays, book reviews, travel pieces, conference reports, political tracts, letters to the editor and occasional short stories—what might be called the written ephemera of exile—for such venues as *Sechaba*, *The African Communist*, *Lotus: Afro-Asian Writings*, *Tricontinental*, *Présence Africaine* and *Moscow News*. The ANC, the SACP, the Afro-Asian Writers Association and other organizations, state and non-state, published these journals.[4] Based around the world, they fostered audiences in Cairo, London, Paris, Moscow, Havana and elsewhere, constituting a counter-public—and now counter-archive—against Western neocolonialism and its various activities. These periodicals contributed to wide-ranging print cultures during the Cold War that sustained political dissidents and exiled writers like La Guma and, in the process, reinvented what African literature and world literature could be.[5]

Yet, despite this geographic reach, the assorted essays, reviews and stories collected here—almost all of which are being published in book form for the first time—have largely been neglected, rendered

---

4 It should be noted that the 'Afro-Asian Writers Association' is sometimes spelled with an apostrophe, i.e. 'Afro-Asian Writers' Association'.

5 On print cultures and South African literature, see Archie L. Dick, *The Hidden History of South Africa's Book and Reading Cultures* (Toronto: University of Toronto Press, 2012); Andrew van der Vlies (ed.), *Print, Text and Book Cultures in South Africa* (Johannesburg: Wits University Press, 2012). On print cultures in Africa and beyond, see Eric Bulson, *Little Magazine, World Form* (New York: Columbia University Press, 2016); Peter Kalliney, 'Modernism, African Literature, and the Cold War', *Modern Language Quarterly* 76(3) (2015): 333–68.

invisible with the passage of time. Indeed, these writings complement La Guma's often forgotten edited volume, *Apartheid: A Collection of Writings on South African Racism by South Africans* (1971), as well as two important posthumous collections—a volume of writings and interviews edited by Cecil Abrahams, entitled *Memories of Home* (1991), and his early pre-exile journalism gathered by Roger Field and André Odendaal in *Liberation Chabalala: The World of Alex La Guma* (1993).[6] These books underscore the vital role of non-fiction throughout La Guma's career. With his highest level of formal education being secondary school, La Guma cut his literary teeth by writing for leftist newspapers, particularly *New Age* (Cape Town) and *Fighting Talk* (Johannesburg).[7] These formative efforts in journalism proved essential to his later fictional depictions of social and political life in Cape Town through such celebrated works as *A Walk in the Night* (1962), *And a Threefold Cord* (1964), *The Stone Country* (1967) and *In the Fog of the Seasons' End* (1972)—the first, third and fourth being canonized through their inclusion in the prestigious African Writers Series edited by Chinua Achebe.[8] During his lifetime, La Guma received a number of awards, including the Lotus Prize for Literature and the Soviet Order of Friendship of Peoples, and he was named a French *Chevalier des Arts et des Lettres*. He posthumously received

---

6 Cecil Abrahams (ed.), *Memories of Home: The Writings of Alex La Guma* (Trenton, NJ: Africa World Press, 1991); Alex La Guma (ed.), *Apartheid: A Collection of Writings on South African Racism by South Africans* (New York: International Publishers, 1971); Roger Field and André Odendaal (eds), *Liberation Chabalala: The World of Alex La Guma* (Bellville, South Africa: Mayibuye Books, 1993).

7 La Guma participated in art classes at the Cape Technical College, but did not complete a degree course.

8 A complete list of his fictional works includes: *And a Threefold Cord* (Berlin: Seven Seas Publishers, 1964); *A Walk in the Night and Other Stories* (London: Heinemann, 1967[1962]); *The Stone Country* (London: Heinemann, 1967); *In the Fog of the Seasons' End* (London: Heinemann, 1972); Alex La Guma, *Time of the Butcherbird* (London: Heinemann, 1979).

the Order of Ikhamanga in Gold from the South African government in 2003, nearly twenty years after his death.[9]

Against this backdrop of acclaim, non-fiction has been an underappreciated, though indispensable, aspect of La Guma's writing life. It provided a first draft for his fiction. As Es'kia Mphahlele, a fellow writer and friend, has written, journalism tests the balance between 'writing as self-expression and writing as objective reporting of the social scene'.[10] La Guma's non-fiction consequently stands on its own, lending an immediate impression of his politics, artistic concerns and personal life. La Guma can be understood as an organic intellectual in Antonio Gramsci's sense, having grown up in the working-class neighbourhood of District Six in Cape Town during the Great Depression and experiencing his intellectual development through factory work, trade union organizing and politically minded parents, especially his father James (Jimmy) La Guma, who was an important figure within the Communist Party of South Africa (CPSA), the original iteration of the party founded in 1921 before it became the SACP in 1953. La Guma's best-known books and stories—especially his first, *A Walk in the Night*, which firmly established District Six within South African literature—drew from this personal background. They also spoke to the immediacy of the political moment. An activist since joining the Young Communist League in 1947, La Guma published *A Walk in the Night* in 1962 during an intense period after the Treason Trial (1956–1961), in which he was one of the 156 accused, and the Sharpeville Massacre (1960), which resulted in the banning of the ANC, the Pan Africanist Congress and other organizations. His second book, *And a Threefold Cord*, which depicted the plight of shack dwellers on the Cape Flats, was published two years later. He also wrote much of his third book, *The Stone Country*, about prison

---

9 For an authoritative biography, see Roger Field, *Alex La Guma: A Literary and Political Biography* (London: James Currey, 2010).
10 Es'kia Mphahlele, *Afrika My Music: An Autobiography, 1957–1983* (Cape Town: Kwela Books, 2013[1984]), 19.

life under the apartheid regime, during this same period, which were to be his final years in South Africa.

La Guma achieved this high level of productivity despite experiences of political detention, solitary confinement and house arrest—disruptive episodes of police brutality he would include in his writing. The initial publication of *A Walk in the Night* in Nigeria and *And a Threefold Cord* in East Berlin resulted from circumstances of state surveillance and censorship. But this situation fortuitously internationalized his work early on: his first readers were not exclusively South African, but cosmopolitan Africans and Europeans alike. His last two novels, *In the Fog of the Seasons' End* and *Time of the Butcherbird* (1979), written and published in exile, built upon this initial legacy by continuing to focus on the South African condition while also more self-consciously addressing a global readership. Like many African writers of his generation and after, La Guma came to depend on this bifocal orientation for the success of his work—a duality that exile only reinforced.

Yet the condition of exile imposed an aesthetic choice. His ambition of pursuing a socialist realism in the vein of Maxim Gorky, a key source of inspiration as cited in several pieces in this collection, was atrophied by circumstances of distance. This conjoined spatial and artistic predicament restricted his creative ability —only two of his five works of fiction were written overseas—but it also encouraged him to reinvent himself, to sustain his political and aesthetic commitments by turning to other subject matter, new genres and literary experimentation, the results of which can be found in this book. As in his early career, non-fiction provided a crucial outlet for him to report on news developments, to test ideas, to publicize the anti-apartheid struggle and to expand his craft of writing more generally. *Culture and Liberation* tells this story about La Guma's career, one different from that found in his fiction. This collection documents, however imperfectly, his life outside of South Africa and his contributions to an emergent postcolonial world literature through a dissident aesthetics, a poetics of exile.

Distant Writing and the Exilic Imagination

Akin to La Guma's recognized fiction, the pieces in *Culture and Liberation* are frequently informed by the intensity of first-hand observation and a political worldview committed to the South African struggle. They possess these qualities despite encompassing a global geography ranging from North Vietnam, to Kazakhstan, Algeria and Cuba, among many locales. La Guma was a Third World internationalist in the most direct sense of the expression, through travels and residences in places such as Addis Ababa, Algiers, Beirut, Cairo, Dar es Salaam, East Berlin, Hanoi, Kingston, Luanda, Maputo, Moscow, New Delhi and Tashkent, in addition to his home of Cape Town and his long stay in London from 1966 to 1978. His final years in revolutionary Cuba—a destination and refuge for many activists, like Huey Newton, Eldridge Cleaver, Angela Davis and Stokely Carmichael (Kwame Ture)—secured these credentials. Indeed, in addition to the Castro government's unwavering support for the anti-apartheid cause, Havana's racial diversity and political outlook bookended La Guma's beginnings in Cape Town. In these opportune ways, his career demonstrates the vital role that individuals, emerging from radical politics and serving as diplomatic intermediaries for political organizations, had in generating the Third World. La Guma did not view the South African struggle in isolation but as part of a broader pattern of activism that pursued decolonization and fought against racial and economic injustice wherever it existed. His writings remain relevant to present-day discussions of these issues for this basic reason.

Exile, of course, is one of the classic themes of world literature. Within African letters it has had the unusual, propitious effect of both restricting many writers from their countries of birth while also enabling successful international careers. La Guma is no exception. Nonetheless, a complex set of tensions emerges in his work between senses of proximity and unfamiliarity, contiguity and detachment, authority and inexpertise—all of which characterize what might be called *distant writing*. In contrast to his earlier work, much of La Guma's exile writing was generated through a view from afar. The concept of distant writing captures this surface problem of geographic estrangement, but it also raises questions about how this predicament of space and alienation informs the engagement of the writer, the affective dimensions of the work produced, and the knowledge imparted—an aesthetic of exile. Such consideration is not reducible to a formula that distance prompts abstraction—a departure from realism. Rather, as La Guma demonstrates, writing can be about seeking political solidarity, collapsing geographic distance and transcending cultural difference as a response to dislocation and exile. Distant writing can exhibit forms of radical empathy—an ethic of identification with social and political conditions beyond one's immediate community—with the resulting literature constituting a third space between 'home' and 'exile'.[11] This politics of recognition, as witnessed in La Guma's writing, frequently occurred by ideological predisposition, but also practical necessity—the result of a complex interplay between inexperience and pre-existing knowledge that inhabited foreignness. This interplay rests at the heart of creativity more generally.

The concept of distant writing can be further situated through several antecedents that meditate on the uses of 'distance'. Mikhail Bakhtin proposed that one fundamental difference between the novel and the epic as genres depended on a distinction of time—an 'epic distance'—with the novel attentive to the contemporary and the epic preoccupied with a past world of unreachable heroes.[12] This temporal 'distance', which related to his idea of the chronotope,

---

[11] Christopher J. Lee, *Frantz Fanon: Toward a Revolutionary Humanism* (Athens, OH: Ohio University Press, 2015), pp. 193–5. See also Lynn Hunt, *Inventing Human Rights: A History* (New York: W. W. Norton, 2007), pp. 28–33.

[12] Mikhail M. Bakhtin, *The Dialogic Imagination* (Michael Holquist ed., trans., Caryl Emerson and Michael Holquist trans) (Austin: University of Texas Press, 1981), p. 14.

pertains to exile with its reciprocal elements of nostalgia, anxiety and uncertain futures. Exile is not solely about space—it is also about time. Bertolt Brecht's theatrical approach of defamiliarization, often referred to as an alienation effect (*Verfremdungseffekt*), illustrates a second example of distance, in this case as a tool for dispelling the illusions of art and heightening an audience's political consciousness. Exile can produce similar effects by making the foreign familiar, but also the familiar foreign to sharp effect, startling the reader. Finally, Franco Moretti, the closest influence to this provisional concept, has more recently urged the adoption of 'distant reading'—a method that reverses the routine technique of 'close reading' to demand that literary production be regarded from further remove, allowing for the materialism of literature to be situated and grasped within broader sociopolitical trends of a world system.[13] 'Distant writing' is an author-focused analogue to Moretti's perspective of the critic. By foregrounding authorial position and intention, this proposed approach can open a space for differentiating a writer's work based on the immediacy of first-hand experience versus work produced as an effect of systemic conditions of global power—the Cold War in the case of La Guma. In sum, while distant writing may suffer from difficult circumstances of exile, it can also retain the potential for penetrating criticism, measured nostalgia, recasting the familiar and mapping universal themes, among other merits, that proximity may not inspire. Distant writing is therefore not about location alone—actual distance—but the qualities of writing incurred, consciously or unconsciously, through separation, progressive disconnection and, at times, permanent remove.

This intersectional approach incorporating time, defamiliarization and the global condition presents one makeshift means for thinking through La Guma's eclectic *oeuvre* in *Culture and Liberation*. It is designed to deconstruct 'exile writing' into several

---

13 Franco Moretti, *Distant Reading* (London: Verso, 2013), p. 48.

component parts and, in doing so, revitalize its possibilities. La Guma's work in exile not only underscores how he shifted focus, but, by extension, also the ways in which African literature was re-invented during the Cold War period. The emergence of the African novel—the paradigmatic genre of the postcolonial period—was attended by smaller genres that went beyond the confines of the nation state. An anti-hierarchical view that accounts for and critically engages with these alternative literary forms is needed. Indeed, the notion of distant writing helps explain the neglect of La Guma's work in exile—why the assorted pieces collected here have remained largely absent from popular discussions of his writing, despite their commitment to broader themes of the human condition. They risk irrelevance through less familiar modes and content. Utilized contrapuntally, however, they productively expand the concerns of his South African fiction through new themes, genres and geographies.[14]

Distant writing thus revisits the issue of absence and the labour of exile. As discussed earlier, absence is an important keyword and recurring sentiment when thinking about Alex La Guma. His books were banned in South Africa during his lifetime.[15] Much of the world that he wrote about—whether the District Six neighbourhood of his childhood or an emergent Third World during the exile years of his adulthood—has vanished. The anti-apartheid struggle itself is over, and many of the values it espoused and that he was stridently committed to—namely, economic justice in concert with political justice—have been marginalized, if not completely abandoned. The Soviet Union, which he visited frequently starting in March 1967 and held in high esteem as a political system that had achieved both kinds of justice through socialism, collapsed six years after his death.[16] The man himself is absent, too, having passed

---

14 Edward W. Said, *Culture and Imperialism* (New York: Vintage, 1994), p. 66.

15 Andrew van der Vlies, *South African Textual Cultures: White, Black, Read All Over* (Manchester: Manchester University Press, 2007), pp. 119–24.

away in Havana, where his body is still buried. Unlike a number of his famed generation who were either released from prison or able to return after years abroad, La Guma is among those who never made it back. He is among those activists whose interred physical remains map a contingent geography of exile and mourning that the apartheid government unduly created.

Compounding these historical conditions of absence and erasure are literary ones. Specific to the writings in this book, many were published in non-South African journals, a number of which have ceased publication since the end of the Cold War. The scattered appearance of La Guma's writing in peripheral or moribund periodicals has retroactively concealed the diversity and extent of this body of work. Reinforcing this situation is La Guma's outlier status within South African fiction. With the exception of having several novels included in the African Writers Series—the most prestigious in African literature and one of the most significant intellectual projects of the twentieth century—La Guma was not part of a clearly defined literary movement like his peers and friends at the Johannesburg-based *Drum* magazine, including Lewis Nkosi, Es'kia Mphahlele, Can Themba and Bloke Modisane. From a political standpoint, his communism has, fairly or unfairly, imparted a doctrinaire quality to his work, with critics interpreting his fiction as too ideological. His descriptions of slums, prison life and police brutality—a South African variation of Gorky's 'proletarian humanism'—are out of fashion with many post-apartheid readers. From a social standpoint, La Guma also stands apart due to his 'Coloured' background. Though of the same generation as the aforementioned *Drum* writers, a number of whom praised La Guma, his Cape Town origins and Coloured identity have marginalized him vis-à-vis these and other black writers, despite

---

16 On his first visit to the USSR, see Field, *Alex La Guma*, p. 172; Christopher J. Lee, 'Introduction. Anti-Imperial Eyes' in Alex La Guma, *A Soviet Journey: A Critical Annotated Edition* (Christopher J. Lee ed.) (Lanham, MD: Lexington Books, 2017), p. 26.

shared themes of urban life found in their respective work—a kind of literary apartheid that he himself wrote against as seen in this book. La Guma's fiction has similarly been perceived as too radical and violent compared to the romanticism of Richard Rive, another friend and Coloured writer, whose depiction of District Six in the novel '*Buckingham Palace', District Six* (1986) has largely replaced La Guma's in the popular imagination. As a final reason for neglect, La Guma never wrote or published in Afrikaans, which has provided a committed audience for some Coloured writers, such as the late poet Adam Small.

Culture and Liberation presents an occasion for correcting this literary and historical absence. These previously uncollected exile writings offer a new means for reconsidering La Guma's literary aims, his political concerns and the progression of his work over the course of a number of difficult, unstable years when personal and political uncertainty was the norm. However, they not only mark the trauma and ambiguity of being an émigré but also the search for new forms of home. This book stresses the ways in which La Guma contributed to the anti-apartheid struggle through artistic means by participating in global literary movements—most crucially the Afro-Asian Writers Association, which was founded in 1958 in Tashkent, Uzbekistan, funded by the Soviet government and based for different periods in Colombo, Cairo, Beirut and Tunis. Indeed, although he carried a British passport, La Guma's political, national and racial identities *enabled* a particular kind of transnational mobility that gave him access to likeminded individuals and conversations—a distinct contrast to conditions in apartheid South Africa. The journalism, literary statements, reviews and intermittent short stories gathered here track this process of creative connection at the same time as they account for the subjective and affective dimensions of expatriate existence, beyond politics.

As such, these assorted pieces provide a more focused sense of his writing life. In La Guma's case as with many others, being a writer did not consist exclusively of working on books, novels or fiction per se. It also meant, among other things, contributing book reviews, sending letters to the editor, reporting on conferences, delivering lectures, answering interview questions, expressing admiration for other authors and reflecting on one's personal life. Too often the novel and other major literary genres take precedent in critical assessments, generating an unspoken hierarchy of what counts as 'literature'. And yet the novel and the fictional mode are frequently inadequate for fully capturing the scale and complexity of a writer's career, let alone a nation or a global geography like the Third World. When taken seriously, this kind of written ephemera can constitute a counter-archive apart from state and party materials, casting vital light on the day to day assignments between major publications—the passing interests, moments of travel, intellectual cul-de-sacs and seeds for future work that, combined, create a mosaic of the obligations, opinions and ideas that define the writing profession. Such tasks sustained La Guma during the final third of his life. A relationship can be discerned between the small genres included here and his international movements. This distant writing represents his constant attempts to maintain his long-term political and artistic commitments, amid the fugitive cosmopolitan lifestyle both forced upon him and which he actively embraced.

Tangential Literatures

How might *Culture and Liberation* be further contextualized beyond La Guma's life? As cited earlier, exile has been a periodic experience for many African writers. Chinua Achebe, Wole Soyinka, Ngũgĩ wa Thiong'o, Bessie Head and Nuruddin Farah are classic examples from across the continent, to name only a few. However, for many readers, the collection of pieces in this book will recall the political writing of other activist-intellectuals from South Africa. Books by fellow SACP member and exile Ruth First, the collected speeches of ANC president Oliver Tambo and the posthumously collected essays of Steve Biko immediately come to mind.[17] The Marxist-inflected Pan-African arguments of George Padmore and the retrospective work of Amílcar Cabral, which influenced La Guma's thinking on culture and revolution, are comparable cases beyond South Africa.[18] Taken together, much of this writing from South Africa and beyond reflects a form of 'combat literature' (*littérature de combat*)—a genre of resistance writing drawn from Frantz Fanon's *The Wretched of the Earth* (1961), which itself echoes Jean-Paul Sartre's notion of 'engaged literature' (*littérature engagée*).[19] In his final book, Fanon wrote of 'a third stage, a combat stage' when 'the colonized writer, after having tried to lose himself among the people, with the people, will rouse the people.' 'Combat literature, revolutionary literature, [and] national literature' emerge at this time.[20] This literary genre of decolonization, which as non-fiction has commonly been neglected by scholars of world literature, presents a means for naming and framing the work of La Guma and other exiles, Fanon himself being a paradigmatic example. Indeed, an argument can be made that non-fiction has been the dominant mode for writing decolonization. It formed a vital part of the re-invention of African literature during the Cold War period.

---

17 Steve Biko, *I Write What I Like: Selected Writings* (Aelred Stubbs ed.) (Chicago: University of Chicago Press, 2002); Ruth First, *117 Days: An Account of Confinement and Interrogation under the South African 90-Day Detention Law* (London: Penguin, 2009[1965]); Oliver Tambo, *Oliver Tambo Speaks: Preparing for Power* (Adelaide Tambo ed.) (London: Heinemann, 1987).

18 Amílcar Cabral, *Unity and Struggle: Speeches and Writings* (Michael Wolfers trans.) (New York: Monthly Review Press, 1979); George Padmore, *Pan-Africanism or Communism? The Coming Struggle for Africa* (London: D. Dobson, 1956).

19 Frantz Fanon, *The Wretched of the Earth* (Richard Philcox trans.) (New York: Grove Press, 2004[1963]); Jean-Paul Sartre, *What is Literature?* (London: Routledge, 2001[1948]).

20 Fanon, *The Wretched of the Earth*, p. 159.

In this sense, the writing of La Guma and others, including Fanon, should not be read reductively as merely intellectual resistance to situations of colonial dominance. Their work reported on social and cultural conditions in addition to political ones. They sought to create new traditions of global humanism. Though South Africa was not yet postcolonial, La Guma, like his peers elsewhere, looked to the future, identifying impending risks of postcolonial power along with supplying critiques of contemporary inequalities. Attempting to capture a history of the present, their writing fostered solidarity and built new forms of community; it did not solely seek to provoke division and promote conflict. Always aspirational in scope, La Guma and his counterparts sought cultural revolution concurrent with political revolution. In form and content, *Culture and Liberation* seeks to resemble Fanon's *A Dying Colonialism* (originally *L'An V de la Révolution Algérienne*, 1959) and *Toward the African Revolution* (1964) in particular, both of which are composite works containing short opinion pieces, sociological case studies and political journalism that served as drafts for later arguments found in Fanon's final work, *The Wretched of the Earth*.[21] The writing in this book similarly consists of draft statements, improvised arguments and raw reportage that would find its way into La Guma's fiction.

In this regard, *Culture and Liberation* also represents a kind of 'tangential literature'—writing that digresses from expected narratives through experimentation with new forms, foreign settings, incipient ideas or alternative aesthetics, frequently resulting in its critical marginalization.[22] It provides a second way of approaching La Guma's work in exile. Similar to distant writing, tangential literature abandons routine and can thus be fragmentary and isolated, evincing moments of intellectual and political courage while also

---

21 Frantz Fanon, *A Dying Colonialism* (Haakon Chevalier trans.) (New York: Grove Press, 1965[1959]); Frantz Fanon, *Toward the African Revolution* (Haakon Chevalier trans.) (New York: Grove Press, 1988[1964]).

22 For an earlier elaboration of this idea, see Lee, 'Anti-Imperial Eyes', p. 44.

undertaking risks of artistic failure and disappearance. But it is not exclusively tied to the condition of exile. Concern is placed instead on radical literary experimentation. La Guma's *A Soviet Journey* conforms to this definition, as do Richard Wright's *The Color Curtain* (1956) and W. E. B. Du Bois's *Dark Princess* (1928) to offer two further examples.[23] All are works that test new genres and appear on the surface to be tangential to the established concerns of each author, but in fact reflect a deeper level or new stage in their thinking. These exploratory texts—a literature of departure—point in particular to the mutually constitutive intersections between the Soviet Bloc, the Black Atlantic and the postcolonial Third World, due to their shared confrontation with the effects of Western aggression. As with Fanon, this impulse towards experimentation by Du Bois, Wright and La Guma, involving the depiction of situations beyond the countries of their birth, reflected a planetary condition of imperialism and racial capitalism that demanded a politics of global decolonization to which each were stridently committed.

Further comparisons can be drawn between La Guma and Fanon. Both documented liberation struggles, but they also occupied middle-strata positions within their respective political organizations, resulting in diplomatic appointments towards the end of their lives in Cuba and Ghana, respectively. Above all, they shared a generational point of view. Both were born in 1925, and both witnessed the rise of fascism in Europe and its defeat during the Second World War. They understood the necessity of armed struggle—the liberatory potential of violence—to end authoritarian regimes. Fanon gained this knowledge first-hand as a soldier in the Free French Forces. Though he never experienced military service, La Guma wrote about antifascism and the defeat of Nazism by the Soviet Union. By extension, he advocated armed struggle through Umkhonto we Sizwe (MK), the military wing of the ANC–SACP

---

23 W. E. B. Du Bois, *Dark Princess* (Jackson: University Press of Mississippi, 1995[1928]); Richard Wright, *The Color Curtain: A Report on the Bandung Conference* (Jackson: University Press of Mississippi, 1995[1956]).

alliance, founded in 1961. In an early set of essays for *Sechaba* included here, entitled 'The Time Has Come', La Guma argues, 'The people can no longer stand subservient to tyranny and rule by force and violence,' invoking an anti-colonial spirit akin to Fanon's. 'Violence can only be fought with violence. There is no alternative in South Africa today.' This promotion of an anti-violence violence reflected a shared antifascist orientation—a political like-mindedness drawn from Marxism-Leninism and a generational vantage point of witnessing both the destructiveness and the destruction of global fascism.[24] La Guma would later dedicate *In the Fog of the Seasons' End* to Basil February, a Coloured MK recruit who died during the ill-fated 1967 Wankie Campaign, which had attempted a military incursion of South Africa via Southern Rhodesia.

This analogy between La Guma and Fanon can be extended to the cases of South Africa and Algeria more generally—a comparison made by Nelson Mandela and others.[25] Similar to the Algerian Revolution, a makeshift division can be drawn between those activists who went into exile as part of the ANC's 'external mission'—such as La Guma, First and Tambo, among many others—and those who remained inside South Africa, whether Mandela, Biko or Rick Turner, to name only a few cases from different movements and organizations. This split should not be fixed too starkly. Each group faced conditions of censorship, arrest and imprisonment, with a number falling victim to assassination by the apartheid regime, as in the cases of First, Turner and Biko. Yet these insider–outsider differences, as in the case of Algeria, provide some explanation for the different intellectual fates and historical legacies of these writers and activists, with those remaining inside South Africa arguably receiving greater popular attention after the end of apartheid—a phenomenon that can be attributed to their presence

---

24 On anti-violence violence, see Lee, *Frantz Fanon*, p. 156.
25 Nelson Mandela, *Long Walk to Freedom: The Autobiography of Nelson Mandela* (Boston: Back Bay Books, 1995), p. 298.

in the country, whether through return, release or burial, as well as for the tonal and subjective immediacy of their written work, which had no distance to overcome.

In contrast, the exile writing of La Guma in this collection points to the wider world of South African activism that emerged during the anti-apartheid years and the artistic, intellectual and historical loss when this global dimension remains unaccounted for. Indeed, South African activism during the twentieth century has always had an international orientation, if not always recognized as such. ANC founders John Dube and Pixley ka Isaka Seme studied at Oberlin College and Columbia University, respectively, while Sol Plaatje, another founder, travelled to Great Britain and the United States, where he met Du Bois and Marcus Garvey, after the publication of his landmark book *Native Life in South Africa* (1914). The longevity of struggle against white minority rule during the segregation and apartheid periods meant this internationalization continued into the post–Second World War period, underscoring how the South African situation challenges conventional chronologies of anti-colonialism, decolonization and the Cold War. The last, enduring just over forty years until the 1991 collapse of the Soviet Union, is much shorter than the lengthier, intergenerational South African struggle for democracy. Twentieth-century South African politics underlines the Eurocentrism of many Cold War narratives, and how conventional paradigms of the Cold War do not transfer neatly to non-Western contexts more generally. Furthermore, this long history of activism indicates how a wider world of Black Atlantic politics flowed into a politics of communist internationalism and later a tri-continental Third Worldism. These political worlds were not discrete. They informed and shaped one another, being positioned over time against the multifaceted, exploitative measures of a global capitalist system, as the life and writing of La Guma demonstrates.

Life came first. James La Guma, Alex's father, attended the Comintern-sponsored League Against Imperialism meeting held in Brussels, Belgium, in 1927—ten years after the Bolshevik Revolution. He went on to Moscow with Josiah Gumede of the ANC—an early moment of the longstanding partnership between the ANC and South African communists—where they met with Soviet Politburo member and Comintern General Secretary Nikolai Bukharin. Together, they developed the Native Republic thesis, which built upon Vladimir Lenin's 1920 programme on the national and colonial questions that not only argued for colonial self-determination but also for black self-determination as an integral part of this broader plan. The Native Republic thesis, which argued for black liberation in South Africa, paralleled the Comintern's Black Belt Nation thesis promoted at the same time, which argued that African Americans should seek self-determination and nationhood in the American South. The upshot is that Black Atlantic and Marxist-Leninist politics intersected at an early stage. Moreover, nationalism and communist internationalism were compatible. The Native Republic thesis defined South Africa as a colony, despite its self-governing status in the British Empire as of 1910, and thus in need of a national democratic revolution prior to socialist revolution. This thesis therefore presaged the later alliance of the SACP and ANC during the 1950s, the alliance itself embodying this two-step process of national liberation first, represented by the ANC, followed by a socialist revolution, to be led by the SACP. The Native Republic thesis still casts a shadow over South African politics over ninety years later, with black nationalism having succeeded but class inequalities remaining unresolved.

The thesis also cast a shadow over Jimmy's only son. Alex became involved with the ANC and the Congress Alliance through the South African Coloured People's Organisation (SACPO) after the CPSA was banned in 1950 under the Suppression of Communism Act and reformed underground as the SACP. The ANC and SACPO afforded a public political cover. Alex's fiction eventually addressed different aspects of the 'colonial question' as drawn from Lenin and foregrounded by the Native Republic thesis.

He viewed the racism and class oppression in South Africa as systemic, requiring revolution. But his exile writing, in particular *A Soviet Journey*, also addressed the 'national question', a predicament confronted by the Congress Alliance during the 1950s. It was unclear how a new South African nationhood could be achieved given the country's diversity of ethnic and cultural communities. La Guma believed that socialism as implemented and practiced by the Soviet Union provided an answer. Based on a trip he took throughout the USSR in May, June and July of 1975 for approximately six weeks upon the invitation of the Soviet Writers' Union, *A Soviet Journey* is a travelogue of his journey from the western industrialized cities of Moscow and Leningrad (St Petersburg) to Soviet Central Asia, Siberia and back again. However, it is also a depiction of the economic and political journey of the Soviet Union itself—a vision of progress for a future South Africa. The book is consequently a factographic amalgam of travel description and political treatise with the USSR providing a paradigm of self-determination and socialist development.[26]

A Soviet Journey is a tangent from La Guma's acclaimed South Africa-focused fiction, but one that illuminates his political commitments through a different mirror. It elucidates a Second Worldism that complements the Third Worldism which threads throughout this book. Published in both Russian and English and complete with publicity photographs, *A Soviet Journey* is a forthright promotional account. Nevertheless, the book is important for being La Guma's longest work, fiction or non-fiction. It is La Guma's most joyful book, enlivened with humour and warmth, in which he finds just about everything to be superior in the USSR. Unlike the oppressive writing conditions he encountered in South Africa, *A Soviet Journey* demonstrates a newfound freedom while

---

[26] I use the term 'factographic' as a loose reference to Soviet 'factography'— a trend among the Soviet avant-garde during the 1920s, prior to the establishment of socialist realism as the dominant aesthetic. See Devin Fore, 'Introduction', *October* 118 (2006): 3–10.

in exile and how the USSR in particular supported the anti-apartheid struggle. It is likewise among his most experimental books—an example of an unguarded late style, as described by Edward Said.[27] Using a tape recorder for its composition, the book possesses an organic, fluid narrative, with descriptive and temporal juxtapositions throughout the text between Lenin and Marco Polo, the legendary Silk Road and Soviet silk production, ancient civilizations of Central Asia and Soviet modernity. Unlike fellow travellers such as George Padmore and André Gide, who became disillusioned with the USSR, and others like Theodore Dreiser, whose initial critiques transformed into commitment, La Guma composed *A Soviet Journey* as a culmination of his unwavering lifelong communism.[28] Not only was the USSR anti-fascist, but Soviet political conditions resembled those in South Africa. Both were predominantly rural countries with comparatively small, if not insignificant, industrial bases. The Bolsheviks had confronted the same rural–urban challenges as South African activists, granting a particular affinity between the two countries that La Guma remarked upon. He viewed the Soviet Union in utopian terms, without apology.

Beyond this strategic analogy, La Guma followed in the footsteps of preceding black travellers, such as Langston Hughes and Du Bois, to the USSR and Soviet Central Asia in particular—today, a frequently forgotten contact zone between Europe, East and South Asia, and the Middle East. La Guma's memoir contributes to a deeper history of Black Atlantic engagements with the Soviet experiment, underscoring how south Atlantic activists must be included in this predominantly North Atlantic paradigm and the black radical tradition more generally. The collected writings in *Culture and Liberation* complement and expand upon *A Soviet*

---

27 Edward W. Said, *On Late Style: Music and Literature Against the Grain* (New York: Vintage, 2006).

28 On the disillusioned, see Richard Crossman (ed.), *The God That Failed* (New York: Harper, 1949).

Journey, highlighting a political geography far beyond the South Africa of La Guma's youth and early adulthood. They capture what I have discussed elsewhere as his *fugitive cosmopolitanism*—an expression that draws upon the notion of 'fugitivity' as elaborated by Hortense Spillers, Stefano Harney and Fred Moten, while also underlining the forms of transnational interaction, both political and cultural, that could result from such a condition.[29] Indeed, David Attwell has separately drawn from Es'kia Mphahlele to propose the idea of 'fugitive modernities', a form of counter-humanism devised to elude colonial designs.[30] Fugitive cosmopolitanism plays a similar role, encapsulating the tensions of freedom and duress, mobility and unsettlement, political dissidence and newfound community that La Guma and other émigrés experienced. As an expression, it provides a more active sense of his life than the conditional passivity imparted by 'exile', enabling instead a practice of diversion (*détour*) as described by Édouard Glissant—an exilic exercise of identification and understanding when return may be impossible, when alternative means must be sought in order to grasp conditions of power.[31] *Culture and Liberation* is a book of such detours. These writings mark attempts by La Guma to situate South Africa and the anti-apartheid struggle within a global landscape of decolonization and nascent postcolonial futures—not only to garner international support but also to sustain revolutionary aims through imaginative means.

---

[29] Lee, 'Anti-Imperial Eyes', pp. 4, 24; Stefano Harney and Fred Moten, *The Undercommons: Fugitive Planning & Black Study* (New York: Minor Compositions, 2013); Hortense J. Spillers, 'Chapter 7' in *Black, White, and in Color: Essays on American Literature and Culture* (Chicago: University of Chicago Press, 2003).

[30] David Attwell, *Rewriting Modernity: Studies in Black South African Literary History* (Athens, OH: Ohio University Press, 2006), pp. 23-4.

[31] Édouard Glissant, *Caribbean Discourse: Selected Essays* (J. Michael Dash trans.) (Charlottesville: University Press of Virginia, 1989[1981]), pp.14-26.

Detours of Decolonization

In her wide-ranging and important book *Apartheid and Beyond* (2007), Rita Barnard makes two significant interventions for addressing South African literature after apartheid. The first is that South African literature itself is an elusive subject to define, given the dramatic political history and demographic diversity of the country. The second is the prominence of space in determining South African literature and culture—from the vitality and confinement of township life in the work of Mphahlele, to the middle-class suburbs of Nadine Gordimer, to the rural geographies of J. M. Coetzee, Zakes Mda and Olive Schreiner. Drawing on Mphahlele, she calls this situation 'a commitment to territory'. But, in doing so, she seeks to stress the imaginative limits of this approach. In her view, Mphahlele's commitment, outlined in his essay 'The Tyranny of Place and Aesthetics' (1987), is a product of his experience of exile, which heightened his sense of artistic duty to the South African condition but equally disempowered his ability to portray South African life through concrete details, as he did in his classic memoir *Down Second Avenue* (1959).[32]

La Guma faced the same challenge. Both Mphahlele and Nkosi had praised his ability to render the urban feel of Cape Town in his early fiction.[33] It is also clear, however, that La Guma did not stop writing. As with *A Soviet Journey*, a certain freedom of expression is found in his lesser-known non-fiction and short stories written while in exile. *Culture and Liberation* underscores the autonomy he had, with unsettlement encouraging the creation of new forms of cultural community and new relations of artistic belonging, which

---

32 Rita Barnard, *Apartheid and Beyond: South African Writers and the Politics of Place* (New York: Oxford, 2007), pp. 4–5, pp. 147–8; Es'kia Mphahlele, 'Exile, the Tyranny of Place and the Literary Compromise', *UNISA English Studies* 17(1) (1979): 37–44; Es'kia Mphahlele, 'The Tyranny of Place and Aesthetics: The South African Case' in Charles Malan (ed.), *Race and Literature/Ras en Literatuur* (Pinetown: Owen Burgess, 1987), p. 54.

33 Mphahlele, 'The Tyranny of Place and Aesthetics'; Lewis Nkosi, *Home and Exile, and Other Selections* (London: Longman, 1983[1965]), pp. 137–8.

in turn complicate simplistic renditions of 'exile'. These writings represent 'detours' from his South African novels and even fiction itself. As such, they uncover a wider set of interests through new subject matter and experiences that shared affinities with the anti-apartheid cause, underscoring a broader landscape of Cold War print cultures that La Guma helped to shape and define. A number of pieces reveal his duties as an editor of the journal *Lotus* during the 1970s and his subsequent executive role in the Afro-Asian Writers Association (AAWA) starting in the late 1970s until his death in 1985, after which the organization markedly declined.[34] They also indicate a reprise of his early vocation as a journalist—he at times referred to himself as a reporter, rather than a novelist or writer of fiction, as one of his cancelled passports indicates. His book reviews, often written under pseudonyms, equally demonstrate that he could be a sharp critic of fellow South African writers Athol Fugard, Dennis Brutus and Nadine Gordimer for their work and politics, despite personal connections. On the other hand, La Guma could also be very generous, as he is in reviews of the poet Oswald Joseph (Mbuyiseni) Mtshali, an obituary of fellow exile Alfred Hutchinson and in discussions of poets and writers from across Asia. Taken together, these writings provide a kaleidoscopic view of the life of a writer in exile, demonstrating in palpable fashion how postcolonial literature and criticism must be approached as ongoing practices of commitment, as argued by Ato Quayson, rather than being tied too closely to political events and timelines.[35]

Culture and Liberation comprises sixty-eight chapters divided into five thematic parts. Though correspondences and direct links can be drawn between each part, this organizational format is

---

34 On the history of this journal, see Hala Halim, '*Lotus*, the Afro-Asian Nexus, and Global South Comparatism,' *Comparative Studies of South Asia, Africa and the Middle East* 32(3) (2012): 563–83.

35 Ato Quayson, 'Introduction: Postcolonial Literature in a Changing Historical Frame' in Ato Quayson (ed.), *The Cambridge History of Postcolonial Literature*, VOL. 1 (Cambridge: Cambridge University Press, 2012), p. 6.

designed to bring shape and definition to La Guma's diverse literary output. The pieces in each section are arranged chronologically to give a probative sense of La Guma's evolution in thinking.[36] Part One, entitled 'Political Worlds', maps the political positions as well as the global geography his life encompassed while in exile. The first essays in this section published in 1967, shortly after he left South Africa, outline in particular his arguments for armed struggle and why Coloured South Africans should support this effort. His later essays of the 1960s and early 1970s indicate a continued preoccupation with state racism and 'Coloured' identity, summarized by two reports he prepared for the United Nations Special Committee on Apartheid. La Guma and other writer-activists were frequently tasked to explain what 'apartheid' was to an international audience. However, by the mid-1970s his attention had shifted to the Soviet Union, Vietnam and the African continent more generally. The pieces in this section published after 1978, the year he moved to Cuba, mark a turn to the Caribbean, with discussion of the Cuban experiment and its support for the anti-apartheid struggle. La Guma uses extended quotations from Fidel Castro in his political journalism to amplify shared ideas. He also addresses Israel's invasion of Lebanon in 1982, thus contributing to a long-standing critique of Israel by South African activists, continuing to the present. The summary point of this section—the longest in the book at twenty-five chapters—is how La Guma conjured a political imagination that drew connections between Africa, Asia and the Americas, whether the subject at hand was the apartheid regime's conciliatory gestures toward postcolonial African countries, the end of the American war in Vietnam or intervention in the Caribbean by the Reagan administration.

---

36 It should be noted that the exact chronology of publications within certain years has been difficult to confirm in some cases, given that journals did not always specify the month of publication. In these instances, I have ordered the publications based on issue number when available, as well as taking into account a logical flow between his positions and arguments.

Part Two, 'Cultural Scenes and Arguments', continues this political focus and transnational outlook while stressing the role of culture in activism. These pieces mark events attended in Beirut, Algiers, East Berlin, Tashkent, Luanda and elsewhere, regarding the First Pan-African Cultural Festival, a symposium on Paul Robeson, and La Guma's growing involvement in the AAWA, ultimately leading to his appointment as secretary general for the organization in 1979—his highest profile position while in exile, next to being the ANC's chief representative for Latin America and the Caribbean while in Havana. Of particular interest is a series of four essays—'Culture and Apartheid in South Africa' (1968), 'The Condition of Culture in South Africa' (1971), 'Culture and Liberation' (1976) and 'Has Art Failed South Africa?' (1977)—which describe the deterioration of culture under apartheid and the consequent inseparability of culture from political struggle. Though drawing from similar arguments made by Cabral, these statements by La Guma must be read on their own terms as delineating a cultural programme for the ANC and the SACP: the aim of cultural revolution in parallel with political revolution. This position is elaborated further in two speeches for the AAWA in 1979 when its conference was held in Luanda, Angola—its first event in sub-Saharan Africa. Indeed, these pieces and others in *Culture and Liberation* provide insight into the workings of the AAWA as an organization, in addition to depicting the institutional dimensions of Afro-Asianism as a Third World platform and ideology that defied a conventional continental logic. The final essay in this section, 'Is There a South African National Culture?' (1985), appeared in *The African Communist* under the pen name 'Gala', which he used regularly. Providing a valedictory message the year he died, it summarizes his case against cultural apartheid in South Africa and his hope that a truly South African literature would be born from the anti-apartheid struggle.

Part Three, 'Literary Criticism and the Writing Life', demonstrates this artistic commitment in palpable form. Employing a variety of small genres, this part includes an obituary for his fellow exile Alfred Hutchinson, a tribute to fellow communist writer Pablo Neruda, a speech delivered in New Delhi upon receiving the 1969 Lotus Prize for Literature, an editorial on short stories and a number of book reviews. Why book reviews for *The African Communist* one might ask? Such minor pieces demonstrate in specific fashion how literature, literary criticism and culture more generally sustained the deeper humanism of the anti-apartheid struggle and liberation movements elsewhere. As mentioned, La Guma embraced the idea of a new South African culture being produced during and, more precisely, *through* the struggle, not after. In these reviews and longer critical essays, he promotes the marginalised voices of black writers, such as Oswald Mtshali, while taking harsher views of internationally known South African writers like playwright Athol Fugard and future Nobel Laureate Nadine Gordimer. In 'Against Literary Apartheid' (1974), he critiques Gordimer in particular for failing to imagine a convincing black character in her work, thus tacitly fulfilling a 'separate development' model of South African literature. In a similarly provocative vein, he excoriates Nobel Laureate Alexander Solzhenitsyn for mischaracterizing the Soviet Union—an unsurprising position given La Guma's orthodox communism. His strident defence of the USSR underlines how he was fallible; recent estimates of those who died in the Gulag prison system approach 2.8 million people.[37] Yet, beyond taking a doctrinaire view that clouded his judgement, La Guma aimed to expose the underlying hypocrisy of Western critics for embracing Soviet dissidents like Solzhenitsyn, who were imprisoned for political subversion, while ignoring the similar oppression and imprisonment

---

37 It should be noted that La Guma could not have known these present-day figures, since they were not fully known until after the collapse of the Soviet Union. Nonetheless, the total numbers of those who died during the Soviet period, including the Red Terror, executions, collectivization and so forth, are much higher. See Anne Applebaum, *Gulag: A History* (New York: Anchor, 2004), pp. 578–84.

of South African dissidents like himself. Balancing these political positions are two pieces, 'Literature and Life' (1970) and 'What I Learned from Maxim Gorky' (1977), that detail the influence that Gorky and socialist realism had on his aesthetic development. These vital reflections are suggestive of how Russian and Soviet literature not only impacted La Guma but other African writers as well—a genealogy of influence in the creation of world literature that has fallen into relative obscurity since the demise of the Soviet Union.

Part Four, 'Five Stories and One Play', and Part Five, 'Interviews and Memoir', take a more personal turn while not completely departing from politics. The positioning of his creative work towards the end of this book is intentional in order to stress the value of his non-fiction writing. Nonetheless, these stories demonstrate his fictional experiments such as 'Come Back to Tashkent' (1970), which is set in Soviet Central Asia and told in the second person, and 'Thang's Bicycle' (1976), which takes place in North Vietnam during an American bombing campaign. Both reflect his travels to these places, but also his attempts to contribute to a postcolonial Afro-Asian literature—an idea he was committed to organizationally and artistically. These two pieces and by extension the contributions of other African and Asian writers to *Lotus* underscore the important role that short fiction and poetry had in the making of postcolonial literature. The three other stories and the play 'The Man in the Tree' (1971) are set in South Africa and recall his earlier work. There is an underlying current of exilic reminiscence in these pieces through their setting. However, in keeping with many submissions to *Lotus*, an emphasis on local culture is also witnessed through La Guma's interspersing of *kaapse taal*—local Cape street slang—in the speech of his characters in 'Late Edition' (1972) and 'Blankets' (1978).

Tones of nostalgia and melancholy, though always tempered by political commitment, can also be discerned in Part Five. The assembled pieces in this section include an interview he gave shortly after arriving in London in 1966—the oldest document in this book—as well as a lengthy speech he delivered to an AAWA conference in Tashkent in 1983, which I have selected to conclude the book, given its publication in 1985 and its sweeping summation of La Guma's political and artistic concerns at the end of his life. Between these two pieces are other interviews, a bitter satire on prison life from 1969, two letters to the editor of *Sechaba* regarding Coloured identity and two memoir essays sharing the same title 'Why I Joined the Communist Party' (1971 and 1982), which provide insight into his childhood and upbringing in District Six—a world that, at the time of the publication of these essays, was being destroyed through forced removals after being declared a 'whites only' area in 1966. Indeed, their timing in retrospect appears to be more than coincidental. Combined, these writings in Part Five offer an outline of La Guma's personal concerns and his emotional life, a framework for an autobiography that he never had a chance to write.

In this sense, *Culture and Liberation* is a 'shadow book' in the expression of the African-American poet and critic Kevin Young—a provisional genre that includes books never finished, books that have suffered censorship and books that have been completed, but are lost.[38] Similar to posthumous collections by Fanon and Biko, *Cultural and Liberation* is an attempt to realize and fulfil a political and literary project that La Guma himself was unable to complete. In this regard, it must be stressed that the pieces included here were ones published in his lifetime. This project is not about publishing draft manuscripts or other material, such as political speeches, for which he did not approve publication. Though La Guma did not endorse this book, it has been undertaken with the approval of his wife, Blanche, as well as with attention and care to what his views and beliefs were. *Culture and Liberation* reflects a comprehensive approach to his materials in order to highlight the diversity and

---

38 Kevin Young, *The Grey Album: On the Blackness of Blackness* (Minneapolis, MN: Graywolf Press, 2012), pp. 11–14.

talent of the man—his wide-ranging interests and his facility with a spectrum of literary forms and topics—rather than pick and choose work, which would inevitably leave unanswered questions. Taking different tangents from his better-known fiction, this collection reveals more explicitly La Guma's political views, his approaches to literature and the writing life, and his experiences in South Africa and the rest of the world. Contingency and a complex individual itinerary define these writings. Many read like first drafts—La Guma likely had little opportunity to revise, and the editorial process for many of these journals was probably minimal. A number of essays possess the rhythms of thought and speech as a result. They demonstrate both evolution and recurrence in his views, reflective of the broader experience of exile.

Culture and Liberation ultimately points to a wider world of activism and intellectual engagement—the multidimensional conversations between Black Atlantic, Second World, Third World and southern African political communities. The best of these essays outline and analyse the conjunctures between these realms. But his life also instantiated such encounters. These writings not only recover his voice—they also track his movements across time and place, which he could, at times, be surprisingly elusive about. These pieces further underscore the role that institutions and movements like the UN, the Organisation of African Unity and the Non-Aligned Movement had on his thinking and the importance of international conferences in the making of world literature. They trace the complex itineraries of Afro-Asianism beyond the seminal event of the 1955 Asian-African Conference in Bandung, Indonesia —itself a moment that defies easy narration—to include the Middle East and the Soviet Union, which stretched across the Asian continent. Indeed, La Guma's exile writings emphasize how the anti-apartheid struggle cannot be reduced to South Africa alone, as counterintuitive as that might sound. It must be understood as part of a broader conjuncture tied to global efforts against neocolonialism in such places as Palestine, Southeast Asia and the Caribbean.

A different cultural world linked to the Soviet Union and Eastern Bloc also comes to light that contrasts with the Western-oriented, liberal democratic world embraced by acclaimed writers like Soyinka and Achebe. As a communist internationalist, the world was La Guma's canvas, and these writings demonstrate this cultivated sensibility. Anti-apartheid activists looked to the USSR and elsewhere, not just the US and the African-American civil rights struggle as so frequently addressed. La Guma accounts for these alternative cultures of decolonization.

But more than these political horizons, when we neglect the ephemera of writers, we neglect their working lives—whether as activists, journalists, book critics or writers simply on short-term assignment. Such ephemeral writing provides a sedimented, material sense of the freedom and precarity of lives in exile. It can sketch the contours of thought between political moments, akin to Gramsci's thinking through the interregnum. Similar to the relative critical neglect of Soviet influence on African writers and other artists elsewhere in the world, *Culture and Liberation* points to anti-colonial liberation struggles, global decolonization and their roles in the creation of world literature—a decolonial epistemology shaped by the Cold War.[39] World literature should not solely regard questions of translation, genre and scale, as important as those issues are, but also account for the preceding historical elements and how they informed the intellectual labour, politics and life situation of the writer.[40] These writings produced under conditions

---

39 On South African literature and the Cold War, see Monica Popescu, *South African Literature Beyond the Cold War* (New York: Palgrave Macmillan, 2010).

40 For recent discussions of world literature, see, for example, Emily Apter, *Against World Literature: On the Politics of Untranslatability* (London: Verso, 2013); Pheng Cheah, *What is a World?: On Postcolonial Literature as World Literature* (Durham, NC: Duke University Press, 2016); Aamir Mufti, *Forget English!: Orientalisms and World Literatures* (Cambridge, MA: Harvard University Press, 2016); David Palumbo-Liu, Bruce Robbins and Nirvana Tanoukhi (eds), *Immanuel Wallerstein and the Problem of the World: System, Scale, Culture* (Durham, NC: Duke University Press, 2011).

of revolutionary struggle illustrate the cultural programme of the ANC as found in the Freedom Charter ('The Doors of Learning and of Culture Shall be Opened!'), and, as a result, contribute to a new humanism as aspired to by Fanon, Cabral and others during the revolutionary period of decolonization. *Culture and Liberation* provides another glimpse of this new Cold War humanism. La Guma must be included among their ranks.

Cold War Codas

As Jacques Derrida argued shortly after the end of the Cold War in *Specters of Marx* (1993), Marxism has frequently involved a notion of haunting. Whether the spectre haunting Europe in *The Communist Manifesto* (1848) or Friedrich Engels' well-known graveside speech at Karl Marx's funeral in 1883, this feature has formed a recurrent theme in the history of Marxist thought and praxis.[41] South African politics remains haunted, too, by its radical past, with the SACP still aligned with the ANC through the Tripartite Alliance, though greatly diminished in its influence. The ANC today has largely, if not completely, rescinded its socialist past. Yet inequalities—social, economic and political—persist in South Africa.

Culture and Liberation is positioned against this backdrop of forgotten ambitions, of a revolution deferred. These writings provide a vital outline of the nearly two decades La Guma spent in exile, and they will, I hope, grant him a new afterlife among contemporary readers and critics. With the exception of *A Soviet Journey*, he left no other memoir or autobiography. These writings accomplish this task, delineating perspectives, experiences and an emotional life that help complete his personal history, given that the South African focus of his popular fiction does not directly address his time in exile. By the same stroke, these writings are

---

41 Jacques Derrida, *Specters of Marx: The State of the Debt, the Work of Mourning and the New International* (London: Routledge, 2006[1993]).

compelling historical and political documents of a period when a generation of activists left South Africa. This book highlights the complex politics of the ANC and the SACP during the Cold War, when the anti-apartheid struggle intersected with a broader set of Second World and Third World politics. *Culture and Liberation* points to the indispensable role of individuals as political and intellectual intermediaries in the articulation of what is today the Global South. These political geographies elude simple narration. La Guma's work offers one way of chronicling and thinking through such terrains, with insight into these global political communities and a distinct internationalist political imagination that challenges many national understandings of the period.

As a consequence, through republication, the afterlife of La Guma's writing holds not only the opportunity to think anew about the historical geographies and themes of South African literature through the genre of exile writing but also the potential to challenge state narratives—and academic narratives—of the post-apartheid present. *Culture and Liberation* provides a minority discourse, which confronts popular perceptions of the anti-apartheid struggle, especially its nationalist focus. Indeed, La Guma's life points to the problem of the archive—how it favours the settled, the powerful and those receiving the sanction of states. *Culture and Liberation* traces La Guma's transition from a Cape Town-based organic intellectual to a global internationalist, and, in doing so, it indicates how the 'archive' can be reconfigured to account for lives placed under constant duress—how the varied pieces of ephemera included here reflect the dislocation and dispossession La Guma experienced. They represent the fragmentation of his biography. Collecting these writings is thus an attempt to make sense of his life, to make it whole, while retaining the gaps, the breakdowns and the silences between pieces that express the incompletion and destabilization of exile.[42] Journals like *Sechaba*, *The African Communist* and *Lotus*

---

[42] My thoughts here reflect: Premesh Lalu, 'Incomplete Histories: Steve Biko, the Politics of Self-Writing and the Apparatus of Reading', *Current Writing*

served as venues for propaganda and politically minded fiction and poetry, activating a global counter-public against forms of neocolonialism. But they also documented creative lives, fostered personal relationships and sustained political and artistic communities, however imperfectly. Their routine publication and distribution, if at times haphazard, nonetheless materialized transnational print cultures that have too often been forgotten. They point to the multiple fronts and forms in which African literature was being invented and reinvented during the postcolonial Cold War era.

La Guma's writing demands that we take these issues seriously—these alternative political imaginations and their implications for redefining the territorial boundaries and content of South African literature and cultural history more generally. The point of literary criticism or historical work should not necessarily be to recover what we already know or agree with, but to restore what can challenge consensus in the present. As Andrew van der Vlies has written, La Guma's body of writing is representative of this problem of definition, constituting 'both an exemplary and an aberrant case study of the disputed nature of writing by a South African writer, which might or might not be "South African" and might or might not be "literature."'[43] Approached differently, like the AAWA project itself, *Culture and Liberation* contests the national allegory paradigm for world literature once argued by Fredric Jameson, as well as broader Euro-American configurations of the non-Western world.[44] With recent scholarship pivoting from metropole-colony

---

16(1) (2004): 107–26; Ciraj Rassool, 'Rethinking Documentary History and South African Political Biography', *South African Review of Sociology* 41(1) (2010): 28–55.

43 Van der Vlies, *South African Textual Cultures*, p. 127.

44 Fredric Jameson, 'Third-World Literature in the Era of Multinational Capitalism', *Social Text* 15 (1986): 65–88. For critiques of Jameson, see Aijaz Ahmad, 'Chapter 3: Jameson's Rhetoric of Otherness and the "National Allegory"' in *In Theory: Classes, Nations, Literatures* (London: Verso, 1992), pp. 95–122; Susan Z. Andrade, *The Nation Writ Small: African Fictions and Feminisms, 1958–1988* (Durham, NC: Duke University Press, 2011).

circuits of knowledge to postcolonial South–South networks, La Guma's life and movements from South Africa, to London and to Havana exemplify the potential of this research turn and its relevance. His writing not only depicts but also instantiates the labour of such connections. La Guma wrote with concern for South Africa, but also for this wider world in political transition, as he experienced it. Whether comparing the assassinations of Martin Luther King, Jr., and Patrice Lumumba, arguing for the need to answer fascist violence with revolutionary violence or maintaining that racism was a consequence of capitalism, La Guma spoke to a global audience.

Stepping beyond conventional considerations of literary posterity, the specific kind of editorial work I have undertaken in *Culture and Liberation* is therefore to raise questions about how granting an afterlife to voices of the past can help recuperate a political unconscious, reinstate lost political futures to the historical record, and, in doing so, confront predicaments of the present. Es'kia Mphahlele once wrote of the 'literary compromise'—that a writer must decide how to prioritize 'the inner compulsion to create' versus 'social action'.[45] This observation has been taken further by Albie Sachs—who, during South Africa's transition to democracy, once argued that art must be more than an instrument of struggle—and Njabulo Ndebele, who has equally urged that post-apartheid writing engage in the 'rediscovery of the ordinary'.[46] Though La Guma did pay close attention to the details of everyday life, these positions that have augured an aesthetic shift in South African writing suggest the limits of La Guma's politically minded writing, of being out of step once again with South African literature.

---

45 Mphahlele, 'Exile, the Tyranny of Place and the Literary Compromise', p. 43.

46 Njabulo Ndebele, *Rediscovery of the Ordinary: Essays on South African Literature and Culture* (Pietermaritzburg: University of KwaZulu-Natal Press, 2006); Albie Sachs, 'Preparing Ourselves for Freedom: Culture and the ANC Constitutional Guidelines', *TDR* 35(1) (1991): 187–93.

Yet recent debates over public history in South Africa have returned to ideas of 'decolonization', indicating the perils of political triumphalism and the recurrent legacies of silent colonial pasts. This re-emergent set of politics resonates with the idealism found in La Guma's writing and the emancipatory project that he committed his life to. Those involved in present-day social movements would gain significantly from reading him closely. His broader literary talent—what Lewis Nkosi once described as 'his enthusiasm for life as it is lived'—should also not be overlooked.[47] Life, for La Guma, was the source of all art. However, for those who never returned, who never had a chance to see their efforts and commitments fulfilled, such contemporary political and cultural resonance offers a provisional source of redemption. Books go out of print, and authors can be forgotten. But they can also be restored.

---

47 Nkosi, *Home and Exile*, p. 137.

PART I

Political Worlds

CHAPTER ONE

Great Power Conspiracy: Review
(January 1967)

This short review for the first issue of Sechaba, *the official organ of the ANC during the anti-apartheid struggle, is perhaps an inauspicious beginning for Alex La Guma's writing career in exile. However, it underscores several key points. First, La Guma was an early contributor to and promoter of the liberation writing of the ANC. Second, it highlights the role that smaller genres, such as the book review, had in cultivating a political culture of letters among activists and to which La Guma would remain committed throughout his exile years. Third, it is also a good example of how many pieces by La Guma were intended to 'explain' apartheid to an international audience. Overall, despite its brevity, it foreshadows his* oeuvre *in the decades ahead.*

The man in the street in Southern Africa has always been puzzled by the contradictions in attitudes of governments and government leaders of the West in particular. The African victim of South Africa's pass-laws, the Indian and Coloured dispossessed under the Group Areas Act have flushed with pleasure at the condemnation, by world leaders, of the Nationalist Government's policies of apartheid. Then their joy has turned to consternation by the stand taken by these same leaders or their representatives in such forums as the United Nations.

To the ordinary person in South Africa, Britain, France and the United States have been countries where the rights of non-whites are upheld; they have been identified with non-colour-bar democracy in their countries. Yet in November 1962, for example, oppressed South Africans were dismayed when 67 countries voted for sanctions against racist South Africa, and Britain, France and the US all voted against. Again, in the Security Council in 1963, Britain and France abstained. When the UN voted for the end of the South African mandate over South West Africa, Britain did not see fit to support the resolution which would have meant a step forward on the road to freedom for the non-whites of South West Africa.

Speeches and promises made by Western statesmen in public have not been fulfilled when these same statesmen were confronted by the task of upholding what was believed to be their word of honour. The oppressed African naturally asks in puzzlement, 'How come?'

The African National Congress of South Africa, in its latest booklet *Great Power Conspiracy*, gives the explanation. In 43 pages of exposure, it reveals how the accumulation of wealth in southern Africa means more to the ruling classes of the Western world than the lives of the subject millions of Africans.

Detailing the extent to which the Western colonialists gain profits from apartheid and race domination, *Great Power Conspiracy* shows, for example, that Britain today has over 1,000,000,000 invested in the Republic of South Africa, and some 200,000,000 in Rhodesia. In fact, Britain's interest in South Africa is greater than in all the rest of the continent together.

A study of US relations with South Africa points out that close connections exist between policymakers in the US administration and financial interests in South Africa. The extent of US involvement in the exploitation of cheap labour in South Africa is shown in concrete terms of figures involving several millions of dollars and numbers of private companies. Apart from this, there are examples of banking loans from the US, which assisted the South African economy during the post–Sharpeville Massacre.

France is a new member of the conspiracy to uphold the racist regimes in southern Africa. When Britain was compelled to impose sanctions against the illegal Smith regime, the reaction of the

French government was apparently to ignore them. French businessmen have continued to operate freely there, while between 1958 and 1962 French imports from South Africa rose from some 10 million to nearly 14 million per year. We are shown that by 1965 France rose to seventh position in the list of world traders with apartheid. Thus Britain, the US and France are three powerful allies for Southern Africa's ruling minorities. What is less known is the existence of a fourth ally, almost a secret ally—the Federal Republic of Germany.

It is well known that Germany and white South Africa first found common ground when the rise of the Nazis in the 1930s found response in the Greyshirt, Ossewabrandwag and Broederbond movements, members of which today rule South Africa. We are shown in *Great Power Conspiracy* that today the stake of the European Common Market countries in South Africa has reached £162,500,000. Among them, West Germany increased its share from £14 million to £28.5 million. West Germany maintains the leading position among the EEC in trade with South Africa. At the same time, the Federal Republic's policy towards Portuguese colonialism in Africa is consistent with its policy on South Africa. Apart from its economic stake in the south of Africa, the West German supply of arms to Portugal has helped Salazar's war against the liberation forces in the Portuguese-held countries.

The African National Congress of South Africa has done an important service in producing *Great Power Conspiracy*. The 43-odd pages expose concisely the reasons for the double-tongue attitudes of those who profess the defence of a 'free world', but whose highwayman interests mean more than the freedom and lives of Southern Africa's millions.

GREAT POWER CONSPIRACY
Published by the ANC of South Africa
PO Box 2239, Dar es Salaam, Tanzania
Price 1/-.

CHAPTER TWO

The Time Has Come

New Forms of Struggle Face the South African Coloured Community
(March 1967)

This article is the first in a series of four articles published in Sechaba in 1967. The series promoted the ANC's armed struggle and sought to rally Coloured support for it. This introductory piece addresses the limits of Coloured politics at the time.

On the night of 16 December 1961, a public holiday known as the Day of the Covenant to Afrikaners, a series of explosions in Johannesburg and Port Elizabeth hailed the birth of Umkhonto we Sizwe (Spear of the Nation). A proclamation issued by Umkhonto stated:

> This is a new, independent body formed by Africans. It includes in its ranks South Africans of all races. Umkhonto we Sizwe will carry on the struggle for freedom and democracy by new methods which are necessary to complement the actions of the established national liberation organisations [. . .] We believe our actions to be a blow against Nationalist preparations for civil war and military rule. In these actions we are working in the best interests of all the people of this country, Black, Brown and White, whose future happiness and well-being cannot be attained without the overthrow of the Nationalists . . . The people's patience is not endless. The time comes in the life of any

nation when there remain only two choices . . . submit or fight. That time has now come to South Africa.

The adoption of methods of armed struggle 'to complement the actions of the established national liberation organizations' came after a long period of non-violent struggle by the non-whites of South Africa, led by the African National Congress, for the overthrow of white supremacy. It is not known to what extent members of the Coloured (mixed blood) population participates in Umkhonto, but the statement that it 'includes in its ranks South Africans of all races' is enough to assure us that non-Africans are taking part in the armed struggle in South Africa today.

At the same time it is possible to point out Coloured people arrested and imprisoned for sabotage who have been associated with other minor movements such as the National Liberation Front and the African Resistance Movement, as well as others who apparently acted individually. For these people, patience was not endless.

Today it should occur to the Coloured community as a whole, as it did to the African people, that the time has come for the acceptance and support of new methods, those of armed struggle, for their emancipation from the yoke of white supremacy and the attainment of a status of equal and unconditional citizenship in South Africa.

The history of the Coloured people's efforts for the extension of the meagre political rights which they possessed in the past, and for the right, with other racial groups, to live as citizens of a truly democratic state, is one of struggle in the face of an opposition holding the reins of government and the State for itself exclusively and determined to surrender nothing, while maintaining the Coloured community permanently in the position of inferiors.

Whatever illusions some Coloured politicians might entertain about eventual 'fair play' on the part of the white supremacists, it should be quite clear that from the very inception of the Union of South Africa in 1910, successive ruling governments showed no intention of including the community in direct and equal participation in the affairs of their country.

The South African constitution was the exclusive creation of whites of which there were those representing the former Transvaal and Orange Free State Republics who accepted as a matter of principle that 'the people will not permit the equalization of Coloured with white inhabitants'. The 'people' meaning whites only and 'Coloured' all non-whites. Likewise, the present Republic was established in 1961 without participation or consultation of the non-white population.

Prior to the establishment of the Union, the Coloured men of the Cape had been granted franchise rights which, even though on paper only, granted them direct representation. When the four provinces were united in 1910, it was agreed as a compromise to the Afrikaners of the Transvaal and Orange Free State that there were to be no non-whites in Parliament. Those in the Transvaal, OFS [Orange Free State] and Natal who did not have the vote would not get it.

Some Cape liberals protested at this arrangement and Mr W. P. Schreiner led a deputation of Coloured men, including Dr A. Abdurahman, to London to petition the British Parliament, without success. This was the first, in modern history, of many peaceful deputations to governments for the preservation of rights. They were all in vain.

In order to further entrench white supremacy in South Africa, white women were given the vote in 1930.

Typical Cynicism

When the Nationalists came to power in 1948, they had a majority of only three in Parliament. Apart from the fact that they are against the non-whites having the franchise anyway, it was clear that the Coloured men's vote in the Cape and Natal had gone against the Nationalist Party, and these votes had to go.

The Nationalists with typical cynicism therefore claimed that a two-thirds majority of both houses was not needed to change the entrenched clauses of the Constitution which guaranteed Coloured men the vote, since to place them on a separate voters roll and give them four white MPs as representatives would not mean diminishing their rights.

The Coloured people replied with a massive campaign led by the Franchise Action Council. They acted on the standpoint that while current rights were not satisfactory, they were not prepared to retreat from that position to one of further political inferiority, but rather demanded the extension of their rights. Mass meetings and a general strike of workers in 1951 could not move the Nationalists.

A deputation led by the late George Golding went to Pretoria to see the prime minister. When confronted in Parliament by so many statements made by himself, Havenga, Stals and other Nationalists that the Coloured people should remain on the common roll, Malan merely waved them aside as 'the dead hand of the past'.

Political Trickery

In spite of protests, the Bill to remove Coloured voters from the common roll was passed. Then four Coloured voters, Messrs E. A. Deane, W. D. Collins and two others instituted Supreme Court proceedings to declare the Act invalid. Their action was upheld in the Supreme Court of the Cape and again in Bloemfontein when the Government appealed. The law was thrown out.

The Nationalists then simply passed a law setting up Parliament as a High Court to try constitutional matters of this kind. This 'court' declared the Separate Representation Act legal. Coloured voters again took the Act to court and won their case again.

The Nationalists then passed the Senate Act and increased the Senate from 48 members to 80 and filled extra seats with their members. They then called a joint session of both Houses and obtained the required two-thirds majority. This time the courts ruled in favour of the Government.

Thus by means of the crudest bits of political trickery, in the face of every protest, the Coloured voters were removed from the common role.

The Nationalists are by no means satisfied with even the mock rights, which the Coloured people possess today. Since the institution of separate representation by four white Members of Parliament, the Coloured voters have consistently returned non-Nationalist candidates to Parliament and the Provincial Council of the Cape. The latest acceptance of Progressive Party members, even though they stand for equality only on certain conditions, has irked the Government to the extent that it will now not tolerate whites (i.e. anti-Nationalists) from 'meddling in Coloured politics'; and threatens to abolish even the present farcical representation.

Third-Class Citizens

Along with the emasculation of standing political rights and the enforcement of 'separate development' have come other methods of reducing the Coloured people still further to a status of third-class citizens.

It was the United Party government, while claiming to champion the cause of the Coloured people, which brought into existence the Coloured Advisory Council and the Coloured Affairs Department (CAD), thereby manifestly proclaiming that the Coloured community is a sort of orphan or retarded child who must receive some kind of separate and special treatment in the same way as the SPCA cares for homeless animals.

This Council was supposed to 'advise (the Government) in matters affecting the Coloured people', but when even its lackeys in the CAC [Coloured Advisory Council] made 'urgent representations' to the United Party government to extend the Coloured vote to the Northern Provinces, it was not prepared to accede. (Second Annual Report of the CAC)

The establishment of the CAC and CAD was met by public outcry on the part of the Coloured community, but as usual white supremacy turned a deaf ear to any opposition.

The Nationalist government, taking over where the United Party had left off, extended the 'Coloured Council' into a Council of Coloured Affairs under a complete Ministry of Coloured Affairs which would control the future of the community under apartheid. In order to give this new apartheid institution a semblance of democracy the people would be able to elect some members to the CCA [Council of Coloured Affairs], the majority being appointed by the Government.

Again the Coloured people demonstrated their rejection of this travesty of political rights. The Coloured people boycotted the elections, and 'candidates' who supported the Government policy were duly declared elected unopposed. They took their seats in spite of their rejection by the people. Such was the opposition to the CCA that the Government refused the public admission to its sessions and all meetings of the Council had to be held in private.

CHAPTER THREE

The Time Has Come

S. A. Coloured People's Social and Economic Deterioration
(April 1967)

This article is part two in a series published in Sechaba, *with the intention of rallying Coloured support for the ANC, MK and the armed struggle. La Guma's discussion focuses on the economic impact of apartheid.*

Forging ahead with its policy of 'separate development', the Nationalists have instituted the Coloured Representative Council which it hopes will serve as a Coloured 'Parliament' in the same way as it expects the Transkei 'Bantustan' Parliament to operate. Sixteen members of the CRC [Coloured Representative Council] will be appointed by the Government and 30 elected by the Coloured people of the Republic.

The CRC will however be responsible to the Central government, and any resolutions it might pass must be considered by the Minister of Coloured Affairs. The Nationalists have made it clear, in any case, that 'the rights of Indians and Coloureds will remain limited'.

Addressing Parliament in April 1965, the late Verwoerd said that 'if the Africans are eliminated from our political life [...] then the position is that we have a White majority in South Africa and two minority groups (Indian and Coloured people) [...] Surely it is much better than to give a minority group limited powers and opportunities. That is the basis of our policy.'

Further inroads have been made into the last institutions where the Coloured people of the Cape have enjoyed direct representation ... the City Councils. In the future, Coloured people will no longer be elected to the central local governments, but will be 'represented' by Management Committees in the Coloured areas.

Parallel with the destruction of whatever political rights the Coloured people possessed within the framework of the white-supremacist society, social and economic conditions have rapidly deteriorated.

Under the Group Areas Act, thousands of non-white people have been removed from long-established homes in 'mixed' areas to racial ghettos. The Group Areas Amendment Act makes it clear that the Minister of Planning is responsible for planning Group Areas for Whites, Coloureds and Asians through the Group Areas Board. As far as African areas are concerned, the responsibility rests with the Minister of Bantu Administration and Development.

Numerous examples of invasions of the people's residential rights can be mentioned. In 1965, the whole of the central area of Cape Town, where non-whites have lived for centuries, and where a large number have businesses, was declared for whites only. From one district—District Six—more than 60,000 people are to be moved. Statistics show that over 100,000 non-whites in Cape Town will be affected by group areas proclamations. In Port Elizabeth, where the second largest concentration of Coloured people lives, the situation is the same. In and around Johannesburg, places like Albertsville, developed by Coloured people over many years, have been taken over by whites. From all parts of South Africa, the names of places, both well-known and obscure, find a position on the group areas map.

Humiliation and Tragedy

Humiliation and tragedy have followed in the wake of the Nationalists' 'separate development' policy. Houses, schools, churches, mosques, human beings suffer equally: the Christian Council of South Africa estimates that at least £3 million is required to build new churches to serve communities moved under the group areas proclamations; when the century-old tiny Coloured community of Sea Point was ordered out of that part of Cape Town, one man, unable to face the prospect of starting life anew in some unfamiliar place, went out and hanged himself.

Beaches, entertainment and meeting halls, public parks, used for generations by non-whites, have been barred to them. The Coloured people, angered by these encroachments on their rights to live and die where they please, have launched campaign after campaign in protest, only to be met with the disdain and intimidation of the Nationalists.

Trade unions have been broken up on racial lines, thereby crippling the power of workers to bargain collectively with employers. Jobs have been reserved for particular races. From driving heavy vehicles in the Orange Free State to posts as traffic policemen, the 'white-only' proclamations have frustrated the ambitions of non-whites for higher standards of living.

Job Reservation

In the building trade, which employs thousands of Coloured artisans, avenues of skilled employment have been closed to them in terms of work reservation decrees. According to the job reservation determinations, work normally performed by a skilled artisan in the following centres is reserved for white persons only:

Durban and Maritzburg—carpentry, joining, wood machining, plumbing, plastering and electrical wiring;

Port Elizabeth—same as for Durban and Maritzburg except for carpentry and plastering;

East London—all skilled trades;

Cape Peninsula area, Paarl, Wellington, Stellenbosch and Worcester—stone masonry, marble masonry, joinery, wood machining and electrical wiring.

In the OFS, no Coloured may work as a building tradesman, even though there is a major shortage of building workers on the goldfields. Job reservation in public transport in Cape Town allows only 16 per cent of the total force of bus drivers to be non-white in spite of the service's complaints of shortage of staff. From most skilled spheres, the barriers of apartheid are diverting the people to the dead-end of unskilled labour.

In the face of increasing forms of apartheid and racial discrimination in politics and economics, it is not surprising that the physical and social life of the Coloured community is deteriorating to an alarming degree, while vast numbers in the lower-income groups are hit first and hardest. Social problems, which might exist under 'normal' capitalistic conditions, are aggravated seriously by racial discrimination.

It should not be assumed that only under Nationalist rule has the position of the Coloured people deteriorated. Statistics reveal that in 1939, 53 per cent of the community lived below the breadline. Today the position is no better since no white-supremacist society, ruled either by the Nationalists or any other government, holds any promise of progress for the non-white people. Nationalist policy has only worsened the position.

Recent observations by sociologists (*Cape Times*, 2 June 1966) show that increased prices of food and higher transport and other costs were widening the already considerable gap between unskilled wages and the rising cost of living. Approximately 150,000 people are dependent on the earnings of Cape Town's 40,000 unskilled workers . . . and 'a marked increase in the incidence of malnutrition' is imminent. Official figures showed that the cost of living had risen by 69 per cent since 1948. In the same period, basic wages had gone up by only 50 per cent so that the unskilled worker was 19 per cent worse off today than he was 18 years ago.

'Reports of medical officers of local authorities in the Cape showed that the infant mortality rate among non-Whites was 4 to 10 times greater than among Whites and that the incidence of diet deficiency diseases was 10 to 20 times greater.'

'In 1965, an average of 185 new cases of tuberculosis a day was notified in South Africa—a total of close to 68,000. About 56,000 were African, 9,000 Coloured, 1,300 Asian and 1,260 White [. . .] Among the Coloured group a comparatively stabilized four-year run has been dramatically broken by an increase of 16 per cent— from 7,800 cases in 1964 to 9,000 last year' (*Cape Argus*, 14 June 1966).

Figures issued by the Cape Town City Council's Health Department show that of those who died in 1963–64, 53 per cent of the Africans, 39 per cent of the Coloureds and 24 per cent of the Asiatics were under the age of 5 years. Thus nearly half of those non-whites who died were infants. The comparative figure for whites during the same period was less than 5 per cent.

According to the Minister of Planning, Mr Haak, the life expectancy of Coloured men is 44.82 years while that of whites is 64.57. Asians are expected to live to the age of 55.77. White women can expect to live to 70.80 years. Figures for African men and women were not available, the Minister said (*House of Assembly*, 16 March 1965).

CHAPTER FOUR

The Time Has Come
(May 1967)

This article is the third in La Guma's Sechaba series on the struggle of Coloured people in South Africa in which he pays particular attention to issues of social welfare.

Sociologists cannot avoid coming to the conclusion that the rapid increase in crime and drunkenness among the Coloured community is linked with poverty and insecurity. Of the daily average of almost 70,000 prisoners in South African jails, approximately 11,000 are Coloured and Indian. A sociologist commenting on the crime incidence in Cape Town said: 'It is poverty that forces both mother and father out of the house, leaving children unattended and often underfed. That is where juvenile delinquency begins, and the delinquents of yesterday are the rapists and murderers of today.'

A large percentage of those who appeared before courts on charges of housebreaking and theft were youngsters—even as young as eight, said the sociologist. 'They steal things to sell and with the money they buy food. And once they have started on this road, it is not easy to stop them' (*Cape Argus*, 11 February1965).

Escape in Liquor

In the same newspaper Dr O. D. Wolheim, for many years warden of the Cape Flats Distress Association and former chairman of the S. A. Council of General Welfare, stated that 'the insecurity caused by the breaking up of settled communities, poverty and ignorance were among the main causes of the problem of lawlessness in the Coloured Townships'. Drunkenness was undoubtedly allied to insecurity. 'They seek escape and compensation in liquor.'

The pattern of apartheid spreads into all spheres of life, and the spheres of culture and education are as important to the white supremacists as that of politics. Hence separate schools, universities and special education for non-whites under their various ministries and departments. Separate and special education for the different racial groups can mean nothing else but preparation of the minds of South Africa's youth for their special places in apartheid society.

Christian National Education

The Nationalists boast of their Christian National state and their Christian National 'philosophy'. Vorster said once that in Hitler's Germany it was called Nazism, in Italy Fascism, and he and his associates call it Christian Nationalism. So in 1949, an Institute for Christian National Education (ICNE), established ten years earlier, made recommendations for the education of South Africa's non-white children. On the education of the Coloured child, it stated: 'The education of Coloureds should be seen as a subordinate part of the Afrikaner's task of Christianizing the non-white races of our fatherland. It is the Afrikaner's sacred duty to see that the Coloureds are brought up Christian-Nationalist . . . The welfare and happiness of the Coloured lies in his understanding that he belongs to a separate racial group and his being proud of it.'

Education should therefore serve to make each group 'proud' of his place in the apartheid structure. Hence Coloured, Indian and 'Bantu' education in separate schools and universities.

But even if he had no objection to his children receiving this type of education, the position of the Coloured person today is such that he can hardly afford it.

The Minister of Coloured Affairs said in the House of Assembly (2 June 1965) that between 86 and 90 per cent of Coloured children of schoolgoing age attended school. Of these, only 40 per cent reached Standard 2, 27 per cent Standard 5, and 2 per cent Standard 10 (matriculation).

Of Coloured persons enumerated at the 1960 Census, it appears that only 19.4 per cent of the total Coloured population had passed Standard 5, and 0.54 per cent (half a per cent) has passed Standard 10. (Calculated from *1964 Statistical Yearbook*.)

Resisting Oppression

The Coloured people have never taken their degradation at the hands of the white supremacists lying down. In spite of political and social fragmentation in the community, the history of the struggle for justice and equality has shown a progressive development: from requests for reforms in the past, to militant demands for full and equal participation in the government of South Africa.

Descendants of slaves, the Coloured people have engaged in many active campaigns. With each stage in the development of political consciousness new forms of struggle have been adopted. We can point out examples like the strike of garment workers in 1931; the mass demonstrations and clashes with armed police arising out of the anti-segregation struggle of 1938; the general strike led by the Franchise Action Council in 1951; the strike led by the Coloured People's Congress against the establishment of the Verwoerd Republic in 1961; the campaigns against the CAD [Coloured Affairs Department], group areas and population registration. Every one of these efforts gained for the community organizational experience and ever-increasing political consciousness.

But on every occasion they, like the African people, have been met by the armed might of the white state. Faced with the guns and troops of the police, army and security forces, they have been prevented from forcing their rulers to accede to their demands.

It has become abundantly clear to the oppressed non-whites that the only way to achieve justice and democracy in South Africa is to seize power by force of arms. What other alternative is there for the Coloured people comprising 1,703,000 of the South African population?

Hypocrisy of United Party

The voters of the Cape for a long time placed their faith in the United Party, hoping that in this 'opposition' to extreme reaction they would find a solution.

The United Party has pretended to be the champions of the Coloured people. They objected to the removal of the Coloured men from the common voters' roll, but only because they saw a section of their electoral support being cut off. Today, when the Coloured community is making greater demands for full and unconditional democracy, the United Party (the official white 'opposition' party in South Africa) offers only a return to the old order of things: the common roll, to vote for white representatives.

When the Group Areas Act was passed, the United Party did not oppose it on principle, but asked that it be administered 'with justice'. Can an unjust law be administered justly? While pretending to champion the cause of the Coloured community, the United Party showed no compunction in conveniently shelving their Coloured 'policy' and contesting the 1965 General Elections under the slogan of 'White Leadership over the Whole of Southern Africa'.

When the Progressive Party decided to contest the separate elections for Coloured seats in the Cape Provincial Council, the United Party had no hesitation in joining the Nationalists in attacking the Progressives who stood for a small measure of equality, albeit with qualifications. Mr Abe Bloomberg, a Coloured's representative in Parliament, charged the Progressive Party with hypocrisy, 'making "eyewash" cocktail-party promises and using "Coloured ex-communists" in its drive. Mr Bloomberg was immediately congratulated for his attack by a Nationalist MP, Mr J. W. van Statden' (*Cape Times*, 9 June 1964).

De Villiers Graaff, leader of the UP, stated at Bredasdorp (*Cape Times*, 24 April 1965) that the United Party was still 'prepared to accept the Coloured people as part of the Western group in South Africa', but he 'prayed that their conduct will not make this impossible for us'.

Indeed, there is no difference between the United Party and the Nationalist policy towards non-whites other than that of method. It is a case of 'anything you can do, I can do better'.

Colonel J. R. Bowring, United Party MP, expressing 'United Party Viewpoint' (*Cape Times*, 14 June 1965), wrote: 'In spite of the great difference between the United Party and the Nationalist Party policies, both have the same aim—the safeguarding and maintenance of White political control.'

While Parliament remains in the hands of the white minority, the non-whites can expect nothing from it. The white electorate, determined to maintain their position of superiority, have rejected even the lukewarm 'democracy' offered by the Progressive Party, and have continued to share their votes between the upholders of apartheid and 'white leadership'.

Coloured Parties

Within the Coloured community itself various groups suggest solutions to the problem, ranging from those who advocate militant action to those who call for acceptance of the status quo and making the best of whatever can be got out of it, or those who preach outright adherence to the Nationalist policy of 'separate development'.

In the latter category are such groups composing the Federal Coloured People's Party (led by Tom Swartz, former chairman of the now dissolved CCA), which hopes to serve as the 'government party' in the Coloured Representative Council. These elements we can dismiss.

Hoping to capture the Coloured Representative Council, or at least become the 'official opposition', is the 'South African Labour Party' under the leadership of Dr R. E. van der Ross. While claiming to be against apartheid, this 'Party' has no hesitation in adopting the outright opportunist line of 'using the instruments available to us', without even challenging the system; saying this was the 'only way the Coloured people can organize themselves under the present system' (Dr van der Ross, *Cape Argus*, 14 November 1965).

Further, the Constitution of the 'Party' says that as there are legislative restrictions on the activities of political parties according to their membership, only people who would not prevent it from carrying out its avowed aims in regard to the Coloured people would be admitted.

Not only accepting the 'instruments available to us', but also racialist 'restrictions according to their membership' of the apartheid dictates of the Nationalists as to what forms of representation and political organization they will tolerate!

The 'S. A. Labour Party' was also speedy in giving the assurance that everything they did would be above board and that they did not object to Security Police surveillance, since they had nothing to hide. But these assurances did not help.

Acceptance of the 'instruments available to us' was not enough for the Nationalists. No sooner was the 'S. A. Labour Party' formed than the Security Police were on its doorstep. Members have been arraigned and warned against 'furthering the aims of communism', and the treasurer resigned. People once active in politics were approached to join the 'Party' and spy on it for remuneration.

So much for the Labour Party's kowtowing to the Nationalists with hopes that they could win anything for the Coloured community by waving about racialist and opportunist policies and rejecting any unity with other groups.

CHAPTER FIVE

The Time Has Come

*The Coloured People Must Prepare
to Bear Arms for Liberation*
(June 1967)

The fourth and concluding article in La Guma's Sechaba *series to rally Coloured support for the ANC. He makes an explicit appeal for armed struggle based on what he sees as 'military traditions' among Coloured South Africans.*

The only uncompromising formula for complete equality and unconditional democracy for all people who inhabit South Africa has been offered by the Congress Movement, led by the African National Congress. The Freedom Charter, which is its programme, sets out the principles on which all people will be able to share in the creation of a united country based on the will of all the people, with guarantees against all forms of racial discrimination.

The Coloured People's Congress, allied to the Congress Movement, accepts the Freedom Charter as its programme, and it is in support of such a policy that the Coloured community can finally come into its own, side by side with the rest of the oppressed people. It is only in a State as envisaged in the Freedom Charter that all the degradations of inferior political rights, social decay, poverty and malnutrition, crime and drunkenness and frustration, to which the Coloured community has been victim, will be swept away.

New Methods of Struggle

But the CPC, although a legal organization, cannot hope to lead and unite the community in the face of the fascist methods of the Nationalist government by adhering to its position as an openly public body, thereby exposing itself to the attacks of the Nationalists.

At the same time, it cannot avoid the standpoint that the seizure of power by the oppressed can only come through armed struggle, in view of the prevailing tyranny in South Africa. It must consider new methods of struggle and new forms of organization. The Coloured community as a whole must be made to realize that the course adopted by the African people led by the African National Congress is the only course open to the oppressed of South Africa.

The Nationalists will tolerate nothing but the grovelling acceptance of apartheid, and the white population have adhered for generations to their position of superiority. By using bannings, house arrest, imprisonment, outright police terror, the white supremacists have stifled every form of opposition to their policies. Coloured city councillors, direct representatives of their people, have been warned to keep in line; such units as the District Six Committee against Group Areas removals, and others, have disintegrated under the intimidation of the Security Police; teachers opposing the Government have been banned and dismissed from their posts.

Members of the Coloured People's Congress, which has shown consistent militancy in its approach to the problems of the community, have been immobilized by imprisonment, bannings and confinements, house arrest, thus bringing all activity of the organization to a halt.

What other recourse have the people then, but to adopt and support new methods of struggle for their freedom?

Underground Organization

'The Coloured people have never been given to working underground,' stated Dr van der Ross (*Cape Argus*, 14 November 1965). We say that *NO* people have been 'given' to working underground. The people of Europe had no natural aptitude for pursuing their underground activities against the Nazi occupation. They had to submit or fight, so they fought underground. So did the people of Asia and so do the people of Latin America. The people can no longer stand subservient to tyranny and rule by force and violence. Violence can only be fought with violence. There is no alternative in South Africa today.

On the international front, there have been numerous resolutions of support for the non-white peoples' demands for justice in South Africa, but such resolutions, while welcome, are only supplementary to the defeat of white supremacy in our country. Vorster, on being elected prime minister, stated that South Africa's problems will be solved in South Africa. We agree, they shall, finally, be solved there.

Today, the feasibility of waging armed struggle for freedom is no longer the dream it has been in the past. South Africa is being rapidly isolated in the international political arena; the emergence of sympathetic African states on the borders of white-ruled southern Africa and the existence of the powerful Socialist world make armed struggle a reality.

In the Portuguese colonies, the African forces of liberation are actively engaged with Portuguese troops; the people of South West Africa have started to embark on guerrilla warfare; the people of Zimbabwe are waging a fierce struggle; in South Africa itself, Umkhonto we Sizwe has emerged as the military wing of the oppressed people.

Fighting Record

The Coloured people number 1,703,000 of which 1,449,000 live in the Cape Province alone. The 1960 Census put the Coloured population of Cape Town as 417,881, estimating an increase to 553,000 by 1970. In Cape Town alone, the Coloured community man 80 per cent of the city's manpower. There on the southernmost sector of South Africa, this vast number of antagonized people stands in the rear of the forces of white supremacy, constituting a potentially formidable ally of the forces of democracy.

Warfare is not new to the Coloured community. Their military traditions are enshrined in the country's history. Albeit under the false colours of imperialism's 'freedom and democracy', the community's contribution to South Africa's defence is recognized.

The military annals of South Africa bear proof of this, since the first Coloured men were called to arms in 1795. Their dead are buried in Europe, the Middle East and Africa. Of their sacrifices in the 1914–18 War, particularly at the battle of Square Hill, Palestine, Brig. Gen. J. W. Walker wrote: 'The gallantry displayed by the Cape Corps Battalion was of the highest order and beyond all praise.'

Fought Against Fascism

In the war against Nazism and fascism, Coloured men of the Cape Corps (including the Indian and Malay Corps) served from South Africa to North Africa, Italy, the Western Desert, Madagascar. The Director of Non-European Army Services, Col. E. T. Stubbs, said: 'On the battle fronts, in fact wherever men of the Union Defence Forces were serving, large numbers of the Cape Corps were to be found' (*Cape Corps Souvenir*, 1945).

'Both out of the line and in the line their soldierly behaviour has been exemplary ... and in no single instance have I ever seen any of my Non-European personnel behave in any way other than in the highest traditions' (Lt Col. C. L. Parkin D. C., 2nd Anti-Tank Regiment, S. A. A.).

Nine Military Medals were won by members of the Cape Corps during the Second World War; four British Empire Medals; fifty-one Mentions-in-Despatches, two King's Commendations and eight Commander-in-Chief's Commendations. The battles of Keren in the Sudan, the capture of 24 officers and 766 men by two officers and 16 men of the Cape Corps at the 'Awash' River area, are only two operations associated with the Cape Corps.

One of the first acts of the Nationalist government when it came to power was to abolish the Cape Corps. This was an act typical of those who supported Nazi Germany when Coloured men were dying to defeat it. Today, the Nationalists cynically expect them to defend apartheid and all its attendant evils through a 'Coloured Corps' created for the purpose of guarding installations at home.

We Must Bear Arms Again

The Coloured people will never defend apartheid. With military traditions behind them, traditions which they created in the hope that their contributions would be justly rewarded, they can continue their heroic service for the victory of real freedom and democracy.

The patience of the people is not endless. The time has come when they, side by side with the other oppressed people, must prepare to bear arms again, this time for the liberation of their country.

CHAPTER SIX

The Coloured Cadets Bill
(October 1967)

This article published in Sechaba *discusses how the apartheid government sought to control Coloured South Africans through pass laws and labour regimes. La Guma outlines how the 'colour bar' was being applied more aggressively to Coloured men, in particular, through new labour legislation. Building on the discussions from 'The Time Has Come' series, this piece is notable for being an early example of his concern for the economic effects of apartheid, not just its political impact, which would later inform his provisional views on racial capitalism.*

The tentacles of passes and forced labour are extended to the Coloured people under the Coloured Cadets Bill.

For more than a century, the African people of South Africa have been forced to leave their homes to engage in work for whites, on farms, in the mines, in industry and in homes. As the pass-law system became more and more brutal under successive governments maintaining cheap non-white labour and upholding white political and economic superiority, millions of Africans have been forced into a life of appalling poverty and police terror raids for passes and permits.

Today the tentacles of this vicious system are commencing their inevitable reach into other sections of the non-white communities, their suckers preparing to seize and grip more and more lives in the stranglehold of enforced labour at the cheapest rates, police searches and labour transit camps. For the South African government has recently introduced a so-called Coloured Cadets Bill.

More Whitewash

Mr N.F. Treurnicht (MP for Picketberg) explained the Bill as 'a measure that would prevent their (Coloured people's) children succumbing to bad habits and eventual delinquency . . . A good start to incorporate the Coloured youth in a positive labour plan.'

It needs only to compare Mr Treurnicht's watery whitewash with the gallons which have been used over the years to glorify the Bantu Administration Act without success. No amount of colourful descriptions have been able to hide the festering horror of South Africa's pass laws for Africans. And it needs only to glance at the words which have become notorious in South African legislation: 'registration', 'empowered', 'penalties', 'compulsory', to realize that an existence under the pass laws now awaits the Coloured people unless they gird up their loins to fight it.

Registration, Compulsory Work

The Coloured Cadets Bill provides for registration of all Coloured men between the ages of 18 and 24, and the training in employment of all those not at school and those who are unemployed. Thus, apart from already having to carry an Identity Card which places a person in his racial category, the Coloured man, whether he is employed or not, will have to register and *will obviously have to carry some sort of document which will prove this*—as does the African.

Having been registered, these men can be called upon to enter a compulsory work-training camp, where training can 'include any work done inside or outside the work-training centres.' Penalties for disobeying call-up orders or failure to register will range from fines to imprisonment or both.

A selection board will be empowered to 'exempt' those who are engaged in full-time study at school or university, and those in permanent employment serving apprenticeships. Thus, as applies to Africans under the Bantu Administration Act, the Coloured men exempted will have to carry a farcical 'exemption document', which he will in any case have to show to anybody in authority, for example, a policemen, to prove that the pass law does not apply to him!

Minister's Discretion

But, the Bill also adds, the authorities concerned are *not compelled to exempt* anybody whether he is studying full-time, or is working in permanent employment or studying as an apprentice. At the same time, it is not the selection board who will be empowered to decide how many people shall be forced into the compulsory labour-training camps, but the Minister of Coloured Affairs who will have sole discretion. Neither does the Bill distinguish between a youth who might honestly be unemployed and seeking work through the normal channels, and one who might be a delinquent. The labour camps await all and sundry who might be gathered into the Minister's net. It means, in effect, that Coloured men will not be in a position to seek work of their own choice—they will be forced into a work category decided upon by those who run the labour camps.

The Coloured man will have no say in his own destiny.

No Parental Control

The Coloured Cadets Bill likewise removes all parental control over Coloured youth, except where property rights and consent to marry are concerned. Thus, parents will have no more say over the future of their sons. Under this Bill any hopes of economic advancement for young people hang forever in the precarious balance of forced-labour authorities and camp commandants.

'Re-trained'—For Unskilled Work

What lies immediately behind the Coloured Cadets 'Forced Labour' Bill? Mr Coetzee, deputy minister of Bantu Administration, stated that the legislation was intended as a means of filling the labour gap in the Western Cape caused by the Government's decision to expel 5 per cent of Africans from the area each year until all Africans are finally expelled from the area. Thus, it means clearly the replacement of African unskilled and poverty-line labour by Coloured labour. It means the relegation of Coloured workers to the grinding economic position that Africans have endured for generations.

Coloured workers, for example, finding themselves retrenched from higher paid, skilled or semi-skilled jobs (a position they have tenuously held due to historical factors), can find themselves forcibly engaged in labouring work at the lowest wages. Trained workers forced out of employment through Job Reservation (which determines that certain skilled jobs are for whites only), will find themselves forced into labour camps where they will be 'trained' for unskilled labour.

Call For Farm Labour

For a long time, farmers of the Western Cape have been clamouring about the shortage of farm labour. In June 1964, for example, the *Cape Argus* complained: 'Western Cape Farmers Badly Hit by Labour Shortage. Alarming Loss of Coloured Labour.' Again, in August 1964, the same paper reported:

> The Winter Rainfall Union and the Cape Province Wool Growers Association have on the agenda a motion asking for the appointment of labour committees to make a study of labour matters in Regional Union areas. The motion says positive steps must be taken to create conditions that will not only keep labourers there but will draw these people from elsewhere.

In February 1965, the paper reported that 'a steadily rising shortage of Coloured labour on farms in the Western Cape is forcing a relaxation of influx control of farming industry . . .' In June 1964,

G. A. Theron, MPU Ceres, had stated at Tulbagh in the Cape: 'I would like to see the thousands of Coloured "won't-works" in the cities transported to the Platteland.'

The Coloured Cadets Bill dooms thousands of Coloured youths to a future as permanent unskilled workers, and as farm labourers toiling for the miserable pittance of £2 or £3 a month. It requires only an amendment to the law to extend the forced-labour regulation age beyond 24 years, and to extend it to Coloured women as well.

Greater Unity Is Called For

The Coloured Cadets Bill will place every Coloured person in the front line of humiliating demands for passes by patrolling policemen. It places every Coloured home in the line of police raids. The Coloured people cannot submit meekly to the degrading life under the pass laws. The Coloured people cannot submit willingly to regimentation by forced-labour officials, to work camps and police raids.

The threat of this new kind of slavery for the Coloured people calls for greater unity with the African people, and renewed and unified struggle to end forever the whole rotten system of cheap labour, indignity, frustration and poverty.

CHAPTER SEVEN

The Coloured People of South Africa
(1968)

This article appeared in The African Communist *under the pseudonym Willem Abram Malgas. Beyond offering an overview of South Africa's Coloured population, what is noteworthy are its remarks regarding the Coloured People's Congress (CPC), which had suffered internal divisions between those who supported the ANC and the Congress Alliance versus those who supported the Pan Africanist Congress. The CPC was the successor to the South African Coloured People's Organisation (SACPO, 1953–59) that La Guma led with Reggie September (1923–2013). Similar to his earlier series 'The Time Has Come', this article indicates a continued attempt to sustain aspects of the CPC's programme and its ties to the Congress Alliance, despite its decline.*

This year, further government attacks on the Coloured community in South Africa resulted in legislation for the final removal of Coloured representation in Parliament, and the expansion of the Coloured Representation Council to serve as a centre of Coloured 'representation' within the framework of apartheid.

Thus, Acts of Parliament were passed to (a) abolish the present representation of Coloured voters by four white MPs (These will serve until 1971 after which date the vacancies will not be filled.) (b) enlarge the present CRC and give it some control over Coloured group affairs, the administration of funds, education, pensions, etc.

In order to give this arbitrary and cynical arrangement an aura of democracy, the legislation allows for the compulsory registration of voters, both men and women, and makes the Council predominantly elective. Needless to say, the Council will remain at the beck and call of the Central Government through the relevant minister, that of Coloured Affairs.

To turn the screws a little tighter, another law has been enacted simultaneously, to prohibit (a) the participation in political parties of one racial group by members of another group; (b) multiracial membership of political parties; (c) the acceptance by South African political parties of funds from abroad.

It would be wishful thinking to say that this latest attack on the Coloured community is the ultimate one on their political life, for who knows what might develop even within the CRC and its elections, and what other 'preventative' measures the Nationalist government might have up its collective sleeve? Thus the continued preparedness of the people and militant leadership, particularly of the Coloured People's Congress, is essential.

The white supremacists have a long record of attempting to relegate this minority community to the status of virtual 'non-people' in the same way it has the Africans. But the insatiable altars of the apartheid Moloch and Baal have history to reckon with, and the determination of people to survive and win.

It would be appropriate and important at this stage to give some further consideration to the complex question of the origin, nature and aspirations of the Coloured people, and their role in the national liberation struggle for the overthrow of apartheid and white minority domination. It is hoped that the following thoughts on this subject may stimulate some debate and discussion in the columns of this journal and elsewhere.

Historical Origins

As a community and part of the South African population, these people generally and officially known as 'Coloured' have a history which cannot be separated from that of the other sections inhabiting the subcontinent.

Latest figures show that this community now totals 1,859,000 persons, the majority of whom are concentrated in the south-western part of the Cape Province. Various statutory definitions have tried to identify the 'Cape Coloured' or 'Coloured' (for while the majority live in the Cape Province, the community is scattered throughout the Republic), but these vague and negative definitions become more inexplicable in the light of any examination of the history of this people.

The main ingredients of the Coloured people of today are (a) slaves brought from abroad; (b) local aborigines (the Khoin [sic] people); (e) white colonists; (d) indigenous Africans to a lesser extent.

The slaves seem to have outnumbered the local Khoin inhabitants, commonly referred to as Hottentots and Bushmen.[1] These latter were decimated by the incoming white colonists, and those not taken as slaves were driven from the area. With the demand for labour increasing as the outpost at Cape Town developed, slaves were brought in by the Dutch East India Company.

There were two main sources of slaves: the East Indies and East Africa including Madagascar. Slaves from the latter were apparently in the majority, and were brought to perform agricultural work mainly in the colony, the pastoral, easy-going Khoin having been found unsuitable. These slaves were 'Negroid by race, with an infiltration of Indonesian blood and an Indonesian language (Malagasy) with remnants of a few Bantu words'.[2]

The Asian slaves, though fewer in number, were the 'aristocracy' of the slave population. They came mainly from the Malay Archipelago. Some were convicts who, having their time, became 'Free Blacks' and chose to settle in the Cape Colony and later formed the nucleus of a small artisan group. Others were political

---

1 The census of 1805 gives the number of slaves as 29,545, and Hottentot and Bushmen, 20,000. In 1821, there were 35,698 slaves.

2 G. B. Lestrade, University of Cape Town.

exiles with their attendants. Many of these were Moslems, and the term 'Cape Malay' (now considered a derogatory term) denotes a religious rather than an ethnic group.

Many of these were skilled craftsmen, builders, masons, carpenters, etc.

The white colonists were farmers, artisans, soldiers, clerks, and there were of course uncounted sailors who passed through. The cultural gap between the lower strata of the colonists and the slaves was probably not very great.

In the original contact situation, the most important mixtures were those between slave men and aboriginal women, and European men and slave and aboriginal women. In both the slave and European communities, men far outnumbered women for a long period, and the relatively few European women were not likely to risk their higher social status for the sake of casual, much less permanent, intercourse with slaves or the despised Hottentots. Even today it is usually the white man and the non-white woman who seek association outside their group.

Thus three-quarters of the children born to slave mothers at the Cape by 1671 were found to be half-breeds.[3] Many of these and later half-breeds, quarter-breeds, etc., may also be the ancestors of the present white population. The intermarriage between historical figures like Van Meerhof, van der Kemp, James Read and others, and non-white women are well known, but it is obvious that it was not only a few potentates who took non-white women.

On the whole, the original intercourse between white and non-white took place mainly between the colonists and slaves, the Hottentots being generally considered with contempt—a 'stinckcne natie' (stinking people) as van Riebeeck described them.

Nevertheless, as the colonists trekked further away from the civilized Cape their way of life forced them to shed many of the little niceties of European culture, for they became as nomadic as

---

3 Prof. I. D. Macrone.

the despised Hottentot, while at the same time the chronic shortage of women compelled many informal, sometimes permanent, unions with the womenfolk of these people.

By the beginning of the nineteenth century, the pure aboriginal had practically ceased to exist in the Colony, and the second, third and fourth generations of mixed breeds were breeding among themselves and increasing their numbers.

In spite of the fact that by this time colour prejudice had hardened, the white contribution to the mixed-breed community seems not to have diminished greatly, and with migration a further mixed-blood community was added—by white and African 'miscegenation', particularly in the Eastern Cape, and in Natal and Transvaal.[4]

In short, the Coloured people are the products of an early series of mixed unions between Europeans and slaves, slaves and Europeans, slaves and aborigines, and Europeans and aborigines, and on a smaller scale between Europeans and Africans and Coloureds and Africans.

The slaves having been transported from their homelands naturally adapted themselves to their new environment. Being at the beck and call of their master, they had to learn his language, pander to his customs and follow generally the course laid out for him. The white slave owners and the colonists, consciously or unconsciously rationalizing their superior status, saw to it that the slave recognized the value of the masters' 'civilizing' influence. The growing community of mixed-bloods gradually accepted the languages, the customs and culture of the whites.[5]

---

[4] The present Coloured population in the Eastern Cape and Natal is estimated at one quarter million, approximately 8,000 living in the Transkei (not taking into consideration removals under the Group Areas Act, etc.), while another 25,000 live in the Orange Free State.

[5] According to the Bureau of Census and Statistics in 1946, languages spoken by the Coloured people in the Cape Province were: English 7.3 per cent; Afrikaans 91.5 per cent; Other 1.2 per cent. In Cape Town only, the

The missionary societies brought Christianity and the beginnings of formal European-based education, and it might be added that today (except for the small Moslem community) the churches of European origin include membership of 90 per cent of the Coloured people.[6] The Dutch Reformed Church has the largest percentage (almost 40 per cent) of Coloured Christians, the rest being divided among the other churches.

Colour—The Basis of Discrimination

No trace is left among the Coloured people of the culture of their slave ancestors, apart from some words and cuisine of Indonesian origin. Names, languages, clothes, customs, art, literature are all shared with white South Africans. '[T]he Coloured do not appear to differ from us today in anything except their poverty . . . A Coloured does not exist in any realistic interpretation of the term', states Prof. J. S. Marais.

Discrimination against the Coloured people has been based on colour rather than on culture, for while the pigmentation and physical characteristics of the community might range from Caucasian to Negroid, no real cultural or language difference between them and the whites can be pinpointed. Indeed, in spite of the attempted definitions of 'Coloureds' for purposes of various laws, the authorities dare not go too far back into the ancestry of either white or Coloured peoples for fear of being confronted with startling revelations.

---

percentages were: English 21.07 per cent; Afrikaans 77.26 per cent; Other 1.67 per cent. The Cape Library Services state that in 1964 in one month (June) 10,446 Coloureds, including juveniles, read Afrikaans books, as against 2,179 whites.

6 The first school for young slaves of the Dutch East India Company was established in 1658. The purpose of the school was to teach the slaves Dutch and to give religious instruction. In 1663, the first mixed school was established with 18 Europeans, 4 slaves and 1 Hottentot. To this, girl slaves were admitted in 1665. By 1823, it was estimated that 1,551 slaves were attending school in Cape Town.

Although slavery was abolished in the British Empire in 1833, it proved difficult to eradicate from the mentality of most white South Africans the conception that the main function of the non-white is to provide cheap labour for the European. The slave-owning mentality was built up long before the African became a source of labour for the white. The distinction between work that was proper for a white person and what subsequently came to be known as 'Kaffir work' was thereby drawn for centuries to come.

The idea that skin colour and not skill should be the determining factor in the economic hierarchy thus became an integral part of white attitudes and support for the colour bar, segregation or apartheid.

From the earliest times, labour restrictions were practiced, and the statutes of the first parliament of the Cape of Good Hope (1854–58) contain 'An Act for encouraging the Importation of European Labourers into this Colony' and others restricting African movement, while earlier, in 1809, labour laws provided for passes for Hottentots.

An examination of the activities of the earliest organizations of the Coloured people show that these generally centred on demands of a political and economic nature rather than cultural. Already sharing a common language and cultural background with the whites, the Coloured community's struggle reflects essentially a desire to return to the fold from which they have been ejected. Politically they had enjoyed political rights in the Cape and Natal equal with the whites since the Charter of 1856.[7] When there were indications that these rights were in danger, as an anonymous Coloured historian put it in the *APO* newspaper in 1909, 'it would be necessary to safeguard their interests', i.e. their equal political rights with the whites.[8]

---

7 In the Cape and Natal, there was no constitutional discrimination between white and Coloured persons. There was however a hardening of attitudes towards non-whites even before Union. e.g. Laws in 1865 and 1896 excluded Africans and Indians from political rights.

Coloured political leaders continued to show a growing ire against being excluded from the fold. In 1938, Dr Abdurahman complained: 'As far as I know, no leader or spokesman of the Afrikaner community during the present [Voortrekker Centenary] celebrations has uttered one word of appreciation of the loyalty, kindness and heroism displayed by the Coloured people and other Non-Europeans who stood by the side of the Voortrekker [. . .].'[9]

Later campaigns reflected this demand for a return to equality with whites. For example (a) the protests against the introduction of residential segregation in 1939; (b) segregation on the trains; (c) removal of the Coloured voter from the common roll; (d) the Anti-CAD movement which saw the Government treating the Coloured people as separate and inferior.

Is It a 'National' Struggle?

There is no basis, and there never has been, for the 'national' struggle of the Coloured people (as we loosely term it) to include the right 'to speak a single language, with all obstacles to the development of that language and its consolidation in literature eliminated'.[10] The history of the community shows that it is part of the English and Afrikaans-speaking communities by virtue of language and culture, sharing with them the common territory of South Africa. By means of their colour they are discriminated against in the interest of the white bourgeoisie, and this discrimination gave rise to a community self-consciousness and demands which cannot be considered 'national' in the strict sense of the word.

Apart from a few minor businessmen and property owners, a Coloured economic bourgeoisie is absent. On the whole, the community provides the labour force in the areas which they occupy. In the Cape Peninsula alone, the Coloured population of over

---

8 Lionel Forman's *Notebooks*.
9 *Cape Argus*, 17 December 1938.
10 Lenin, *The Right of Nations to Self-Determination*.

500,000 provides 80 per cent of the manpower required to keep the area's secondary industries going, with the rest occupied in other work and in the professions. In the Western Cape countryside, they form the bulk of the rural working population. The Coloured people, workers essentially and discriminated against on colour lines, demand 'as a matter of principle, that there should be no privileges, however slight', and consequently what they demand is that they be given the same rights as their white counterparts.[11]

However, the rise of the African liberation movement enforced upon Coloured political thinkers the consideration of the common basis of African and Coloured struggle, against the barriers of race and colour oppression.

Efforts for Coloured–African unity are not recent ones. The *APO*, dealing with the question of the Act of Union, stated: 'We the Coloured and Native peoples of South Africa have a tremendous fight before us. We have the war of wars to wage'. And again, by the *APO* Johannesburg correspondent:

> The fight must begin somewhere and it seems to us that the Pass Regulations is a good battleground for the first struggle. When once it has begun, consolidation of native forces will be the result. Success must not be looked for immediately, but the Coloured people must remember that the fight for freedom, national, social, political or economic, 'though baffled oft' is ever won.[12]

The struggle for freedom in South Africa is inclusive of similar calls and practical efforts for unity of struggle. But the development of the struggle, under the leadership of the militant African liberation movement, has given rise to advanced conceptions of the goal of the struggle. The ultimate [aim] of a united South African nation arising from the equal participation of all groups has been something minority groups, especially, have had to chew upon.

---

11 Lenin, *The Right of Nations to Self-Determination*
12 *The Working Class Is Born* (New Age pamphlet).

The white racists of course reject this conception. The more conservative thinkers in the Coloured community hesitate, but the pressure of the African people was felt, and thus the Coloured Convention of 1961 'proclaimed a new dynamic for the South African *nation* . . . a dynamic that will bring every single person who comprises the South African *nation*, peace, justice, honour, happiness, security and prosperity'.[13] Other politicians of the Coloured Left adopted a similar standpoint. 'The South African *nation* is thus made up of people of *various* "racial" and cultural origins *who have undergone* an irretrievable process of assimilation [. . .].'[14] [Our emphases]

Both these groups jump the gun, for they already speak of 'the South African nation' as if this already exists, as if the evolutionary process has already taken place. Of course, the principle of a common South African nation is accepted by far thinking people, but hasty proclamations of its existence do not bring it about.

For the generally unorganized Coloured community with its cultural and historical base in the white groups, the conception of real unity with the Africans has always been a difficult one to bring to practicality. While unity with the African people has been theoretically accepted as an essential for the overthrow of economic and political barriers, there exists the subconscious fear that this unity would result in a total alienation from the base. This fear has also resulted in a failure to maintain sustained political organization on a community basis, other factors aside—organization which might involve antagonizing those who are in fact 'blood brothers' of the Coloured people. Organization of the Coloured people on the basis of the community, while essential in the light of colour discrimination, will continue to be hampered by this blockage, and principled enunciations about the 'South African nation', present or future, will not help to remove it.

---

13 The South African 'Coloured' National Convention. Preliminary Report.
14 *Towards a Modern South African Patriotism*. A *Citizen* Pamphlet.

While the ultimate goal of all the South African peoples is a single unified South Africa, the first consideration of the Coloured people is a return to their base to become integrated with their English and Afrikaans counterparts. While those who hope to see Coloured participation in the struggle against the white supremacists do not take this into consideration, difficulties will continue to be met.

Class Factor Is the Key

But the blockage can be bypassed only by the correct orientation of the progressive leadership within the Coloured community. The difficulties experienced in creating sustained organization, in creating political unity with the African people, can be overcome by a greater consideration of the Coloured people's *class* position and the relationship of that position to its community position. We have pointed out that the Coloured community is essentially a working-class community. Since the period of slavery, the Coloured people have been a labour force, and today they form a proletariat reduced to a source of cheap labour by virtue of their colour. On the class basis, their demand is 'that there should be no privileges (for whites only) however slight'. Coloured workers are found in every branch of commerce and industry, particularly in the Cape, as has been pointed out. Coloured trade-union membership in that Province is extensive to the extent that they can cause considerable consternation for the ruling class. This has been shown during such periods when protest strikes were waged. They are the pioneers of the garment workers' union formed in the 1930s, one of the biggest in the Cape. On this class basis, they are far better organized than on the 'Coloured', and experience has shown that it has been on this basis that they have reacted during periods of militant struggle against community oppression.

It is in the field of class struggle where what we claim is a psychological blockage, the fear of alienation as a community, has been overcome.

Scant attention has been paid by the *political* movement of the Coloured people to this aspect of the community's organized life, and far greater effort should have been made to overcome the deficiency. It is hoped that, in spite of the violent repression existing in the country, that the task can still be undertaken.

By this alliance of the class interests with the community interest can the Coloured people win the equality they desire and take their place within a common community of white and Coloured, and contribute towards the creation of the eventual South African nation.

The Freedom Charter of the Congress Movement provides a realistic programme for the ultimate united South Africa. It recognizes the diversity of the peoples of South Africa and provides for the fulfilment of their immediate aspirations. 'All people shall have equal right to use their own languages, and to develop their own folk culture and customs; all national groups shall be protected by laws against insults to their race and national pride.'

The Coloured People's Congress, in adopting the Freedom Charter, and allying itself with the Congress Movement, showed its willingness to organize the Coloured community on the basis of a realistic programme. But what is basically required of the CPC is a detailed and scientific examination of the community's past, its present aspirations, and its destiny. This is essential for future organization and cooperation in the struggle for a new South Africa.

CHAPTER EIGHT

Pumpkins and Dark Skins
(May 1969)

This fable-like article appeared in Sechaba, distilling the absurdities of South African racial categorization through a journalistic narrative approximating a short story.

On a smallholding in the Western Transvaal, Mrs Maria Haasbroek raises pigs, turkeys, and hens, and grows vegetables. She has been separated from her husband for the last six years and apart from the sales of farm produce, gets a welfare grant and some money from her husband.

One day a four-man deputation, including a dominee from the Dutch Reformed Church, the Deputy Director of Education in the Transvaal, and the Inspector of Education for Potchefstroom, advanced on the small farm.

The dominee was the first to speak, addressing Mrs Haasbroek with prescribed unction. He said that God had sent them to help her in her troubles. He would open the discussion with a prayer, asking God to help, as the woman stood in the place of her husband and she had 'Hell to fight through'.

It appeared that the 'troubles' all revolved around the fact that while Mr and Mrs Haasbroek were 'White' according to South African standards and carried the appropriate identity cards, one of the sons, Flippie, aged 13, was creating 'hell' not only for Mrs

Haasbroek but for the whole Apartheid State, including the Population Register and the Transvaal Education Department.

The fact of the matter is that Flippie looks Coloured, has a dark skin and kinky hair, and while he is described as a bright and appealing boy, his looks are enough to upset the whole Apartheid applecart.

His parents having registered him as 'White', he was sent to a White school for the benefits of a 'White' education. But problems arose when his schoolmates, no doubt acting in the best interests of White civilization, turned upon him and made his life difficult with taunts of 'Coloured'. In any event, Flippie's presence at the Ventersdorp High School became an embarrassment to all and sundry involved in his education, and ways and means had to be found of getting rid of him.

Flippie was thereupon expelled for stealing pumpkins.

But his brother Lewies was also found guilty of stealing pumpkins, but was not expelled from his school. Lewies is fair-skinned. 'I see this whole thing as the victimization of my son on account of his appearance,' Mrs Haasbroek told the Johannesburg *Sunday Times*.

When he was at junior school, the principal and members of the school committee had approached Flippie's mother, asking her to withdraw him because, they said, other parents were threatening to send their children away if Flippie stayed. When Flippie passed to high school, the 'problem' went with him.

Finding it difficult to make 'Operation Pumpkin Stealer' work, the panjandrums of the Transvaal Education Department took a new course. They would offer to send Flippie, an 'expelled' pupil, to a private school and pay all the expenses. This is a departure from the normal treatment of expelled children.

It is not difficult to imagine the furtive running around to find a White private school that would be willing to gulp down its race pride and admit Flippie into its hallowed Aryan environs. After many refusals and much juggling, the deputation advanced in triumph upon the Haasbroek household, waving aloft an offer from a school, 'Not one where fees are necessary, but no doubt a donation will be made to the school by the department.' It was emphasized that it was a school for Whites.

However, Mrs Haasbroek, almost gummed up the works. She did not want to sign any papers before she had inspected the school herself. No matter what persecution her child was undergoing for not being the right colour, she wasn't going to let the side down. She was a good White South African.

'I feared that they would send Flippie to a school for Coloureds. I asked them what pupils attended the type of school they had in mind for Flippie, and they said there were mostly English-speaking children, including Roman Catholics and Jews. I said I was afraid Flippie would be influenced at a school like this and become a liberal. I don't want him to become a liberalist. Flippie is a good Afrikaner boy and that's how he should be brought up and that is how I want him to be educated.'

Faced with this outburst of patriotism, the deputation promised to investigate further. The Director of Education for the Transvaal subsequently stated, with official pomp not unmixed with relief and glee, 'The department has obtained the cooperation of the mother of Phillipus Haasbroek in connection with the placing of her son in a school which is regarded in the best interests of the pupil. Both the mother and the school concerned have, at the Department's request, given their wholehearted cooperation and the matter has been settled to the satisfaction of all the parties concerned.'

Flippie went to his new school. The pumpkins have been carefully stored away. What will happen when Flippie finally wants to realize his boyhood ambitions is another bridge to be crossed. When he grows up, Flippie wants to be an airline pilot.

One can almost imagine the Ministers of Transport and of Labour already reaching for their aspirins.

The story of Flippie is really not a new one in the lurid pages of South Africa's cloud-cuckoo anthology of Apartheid. As Mrs Haasbroek herself remarked, it is another 'Sandra Laing' tale, referring to the girl removed from her White family because she was dark-skinned. The chapters can become more grimmer when one looks back on such incidents as that of a 12-year-old 'Coloured' boy who hanged himself because he could not adapt to his 'White' family. The fact is that in spite of claims of White supremacy, there are really few pure White South Africans, a great deal of miscegenation having taken place between settlers and slaves during the early days of South Africa's colonization. So that 'throwbacks' can occur within a 'White' family, leading to consternation in the offices of the Population Register and the Ministry of the Interior.

When the Race Classification Act was first enforced, officials took it upon themselves to decide who belonged to which racial group. They ran pencils through the hair of their victims. If the hair was kinky and the pencil did not go through smoothly, the victim was Coloured, or African as the case may be. By forcing a victim to repeat a tongue twister, they could discover, by his accent and pronunciation, his category.

Later, the legislature had to enact a series of definitions, which rapidly became meaningless, involving 'appearances', 'associations' and a host of other stipulations.

Recently, Mr Justice Hiemstra wearily criticized 'sterile legalisms' in the Race Classification Act that led him 'with the greatest regret' to reject an appeal by a mother and her adopted daughter to be reclassified White (the husband is classified White) although they are in appearance White and accepted as White.

The adopted daughter, the mother told a welfare officer, had been born illegitimately, and the father might have been Chinese, although the child in everyday life benefits from all those good things reserved for the master race. The Justice declared, 'The fact that a man and a wife are now classified into different race groups is highly unsatisfactory, and must be utterly mystifying to them.'

Not only to them. The pretexts for racial divisions and discrimination must be mystifying to any sane person. But then in South Africa one must expect the standards of a lunatic asylum when it is run by those who are fit more to be the inmates of such an institution rather than its governors. There is even more bewilderment caused by victims such as Mrs Haasbroek who proudfully proclaims that young Flippie's heroes are the late Dr Verwoerd, former President Swart and the wrestler Vrystaat (FREEDOM!).

CHAPTER NINE

On the Coloured People
(1970)

This short piece from The African Communist *is a letter to the editor written under the pseudonym Willem Abram Malgas, in response to comments made on his earlier piece 'The Coloured People of South Africa' (1968).*

Allow me to reply shortly to Comrade P. Mthikrakra and S. Dlandlayo who contributed on my article 'The Coloured People of South Africa'.

I am surprised at the host of misconstructions of opinions, and the amount of words put into my mouth by these comrades. I can only take up their own hope and supposition regarding my article, that is, that they distorted the sense in order to afford themselves an opportunity of arguing with me.

Permit me then to point briefly at their 'arguments'.

They are such that one finds it difficult to decide which should be given first preference. Let me say then, in the first place, that I have never disavowed the 'programmatic demand' put forward both in the Freedom Charter and the proposals of the South African Communist Party. But these are both generalized statements with regard to the minorities in South Africa. They are not specific analyses of the question of these minorities.

For instance, the SACP programme states, as the two comrades quote: '(the national democratic state must) uphold the rights, dignity, culture and self-respect of all national groups inhabiting our country.'

Agreed! But all I contend is that given equality, the Coloureds and whites will no longer be separate minorities.

It is Mthikrakra and Dlandlayo who refer to the Coloured people as a 'national group'. They do not say why. But if they read their own quotations from the SACP programme, they will see that nowhere do these quotations refer to the Coloureds in that way. And I do not believe it is only a matter of semantics.

Our comrades may rest assured that I have 'checked Marxist–Leninist writings on the national question'. Even if we should mechanically apply Stalin's definition of a nation, what would it prove? That allowed all the conditions for the formation of a nation as set out by Stalin, the English-speaking whites and Coloureds, and the Afrikaans-speaking, will find themselves associating in the formation of nations? In the same way as we foresee the eventual union of all groups comprising the South African people? And need we stop there?

I am also at a loss to see why the 'historic-biological' origin of the Coloured people quoted from E. Roux should be accepted as 'more correct' than the conclusions drawn by me from my own researches. After all, Roux was not dealing with the history of the Coloured people in *Time Longer than Rope*, and his references to their origin does not make the extract more authoritative. Nor do our comrades' statistics as to what percentage of Coloured belong to what church. They do not try to debate the 'psychological make-up, manifested in a common culture' of the people. So they cannot blame me if I suspect that they are merely attempting to score points.

I will not deal with all the other attempts, by way of quotations and historical data, to assail me, since they generally tend to support my contentions rather than to dispute them.

However, I must state that, in my ignorance, I fail to see how the 'political struggle' is liquidated on the basis of an appeal to a 'greater consideration of the Coloured people's class position'. And to conclude bluntly that this 'class position' means 'Nothing but trade unionism, *pure and simple*' (my emphasis) is, to say the least, fantastic. Why should the demand for 'no privileges however slight' mean only equal pay for equal work? That I seek to '*raise trade union politics* (!) to a predominant position' is utter nonsense. And their allegation that I propose we must 'confine ourselves *only and mainly* to developing this particular means of struggle (strikes, etc.)' and turn away from 'armed detachments' is nowhere near the subject under discussion.

We are concerned with my contention (let us put it shortly) that, under the equal status afforded by the democratic revolution, the white and Coloured communities will fuse to form English-speaking and Afrikaans-speaking national groups before the one unified South African nation evolves.

But the white people today are allies of the reactionary capitalist class which stands in the way of this unity which is the basic aspiration of the Coloured people since they are historically and culturally bound to their white counterparts. Only alliance with the African majority to overthrow the white ruling class will achieve this unity. As the original article states, inter alia, demonstrations of this alliance and attempts at 'national' organizations have been sporadic and inconsistent, because of there being 'no basis for the "national" struggle of the Coloured people' in the accepted sense of the word, such as exists in the case of the African people.

The Coloured are essentially part of the English and Afrikaans working class, discriminated against by way of their colour. Thus the emphasis of the movement should be on the class position of the Coloured community in directing the 'national' struggle (if we must call it that).

So I find it strange that anybody advocating more attention to the class struggle can be accused of 'being led straight into the positions of the bourgeois nationalist'.

No, I will not continue to belabour the hodgepodge of word-spinning and misplaced quotations, as well as misrepresentations, which I am afraid forms the 'reply' of our comrades.

Far better that we hear more about the 'national question' as it concerns the Coloured community. It is not enough for our movement to talk of one-man-one-vote or to place on record the contributions of the Coloured people to the struggle for freedom.

I am pleased, however, to see that my contribution has provoked some attention to the question. This at least shows that we may be on the threshold of a debate that will stimulate further consideration of the destiny of 'God's Step-Children'.

CHAPTER TEN

The Immorality Act

South Africa's Sex Law
(August 1970)

This academic report was produced for the Notes and Documents series (1968–91) of the Unit on Apartheid (later renamed the Centre Against Apartheid in 1976), which was located within the Department of Political and Security Council Affairs at the United Nations. The series was initiated by E. S. Reddy (1924–2020), who led the Special Committee Against Apartheid (established in 1963) from its founding until his retirement in 1985.

Against the background of innumerable laws enacted by successive South African Governments to uphold the myth of white supremacy and to exclude all non-whites from the spheres of privilege commanded by the 'master race', there stand those which compare with the Nazi enactments of Hitler's Germany to prevent so-called 'race pollution'.

The Mixed Marriages Act prohibits marriage between white and non-white, and such marriages entered into outside South Africa are considered null and void.

The Immorality Act (Act No. 23 of 1957), also referred to in an ironic pun as 'The Sex Act', makes it an offence for whites and non-whites to enter into illicit carnal intercourse. The Act also makes it an offence to conspire or incite to have interracial carnal intercourse, so that the mere solicitation to commit an illicit sexual act by a member of one race to a member of another race itself constitutes an offence.

In addition, apart from actual intercourse or incitement to enter into it, the Act also prohibits 'any act of indecency' which is not defined but which could be interpreted to mean any erotic action involving bodily contact, even with consent. Thus a kiss or ordinary petting could become an offence under the Immorality Act.

While the Mixed Marriages Act is a relative newcomer (1949) to the statute books of South Africa, the Immorality Act was first passed in 1927. It then prohibited extramarital intercourse only between white and African. With the ascendance of the Nationalist Party to power, the law was amended in 1950 to apply to all non-whites. In 1957, another amendment raised the penalties for contravening the Act from four years for women and five years for men to a maximum of seven years compulsory hard labour, and added the 'petting clause'.

It is significant that the original Act of 1927 had been introduced under the 'Pact' government, which included the Nationalist Party.

Prosecutions under the Act

The original law was not really applied with vigour. Prosecutions on the whole involved those actually caught by chance, but with the rigorous application of segregation and apartheid generally since the election the Nationalist Party and the widespread implementation of its policies, prosecutions under the Act have increased considerably.

According to the *Rand Daily Mail* of Johannesburg, 17 April 1970, statistics available showed that from 1950 to 1961, 4,379 persons were convicted under the Act. It stated that there was mounting evidence that the number of convictions has almost doubled since prosecutions started in earnest in 1950.

At the same time, the paper noted, concern has been voiced at the number of people arrested who were not convicted. In the period 1962 to 1967, 3,871 were arrested and 2,055 convicted, but from July 1967 to June 1968, 911 were arrested and 459 convicted.

Racial Categories Involved in Prosecutions

The Annual Report of the Commissioner of South African Police for the year ended 30 June 1957, the year of the last amendment to the Act, gives the following figures of convictions broken down into racial groups.

> 183 white men
> 19 non-white men
> 7 white women
> 157 non-white women

The Police Report for 1963–64, showed that the following were convicted under the Immorality Act on being found guilty of inter-racial carnal intercourse:[1]

For intercourse between	Whites		Non-Whites	
	Men	Women	Men	Women
White men and African women	141	—	—	110
African men and white women	—	1	4	—
Whites and other non-whites	67	1	3	174

The Minister of Justice gave the following statistics for the year (1 July 1963 to 30 June 1964):[2]

	Prosecuted	Convicted
Whites	426	205
Africans	211	110
Coloured persons	145	63
Asians	8	4

---

1 *1965 Survey of Race Relations in South Africa* (South African Institute of Race Relations, Johannesburg, 1966), p. 113.
2 *House of Assembly Debates* (Hansard), 9 March 1965, columns 2481–2482.

In 1968, the minister reported the following figures for the year (1 July 1967 to 30 June 1968):[3]

	Charged		Convicted	
	Men	Women	Men	Women
Whites	452	16	238	6
Africans	9	230	6	116
Coloured persons	10	184	4	84
Asians	3	7	2	3

In the vigorous application of the Immorality Act, no age or occupation has been spared. Those who have been arrested and who appeared in the courts include farmers, educators, clergymen, sportsmen, businessmen, attorneys, civil servants and even policemen.

In order to trap suspects, police have resorted to climbing trees, hiding in the boots of cars, feeling beds for warmth, peeping through keyholes and windows. Non-white women have also often been used as traps.

The types of cases involving contraventions of the Immorality Act dealt with in the courts can generally be divided into (a) casual relationships, and (b) genuine love relationships. While the problem of prostitution, which falls under casual relationships, does not fall within the scope of this paper, it must be noted briefly that, because of the extreme poverty of the African urban population, and the Government's policy of breaking up African families through its migrant labour system, prostitution is not uncommon among non-whites, and since it is the white man who has the money, contravention of the law is frequent.

On examination it will be seen that the great majority of cases involves white men and African or Coloured women. White women are rarely involved. Throughout South Africa's social history, white women have been instilled with an abhorrence of Africans in particular, and their menfolk have traditionally maintained an

---

[3] *House of Assembly Debates* (Hansard), 13 May 1969, column 5817.

excessive protectiveness over them, actually restricting them in many respects.

Genuine Love Relationships

Generally, Immorality Act offences committed by whites cause unusual concern among the regime and its supporters. But what raises the ire of white racists to fever pitch are those cases of genuine love relationships between white and non-white of the opposite sex. It is unimaginable in the eyes of the white racists for whites and non-whites to set up house and live happily. The press in South Africa usually gives such revelations greater coverage than those concerning prostitution. The authorities do their utmost to break up such relations. Here we mention only a few such cases as examples:

* In 1954, a German sailor on leave in Cape Town fell in love with a Coloured girl. Back in Germany, he heard that a child was to be born. Unable to pay his own way back to South Africa, he made use of an immigrant miners scheme to enter the country. The law forbids mixed marriages, but the couple set up a home nevertheless.

* In 1959, when a second child was on the way, the man was prosecuted under the Immorality Act. Because he begged for the chance to leave the country with his family, he was given a suspended sentence. A Berlin newspaper offered to pay their travelling expenses and guaranteed employment in Germany.[4]

* The *Rand Daily Mail* reported that Yvonne King, a Coloured woman, and Griffen Walter Smith, a white man, went to bed in their small Durban flat 'not knowing whether a rap on the door would start all their race-law troubles again.'[5] The previous day they had been acquitted in the Magistrates Court through what amounted to a technicality. The magistrate said had the charge been framed in another way, 'the result of the trial would have been different.'

---

4 *1958–1959 Survey of Race Relations in South Africa* (1959), p. 321.

5 *Rand Daily Mail*, Johannesburg, 13 January 1970.

Cradling their four-week-old baby in his arms, Mr Smith told the reporter: 'We are worried that at any time a policeman could knock on the door and charges be laid all over again. We don't want to split up now that we've got the baby. We are very happy to live together. The only thing that's in the way is the law.'

* The 1969 Race Relations Survey states: 'A case reported during the year under review originated when a Chinese man befriended a distraught white teenager who had run away from a most unsatisfactory home. They fell in love and, unable to marry, lived as man-and-wife for five years and had three children. Eventually, they were charged under the Immorality Act and were given suspended sentences.'[6] (The woman eventually applied to be reclassified Chinese in order to enable her to marry the man.)

* The same issue of the Survey reports the case of a man born in South Africa, but of Lebanese descent, who was educated in England and married an English girl. During 1969, the couple and their child visited Krugersdorp (Transvaal) to help the man's father in business difficulties. While there the man received an identity card for which he had applied earlier to the South African authorities. This stated his race to be 'Coloured'. The couple were then charged with contravening the Immorality Act. However, they were acquitted on a technicality, the judge finding that they were not in fact domiciled in South Africa at the time of the alleged offence and that they intended returning to England.[7]

Police Methods

As has been pointed out, the police in South Africa go to extraordinary lengths to make arrests under the Immorality Act. Any hint or suspicion that a breach of the law might be committed sets the wheels of the anti-sex law in motion. Traps are set, volunteers

---

6 *1969 Survey of Race Relations in South Africa*, p. 29.
7 *1969 Survey of Race Relations in South Africa*, pp. 29–30.

are recruited to compromise potential offenders and reports reveal that the police actually engineer breaches of the law to gain arrests.

The 1969 Race Relations Survey mentions that 'during May, four white men and a youth were charged under the Act as a result of evidence given by an African woman who had "volunteered" to the police to allow herself to tempt men.'[8]

Police of the 'Immorality Squad' have themselves 'picked up' African and Coloured girls and have then charged them. The *Rand Daily Mail* reported on 14 October 1969:

> Diane Jacobs, 31, was sentenced to two years' imprisonment yesterday for soliciting a white policeman for immoral purposes [...] The court heard earlier that Jacobs 'nodded and winked' at Detective Sergeant J. L. Kleynhans of the Liquor, Gambling and Immorality Staff, while he was on patrol in Jeppe Street on July 30. Later she climbed into his car. She said, 'Let's go to your place but you must pay me four Rand,' Sergeant Kleynhans told the court. He said he understood she wanted him to pay for intercourse. 'I immediately revealed my identity and arrested her for soliciting.'

It was also reported that W. J. Scheepers, a Bantu Affairs Commissioner, was arrested when an African schoolmistress to whom he had made overtures allowed herself to be used to trap him. At the appropriate moment 'she gave the prearranged signal to the police and Sergeant P. Ras came into the room. After taking a picture of the partly undressed Scheepers and herself, Sergeant Ras arrested Scheepers.'[9]

---

8 *1969 Survey of Race Relations in South Africa*, p. 30.
9 *Rand Daily Mail*, Johannesburg, 8 November 1969.

Disparity in Sentences

A striking feature of convictions under the Immorality Act is the obvious discrimination in sentencing couples involved. While the maximum penalty of seven years compulsory hard labour has never been invoked, non-whites have generally received higher sentences than their white co-accused in the same trial. At the same time, it has become usual for separate trials to be ordered. Most Immorality Act convictions result in what the public has come to regard as 'apartheid sentences'.

Giving figures for convictions under the Immorality Act in 1964, the Minister of Justice stated that, in six cases, an African woman was convicted while the co-accused white man was discharged.[10]

In the case of the Chinese man and the white woman mentioned above, the man received a suspended sentence of eighteen months and the woman six months. The charge against them was the same.

In another case, the woman involved had already served two months of her six-month sentence before the man's trial took place.

Publicity was given during May 1969 to two cases in which African women were convicted and jailed, while the white men charged with them were acquitted. Such cases may indeed occur when the woman pleads guilty and the man pleads not guilty and a separation of trials is ordered. The woman may have no option if, for example, she has a child who is Coloured in appearance.

Effects of the Act

Such is the concern of white South Africa for its status as overlord of the 'inferior' non-whites that it has little toleration for those of its membership who consort, particularly sexually, with members

---

10 *House of Assembly Debates* (Hansard), 9 March 1965, columns 2481–2482.

of other race groups. Social ostracism, both by the authorities and the public, of whites who have been charged under the Immorality Act has therefore become an accepted practice, and several victims of the Act have even taken their own lives in preference to the stigma of prosecution.

* The *Rand Daily Mail* reported: 'To avoid the malevolent stigma left by the Act, many people—a large number of them fathers of families—have hanged, drowned or shot themselves after being charged. One man poured petrol over himself and set himself aflame.'[11]

* In February 1970, Mr Z. E. Botha, 35, a father of four children was found hanged in a Vanderbijlpark (Transvaal) police cell. His widow said after the funeral: 'We are convinced that Sakkie died to spare me and the children the humiliation of facing a charge under the Immorality Act.'[12]

* Mr Gerhard Moll, 59, the Johannesburg school principal, suspended from his post after his wife laid charges under the Immorality Act against him during a fit of 'pique and jealousy', stated: 'There is a terrible stigma attached to anything concerning the Immorality Act, and it is dreadful to have your name dragged through the mud when you know you are innocent. People treat you as though you had leprosy.'[13]

* In the case of the Bantu Affairs Commissioner, Scheepers, mentioned earlier in this paper, the Public Prosecutor stated that previously another official of the Bantu Affairs Department had been found guilty under the Act of 'attempting to commit immorality' and was jailed for three months. Both men were dismissed by the Department.

* Mrs J. L. Smith who admitted to having contravened the Immorality Act with an African sent her two youngest children,

---

11 *Rand Daily Mail*, Johannesburg, 17 April 1970.
12 *Sunday Times*, Johannesburg, 15 February 1970.
13 *Rand Daily Mail*, Johannesburg, 3 December 1969.

Buksie (6) and Sussie (4) into hiding 'for fear they would be taken away from her by the authorities'.[14] The magistrate in the case said that the Social Welfare Department would be informed, and they would decide what to do with the children.

Mrs Smith and her children lived happily on the farm until Buksie started school. Mr T. F. J. van Aarde, headmaster of the school, said: 'I saw Mrs Smith with her son on the first day of school ... I noticed that the boy was different from the other children.' The newspaper stated that one of the school parents laid a complaint with the police. Mrs Smith and a farm labourer were subsequently arrested under the Immorality Act and sentenced.

The *Sunday Express* added: 'After the court finding, Naboomspruit parents refused to allow the dark-complexioned Buksie to share a classroom with their children.'[15]

A commentator for the South African Broadcasting Corporation's Current Affairs programme said the Act was necessary to preserve the nation, but it should be called what it was, the 'Anti-Miscegenation Act', and further, that there should be an 'appropriate limitation' of permitted publicity.[16]

Opposition to the Act

There are no signs that the Government intends relaxing by any degree the harsh provisions of this unjust law—a law which has trailed in its wake, misery, death, unhappiness and suffering to those caught up in its tentacles.

Pleas for the abolition of the Act have attracted little attention, although there have been signs of concern in certain Nationalist circles at the present policy. The Afrikaans churches, however, have remained silent on the issue.

---

14 *Sunday Times*, Johannesburg, 15 February 1970.
15 *Sunday Express*, Johannesburg, 15 February 1970.
16 *1969 Survey of Race Relations in South Africa* (1970), p. 30.

Die Kerkbode, organ of the Nederduitse Gereformeerde Kerk (Dutch Reformed Church) fully supported the Act in an editorial in 1950. In July 1969, it expressed strong disapproval of the use of African women as traps, but it went no further than that.

In contrast, the independent *Pro Veritate*, which is associated with the Christian Institute, stated in April 1969 that the State had no right according to the Scriptures to regard extramarital intercourse across the colour line as more immoral than within the limits of one race.

Mr Japie Basson, of the United Party, said, 'The Immorality Act must be scrapped. It involves a hunting down of people in their most private lives and a cruel and sordid invasion into relationships which concern individuals alone.'[17]

---

17 *Rand Daily Mail*, Johannesburg, 17 April 1970.

CHAPTER ELEVEN

Dialogue 'A Gross Betrayal'
(February 1972)

The article appeared in Africa Report *as a critical response to a new diplomatic approach within the international community of 'dialogue' with the apartheid government. The 1969 Lusaka Manifesto signed by thirteen African countries presented a softer approach to the South African regime, advocating diplomacy over armed struggle in order to bring change. This position shifted after the rejection of its terms by the South African government, resulting the Mogadishu Declaration of the Organisation of African Unity (OAU) in 1971, which called for the liberation of southern Africa by force.*

No one who examines the situation in South Africa can believe that any fundamental or substantial change has been wrought in the lives and conditions of black South Africans through cooperation with apartheid. Likewise, the belief that the only prospects for economic progress for black South Africans lie in an economy whose needs for skills and manpower will break through colour-bar laws is shattered by the realities of African life in spite of the economic boom.

All the proponents of dialogue must be aware that no dialogue with Vorster will change anything in South African society. Vorster himself said it in the London *Daily Telegraph* of 16 November 1970, which reported an interview with him: 'Any relationship South Africa enters into with black African states will be made on the basis that there will be no interference with the Republic's domestic policy of apartheid.'

Why then the dialogue, and what would it involve? If it ever got to a round table, it would have to be about trade, finance and other matters relevant to the future of the black states themselves rather than the future of blacks in South Africa.

Who gains from dialogue also becomes obvious when we discover what has gone on between South Africa and those countries that have already entered into economic and political relations with Pretoria.

Lesotho and Swaziland have become virtually other 'Bantustans' attached to South Africa. Malawi has trade with the Republic, but while the figures show a steep rise in South African exports to Malawi, the latter's main export to South Africa remains her people —men to work in South Africa's mines and Rhodesia's farms.

In exchange, Malawi receives investment capital from South Africa. But the investment is not designed to raise the living standards or to assist economic self-sufficiency. South Africa's advance of R8 million (approximately $10.5 million) towards Banda's prestige capital at Lilongwe, or a further R11 million ($14.5 million) for a rail link to Mozambique (strategically important to the southern African white bloc) will not ease Malawi's poverty and backwardness.

The much-vaunted deal of £2.7 million (approximately $7 million) with Madagascar is, by international finance standards, small time. Its purpose is to develop 'tourism'—a single tourist hotel at Nossi-bé Island. This small venture is the start perhaps of something more, rather for South Africa than for Madagascar. A Johannesburg *Sunday Times* commentator stated: 'Industrialists, as they explore the island [Madagascar] are certain to realize the potential that lies in the low cost of labour. For it may be cheaper to manufacture in Madagascar than in South Africa's cities and border areas.'

Madagascar, like Malawi, also has a strategic purpose for white South Africa. There are plans to develop a large repair-and-servicing base for naval vessels, and the participation by South Africa in this project, which will cost between £30 and £40 million (between $80 million and $100 million), will provide the white Republic and her allies with a hostile base off the shores of Tanzania.

Behind the screen of 'dialogue' must be seen the strategic objective, both short term and long term, of the South Africans vis-à-vis the African continent.

The objective is to create client states among the independent African countries, with the aim of cutting off the South African national liberation movement from all sources of assistance; to compel such client states to participate actively in the destruction of the liberation movement; and to ensure the preservation of apartheid.

The strategy is further aimed at cutting short Africa's striving to establish for herself an independent and equal position in the world's economy and the international political system.

White South Africa uses many and diverse means in the attempt to fulfil her objectives. To begin with, South Africa is economically the most powerful country in Africa and thus seeks to expand trade relations with the rest of Africa. Her exports to Africa, more than doubled between the years 1964 and 1968, while her imports from Africa grew by about one-third. South Africa uses Africa as her market for manufactured goods while the African countries serve her as sources of cheap raw materials. All these trade relations increase Africa's dependence on South Africa and help maintain the African economies at a low level of development. In addition, South Africa already has large investments in mining in all the countries of southern Africa. Her companies have reached as far north as Mauritania.

It is necessary to point out that the economic processes dealing with South Africa's external economic relations are organically linked with apartheid insofar as it is an internal South African system of economic relations. As a system, one of whose central features is the exploitation of the African people, apartheid results in certain economic consequences.

One of these is that, since the earnings of the African majority are kept at the bare minimum level, the internal market for industrial goods is extremely limited. This is particularly important in the situation that obtains today wherein manufacturing contributes more to the gross domestic product than mining and agriculture.

Mining and agriculture have, of course, been traditionally export oriented. A limited home market was therefore of no material significance to their development. The contrary is the case with regard to manufacturing. The restricted nature of the home market impedes the development of this sector. Hence the necessity to find external markets for manufactured goods.

The second of these economic consequences is that very low wages mean very high profit rates. South Africa therefore generates investment funds internally. In addition, the influx of capital from abroad adds up to large amounts ($2 billion from 1956 to 1968). And what attracts such large sums is the fact of low wages and correspondingly high profit.

Thus a situation arises in which South Africa finds herself burdened with an 'embarrassment of riches'. She therefore exports her 'excess' capital. Thus it is that South Africa's internal economic processes are organically linked with the external.

In her strategy to acquire client states in Africa, South Africa has also been preparing and continues to prepare for war, for the continuation of her political and economic policy by other means. The regime has adopted a military posture aimed at keeping the white-dominated south of Africa intact while simultaneously pushing the regime's military defence line far to the north, creating a protective system of buffer states around itself.

South Africa has a military presence in Zimbabwe (Rhodesia), Mozambique and Angola, and political, military and intelligence agreements with Rhodesia and Portugal. She refuses to relinquish Namibia (South West Africa) in spite of the United Nations and the verdict of the World Court and has built a major military base in the Caprivi Strip, in the northernmost tip of Namibia, 1,000 miles from her own borders with that territory. From this base she can strike quickly and suddenly at countries far to her north. The new airport being built at Lilongwe, Malawi, will be open to aircraft of the South African Air Force, and South Africa also openly maintains a military attaché's office in Malawi.

However, South Africa cannot deal from strength alone. Thus, as part of her campaign, she has put out the idea of a dialogue.

Africa's already fragile political cohesion is in danger of further subversion from the south. Operating with the close diplomatic and political support of the French, British and the United States, white South Africa is taking the initiative to destroy African unity. The stakes are high: no less than the control of Africa.

Dialogue will not bring about a withdrawal of South African advance forces from Caprivi or from Zimbabwe, where they threaten not only the liberation forces but also Zambia herself. Dialogue will also not inhibit Vorster from building a base at Lilongwe from which South African planes will dominate the skies of the whole of southern Africa and beyond.

No, there must be no talks with South Africa. Let Africa take heed from the Guinea invasion and prepare to defend herself. In addition, there is needed a greater recognition of the role of the liberation movements and their consequent admission to the relevant councils of the OAU.

Let the United Nations move seriously towards carrying out in practical terms the numerous resolutions passed against South Africa, and let it take steps to isolate South Africa from all the political and diplomatic support she is receiving in the world body.

In a recent speech, Alfred Nzo, secretary general of the African National Congress of South Africa, condemned those who are working for a policy of fraternization and accommodation with Pretoria.

'The substitution of dialogue for armed struggle,' he declared, 'is a gross betrayal of the people of South Africa.'

CHAPTER TWELVE

Apartheid and the Coloured People of South Africa
(September 1972)

Similar to La Guma's analysis of South Africa's Immorality Act, this report was prepared for the Unit on Apartheid at the United Nations. It bears traces of his preceding 1968 essay on Coloured South Africans for The African Communist.

Introduction

The indigenous African people, although subjected to the most intense oppression and exploitation, are not the only oppressed group in South Africa. The 2 million Coloured people and more than a half million Asian people suffer varying forms of race discrimination, humiliation and oppression in the Republic.[1] They are part of the non-white base upon which rests white privilege. As such, they constitute an integral part of the social forces ranged against white supremacy. Despite deceptive and often meaningless concessions, they share a common fate with the African people, and their own future in a free South African society is inextricably bound up with the liberation of the African majority.

Minor concessions and dubious privileges, an illusory social superiority over the African population, have been embodiments of attempts on the part of successive governments of South Africa to woo the Coloured people to the side of the whites in the confrontation with African opposition. However, the advent of the

---

1 1970 population statistics released by the Department of Statistics: Whites 3,751,328; Coloured people 2,018,453; Asians 620,436; Africans 15,057,952.

National Party government in 1948 and its policy of apartheid soon revealed to the non-white population as a whole the true nature of white supremacy. 'Separate development' and apartheid meant the final negation of those already much-eroded minor privileges which the Coloured people possessed, culminating in the plans for the destruction of the last vestige of democratic process, the municipal franchise, in 1972. Thus apartheid finds little support in the community, and even those Coloureds who do cooperate with the Government for one reason or another are today finding 'separate development' a bitter pill to swallow.

But after more than 20 years of the application of their policy of apartheid, the rulers of South Africa themselves now find that they have arrived at an impasse vis-à-vis this community and a pretext for the implementation of the final objectives of apartheid, not only because of the opposition from the community and the basic falsity of the concept of white supremacy but also arising out of the sociohistoric background of the Coloured people, resulting in the difficulty of finding a 'solution' to the problem of fitting them into the black and white jigsaw pattern of apartheid. While hoping to use the Coloured community to widen the anti-African base, in the face of the people's rejection of apartheid, the racists have instead run aground on the rocks of their own making.[2]

The Johannesburg daily newspaper, the *Rand Daily Mail* reported:

> Quite casually and without any apparent, signs of conscience about it, three Cabinet Ministers last week admitted

---

[2] Early in 1971, the Afrikaans Calvinist Movement suggested a 'three-stream' policy patterned on Hertzog's 'two-stream' policy for white English and Afrikaans sharing of political rights. At the end of July 1971, 10 Transvaal professors and 19 lecturers from the University of South Africa and [the University of the] Witwatersrand issued a public 'declaration of faith', appealing to South Africans to think again, especially about the eventual achievement of full citizenship by Coloured people. The Coloured people would have to be accepted as a full and equal element in the 'Western community' in South Africa, they said.

to the raw deal being given [to] the Coloured people. The Minister of Defence, who is also leader of the National Party in the Cape and a former Minister of Coloured Affairs, said in the most emphatic terms used on the subject so far, that the Government would never give the Coloured people a homeland of their own ... The Minister of Information meanwhile was admitting at a meeting in Durban that the Government really didn't know what it could give the Coloured people in lieu of a homeland. All it was sure about was that they had to be led along a path away from the whites; but what that path was leading to he couldn't say.[3]

The Foreign Minister, Dr Hilgard Muller, when questioned by Mr Colin Eglin, Progressive Party, admitted that since the Coloured could not develop fully either within 'white' South Africa or in a homeland of their own, they would in fact have even less freedom than the Africans. When the question was put to him in so many words, he replied, 'Yes, I agree with that 100 per cent.'

Later that year, another newspaper stated:

The Nationalist government has finally told South Africa's 2 million Coloured people what their political fate is to be: it is to wander forever along an unending road which will lead them neither to separate Coloured-stans nor to any meaningful share of rights in the Republic itself. Stripped of its frills, this is the real message of last night's Cabinet statement issued by the Minister of Coloured Affairs, Mr Jannie Loots ... The best they can hope for is mainly local authority rights, always under the control of the white Government. In reality this adds up to permanent white *baasskap* over the Coloured people.[4]

---

3 *Rand Daily Mail*, Johannesburg, 26 October 1970.
4 *Sunday Times*, Johannesburg, 6 December 1970. *Baasskap* is a term referring to white domination.

1. Background

LEGAL DEFINITION

The basis of apartheid legislation is the classification of the South African population into racial categories. The Population Registration Act of 1950 aimed at a rigid system of race classification, defined white, Coloured and African, and empowered the Governor General (of the then Union of South Africa) to make further subdivisions. This was done in 1959 when the Coloured people were divided into Cape Coloured, Cape Malay, Griqua, Chinese, Indian, 'other Asiatic' and 'other Coloured'. Until 1962 acceptability by the community was the main test used by officials engaged in race classifications, but the Amendment Act of that year altered the definition of a 'white' person and made it obligatory for appearance and acceptance to be considered together. Further additions to the Act were made in 1969, which made lineage the sole criterion.

Thus, according to law, a Coloured person is a 'person who is not a white person or an African' while also subject to the subdivisions described above. Likewise a man 'who in appearance obviously is white' must be classified as a Coloured person if one of his natural parents has been classified as a white person and the other as a Coloured person. Further, if a person is unable to prove that he 'is generally accepted as a white person', he is assumed to be 'generally accepted as a Coloured person' unless he is 'in appearance obviously an African'.

However, the legal definition does not adequately identify the Coloured person, but suffices, in the eyes of the authorities, in order to place him in the orbit of the various discriminatory laws operative in South Africa. A brief glance at the early history of this people gives them a more meaningful identity.

EARLY HISTORY AND DEMOGRAPHY

As a community and part of the South African population, any study of the people generally and officially known as 'Coloured' must take into account their origin, historic and cultural background. Many strains have blended in forming the Coloured people of today: Negro slaves, Malay, English and Dutch, Bushman and Hottentot. The main ingredients of the Coloured people of today are:

(a) slaves brought into the country from abroad;
(b) Khoin [sic] and Nama people, the local aborigines commonly known as Bushmen and Hottentots;
(c) white colonists;
(d) indigenous Africans.

Slaves were brought in by the Dutch East Indian Company which established the first European colony on the Cape Peninsula, in order to supplement the labour supply, particularly agricultural, the Khoin people having either been decimated or driven from the region. There were two main sources of slaves—the East Indies and East Africa, including Madagascar. Slaves from the latter were apparently in the majority and were 'Negroid by race, with an infiltration of Indonesian blood and an Indonesian (Malagasy) language with remnants of a few Bantu words'.[5] The Asian slaves, though fewer in number, were the 'elite' of the slave community. They came mainly from the Malay Archipelago. Some were convicts, others were political exiles with their attendants. Many were skilled craftsmen, builders, masons, carpenters and so on. The white colonists were farmers, artisans, soldiers, clerks and there were of course innumerable sailors passing through.

In the original contact situation, the most important mixtures were those between slave men and aboriginal women, and European men and slave and aboriginal women. On the whole, the original intercourse between white and non-white took place mainly between the colonists and slaves, the Khoin people being generally considered with contempt—a 'stinking nation' as Jan Van

---

5 Sheila Patterson, *Colour and Culture in South Africa* (London: Routledge, 1953).

Riebeeck called them. Nevertheless, as the colonists trekked further away from the civilized Cape, their way of life became as nomadic as the despised Khoin and San while at the same time the chronic shortage of women caused many an informal, sometimes permanent, union with the womenfolk of these people. The Griqua group of the North Cape resulted mainly out of such unions. The entry of French Huguenot refugees, the annexation of the Cape by the British introduced further European blood into the growing community.

By the beginning of the nineteenth century, the pure aboriginal had ceased to exist in the Colony and the second, third and fourth generation of mixed-blood people were increasing their numbers among themselves. In spite of the fact that by this time colour prejudice had hardened, the white contribution to the mixed-blood community seems not to have slackened greatly, and with the migration from the Western Cape eastwards, a further mixed-blood community was added—by white and indigenous African union, particularly in the Eastern Cape, Natal and Transvaal.

In short, historians agree that the Coloured persons are the product of an early series of mixed unions between Europeans and slaves, slaves and Europeans, slaves and aborigines, and on a lesser scale between Europeans and Africans, and Coloured persons and Africans.

CULTURAL BACKGROUND

Having been transported from their countries of origin, the slaves naturally adapted themselves to their new environment. Being at the beck and call of their master, they had to learn his language, pander to his customs and follow generally the course laid out for him by the master. The white slave owners and the colonists, consciously or unconsciously rationalizing their superior status, saw to it that the slave recognized the master's 'civilizing' influence. The growing community of mixed-bloods gradually accepted the languages, the customs and the culture of the whites. The missionary societies introduced Christianity and the beginnings of formal European-based education, and today, with the exception of the small Moslem community, 90 per cent of the Coloured people belong to churches of European origin.

2. The Coloured People in Economic Life

Although slavery was abolished in the British Empire in 1833, it proved difficult to eradicate from the mentality of most white South Africans the conception that the main function of the non-white is to provide cheap labour for the European. The slave-owning mentality was built up long before the African became a source of labour for the white. The distinction between work that was proper for a white person and what subsequently became known as 'Kaffir work' was thereby drawn for centuries to come. The idea that skin colour and not skill should be the determining factor in the economic hierarchy thus became an integral part of white attitudes and their support for the colour-bar segregation and apartheid.

While emancipation opened a new stage in the relations between whites and Coloured persons, it did not revolutionize the society or abolish discrimination. Few settlers in the Cape accepted the humanitarian's ideal of racial equality. An ordinance of 1835, which was supposed to prepare the slaves for freedom, changed little more than their name. Now called apprentice labourers, they continued to work for their former owners, without wages and on the same terms of food, clothing and medical care.

While the absence of a colour bar in the Cape's labour legislation had a marked liberalizing effect on industrial relations in the Colony, wages and working conditions, however, were always adjusted to the conventionally low standards of ex-slaves, free Coloured and tribal peasants.

In the last half of the nineteenth century, most of the Coloured people remained as farm labourers with barely increased remuneration, and that largely in kind. At the same time, the increasing use of cheaper African labour, particularly in the Eastern Cape, caused a drift to the villages and the towns and the formation of an unskilled urban Coloured proletariat. In Cape Town especially, former skilled slaves had also emerged as a relatively well-to-do urban artisan class.

The discovery of gold and diamonds, the opening of a new era of an industrial economy in South Africa and its attendant labour laws which ensured the supply of cheap non-white labour naturally affected not only all Africans, but the minority groups, the Indians and Coloureds, as well.

THE 'CIVILIZED LABOUR' POLICY

The repeated subdivision of farm holdings and the prevalent, highly uneconomic methods of farming had also, by the end of the nineteenth century, created a large and increasing group of impoverished white persons. The latter, unable to survive any longer on the land, were flooding into villages and towns to offer themselves as unskilled labourers on the open market. The 'poor white' as he came to be called was only equipped to enter the unskilled market, which was the almost exclusive preserve of African and Coloured. The Nationalist–Labour coalition of the 1920s, adopting the attitude that prosperity must be redistributed with a greater emphasis on lightness of skin, thus instituted what was called the 'civilized labour' policy.

This official action was directed mainly against the Africans, but in those areas of the Cape where Coloured people constituted the bulk of the unskilled labour force, it was natural that they should suffer too. Civilized labour was defined as 'the labour rendered by persons whose standard of living conforms to the standard generally recognized as tolerable from the usual European standpoint. Uncivilized labour is to be regarded as the labour rendered by persons whose aim is restricted to the bare necessities of life as understood among barbarous and undeveloped peoples.'

Thus, vast numbers of unskilled non-whites, in government-owned employment particularly, were replaced by whites, who while traditionally abhorring 'Kaffir work', were however compelled to enter it. The difference was, however, that whites would not receive 'Kaffir' wages.

To extend the 'civilized labour' policy into private industry, such officially colour-blind Acts as the Apprenticeship Act of 1922, the Industrial Conciliation Act of 1924, and the Wage Act of 1925 have all acted as barriers to the economic progress of both Coloured and African.

COLOURED PEOPLE IN INDUSTRY

Because of a shift in attitudes and circumstances during the Second World War, the Coloured people were able to hold their own in industrial employment. They have, nevertheless, been gradually ousted from higher levels of skilled work. Coloured apprenticeship hardly exists outside the Cape, where it is mainly confined to the traditional centre of Coloured skilled trades in Cape Town. Even here, however, the position has deteriorated, and although Coloured people might have held their own in building and furniture trades, they have lost ground in the vastly expanding technical industries.

Most of the pressure for the introduction of statutory restrictions on the employment of non-whites has emanated from white labour and their leaders, often in a bid for support in party politics or trade-union organization. Labour leaders claimed credit for the fall in unemployment during an upward swing in the economy between 1925 and 1930 and urged more vigorous action to prevent Asians, Coloured people and Africans from competing against wage earners, who formed 90 per cent of the electorate in Transvaal urban constituencies. Likewise, the Pretoria Coordinating Council formed in 1948 by white trade unions, which broke away from the Trades and Labour Council, recommended to the Industrial Legislation Commission:

> European trade unions should have guardianship over the Natives in each industry, and that in the instances of mixed trade unions, the Coloured and Asiatic workers should be placed in separate branches with their own committees, which should serve in an advisory capacity. They should not, however, have representation on the contracting body of the European trade unions.[6]

In the House of Assembly on 23 February 1971, Mr W. S. J. Grobler of the National Party said:

> In the political sphere, this Government will have to continue taking steps which will keep the position of the white worker in South Africa entrenched by law—and in saying this I believe I am speaking on behalf of every white worker in South Africa.[7]

The concept of 'civilized' labour has always been a characteristic of the distribution of employment, and the practice has been reinforced by law. Thus 'job reservation' of today can be seen as a further projection of this racist concept and its enforcement by law through the enactment of the Industrial Conciliation Act of 1956, a further development of the colour bar in industry.

Coloured and Indian workers are allowed to belong to registered trade unions, but with fewer rights than whites. After 1956, further registration of racially mixed unions (i.e. consisting of white, Coloured and Indian members) was prohibited. All mixed unions that were already registered at that time were ordered to form separate racial branches and to hold racially separated meetings. The executive committees of such unions were to be exclusively white and they were not to extend the union's interest on behalf of one racial group only. Thus Coloured or Indian workers in the union are represented by whites. The Coloured and Indian

---

6 *Cape Argus*, 26 August 1949.

7 *House of Assembly Debates* (Hansard), 23 February 1971, column 1446.

workers are further discriminated against by wider laws such as those depriving them of the right to vote.

Under the 'job reservation' regulations of the Act, Coloured workers have suffered drastically. From driving heavy vehicles in the Orange Free State to posts as traffic policemen, the whites-only proclamations have caused anger and frustration within the community. In the building trade, which employs thousands of Coloured artisans, avenues of skilled employment have been closed to them.

By June 1970, 26 job reservation determinations were made in terms of section 77 of the 1956 Industrial Conciliation Act. More than 105,000 African, Coloured and Asian workers were denied jobs by these definitions . . . In almost every case, the initiative for an investigation came from a white trade union or a group of white workers. Indeed, no section of the white trade union movement can be acquitted of responsibility for this enormous injustice to the millions of African, Coloured and Indian people.

In March 1969, a leading commercial bank in Cape Town provisionally recruited twenty Coloured girls as clerks and machine operators. On applying for the necessary permits, the bank was informed by the Divisional Inspector of Labour that there were unemployed white women who were available. The educational qualifications of these white women were considerably lower than those of the well-qualified Coloured women, but the latter's recruitment were nevertheless withdrawn.

Even where Coloured workers are allowed to occupy positions normally held by whites due to recent shortage of labour, the jobs are usually downgraded so that wages are lower than those of the white workers who formerly performed such work.

Wage differentials are based on race, with the white worker often earning up to ten times as much as the African and five to eight times more than Indians and Coloured people. The average gross wages in the mining industry are R371 for whites and R82 for

Coloured persons. Africans earn only R18 with another R30 estimated in 'fringe benefits'. Differential rates are not simply for different kinds of work. They are also applied in instances where people of different racial categories are doing identical work.[8]

In the two professions, nursing and teaching, which Coloured people favour due to their accessibility, the situation is no different. A white trained nurse earns R2,280 to R3,450 a year, Coloured or Indian nurses earn R1,620 to R2,040 a year and African nurses earn only R1,170 to R1,620 a year.[9]

In May 1969, the Cape Teachers' Professional Association adopted a resolution expressing disappointment with the salary increases received by Coloured schoolteachers at the end of April. The resolution said that the gap between Coloured and white teachers had widened and that Coloured teachers received 54 per cent of the pay white teachers received.[10]

While the economic boom of the past decade resulted in a substantial increase in employment and earnings in South Africa, the gap between white and non-white earnings, however, increased. Average monthly earnings of whites in the manufacturing industry, for example, increased from R163 ($228) in 1962 to R238 ($333) in 1967, or by 8.6 per cent per year. The earnings of non-whites increased from R37 ($52) to R49 ($69) or by 5.8 per cent a year. Earnings of whites averaged 440 per cent of earnings of non-whites in 1962 and 485 per cent in 1967.[11]

---

8 Figures of the South African Department of Statistics, analysed in the *Rand Daily Mail*, Johannesburg, 2 July1971. One Rand (R) is equivalent to $1.40 until December 1971. It is now $1.33.

9 Replies to questions in Parliament by the Minister of the Interior, *House of Assembly Debates* (Hansard), 17 February 1972, columns 235–238.

10 *Cape Times*, 24 May 1969.

11 United Nations Unit on Apartheid, 'Facts and Figures on South Africa', Notes and Documents No. 7/71.

The government's wage determinations made at the beginning of 1972 for the Cape Peninsula, which set a minimum wage level for unskilled labour below the poverty datum line, was severely criticized. The new wage scales were based on an eight-and-a-half hour working day and would bring unskilled workers R11.64 per week. Yet surveys by the University of Cape Town, for example, had shown the poverty datum line to be R17.97 weekly in Cape Town areas.[12]

RURAL CONDITIONS

Industry is not the only major sphere of Coloured employment. The provisional estimated number of economically active Coloured people at the end of 1970 was 708,000.[13] On 18 December 1970, the Johannesburg *Financial Mail* carried an article on farm population in the Republic, which contrasted the results of the 1959–60 Agricultural Census with a survey taken in 1969 by the South African Agricultural Union. The 1959 Census gave the figure for the Coloured farm population as 356,000 and the survey as 452,000.

It has been charged that the economic conditions of Coloured rural workers in the Cape have changed but little over a century. Their status as labourers in the main, in contrast to their minimal numbers as actual farmers, has been perpetuated 'with little heed for formal sanctions, save the Masters and Servants Act. It has been perpetuated through the determination and unity of white rural society, often supported by the spiritual authority of the Dutch Reformed Church.'[14]

The Race Relations Survey also refers to a report in the Johannesburg *Star* of 10 December 1970, describing farm labour

---

12 *Rand Daily Mail*, Johannesburg, 12 January 1972.
13 *1971 Survey of Race Relations in South Africa* (Johannesburg, 1972).
14 Patterson, *Colour and Culture in South Africa*.

conditions in certain areas of the Cape where Coloured labourers earned 70 cents a day, while a report on 19 December 1970, referred to conditions in the Transvaal districts. [...] Farm workers claimed that they earned between R5 and R8 in cash and were given a bag of maize meal every month. No annual holiday was permitted and workers could only take time off from their twelve-hour shift if there were other members of their families to replace them. Employers allowed the workers to build their own homes, usually mud huts, allocated small plots on which crops could be cultivated, and some had schools built for the children of farmhands. Casual labourers earned 20 cents a day.[15]

Another aspect of Coloured rural life is centred in the Coloured reserves, the basis of which are those areas settled by aboriginals under missionary auspices in the nineteenth century and formalized by the British administration of the Cape Colony. Coloured reserves are scattered areas mainly in the Northern and Eastern Cape. According to the report of the Department of Coloured Affairs for the period January 1962 to 31 March 1964, their total area is 1,903,318 morgen; there are 7,516 registered occupiers; and the total population is 40,289.[16] Mr W. P. Carstens has stated, however:

> Taking the population as a whole, there is a strong suggestion that at least three quarters of all families (in the Northern reserve, Namaqualand, Cape) are unable to make a living out of mixed farming alone and must therefore find work to augment the family budget.[17]

He goes on to reveal that Coloured rural workers employed on the mines earned £5.14 ($16) a month up to 1952, and by 1958 the

---

15 *1971 Survey of Race Relations* (Johannesburg, 1972).

16 *1965 Survey of Race Relations* (Johannesburg, 1966).

17 W. P. Carstens, *The Social Structure of the Cape Coloured Reserve* (Cape Town: Oxford University Press, 1966).

figure had risen to £10 ($28).[18] The conclusion the reader must inevitably draw from reading this book is that there is no difference between a Coloured reserve and that of the African—both are areas of dire poverty and both serve a main function: to serve as reservoirs of cheap migrant labourers.

A new and sinister encroachment into the economic status of the Coloured people was made with the Coloured Cadets Training Act, 1967, which has been seen to be a means of procuring forced labour for the white employers, particularly on the farms. This contention seems to be adequately justified since the Act came in the wake of numerous complaints of a serious shortage of labour by farmers, mainly in the Western Cape where the majority of the Coloured people live. In fact, the Deputy Minister of Bantu Administration stated at the time that the legislation was intended to fill the gap in the Western Cape caused by the Government's decision to expel 5 per cent of Africans from the area each year.

Men who have registered under the Act will obviously, too, have to carry proof that they have so registered or had been exempted. This also reveals the commencement of the extension into the Coloured community of the pass laws and forced labour system as applies to Africans. The initial reluctance of the Coloured men to register quickly was met with intimidation by the authorities who used helicopters to scatter thousands of leaflets over Coloured areas, threatening them with the penalties of the law which provides for a fine not exceeding £250 or three years' imprisonment or both. The Minister of Coloured Affairs stated in the South African House of Assembly that the first registration would draw in approximately 90,000 persons and that after that approximately 20,000 persons would be drawn in per year.[19]

---

18 Prior to 1961, the unit of currency in the then Union of South Africa was the pound sterling, equivalent to $2.80.

19 United Nations, Office of Public Information, *Infringements of Trade Union Rights in Southern Africa* (Report submitted to the Economic and Social Council by the Ad Hoc Working Group of Experts appointed by the Commission on Human Rights, 1970).

DEVELOPMENT CORPORATION

In the hope of giving the impression of economic favour for the Coloured community and at the same time strengthening the small middle-class, the Government established a Coloured Development Corporation for the purpose of giving financial assistance to would-be Coloured entrepreneurs in their own areas.

The Minister of Coloured Affairs stated that, during 1970, the Corporation had granted 32 loans with a value of R53,375 to Coloured businessmen. The Corporation had itself spent R1,489,680 on establishing a property company, a supermarket, the Spes Bona Bank and a block of flats. The Corporation, or with its assistance, Coloured men had established or taken over eleven hotels, three of them in the Cape Town area. According to a member of the Coloured Representative Council, the Development Corporation was a 'massive move to help the wine farmers'.[20] It is from among this small section, which rotates around the Corporation, that the Government is assured cooperation.

In the realms of higher finance, however, a somewhat different picture is seen, with favour going to whites even in the so-called Coloured areas. Prospecting rights for base metals had by 1971 been granted to nine Coloured persons and nineteen white persons. Prospecting rights for precious stones were held by the Corporation, assisted by five white and one Coloured contractor and one firm jointly owned by white and Coloured. The Corporation held mining rights in Komaggas and Richtersveld in the Northern Cape and was being assisted by two white contractors.[21]

SOCIAL EFFECTS

In spite of the claims by the protagonists of the colour bar that the Coloured people enjoy a privileged status within the black–white

---

20 *Rand Daily Mail*, Johannesburg, 21 August 1971.
21 *1971 Survey of Race Relations* (Johannesburg, 1972).

arrangement in South Africa, facts continuously reveal quite the opposite. Neither should it be assumed that only under the present National Party rule has the position of the Coloured people deteriorated economically and socially. Statistics show that in 1939, 53 per cent of the community lived below the breadline. Today the position is no better and the Government with its policy of extreme racism has only aggravated the situation.

Whites who form 19 per cent of the population of South Africa control 69 per cent of the national purchasing power... Coloureds form 10 per cent of the population only control 6 per cent of purchasing power.[22]

It has been reported that approximately 150,000 people were dependent in 1966 on the earnings of Cape Town's 40,000 unskilled workers and that 'a marked increase in the incidence of malnutrition' was imminent.[23] A comparatively stabilized four-year run in the incidence of tuberculosis was dramatically broken by an increase by 16 per cent in cases of the disease.[24] In 1970, 6,608 cases of tuberculosis among Coloureds were notified, as against 824 whites.[25] 'Kwashiorkor, a disease caused by malnutrition, affects mainly the Africans and Coloured people. The incidence of the disease in 1967 was: whites 7; Coloured people 1,046; Asians 12; Africans 9,675.'[26] Fifteen thousand Coloured children die of malnutrition a year.[27] In 1970 the Minister of Statistics stated that the infantile mortality rate was 21.1: 1,000 for whites and 136.2: 1,000 for Coloured people.[28]

---

22 United Nations Unit on Apartheid, 'Facts and Figures on South Africa', Notes and Documents No. 7/71.

23 *Cape Times*, 2 June 1966.

24 *Cape Argus*, 14 June 1966.

25 *1971 Survey of Race Relations* (Johannesburg, 1972).

26 United Nations Unit on Apartheid, 'Facts and Figures on South Africa', Notes and Documents No. 7/71.

27 United Nations Unit on Apartheid, 'Facts and Figures on South Africa', Notes and Documents No. 7/71.

Sociologists cannot avoid coming to the conclusion that the rapid increase in crime and drunkenness among the Coloured community is linked with poverty and insecurity. A social worker commented on the large percentage of those appearing before courts on charges of housebreaking and theft being young people, who steal things to sell so as to buy food. 'And once they have started on this road, it is not easy to stop them,' a newspaper commented.[29]

It has been estimated that each year one out of every six Coloured men is convicted of a crime. The crime rate among the Coloured people is 5.5 times that among whites.[30] According to the report of the Commissioner of Prisons, of the 484,661 sentenced prisoners for the year 1 July 1969 to 30 June 1970, 409,534 were Africans, 64,504 Coloured, 2,225 Asian and 8,408 whites.[31]

3. *Education of the Coloured People*

Mr Billy Nannan has written:

> The educational system for non-whites in South Africa, far from universalizing knowledge and experience, seeks artificially to isolate each racial group and reinforce tribalism in accordance with the Government's policy of apartheid. The enforced isolation and police state environment of the African, Indian and Coloured colleges condemns the students to an inferior system of higher education.[32]

Before the advent to power of the National Party in 1948, education remained in the hands of the respective provinces, and in

---

28 *1971 Survey of Race Relations* (Johannesburg, 1972).

29 *Cape Argus*, 11 February 1965.

30 United Nations Unit on Apartheid, 'Facts and Figures on South Africa', Notes and Documents No. 7/71.

31 *1971 Survey of Race Relations* (Johannesburg, 1972).

32 United Nations Unit on Apartheid, 'Discrimination and Segregation in Education', Notes and Documents No. 14/71.

spite of general adherence to racially segregated schools and differences in standards and facilities from province to province, the education offered to the various racial groups was the same in terms of content and academic standards, and a common educational system applicable to all the people of South Africa was the basis of educational policy.

In 1939, a congress of Christian National Education, sponsored by Nationalists in the main, was held at Bloemfontein and set up an Institute of Christian National Education, which in 1949 recommended the basis for future education of the population.

The method selected by the Government to implement its educational policy for the Coloured people was much the same as in the case of the Africans. A Commission was appointed in 1953 to investigate 'Coloured education' and its terms of reference included the consideration of the question 'whether the nature and direction of the present educational system fulfil the needs of the Coloured population, or whether the system with its emphasis on the academic side does not lead to a feeling of frustration.' The Commission concluded accordingly:

> A large part of the population of this country makes a living by the use of its hands. The Coloured people are certainly no exception to this; indeed under present circumstances most of the opportunities for employment open to them are in those fields of industry and agriculture where manual labour plays the chief role, the development of their manual skills should therefore be emphasized.[33]

In 1961, Coloured vocational and technical training was transferred to the Coloured Affairs Department, and in 1963 the Coloured Persons Education Act transferred Coloured primary and secondary education as well. In October 1962, the then Minister of Coloured Affairs, Mr Botha, re-echoing Nationalist views on

---

33 'The Transfer of Coloured Education to the Coloured Affairs Department'. Leaflet issued by the Anti-Transfer Action Committee (ATAC), Cape Town.

African education, said: 'It would not help to give them only academic education and then throw them on the market as frustrated people.' Opposing a clause that would amend the Act to give Coloured the same education as whites, Mr Botha claimed that many Coloured people could not cope with the education whites received and that many teachers had only reached Standard 8.

In 1959, the Government had passed the so-called Extension of University Education Act, which provided for the establishment of special university colleges for non-white students, who were to be separated on racial and ethnic lines. The University College of the Western Cape was officially established on 1 November 1959 to serve the Coloured (including Malay and Griqua) community.

It is not the intention of this paper to enter into a detailed analysis of the effects of 'Coloured' education on the community. However, attention must be drawn to certain facts related to the education of Coloured children and students.

School attendance is compulsory for white children, but is compulsory for Coloured children only where accommodation permits. In the Cape Province, where the overwhelming majority of Coloured people live, there are only four primary schools, one secondary school and one high school at which attendance is compulsory for children resident within three miles of the schools.[34]

Per capita expenditure on education for white children is R114.1 ($159.74) and on Coloured and Indian children it is only R74.5 ($104.30). The number of candidates for matriculation examinations in 1968 was: 39,637 whites and only 3,446 Coloured. Among the economically active whites in 1960, 18.5 per cent were engaged in professional, technical and managerial occupations, while 18.9 per cent had school-leaving or matriculation certificates. Of 551,750 economically active Coloured persons, only 3.7 per cent were

---

34 United Nations Unit on Apartheid, 'Facts and Figures on South Africa', Notes and Documents No. 7/71.

engaged in professional, technical and managerial occupations and 1.4 per cent had school-leaving or matriculation certificates.[35]

Insofar as the political system of South Africa has always been geared for the maintenance of white supremacy, the educational systems therefore are recognized to be different: the one for the education of the sons and daughters who are to occupy the positions of mastery; the other to provide for those who are to live in servitude and subjection.

4. *The Coloured People in Political Life*

THE CAPE LIBERAL TRADITION

Participation by Coloured people in the affairs of government, albeit on a limited and conditional scale, has its origins in the early days of colonial settlement. As far back as 1799, Coloured riflemen joined the British in putting down a rebellion of descendants of the original Dutch who turned against the administration for alleged partiality to the Coloured and Xhosa in the Cape.

The British Empire, which backed the emancipation of slaves, generally maintained an attitude of liberalism in the Colonies. Cape liberalism, which stood for racial tolerance, however, was not a general characteristic of the white population. British immigrants rapidly absorbed the racial prejudices of the older white inhabitants. Nevertheless, as the Simons point out, 'liberalism took root in the Western Cape because of the region's peculiar history, relative tranquillity, racial composition and cultural cleavages.'[36]

The policy resulted in minor concessions for the Coloured population, but did not manifest itself in any far-reaching uplifting of their conditions, material or political.

---

[35] United Nations Unit on Apartheid, 'Facts and Figures on South Africa', Notes and Documents No. 7/71.

[36] H. J. and R. E. Simons, *Class and Colour in South Africa (1850–1950)* (Harmondsworth: Penguin, 1969), p. 20.

The constitution of 1853 gave the Cape a system of representative government and a franchise open to any man with certain economic qualifications. But the constitution was colour blind only in form. The Coloured people made up the great bulk of the poor and, consequently, few qualified for the vote. Even in later years, when Coloured voters were marginally important in a dozen or more constituencies, they never succeeded in returning any of their own people to Parliament.

In the General Election of 1893, an attempt was made for the first time to put up non-white candidates. In Paarl in the Western Cape, moves were made to unite everybody in support of James Curry, the Coloured candidate. In Cape Town, the Malay community prepared to nominate A. M. Effendi, who was of Turkish extraction. At that time, there existed in the Cape a form of proportional representation known as the cumulative vote. Certain large constituencies returned more than one candidate, and every voter was allowed to cast as many votes as there were candidates, and voters could, if they chose, cast all their votes for the same candidate. To prevent this from happening in the case of the non-white representative, a Constitutional Amendment Act was rushed through Parliament, which abolished the cumulative vote.

In Natal at the time of the Union, there was, as in the Cape, no constitutional discrimination between white and Coloured people from the time of a charter in 1856. There was, however, a hardening of attitudes even before Union, and laws in 1865 and 1896 excluded Africans and Indians respectively from political rights.

In the Orange Free State and Transvaal, the Coloured people had not enjoyed political rights from the time of the establishment of these republics to the time of Union. The Transvaal Republic laid down that no 'bastard' could sit in its meetings as a member or judge up to the tenth generation.

The South Africa Act of 1909, passed just prior to the formation of the Union of South Africa, finally removed the right of

Coloureds in Natal and the Cape to stand and serve as elected or nominated representatives in both Houses of Parliament.

Just before Union, some Coloured leaders decided that their interests were not fully safeguarded by the white political parties, and, in 1902, the African Political Organisation (APO) was formed.[37] Despite its name, the APO was composed of an entirely Coloured membership.

At a conference in 1905, Dr A. Abdurahman, the first Coloured (Malay) member of the Cape Town Municipal Council, was elected president of the APO. In 1906, when the British handed power back to the Transvaal whites, the APO put forward a demand for the vote for Africans and Coloureds, and sent Dr Abdurahman and two others to England on a deputation to present their case to the British public.

Coloured progressive thought was already turning towards an alliance with African organization and opinion in the confrontation with the segregationist policies of the newly formed Union. Already in 1907, the APO had attended a joint conference of Africans and Coloured people in order to discuss a common attitude towards the Cape elections the following year. An extract from an APO editorial, written on the approval by Britain of the colour-bar Act of Union gives an idea of how far advanced the APO in fact was. The editorial stated:

> The struggle has not ended. It has just begun. We the Coloured and Native peoples of South Africa have a tremendous fight before us. [. . .] No longer must we look to our flabby friends of Great Britain. Our political destiny is in our hands; and we must be prepared to fight with grim determination to succeed.

It was of course not in the favour of the white people to see the Coloured people siding with the African majority. The whites meant to ensure that all power remained in their hands, and every

---

[37] Later known as the African Peoples Organisation.

effort would be made to split the potential forces of non-white opposition. To this end the whites could make use of the Coloured people's history and cultural affinity with them in order to gain support. Hertzog told Parliament in 1929 that it would be 'very foolish to drive the Coloured people to the enemies of the Europeans—and that will happen if we repel him—to allow him eventually to come to rest in the arms of the Native.'

On the electoral front, the fear of driving the Coloured people to rest in 'the arms of the Native' lost intensity as successive measures disfranchised Africans and diminished the relative importance of the Coloured vote. The Women's Enfranchisement Act, which gave the vote to white women, at one blow halved the importance of the Coloured vote. It was further diminished by the Franchise Laws Amendment Act of 1931, which brought the white male franchise in the Cape in line with the rest of the Union by abolishing the property qualification and extending the franchise to every white male over twenty-one years.

THE NEW GENERATION

Teachers, students, university graduates, journalists and a handful of artisans produced a new generation of radicals in the Western Cape during the 1930s. Like Dr Abdurahman thirty years before, they refused to take second place to the whites, but they turned their backs on his policies and strategy. Abdurahman had discredited himself and his organization by clinging to the white liberals when they followed Smuts into Hertzog's camp. The younger generation disputed his leadership and authority and made a bid to create anew on their own account. By the 1930s, the APO had degenerated into hardly more than a benefit, burial and building society.

In December 1935, the National Liberation League of South Africa was founded, with Mrs Z. Gool, Dr Abdurahman's daughter, as president and James La Guma as general secretary. Coloured radicals looked to Africans for mass support, and they drafted the

League's programme with them in mind, although they renewed pleas in the interest of all, black and white, calling on white workers to cut themselves off from the ruling class before it dragged them down to the 'degraded position of the non-European'.

At that period of its history, the African National Congress was sluggish and steeped in reformism, and it appeared that from then on Coloured radicals would strive to shape aims and strategy of activity in the Cape.

At that time as well, white politicians were preparing for battle in the impending general election and Afrikaner nationalists set the pace. Thundering against aliens, communists, Jews, men of colour, they publicized the manifesto that was to form the basis of their legislative programme after 1948. The Government of the day was quickly alarmed and attempted to outmanoeuvre them by getting in first.

The Cape Provincial Council passed an ordinance giving municipal councils the power to enforce segregation in public places and residential areas. Stuttaford, then Minister of Interior, gave notice of a scheme of 'complete and parallel' segregation, a forerunner to the present policy of apartheid.

The Non-European United Front, which had been initiated earlier by the National Liberation League, replied with a massive demonstration of Coloured people in Cape Town on 27 March 1939. The police attacked demonstrators outside the Houses of Parliament and continued to assault the residents of District Six, the Coloured quarter, until the early hours of the morning.

The Government vetoed the ordinance and dropped its own segregation proposals, a victory for the mass militancy of the Coloured people.

With the Second World War looming on the horizon, the Government also realized that it would need the full cooperation of the entire population, and it therefore shelved most of its anti-colour policies. The Nationalists, destined to become the party in power after the war, did not let up in their racism and pro-Nazism. While several of those who are today rulers of South Africa were interned for siding with the enemy, Coloured men went off to war, hoping for a better deal for their people on their return.

APARTHEID GOVERNMENT COMES TO POWER

When the National Party came to power in 1948, many of the subtleties which had attempted to disguise the racial policies of previous administrations were stripped away and non-whites were faced with the naked hand of oppression. Apart from the fact that Nationalists were against the enfranchisement of non-whites, it was clear that the vote of the Coloured men in the Cape and Natal had gone against them, and this constituted a danger which in their eyes had to be removed. Likewise the potential strength of the total non-white vote was something Nationalists could not countenance, because it constituted an ominous presence in the body politic; only the white man should govern.

5. *The Coloured People Against Apartheid*

At the very first session of Parliament after the advent to power of the Nationalist Government, it introduced an Electoral Law Amendment Act[38] which provided that Coloured applications to vote must be witnessed and completed in the presence of an electoral officer, magistrate or police officer.[39] The result was of course a serious drop in the number of Coloured voter registrations in spite of the fact that the Coloured community had already acquired an apathy for white-controlled elections.

The next step was the Separate Representation of Voters Act, which removed the Coloured voters from the common roll in the 55 Cape constituencies.[40] Coloured voters were then placed on a

---

38 Act No. 50 of 1948.
39 Previously a voter could complete a form without supervision.
40 Act No. 46 of 1951.

separate roll which would then elect four whites to represent them in the House of Assembly at five-year intervals and two white representatives to the Provincial Council.

The Coloured people replied to these proposals with a massive campaign organized by the Franchise Action Council, a united front of all elements, both white and non-white, who were against the removal of Coloured voters from the common roll.

In spite of widespread protests, including a general strike of Coloured people and court proceedings instituted against the Government, the Bill to remove the Coloured voters from the common roll was passed. This was only accomplished, however, when the Government padded the Senate with its supporters in order to get the required two-thirds majority of both Houses in order to amend the entrenched clauses of the Constitution.

While separate representation in Parliament had been a feature of Nationalist policy since early times, it became clear that even after their common roll 'triumph', in the long run they would not be satisfied with even representation of Coloured people by white representatives. At each election under the Act, pro-Government candidates were resoundingly defeated. The Government was forced, therefore, to contemplate another form of 'representation' and this led to the present Coloured Persons Representative Council.

COLOURED AFFAIRS DEPARTMENT

The basis for the present form of representation under the Nationalist government had indeed been established by the previous United Party government. It was the latter administration, which while claiming to champion the cause of the Coloured community, brought into being a Coloured Advisory Council (CAC). Instead of finding plans to extend the rights of the Coloured people in return for their services in defeating Nazism, Coloured soldiers returning home discovered that the Government under which they had served was prepared to appease the Nationalists who had sided with the enemy. Shortly before the General Election of 1943, Smuts had decided to introduce administrative segregation for the Coloured people. Coloured affairs henceforth would be dealt with by a special section of the Department of the Interior and by a permanent council of Coloured notables.

An immediate and emphatic protest was launched by Coloured organizations, individuals and their supporters. Some 200 delegates attended the first National Anti-CAD conference in Cape Town on 29 May 1943. The conference decided to institute a political and social boycott of the Coloured Advisory Council and to promote a united front against all forms of discrimination.

The CAC, functioning under the Coloured Affairs Department, was composed of members of the community appointed by the Government. It was supposed to advise in 'matters affecting the Coloured people'. However, when even these specially appointed 'representatives' made urgent appeals to the United Party government to extend the Coloured vote to the Northern provinces, they were turned down by the Government.

The CAC continued to function for nearly two years after the victory of the National Party at the polls, in the face of intense attacks from its opponents.

The Nationalist government, taking over from where the United Party had left off, extended the Council into a Union Council of Coloured Affairs (UCCA) under a complete Ministry of Coloured Affairs which would control the future of the community via apartheid. In order to give this new apartheid institution a semblance of democracy, the Government allowed Coloured people to be able to elect some members, but the majority were still appointed by the Government.

Again the Coloured people demonstrated their rejection of this travesty of political rights and boycotted the 'elections'. 'Candidates' who stood in support of this institution were duly declared elected unopposed. They took their seats in spite of bitter opposition from the community, and such was the opposition that the authorities had to refuse public admission to sessions of the UCCA and all its meetings had to be held in private.[41]

(a) *The Coloured Persons Representative Council Elections*

The Coloured Persons Representative Council (CRC) was established by the Coloured Persons Representative Council Amendment Act of 1968. It consisted of 60 members—40 to be elected[42] and 20 to be nominated by the Government. Every Coloured man and woman in South Africa over 21 was compelled to register as a voter under pain of a fine of R50 ($70) or three months' imprisonment.

The establishment of the CRC gave rise to a spate of political parties among the Coloured community, organized in the main by those who supported the apartheid policy of the Government one way or the other and saw themselves as participating in their own 'parliament'. The anti-apartheid Coloured Labour Party had been established by moderates who hoped to fill the vacuum caused by heavy Government repression against such organizations as the Coloured People's Congress, the Non-European Unity Movement (of which the Anti-CAD was a unit). This party had originally been under the leadership of Dr R. E. van der Ross.[43] It was formed in order to 'use the instruments available to us', because 'that was the only way the Coloured people can organize themselves under the present system'.[44] The article went on to say that the Coloured people were not 'given to working underground'.

Even though the Labour Party was speedy in giving assurances to the authorities that everything they did would be above board

---

41 CCA after the declaration of the Republic.

42 28 in the Cape Province, 6 in the Transvaal and 3 each in Natal and the Orange Free State.

43 Now advisor to the Government on education for Coloured people.

44 Dr van der Ross, writing in the *Cape Argus*, 14 November 1965.

and that they had no objection to Security Police surveillance, no sooner had it been established than leading members were arraigned before magistrates and warned that they could be banned and proscribed for 'furthering the aims of communism'. Some of the founders then resigned.

The first election of the Coloured Persons Representative Council was held on 24 September 1969. Six parties contested the election, of which only the Labour Party stood on an anti-apartheid platform. There were contests in only 37 of the 40 seats, 3 candidates of the pro-Government Federal Coloured People's Party, led by Mr Tom Swartz, were returned unopposed.[45]

Of the little over 600,000 compulsorily registered voters, only 48.7 per cent went to the polls. Polling of up to 75 per cent was registered in some of the rural areas, where Coloured voters had reportedly been subjected to great pressure by employers and the police, and permission to address meetings in the Coloured reserves was usually refused to anti-Government candidates. In the Cape urban constituencies, where Coloured people had previously had the vote on the common roll, the polls were low, some areas showing a mere 13 per cent, 16.4 per cent, 19.2 per cent and 20.2 per cent.

Nevertheless, the community's rejection of Government policy was shown by the outcome of the election, in which the anti-apartheid Labour Party topped the polls, winning 26 seats. The Federal Party won 11 seats. The Republican Coloured Party, National Coloured People's Party, Independent Federal Party won one seat each.

To secure control of the Council, the Labour Party had to win 31 seats, which it failed to do. The Government then proceeded to appoint Federal Party men to fill the remaining 20 seats of the Council, including 13 candidates who had been defeated in the

---

45 Mr Swartz had formerly been Chairman of the Council of Coloured Affairs.

elections. This gave the Federal Party the necessary votes to control the Council.

Perhaps the worst insult of all to the Coloured electorate and the people at large was the Government's appointment of Mr Tom Swartz himself as chairman of the Council executive. During the elections Swartz was heavily defeated by the Labour Party candidate and got even fewer votes than the Republican Party candidate who came second. Yet this man is being presented to the world as the so-called Prime Minister of Coloured South Africa.

The CRC is totally subordinate to the central Parliament, and its powers are even narrower than those of the Transkei Assembly. It may draft laws on the limited and specified range of matters entrusted to it, but no proposed law may be introduced unless it has the approval of the Minister of Coloured Affairs. The entire budget of the CRC is voted by the all-white South African Parliament, which can for its part legislate on any matter concerning the Coloured people as it sees fit.

The then-leader of the Labour Party, Mr M. D. Arendse, was not exaggerating when he told the annual conference of the party in Cape Town in April 1970 that the Nationalist government had by devious means deprived the Coloured people of all democratic voting rights on every level, thus stripping them of the last vestiges of democratic processes. As a result of the new political dispensation that had been engineered by the authorities, he went on to say, 'we find ourselves now virtually a voiceless people in the land of our birth.'

(b) *Campaigns against Apartheid*

One of the first campaigns launched by the Coloured people against the Nationalist government's apartheid policy centred on the introduction of racial separation on suburban trains in the Western Cape. Here again it was discovered that the new Government's implementation of apartheid on local railways was in fact a follow up of the previous administration's plans. All the technical and organizational wherewithal had been prepared by the United Party administration, and it fell to the Nationalists to merely put them into effect. In 1949, widespread protest against this violation of longstanding rights of the people was led by an ad hoc Train Apartheid Resistance Committee.

Apartheid on local buses was introduced in 1955, and a massive boycott of buses was organized by the Coloured People's Congress (CPC).[46] After the collapse of the National Liberation League in the late 1930s, some of its former members had regrouped after the Second World War and had initiated the Non-European Unity Movement (NEUM) which embraced the Anti-CAD and the Teachers' League of South Africa as its main Coloured affiliates. The NEUM pursued an isolationist attitude and relied mainly on propaganda rather than active struggle. With the Government pressing relentlessly on with its apartheid policy, and with the most militant sections of the non-white population emerging under the leadership of the African National Congress (ANC) and the South African Indian Congress, mass participation of the Coloured community was essential for a united struggle. The Coloured People's Congress provided that participation.

Apart from mass campaigns against the implementation of Group Areas Act,[47] the Population Registration Act,[48] the CPC also participated in the nationwide campaign for the Congress of the People in 1955, which formulated and adopted the Freedom Charter. From 1956 to 1960, several of its leading members were among the accused in the notorious Treason Trial, which resulted from that campaign.

When the ANC called for a national day of protest following the Sharpeville Massacre, the CPC was instrumental in organizing

---

46 The Coloured People's Congress, initially the Coloured People's Organisation, was formed in 1953.

47 Act No. 41 of 1950.

48 Act No. 30 of 1950.

the support of thousands of Coloured workers who struck in alliance with the Africans reiterating their own demands at the same time. The entire CPC leadership was detained during the resultant State of Emergency proclaimed by the Government, the only section of Coloured leadership to be thus imprisoned. Similarly, when the National Action Council of the All-In African Conference at Maritzburg called for demonstrations in support of a National Convention for a new Constitution in reply to the establishment of the white Republic, thousands of Coloured workers again responded to the leadership of the CPC. In the Cape Peninsula alone, between 35,000 and 40,000 Coloured workers engaged in commerce and industry stayed home and virtually crippled the clothing, building, engineering, leather and baking concerns. In Port Elizabeth, where the second largest concentration of Coloured people live, 75 per cent of the Coloured labour force supported African strikers. For the first time, Coloured workers participated in the stay-at-home in Durban and Maritzburg, Natal.

In 1961, a National Convention of the Coloured People was called in order to examine their status in South African society and to formulate common demands which would provide for their future in a democratic state. A wide section of the Coloured population, conservative, moderate and militant, joined in the preparations for the Convention through the participation of political, social, religious, sporting, cultural and trade-union organizations, as well as a number of personalities. On the night of 6 July, the Minister of Justice enforced the Suppression of Communism Act[49] and banned the holding of the Convention within a radius of 30 miles around Cape Town. The organizers moved the assembly to two farms at Malmesbury, just beyond the limits of the Minister's prohibition. In spite of the difficulties entailed by the last-minute ban, all provinces were represented and the Convention proceeded on the 8 and 10 July.

---

49 Act No. 44 of 1950.

Among its findings, it stated:

> The only policy that can succeed in South Africa is one of complete equality for all people [...] the total abolition of the colour bar in every sphere, and full citizenship for all the peoples of South Africa.[50]

Faced with widespread opposition to their policies, the Government resorted to wholesale intimidation of Coloured leaders and organizations. The provisions of the Suppression of Communism Act were invoked in order to ban, confine and house arrest individual activists. The CPC became practically immobilized by the banning of its most active cadres, and although technically still a legal organization, today its activities have to be carried on underground.

After dealing with Congress militants, the Minister of Justice turned upon such Coloured bodies as the Anti-CAD and the Teachers' League of South Africa, banning their foremost spokesmen. Coloured members of the Cape Town City Council, the only institution of direct representation for Coloured people, were prohibited from attending gatherings. Members of the District Six Action Committee, which had been campaigning against Group Areas proclamations, were arraigned before magistrates and warned that they would be dealt with for 'furthering the aims of communism' if they persisted with their protest campaign.

The widespread activities of the Security Police and the Minister of Justice have since that period been used in an attempt to eliminate opposition to apartheid.

6. *Hardening Attitudes*

The application of apartheid has been seen as the ruthless continuation and development of the segregation and colour-bar policies

---

50 *Contact*, Johannesburg, 10 August 1961. *Contact* was itself later banned under the above-mentioned Suppression of Communism Act.

of past South African governments and has emphasized for the non-whites that other parties in Parliament hold no promise of redress for their grievances against the Government, nor agreement to equality for all in South Africa.

The main opposition party in Parliament, the United Party, has for generations made use of the Coloured people's old preference for the British connexion, and in the guise of having the interests of the community at heart, exploited the Coloured franchise for its own parliamentary ambitions. The concern over growing Coloured antagonism to white supremacy as a whole must be seen as anxiety of that section of the whites over the imminent loss of support from a large section of the non-African population in a potential front against the black majority.

Sir De Villiers Graaff, leader of the UP [United Party], stated in 1965 that the Party was still 'prepared to accept the Coloured people as part of the Western Group in South Africa', but he 'prayed that their conduct will not make this impossible for us.'[51]

Today the United Party accepts the principle of the system of separate representation first introduced by the Nationalist government. On 9 June 1971, De Villiers Graaff said:

> The Coloured people should be represented in the central Parliament by six Members of Parliament who could be either Coloured or white persons. They would be elected on a separate roll. The Coloured Persons Representative Council should be transformed into a wholly elected communal council. [. . .] Coloured people should not be deprived of the municipal vote before adequate alternative rights are available.[52]

The more radical of the Coloured political groups have always warned against the basic racist allegiances of the opposition parties. However, today even more moderate elements as well as those who

---

51 *Cape Times*, 24 April 1965.
52 *1971 Survey of Race Relations in South Africa* (Johannesburg, 1972).

had favoured United Party policy in the past have rejected that party and have come out in favour of full equality for Coloured people. Even the pro-apartheid groups in the Coloured Persons Representative Council (CRC) have stated this position.

As the *Rand Daily Mail* reported on 6 March 1972:

> Coloured leaders of the Labour Party told the United Party in strong terms that their political plans for the Coloured people were unacceptable, i.e. plans for separate institutions like communal councils.

The Coloured leaders were also reported to have told United Party Members of Parliament that they objected to the continual stress on the fact that the United Party stood for white leadership and was in favour of separate Coloured areas.

The United Party's policy was rejected by the leaders of both the major parties in the Coloured Persons Representative Council. Mr Tom Swartz of the Federal Party was reported to have said that the Coloured people would never be satisfied with inadequate measures but that they wanted 'full equality'.[53]

GROWING OPPOSITION

Outside the deliberations of the CRC and official meetings, the Coloured community has continued to reveal its rejection of apartheid and a hardening of attitudes to colour-bar attitudes from all quarters of the white front. This is taking place even in spite of the atmosphere of intimidation by the Security Police and the Minister of Justice, which prevails today.

Among the intelligentsia, scholars and students, opposition and protest have been developing openly. During the Government-organized celebrations of the tenth anniversary of the Republic in 1971, reports revealed that the majority of pupils arranged to participate through their schools refused to turn out. On another

---

53 *1971 Survey of Race Relations in South Africa* (Johannesburg, 1972).

occasion, when the whites-only Cape Peninsula Arts Board performed at a high school, Coloured students created disturbances or ignored the performers. At the Coloured University of the Western Cape, students have been consistently resisting a 'quisling' Students Representative Council.

The poet and philosopher Mr Adam Small has written:

Racism is a phenomenon of inferiority. Our blackness is a phenomenon of pride. [...] We can no longer care whether or not whites understand us. What we do care about is understanding ourselves, and in the course of this task, helping the whites to understand themselves. [...] We are rejecting the idea that we live by their grace (i.e. that they have the right to decide our future). We may live by the Grace of God, but we do not live by the grace of the whites.[54]

When Dame Margot Fonteyn, the British ballerina, announced her intention of giving special performances for Coloured people when visiting South Africa, Mr Small said again: 'Here it is all over again—the sickening phenomenon of the patronizing white man or woman graciously condescending to "do something for us non-whites". The business is doubly sickening because it is all happening in the name of art.'[55] The London *Guardian*'s Cape Town correspondent later reported that Dame Margot's action had angered the community and that they were planning a boycott of the performance.

A Coloured Anglican priest has said: 'The black man in South Africa knew no existence but oppression and incarceration.'[56] The Reverend Clive McBride, speaking at a symposium at the University of Cape Town as part of Human Rights Week, has said:

---

54 *Rand Daily Mail*, Johannesburg, 13 July 1971.
55 *Guardian*, London, 17 March 1972.
56 *Star*, Johannesburg, 1 April 1972.

'I cannot distinguish between Nationalist or Progressive. All I see is that there is manifested against me a power, an evil, stunting power—a white power that mercilessly oppresses.' He went on to say that although the non-white had the aspirations and the appearance of a human being, the dignity that made him a human being was taken away.

After the shooting at Gelvandale, Port Elizabeth, in May 1971 mentioned earlier, serious unrest continued for about three weeks. Buses were stoned, and attempts were made to set up roadblocks. More than 40 persons were subsequently charged in court with various offences, such as public violence or malicious damage to property. The Gelvandale community also set aside one day on which they wore black rosettes and armbands to 'mourn the loss of our people's rights'.

In a letter to the Prime Minister, the General Secretary of the Trade Union Council of South Africa urged that a top-level enquiry be instituted into the future of the Coloured people. It was evident, he said, that the community was 'becoming increasingly resentful of the treatment they are receiving, and their frustration is moving towards an explosion point.'[57]

THE REJECTION OF APARTHEID INSTITUTIONS

The predecessors of the CRC, namely, such bodies as the Coloured Advisory Council, the Coloured Affairs Department, the Council of Coloured Affairs and the like, had all been given the cold shoulder by the majority of the Coloured community. As has been pointed out, the majority of the electorate did not participate in the election of the CRC in 1969. In the prevailing atmosphere in South Africa, aggravated by consistent rejection of the demands of the oppressed groups, it is inevitable that those who did believe that redress might be sought within the institutions of apartheid are

---

57 *Star*, Johannesburg, 17 May 1971.

themselves becoming rapidly disillusioned with this approach. Thus inside the CRC the realization that nothing can be achieved for the community within the framework of the Government's policy has been growing.

Mr Sonny Leon was reported to have said in Pretoria: 'The CRC should be scrapped and replaced by Coloured representation at all levels of Government in South Africa, based on a common roll.'[58] He went on to say that the Council was a puppet of the Government without real powers and that even some of the nominated members were beginning to see that the Council was little more than a shop window intended to reflect the progress of the Government's separate development policy.

On 21 February 1972, the *Rand Daily Mail* quoted Mr Leon as saying: 'The CRC has become an acute embarrassment to the Nationalist government because its nominated majority had lost control.'

Because of defections, Mr Swartz could count on only 29 votes from among 60 members. At the last session of the Council, a resolution requested that the Council be converted into an all-elected body because the 20 Government-appointed members 'do not necessarily represent the views of the Coloured.' It stated that the Coloured people had lost confidence and the Council its credibility.

At the proceedings of the Council in 1971, Mr Curry was reported to have said that the Labour Party considered the Government's policy of separate development to be 'pure hypocrisy —a cloak to maintain white political domination'. 'The traditional pattern of South Africa's racial policies', he went on to say, 'was not going to be changed by decisions made in the Coloured Persons Representative Council.' In addition, at the start of the session, Mr Leon introduced a motion calling for the abolition of the Council

---

58 *Rand Daily Mail*, Johannesburg, 10 September 1971.

and for the inclusion of its 40 elected members in the House of Assembly as representatives of the Coloured people.

The Labour Party boycotted the official opening of the Council during August 1971 by the Minister of Defence and the Cape leader of the National Party, Mr P. W. Botha. It also boycotted the budget debate after proposing an amendment that the budget was unacceptable because the Council had no power to change it.

Inevitably disillusionment with the apartheid machinery must compel their participants to consider complete non-cooperation. Thus a decision to call upon the Labour Party to abandon participation in the CRC was taken by the Transvaal region of the party in March 1972. It called on the Labour Party to quit the CRC and to work independently of all apartheid institutions. The national leadership was however not prepared to go so far. The *Rand Daily Mail* reported Mr Leon as having said that the resolution adopted by the Transvaal region reflected the general consensus of opinion that the CRC was a 'meaningless institution'. He claimed, nevertheless, that the Labour Party should remain in the Council to 'expose it for what it was' and that their presence was essential as it provided the party with 'a legal instrument to express the desires of the people'.[59]

Within the ranks of the pro-Government Federal Party, too, disillusionment is taking root. During August 1971, the former leader of that party in the Eastern Cape, Mr P. E. Kievetts, resigned, stating that he could no longer join in any defence of the apartheid policy.[60]

7. *The African Liberation Movement*

The 'extra-parliamentary' mass movements and campaigns against injustice and racial discrimination have been the methods by which

---

59 *Rand Daily Mail*, Johannesburg, 14 March 1972.
60 *Rand Daily Mail*, Johannesburg, 21 August 1971.

the whole people demonstrated in uncompromising terms their rejection of the colour bar, segregation, apartheid or so-called separate development. The struggles against the destruction of the franchise, against Group Areas, against poverty and cultural and educational discrimination as well as support for the Freedom Charter of the Congress Movement, a National Convention and the like—all have registered the Coloured community's rejection of the generations-old system of racism in South Africa.

Most important, these struggles and campaigns were always conducted in cooperation with the African people and emphasized the fact that, in spite of different historical and cultural backgrounds, success for oppressed minorities lays only in alliance with the national liberation movement of the African majority.

In a very real sense, the future of the Indian and Coloured people and their liberation as oppressed groups is seen as being intimately bound up with the liberation of the Africans. Coloured and Indian people are increasingly seeing their liberation as an integral part of the liberation movement and not as a mere auxiliary.

Events such as the distribution of underground literature and leaflets from the Coloured People's Congress and the African National Congress among the Coloured people are evidence of the fact that new cadres are emerging within the community to work for strengthening the democratic alliance, following the suppression of known militants. Indeed, the public demands made today by all non-white oppressed groups are reiterations of the demands unfolded by the liberation movement since its inception.

Coloured youths appear to be preparing for and joining the guerrilla movement of Umkhonto we Sizwe, the military wing of the ANC. A young Coloured man, Basil February, a member of this armed force, was killed by security forces in Zimbabwe in 1967 while making his way to South Africa. In 1971, another Coloured member of Umkhonto, Mr James April, was arrested in Natal while bringing arms into South Africa, was sentenced to 15 years' imprisonment.

Generations of experience show that the ruling white minority has no intention of according the Coloured people any genuine democratic rights in South Africa and is rapidly bringing about the final acknowledgement that only the overthrow of the racist state can lead to the just participation of all South Africans in an altogether new society.

CHAPTER THIRTEEN

Vietnam

A People's Victory

(1973)

La Guma served as the African member on a World Peace Council (WPC) delegation that visited North Vietnam from 13 to 20 January 1973. This article published in The African Communist *is an account of his trip.*

Hanoi is a city of lakes. Once, long ago, the land had been under water, and when the water subsided Hanoi was born. Today, you can still walk down the wide Parisian avenues that are lined with trees, past the yellow French colonial buildings, and stroll along the quiet bank of the Thugen Quan Lake, or visit the Lake of the Restored Sword. Cross the red Huc Bridge that arches over the placid water and you find yourself at the Ngoc Son Pagoda which stands on an island in the lake, among lotus blossoms, under a banyan tree. Or you can visit the temple dedicated to Le Roi who in 1407 led his people against the Ming invaders. Le Roi became king and founded the Le dynasty, you will be told. Then you can go to the one-pillar pagoda. It stands on a single column, the stem, and the building is shaped after the lotus flower. It is the city emblem of Hanoi. You can stroll down the shady avenue Dien Bien Phu and along Hung Vuong towards the palace of the former French Governor General. Everything is peaceful.

Slap in the Face

But turn aside into the working-class areas, the populated districts where the Vietnamese women in their white blouses and black trousers, conical straw hats, trot along with baskets slung from a shouldered bamboo pole, and the streets teem with hundreds of cyclists, and there the aftermath of war strikes you like a slap in the face.

Kham Tien Street in the Dong Ba district is gone. Eighteen blocks of buildings, mostly residential, had been reduced to piles of rubble, the shells of others stood precariously among the mounds of debris. For the length of a kilometre and the width of 600 metres, the storm of explosive from the US Air Force's giant B-52 bombers and F-111s had laid waste this oldest part of Hanoi. Ironically, Kham Tien means 'Watching the Sky', because long ago an observatory had stood there. Thirty thousand souls had lived in the area, and it had been transformed into hillocks of broken bricks and splintered beams. The marketplace had been destroyed, the welfare centres, cinema, the People's Bookshop, restaurants, stores, kindergartens. Fortunately, the high degree of organization of the Civil Defence and the system of air-raid shelters had managed to save more lives than had been lost.

This was the centre of Hanoi, and the other three districts of the four into which the 586 square kilometres is divided had likewise been systematically bombed again and again. Ahn Duong (Peaceful Scene), a residential area along the Red River, was without most of its homes, the primary and secondary schools catering for 5,000 children, the infirmary and the maternity centre.

Everything pointed to the fact that the United States aggressors had been determined to raze the city of Hanoi to the ground, to break the morale of her people, to force them to beg for mercy. It was not a matter of military targets but of political and military blackmail. But the giant bombers and millions of dollars of electronic equipment had foundered on the determination and courage of a people. Imperialism had banked on the racist theory that yellow-skinned people would never stand up to a blitzkrieg, but false hopes crashed down in piles of wreckage that dot the city and the countryside; heaps of aluminium and wire and scorched perspex, some still bearing the shattered insignia—iron gauntlet clutching lightning bolts (and an olive branch!)—of the US 'Strategic Air Command'. All over Hanoi placards proclaimed the toll taken of the 'May Bay My'—United States aircraft.

Hero Cities

We had come to the Democratic Republic of Vietnam in January, just before the ceasefire agreement was about to be signed, as a delegation of the World Peace Council to present the WPC's Lambrakis Medal to the hero cities of Hanoi and Haiphong for 'courage and sacrifice in the cause of national independence'.

These were the hero cities indeed. The outskirts of Haiphong looked like pictures of Hiroshima come to life. Here again the populated areas had been constantly and systematically blasted by planes and naval guns. The Czechoslovak-Vietnam Friendship Hospital had suffered, the Polish ship 'Josef Conrad' listed at the wharf, her upper works blasted, a great hole surrounded by peeled metal gaping at the sky; everywhere the port had been hit, everywhere people wore the white headbands of mourning.

But both Hanoi and Haiphong still stood, scarred, battered, burnt, but they still stood. This was Hiroshima and Nagasaki with a difference—the enemy had been defeated, made to run with tail between legs.

As one of our hosts from the Vietnamese Committee for World Peace put it, 'Imperialism could not afford a direct confrontation with the Socialist powers, particularly the Soviet Union, so it has chosen the front of national liberation. If imperialism could push back the forces of liberation in Vietnam, it would be able to do so to the liberation movements in other parts of the world. But it is necessary for the imperialists to ponder over the advancement made by progressive forces in this period of world history.'

But Vietnam needs peace. It is the demand of the common people whom we spoke to on the streets as they cleared the wreckage, and of those who wear the white bands of mourning; it is demanded by the young men and girls who man the anti-aircraft defences, the soldiers standing by the looming black-and-green surface-to-air missiles; it is the demand of their leaders and their government. It is proclaimed in the shattered Bach Mai Hospital, the bombed dykes and the destroyed villages, the children maimed by pellets and shrapnel from anti-personnel bombs.

In Hanoi, the Commission on US War Crimes in Vietnam has reckoned the cost paid by the people in blood and property. So has the Medical Aid Committee for Vietnam, and the US Committee for Responsibility, and other agencies on both sides. Figures of casualties and destruction of homes and institutions are too numerous to mention. Seven million tons of bombs were dropped on Vietnam by US planes, 3.5 times what was used in the Second World War.

A People's Victory

But peace in Vietnam does not mean the surrender of Vietnam; peace will not be paid for with the freedom and independence of the Vietnamese people. Today, it is not Nixon who has 'peace with honour', it is the heroic people of Vietnam.

Everywhere it was stressed that as the war ends, the vigilance of the world community must not be relaxed, that the democratic forces, the peace-loving people everywhere must ensure that the peace is kept and the terms agreed on adhered to. The people of Vietnam would continue to be on guard, we were told. 'We will be on guard as long as the machinations of the imperialists continue. We are prepared to meet any situation, war or peace.'

Hoang Tung and Pham Hong of the Vietnam Peace Committee told the WPC delegation: 'We must continue to be vigilant even as the war ends. During the past years, a wide and unprecedented world movement has arisen around developments in Vietnam. World opinion helped to stay the bloody hand of Nixon. Now the question is whether the United States and its puppets will carry out the agreement. We are ready to carry out our programme of national concord; we are ready to cooperate provided that there is willingness to build independence, democracy and world peace. We do not entertain a policy of war, and we will not permit the enemy to carry out a policy of war.'

The representatives of the Provisional Revolutionary Government of South Vietnam voiced the same sentiments. In addition, Nguyen Phu Soai, vice president, and Nguyen Van Tien, member of the Paris Conference, stressed the importance of the question of political prisoners held by the Thieu government. The US had tried to avoid this issue during negotiations, they said, but the US was equally responsible for these prisoners. International pressure should be strengthened to ensure the safety of the political prisoners, their release and return to participation in all aspects of Vietnam's future.

The Lessons

Above all there were lessons to be learnt from Vietnam, especially for those engaged in the national liberation struggle in their own countries.

'We owe much to the assistance and support of the Socialist countries, to the Soviet Union and to the worldwide solidarity of all progressive forces,' we were told. 'But most important for victory was the political unity of the Vietnamese people. Even our government and leaders were astonished by the determination, bravery and calmness of every citizen. In spite of tragedy, the loss of whole families, the people stood firm.'

In Vietnam, we saw the results won by the conviction of a whole people in the justice of their cause and the necessity to fight together; by their organization, political and defence, which extended from street to street, to residential quarter, to district, to city; by complete cooperation with their leaders on local, city and national level, with the Fatherland Front and the Vietnam Workers' Party; by the cooperation and solidarity between urban workers and the peasantry.

But perhaps everything was summed up by Prime Minister Pham Van Dong himself, when the delegation met him for an informal chat in Hanoi. He smiled as he replied to a comment from the Latin American delegate, saying: 'THE PEOPLE PLUS MARXISM–LENINISM, THAT IS THE VICTORY.'

CHAPTER FOURTEEN

Whither South Africa?
(1974)

This article was published in The Black Scholar *as part of a special issue on the Sixth Pan-African Congress held in Dar es Salaam. An earlier version of this essay appeared in a 1971 issue of the Cuban journal* Tricontinental *with the title 'Apartheid, Imperialist Monster' (in Spanish, 'Apartheid, Engendro Imperialista'), in which he marked the tenth anniversary of South Africa as a white minority-ruled republic. The existence of a preceding draft highlights how La Guma revised his ideas and writing over time to speak to new events.*

The Sixth Pan-African Congress came in the wake of congresses in held in 1919, 1921, 1923, 1927 and 1945. A foundational Pan-African Conference was held in 1900, though the 1919 meeting is technically the First Congress. Organized by George Padmore (1903–59) and Kwame Nkrumah (1909–72), the 1945 meeting held in Manchester proved pivotal with its promotion of African self-determination—a platform that foreshadowed decolonization after the Second World War. In contrast, the 1974 meeting expressed anxieties over Cold War neocolonialism that had taken hold since decolonization and the early independence period. La Guma's essay captures this mood, especially for southern Africa. Furthermore, it is one of his most direct engagements with the issue of racial capitalism.

Racism in South Africa—the ideology of white supremacy and black inferiority—was born with the invasion of our country by white settlers in the seventeenth century. The capitalists and traders of Europe, dissatisfied with the pillage of their own people, sought new sources of wealth in other parts of the world. By armed force, fraud and intrigue, they plundered the people of Africa, Asia, Latin

America and Australasia. The settlers came to South Africa as the henchmen of the Dutch East India Company.

Jan van Riebeeck, leader of the first Dutch settlers, referred to the Khoikhoi people, the aboriginal people of the Cape, as 'dull, stupid and lazy', and described them as 'a stinking nation'. Thus justified, the settlers organized commandos and hunting parties to shoot adult members of these people. They shot as many as they could and took the younger ones as slaves and cattle herders. Predatory raids against these people who owned large herds of livestock resulted in rich booty for the settlers. Because of inferior weapons, the aborigines naturally lost the battle against colonization.

White settlers gradually penetrated the interior of the Cape and drove the indigenous people from the best farmlands. Slaves were also imported from the East Indies and other parts of Asia and Africa to reinforce the decimated labour supply. The pattern was set for the ruthless colonial exploitation of the country, the expropriation of the land, the enforced harnessing of the labour power of the blacks.

When in 1806 the Dutch colony was seized by the British, the pattern did not change substantially. The British colonialists mounted a series of savage campaigns against the AmaXhosa in the Eastern Cape and the Zulu people in Natal. They imported more white settlers from Britain and extended their conquest further through Bechuanaland, Basutoland and later into Zimbabwe, which they called Rhodesia.

However, as the ranking capitalist country of that time, Great Britain was opposed to direct chattel slavery. When this type of slavery was abolished, large contingents of Boers (farmers, descendants of the original Dutch settlers), who wanted to maintain chattel slavery, left the Cape on 'the Great Trek' and advanced into those areas later named the Orange Free State and Transvaal, and into Natal. In the course of these advances, the Boers conducted repeated aggressive wars against African tribes who owned the land of those regions. The Boers seized these lands, established the Republics of the Transvaal and Orange Free State, based upon white domination, the exploitation of the black populations and the principle of 'No equality in church and state'. The spirit of the white slave-owner remained as the core of their outlook.

The discovery of diamonds and then gold had profound and far-reaching effects: more foreigners flocked into South Africa. British and European financiers exported vast sums of investment capital to South Africa. In order to gain complete control over the gold in the Transvaal, British imperialism invaded the two republics and brought them into the British Empire, but no change in the conditions of the African people followed. Their colonial status and subjugation continued and was in fact intensified. The mining interests were now masters of the country, and they had only one interest as far as the black inhabitants were concerned: to force them into labour in the mines at the minimum rate of pay. The British found the harsh colonial and racist policy of the Boer republics well suited to this purpose. Taxation, the pass laws and land grabbing followed.

New Colonialism

British imperialism and Afrikaner (Boer) nationalism found common ground in the dispossession, oppression and exploitation of the non-whites. On this foundation the Union of South Africa was established in 1910. The racist constitution legitimized racism in the country and prepared the ground for the legalized national oppression, exploitation and humiliation of the black masses, and for all the atrocities committed against the people, individually and collectively.

> The conceding of independence to South Africa by Britain in 1910 was not a victory over the forces of colonialism and imperialism. It was designed in the interest of imperialism. Power was transferred not into the hands of the masses of

the people of South Africa, but into the hands of the white minority alone. The evils of colonialism, insofar as the non-white majority was concerned, were perpetuated and reinforced. A new type of colonialism was developed, in which the oppressing white nation occupied the same territory as the oppressed people themselves and lived side by side with them.[1]

Controlling the all-white Parliament, the Boer landowners and imperialist mine owners combined in a brutal alliance to extract the last ounce of cheap labour out of the African people. The first assault of the new Union of South Africa against the African was the Land Act of 1913. This law prohibited the African from owning land outside the 'reserves', which constituted approximately 13 per cent of the country. The whites seized the remaining 87 per cent of the land, which was naturally the best and most fertile. The reserves, being insufficient and agriculturally poor, were incapable of supporting the population; thus the menfolk were driven by hunger to work for the white-owned enterprises.

The state developed the contract system of migrant labour, which separated the wage earner from his family, so that the bosses would not have to pay for the upkeep of the worker's dependents. The reserves became nothing less than reservoirs of cheap labour and the burial ground of those Africans who worked themselves to death under the semi-slave conditions which prevail in mines and on farms.

The cooperative basis of the old tribal societies was broken down, and the entire African people transformed into a community of impoverished peasants and underpaid forced labourers.

Today, the stratum of 'white South Africa' is characterized by all features of the advanced capitalist state in its final stage of imperialism: highly developed industrial monopolies and mergers of industrial and finance capital; agriculture pursued on capitalist

---

1 Programme of the South African Communist Party, 1962.

lines, employing wage labour and producing for local markets and export. South African monopoly capital is likewise closely linked with British, United States and other foreign imperialist interests in South Africa, and they jointly share in the exploitation of the non-white peoples and uphold the racist apartheid policy.

Foreign investment clearly plays an important role in the economy of South Africa. In 1968, the total of foreign assets in the country was estimated at $6.416 million. The principal creditor countries were the United Kingdom, whose holdings were the largest, accounting for more than half of the total, and the United States. The two countries combined represented about 70 per cent of the total value of foreign investments in South Africa at the end of 1968. There were much smaller, nonetheless significant, investments on the part of international organizations, France, the Federal Republic of Germany, Switzerland and several other countries. Among the major industries, foreign investments concentrated primarily in mining and manufacturing, though they were also of importance in South African finance and trade.[2]

The alliance between local capital and foreign imperialists naturally has developed internal conflicts. These are represented in the main white political parties and groupings, but they find common ground in the continued colonial-type subjugation of the non-white peoples.

* * *

South African monopoly capitalists also export capital, especially in Africa, and their expansionist character is plainly reflected in the inroads made by the regime into South West Africa, the open

---

[2] *Foreign Investment in the Republic of South Africa*, Department of Political and Security Council Affairs, Unit on Apartheid, United Nations, New York, 1970.

threats to African states to the north, and the political and economic interests in former British 'protectorates' and Rhodesia, Malawi, etc. The recent news that South Africa is now also capable of developing the atom bomb is the latest manifestation of the racist republic's imperialist ambitions.

The white workers, on the whole, form the 'aristocracy of labour'. The ruling class has granted numerous concessions to them. They have the monopoly of the best-paid work and are invariably given positions of authority over non-whites. They go regularly to the polls and vote for apartheid or racism in one form or another. The high standard of living and remuneration enjoyed by the whites come from their share in the super profits accumulated by the capitalist class from the exploitation of the non-whites.

The progression of white economic privilege is shown in the widening gap between recent black and white wages. For example:

> [I]n 1945–46 the ratio of white and African wages in private industry was 100:26. By 1957 it was 100:18. Statistics for 1970, which include mining and construction in addition to private industry, show a ratio of 100:12. Figures reveal that a white miner earns 19 times as much as a black miner; a white worker in industry gets five times as much as the black worker; and a white worker in the construction industry over six times as much.[3]

Together with economic privilege and political superiority, the white population is systematically indoctrinated with the creed of white supremacy and regards itself as part of the ruling class; thus it willingly acts as a tool and accomplice in the maintenance of colonialism and capitalism.

The lower strata of 'black South Africa' exhibit all the characteristics of a colony. The indigenous population is subjected to extreme forms of national oppression, exploitation and poverty,

---

3 'African Workers and the National Struggle', *The African Communist* 44 (1971).

lack of democratic rights and the domination by a group advocating its 'European' or 'Western Christian' character and 'civilization'. Characteristic, too, of imperialist rule is the reliance upon brute force and terror, the army and police, and the encouragement of the most backward of tribal elements and institutions.

The African people today constitute 69.7 per cent of the population. The 1970 Census figures disclosed by the Ministry of Statistics give the following population figures: whites, 3,799,000; Africans, 14,893,000; Coloureds (mixed descent), 1,996,000; Asians, 614,000. Total: 21,282,000.

The African inhabitants, living and working in all parts of the Republic, form the basic population and are the main victims of the colonial system. The former divisions of the Africans on tribal lines have steadily broken down. The tribal system was suitable for the simple, self-sufficient economy of the past, but there is no place for it in a modern economy based on large-scale industry, mining and farming. The present government, pursuing the policy of 'divide and rule', is attempting to revive tribalism, but these attempts cannot succeed. The African people are moving inevitably towards the formation of a single modern nation.

Under its so-called Bantustan policy, the Government proposes to partition South Africa. Nearly one-third of the African people live on the reserves. The largest of these are the Transkei and Ciskei in the Cape Province, and there are also others scattered widely in the other three provinces. All these the Government hopes to make the 'homelands' of the African population. But these are unable to sustain the additional population—those Africans in the remaining 87 per cent of the country, whom the authorities consider 'aliens' or 'temporary sojourners' in the 'white' areas. The reserves are grossly overcrowded already and far too small to maintain the present population.

Most of the Africans in the reserves are not independent peasants or do not have sufficient land by which to make a living. To support their families, most of the men in the prime of life are away working for the whites. 'More than 40 per cent of the economically active men in the reserves are absent at any given time, working in the mines, factories, farms and homes in the white areas.'[4] 'About 46.5 per cent of the Africans live in the "homelands", the remainder live in the so-called white areas.'[5]

Likewise, soil exhaustion and lack of opportunity for crop rotation and intensive scientific farming is a feature of all the reserves, which are the most backward and undeveloped areas, typical of colonial Africa. In spite of its boasts, 'the number of jobs created in the past ten years for Africans in industry in the "homelands" is about 2,000.'[6]

* * *

The South African government presents the 'Bantu Homelands' scheme as a concession to the growing freedom struggle among the African people and to world opinion, but it has been rejected with contempt by freedom-loving Africans and even by those who had approved of the racist-colonialist plans. In any case, the regime has no intention of conferring any genuine independence on any sector of the non-white people.

The special character of colonialism in South Africa and the appropriation by the white minority of all those opportunities, which in other colonial countries have given rise to the growth of a national capitalist class, have strangled the development of a class of African capitalists. All positions of economic power and influence are held by members of the white group alone. There are very few Africans who make profits from the exploitation of labour power, since most of them are wage earners in agriculture and

---

4 P. Smit, head of the department of Geography at the Africa Institute, reported in the *Star*, Johannesburg, 12 July 1969.

5 House of Assembly Debates (Hansard), 25 September 1970.

6 J. A. Grobbelaan, general secretary of the Trade Union Council of South Africa, quoted in the *Star*, 16 February 1970.

industry. A few independent farmers own holdings, usually so small that they can only be cultivated by the farmer himself and his family. There are a few African traders and shopkeepers who have to contend with numerous colour restrictions; and their capital is so small that their businesses are rarely profitable. The professional groups, mainly teachers, do not as a rule receive better salaries, nor do they live better, than their fellow Africans.

The coloured people live mainly in the Western Cape Province and comprise workers, farm labourers, professional people and small businessmen. The Asian community, mainly people of Indian origin, are descendants of indentured labourers brought in the last century to work in the sugar plantations. The majority of them are industrial and agricultural workers, and they have also developed a considerable merchant class. Both these non-white minority groups are subject to the various racist laws and restrictions.

The Revolutionary Force

The African workers in the towns comprise the most dynamic and most revolutionary force in South Africa. The wages of urban Africans, in relation to the very high living costs, are scandalously low. In shops and factories, they are relegated to the heaviest and least rewarding forms of labour. Pass laws and urban-areas regulations make the terms of their work and residence precarious, and they are subjected to never-ending raids and persecutions by the police. African trade unions are not given recognition, and it is illegal for an African to go on strike. But despite this, this class, the most numerous and experienced working class on the African continent, has time and again shown that it is in the forefront of the struggle of the African people. It has experience in organization, it is devoted to the cause of African liberation and to workers' unity on the continent and throughout the world.

The system of colonialism and racial oppression in South Africa will be overthrown by the unified struggle of national liberation and working-class movements that have grown in experience and matured and become steeled in many years of difficult struggle.

The crisis in South Africa springs from the fundamental contradictions of South African society between the oppressed people and their rulers; between South African colonialism and the worldwide movement against imperialism and colonialism; between the working class and the rural masses, together with the middle classes, on the one side, and the handful of monopoly capitalists on the other.[7]

This deep-seated crisis will only be resolved by a revolutionary change which will overcome these contradictions by putting an end to the colonial oppression of the African and other non-white peoples; a national democratic revolution to overthrow the colonialist state of the white minority and establish a genuine people's democratic state in South Africa.

In a report on 'Strategy and Tactics of the South African Revolution', the African National Congress (ANC), the main force for national liberation in South Africa, states:

> The main content of the present stage of the South African revolution is the national liberation of the largest and most oppressed group—the African people. This strategic aim must govern every aspect of the conduct of our struggle. [. . .] It demands in the first place the maximum mobilization of the African people as a dispossessed and racially oppressed nation.

Similarly, the programme of the Communist Party says:

> The main content of this revolution is the national liberation of the African people. Its fulfilment is, at the same time, in the deepest interests of the other non-white groups, for in achieving their liberty the African people will at the same time put an end to all forms of racial

---

7 Programme of the South African Communist Party, 1962.

discrimination. It is in the interest of the white workers, middle-class and professional groups, to whom the establishment of genuine democracy and the elimination of fascism and monopoly rule offer the prospect of a decent and stable future.

The African National Congress in the report quoted states further:

> It is a national struggle which is taking place in a different context from those which characterized the early struggles against colonialism. It is happening in a new kind of world—a world which is no longer monopolized by the imperialist world system; a world in which the existence of a powerful socialist system and a significant sector of newly liberated areas has altered the balance of forces; a world in which the horizons liberated from foreign oppression extend beyond mere formal political control and encompass the element which makes such control meaningful—economic emancipation. It is also happening in a new kind of South Africa [. . .] in which the independent expressions of the working people—their political organization and trade unions—are very much part of the liberation front. Thus our nationalism must not be confused with chauvinism and narrow nationalism of a previous epoch. It must not be confused with the classical drive by an elitist group among the oppressor in the exploitation of the masses.

The primary aims of the South African democratic revolution are defined in the Freedom Charter, which is the joint programme of the national liberation organizations of the various non-white peoples. The Freedom Charter is not a programme for socialism.

It is a common programme for a free, democratic South Africa, agreed upon initially by the mass Congress of the People in 1955, attended by thousands of the people's representatives, socialist and non-socialist alike. However, in order to guarantee the abolition of racial oppression and white-minority domination, the Charter calls for distinct economic changes: drastic agrarian reform to restore the land to the people; widespread nationalization of key industries to break the grip of monopoly capital; radical improvements in the conditions and standards of living for the working people.

Armed Struggle

Neither the national liberation movement nor the Communist Party has ever adopted the theory of violent struggle or guerrilla warfare as the only possible road to freedom in South Africa or any other country, irrespective of conditions and circumstances. As is well known, the movement, for many years and particularly during the 1950s, sustained prolonged campaigns of mass political and trade-union activities, embracing hundreds of thousands of people, making the widest possible use of militant but non-violent struggle.

The policies and campaigns in that period were fully justified and correct. It has always been the view of the movement that a revolutionary policy should be that which holds out the quickest and most fundamental transfer of power from one class to another. But in real life such radical changes are brought about not by imaginary forces but by those whose outlook and readiness to act is very much influenced by historically determined factors. To ignore the true situation and to entertain imaginary forces, concepts and ideals is to invite failure. The art of leadership consists in providing leadership to the masses and not only to its advanced elements.

The militant actions and resultant persecutions also purged the South African movement of opportunists, waverers and careerists and gave it its revolutionary character. These struggles convinced the masses of the people and all their honest leaders and spokesmen that there is no other road towards the achievement of their aspirations than that of revolution. Furthermore, the victory of the anti-imperialist forces in the Second World War, and the tide of independence in Africa, Asia and Latin America, combined with the struggles within South Africa in the past 50 years, created in the beginning of the 1960s the possibility and feasibility of the turn in the direction of armed struggle in South Africa.

The establishment of the Spear of the Nation, the military wing of the ANC, in 1961 was recognition that from then on the liberation movement would have to achieve its goals not only by traditional political methods but also by means of armed struggle, by answering fascist violence with revolutionary violence.

'The moulding of mass political consciousness reached a new intensity,' states the ANC report quoted above. 'The response of the authorities was such that the overwhelming majority of the people, through their own participation in the struggle and confrontation with the state, recognized that in the long run the privileges of the minority will only be wrenched away from it by armed combat.'

* * *

In a new year's message in 1968, Oliver Tambo, acting president general of the ANC, declared on behalf of the South African liberation movement: 'For centuries the white oppressors of our country have lived by the sword. Now they shall perish by the sword. For decades, white supremacy has been maintained by the gun. Now freedom shall be achieved by means of the gun.'

Since the launching of the armed struggle in South Africa, the guerrilla detachments of the freedom movement have clashed with the racist troops of Vorster and those of Ian Smith in Rhodesia. The Battle of Wankie in the Zambesi Valley in 1967, between combined ANC and Zimbabwe African Peoples' Union (ZAPU) forces and the white troops was a beginning of hard and serious battles still to come. Reports from South Africa indicate that guerrillas and armed political cadres are now infiltrating into the Republic, after training abroad.

In an illegal broadcast made by means of tape recordings placed at vantage points in several South African cities, the ANC called on the oppressed people to prepare for armed struggle:

> The ANC calls on all the oppressed to organize and struggle and fight in the town and countryside.
>
> We fight a guerrilla war. A guerrilla war is not a war of big armies. We have no big army. We organize ourselves into small groupings. We attack the enemy suddenly, when he is not expecting us. We kill him and we take his guns and disappear.

The countries of southern Africa have yet to break the chains of colonialism and racism which hold them in oppression. In the Portuguese colonies, South West Africa (Namibia), Rhodesia (Zimbabwe) and the Republic of South Africa, white racists and fascist regimes maintain systems which go against the current of the African revolution and world development. But the war of national liberation is on and it will develop and be fought to the finish.

Victory or Death!

CHAPTER FIFTEEN

Apartheid Coloured Council Flounders
(January 1975)

Published in Sechaba, this article points to La Guma's ongoing commitment to the conditions of Coloured South Africans under apartheid, despite the increasing internationalism of his writing during the 1970s. This piece, in particular, addresses the Coloured Representative Council and the ways in which the apartheid government manipulated the Coloured community through false promises of political participation and a divide-and-rule strategy that only multiracial solidarity could work against.

The apartheid government's policy of separate representation for Coloured people in South Africa floundered on the rocks of its own making last July when the so-called Minister of Coloured Relations prorogued the Coloured Representative Council.

At the session held in Cope Town, a resolution introduced by the opposition Labour Party, expressing no confidence in the policy of separate development and 'all its Institutions including the Coloured Representative Council' was carried. The vote was 29 to 25 after Mr Tom Swartz, leader of the Federal Party and chairman of the Council, left the chamber without voting and two of his members did not vote either. This represented the first defeat for the Government-supporting Federal Party.

The fraudulent Coloured Representative Council has always been regarded by radical groups in the community as a crude hoax perpetuated by the Nationalist government to fit the Coloured people into its apartheid schemes. Indeed, a section of the people proposed a boycott of the first election, while only 48 per cent of those eligible actually registered as voters. The election took place in September 1969. Others, like the Coloured People's Congress, pressed that any participation in the elections should become a demonstration against the apartheid policy of the racist government. This was manifested when the anti-apartheid Labour Party emerged as the biggest party with 45.3 per cent of the votes cast and 26 of the 40 elected seats.

The CRC, foisted upon the Coloured people as a substitute for direct representation in the central Parliament after Coloured voters had been removed from the common electoral roll, consists of 60 members—40 elected and 20 nominated by the Government. To secure control of the Council the Labour Party had to win 31 of the total 60 seats. In order to make sure that their stooges retained that control, the Government appointed members of the defeated Federal Party to fill the 20 nominated seats. This gave the Federal Party which had only won 11 seats, the necessary 31 to make the majority, likewise appointing Swartz, who had actually been defeated in the election, to the chairmanship of the Council. Following the adoption of his no-confidence motion in July, Mr Sonny Leon, leader of the Labour Party, called on Swartz to resign. Swartz refused and introduced a motion calling for the Council to adjourn until it could be prorogued, but he had lost his power to get his motion passed. At this stage the minister, Dr S. W. van der Merwe stepped in on the advice of Swartz and announced that he had decided to use his powers to prorogue the Council forthwith.

The State President, Fouche, announced that a second election for the CRC would be held after the completion of the second general registration of Coloured voters.

In spite of the racist government's hopes for the opposite, the CRC has regularly exposed itself as the fraud the progressive and democratic movement had warned it would be. A talking shop wherein those who hoped to operate 'within the framework of apartheid' could achieve nothing concrete, its sterile debates at least revealed to the Coloured community in general that the apartheid central government had no intention of recognizing any of the Council's suggestions, requests or demands. Now it is hoped that leaders participating in the CRC (at any rate, the anti-apartheid leaders) will discard the illusions fostered by the CRC and turn their attention more towards organizing mass activity of their members and the public in general.

Reformist Hopes

When the Labour Party was first formed, its founders believed that the ambitions of the Coloured community might be achieved by working within the institutions provided by the Nationalist government in pursuance of their programme of 'separate development' or apartheid. In spite of this erroneous and reformist outlook, the Labour Party has in fact engaged in numerous public campaigns like bread boycotts, boycotts of stores refusing to employ Coloured labour, protests against the shooting and arrest of demonstrators in the Port Elizabeth area, etc. As the black opposition to apartheid became more and more widespread and militant, coinciding with the emergence of 'Black Consciousness' over the latter years, Labour Party members began to think more and more of black unity and open alliance with the rest of the black oppressed. Branches began to think in terms of scrapping participation in the sterile CRC. The leadership itself voiced their own frustration again and again, and repeatedly denounced the CRC. 'None of the important motions passed by the Council including a call for the abolition of the Immorality Act and job-reservation laws have ever been taken seriously by the Government,' Mr Leon reiterated (*Rand Daily Mail*, 21 August 1974).

Unfortunately, the concentration on the pursuance of their 'parliamentary' life, rather than attention to popular activity and unity, has also led the professed anti-apartheid leadership of the

Labour Party into the trap of Coloured exclusiveness. While on occasion unfolding the banner of black unity, the leaders of the Labour Party demonstrated its confusion by adopting a sort of Coloured 'apartheid' policy.

Talking at times of 'all races' the Labour Party often drops this for a 'Coloured only' stance. Returning from a 'fruitless' interview with Prime Minister Vorster in August, Mr Leon, leader of the Labour Party again said, 'The mushrooming crisis can only be averted by real concessions to the political and economic aspirations of the Coloureds' (*Rand Daily Mail*, 21 August 1974).

Indeed, the motion passed by the CRC the previous July had been, according to reports, the call that the Council be abolished, and direct representation be given to 'all the people' in Parliament and 'all councils of the nation'. When challenged about 'all the people' by van der Merwe, it later turned out that Mr Leon was talking about all the Coloured people, for he said later, 'he would use the coming CRC elections to get a mandate from his people for full parliamentary representation' (*Rand Daily Mail*, 20 August 1974). He repeated, 'What we are seeking is representation in parliament and total equality with whites' (*Rand Daily Mail*, 1 September 1974).

Far from demanding democratic rights for all black people in South Africa, Mr Leon actually warned that 'rejection of the Coloured demands for greater political freedom could lead to a consolidation of Black Power in South Africa' as if 'Black people would avoid in exchange for concessions' (*Rand Daily Mail*, 7 September 1974).

Going even further, Mr Leon manifests an illusory faith in collaboration with the oppressor by requesting that Dr Connie Mulder, Nationalist Party leader in the Transvaal and a Dr Andries Treurnicht, MP for Waterberg, should attend the meeting which the Coloured Labour Party leaders were to have with Vorster. 'These are two men who will dictate the future of the Coloured people. It is only right that they should attend the meeting and spell out our future.'

In the usual cynical fashion of the racists, Vorster replied later in the House of Assembly that 'he was opening the door for Coloureds and Indians to serve on statutory bodies like the Road Safety Council and the Consumer Council.'

The Federal Party, the other major Coloured party has, as stated, acted as the Government's lackeys in the CRC, but even this party, hard-pressed by the events of the day, in its annual congress recently adopted a new manifesto which declares that the party accepts 'nothing less than direct representation in parliament'. But Mr Swartz admitted gloomily, 'The government did not have a good record for doing what the Coloureds wanted' (*Sunday Express*, 1 September 1974). He said elsewhere that they would continue their 'dialogue' with the Government and continue to use the CRC for this purpose.

Another Chance

So, while it appears that the Nationalist government was hoisted on its own petard in the CRC last July, the parties involved have, however, declared their intentions to continue participation in the next session due in November. To unconditionally concentrate on the CRC, must give people the impression that these party leaders are more interested in playing at 'prime ministers' and 'parliamentarians' in their own Bantustan, than in the struggle to overthrow apartheid. The next elections for the CRC will take place in March 1975. The small Social Democratic Party of Mr Eddie Rooks, holding one seat, may call for a boycott on the grounds that the CRC is 'toothless', but the Labour Party wants the election to be a 'referendum' of support for their policy. 'Support for the Labour Party means support for Coloured representation in the Central Parliament,' Mr Leon said (*Rand Daily Mail*, 26 September 1974).

There is no indication that the anti-apartheid section of these parties are in any way going to explore ways and means of making the CRC completely unworkable. It looks as if they are going to adopt the old formula and allow it another chance, for what genuine purpose it is impossible to say. The CRC has been proved a fraud and a diversion, a realization that must strike any honest and courageous leader really interested in advancing the cause of the people to complete emancipation from apartheid humiliation. On the level of public activity, it appears as if the Coloured community will continue to be badgered with the confused policies of the CRC parties and their misguided emphasis on Coloured exclusiveness, while now and then paying lip service to black unity.

Mass Action

The Coloured People's Congress, once the most militant section of political organizations among this people, has been seriously immobilized by banning, imprisonments, intimidation and exile of its members. On the other hand, there has been an underground bulletin in circulation, distributed illegally among Coloured people, called *STRUGGLE* which stated (Issue No. 4, 1974):

> Certainly we have not denied that when the situation demands, the old forms of legalistic activity are useful. But we have never advocated placing all our eggs in one basket. This year of mass action of the oppressed people will have shown our people that it is the might of unified offensive that has shaken the apartheid state to its foundations and not speeches of the 'representatives' in the CRC.

More recently, the bulletin (Issue No. 5) said, referring to the latest postures of the CRC parties:

> We are not interested in having a Coloured Minister of Coloured Affairs and 'direct representation for Coloureds in all councils of the Nation'. Such ideas cannot but perpetuate an exclusiveness of the Coloured people. While the

aspirations of the Coloured people as a community must be recognized, it must also be recognized that they will never achieve these aspirations as long as the African majority in South Africa remains oppressed. The liberation of the African people means the end of apartheid and so too the end of discrimination and humiliation of the Coloured community.

The widespread mass action by black workers, African, Coloured and Indian, have shown the people of South Africa once again that it is the unified power of the oppressed that makes the oppressor tremble. The action of black people who defied the fascist authorities in order to demonstrate in support of the successes of FRELIMO in Mozambique, demonstrates the mounting awareness of the people that in the final analysis it is the overthrow of the oppressor that brings the victory. The participants in the Coloured Representative Council, too, must learn this if they are not to be isolated from the dynamic advance of the people. Or perhaps their isolation might indeed become necessary if they are to be prevented from misleading people further into the meshes of the apartheid machinery which, according to Vorster, 'is still working well'.

CHAPTER SIXTEEN

Africa and the USSR
A Friendly Handshake
(1977)

This article appeared in Moscow News. *Elements of it later surfaced in the travelogue* A Soviet Journey *(1978), which was based on a trip La Guma took in 1975 upon the invitation of the Soviet Writers' Union. Not only does this article capture La Guma's personal experiences in the USSR but it also provides a glimpse of his views on the Soviet Union's role as a supporter and paradigm for African liberation.*

On the road between Dushanbe and Nurek, I stopped to talk to some building workers who were on their way home for the weekend. When they heard I was from Africa they all said they knew of the struggles of the African people from newspapers and TV, and wished us all well and a speedy victory. Their good wishes were only a few of the many received as I travelled about the Soviet Union.

Apart from the representative speeches of Soviet leaders, it was heartening to hear these expressions of solidarity uttered by ordinary working people of the USSR.

The friendly and profound demonstrations of friendship between our peoples are not new. We remember those Senegalese troops of the French forces who preferred to mutiny rather than attack the newly born workers' state during the days of imperialist intervention soon after the Great October Revolution of 1917. Likewise, returning from a visit to the USSR, ten years later, the

South African leader, Gumede, announced enthusiastically albeit theatrically: 'I have seen the new Jerusalem!'

What the workers on the Nurek-Dushanbe road did also add was, 'We hope your problems can be solved peacefully. The Soviet people experienced so much bloodshed during the last war that all we want now is peace for everybody.'

All sane people want problems solved by peaceful methods. The USSR has made the issue of peace a central pillar of its foreign policy, expressing the wishes of those workers on the Nurek road and undoubtedly all Soviet people. From the prairies of Kazakhstan to the oil fields of Siberia, I always met ordinary people who spoke of their great desire to live in peace.

Unfortunately, there are still forces in the world who mouth similar sentiments but rule by terror and armed aggression. Some of them are holding sway in the southern part of the African continent, and the only way the people of southern Africa anyway can bring about peace down there is to destroy them.

Real Friends and Enemies of Africa

Deliberately trying to nullify the Peace Programme of the USSR and the socialist states, the imperialists claim that support for the liberation movements is a negation of peaceful coexistence and détente, and continue to rant fearfully about the 'communist menace' in Africa. The propaganda campaign launched by their press around this 'threat' has recently reached unprecedented proportions. The successes of the liberation movements of Zimbabwe, Namibia and South Africa have all been put down to the mysterious 'hand of Moscow'. Even the breakdown of peaceful attempts at settling Zimbabwe's problems in Geneva has been blamed on Moscow.

We all know that it is not Moscow but the incalcitrance of the racist minority regimes that has left us no alternative but to step up the armed struggle so that one day we might settle down to a peaceful and free life.

In any event, numerous resolutions in the UN have called on all member states to support the just struggles of the colonial peoples for national liberation and independence. It has only been the Soviet Union, other socialist states and countries in Africa and Asia who have implemented these resolutions.

Who must we then regard as our friends?

Imperialism, intent on exploitation and plunder, does not care about the historical process and human development. The inevitability of socialism and communism is written off as a 'plot', and proletarian internationalism they try to disparage as 'violations' of détente.

But for ourselves, can we avoid to echo the sentiments of the Resolution of the CPSU Central Committee 'On the Sixtieth Anniversary of the Great October Socialist Revolution': 'The sixtieth anniversary of the October Revolution is an important milestone [. . .] in the development of the entire world liberation movement.' The Resolution said further, among other things: 'The triumph of the October Revolution is the major event of the twentieth century, which radically changed the course of development for all mankind.' The October Revolution revealed, as Lenin stated, to all countries something—and something highly significant—of their near and inevitable future.

Mr Davidson S. H. W. Nicol of Sierra Leone, chairman of the Special UN Committee of 24 on Decolonization, said at the time of the Lenin centenary: 'Lenin's philosophy, teaching and thought bear a significant relationship to the work of our Committee. He believed in the principles of the right of all peoples to control their own destiny, the full equality of nations and the right of nations to self-determination. Lenin's ideas have influenced the thoughts and practice of men of all nations.'

Perhaps one of the most important developments of the Great October Revolution for the colonial countries was the feasibility of liberated colonies advancing towards socialism without going through the stage of capitalism. As countries of Africa became liberated, many statesmen and leaders gave serious consideration to the building of socialism. Socialism was seen in a different light from leader to leader, country to country, but unavoidably the seed had been sown.

Which Way to Go

Colonialism has been a horrible calamity and a disaster for Africa. When, in the past years, the main imperialist powers with their capitalist bases were compelled by our struggles and the victorious advance of socialism and national liberation on a world scale, to release their formal political control over their African 'possessions' they left behind them a continent virtually in ruins—a continent with the lowest standard of living, of literacy, of health, of longevity, of economic development and social services.

Must we ape the capitalists with their anarchic economy and their predatory morality?

The experience of the Soviet Union and the other socialist countries proves beyond doubt not only that socialism does work, but that it works far better than capitalism ever did. It is the society of our future, a truly just and humane way of life, offering a far richer material and cultural life than ever before, a life of peace, freedom and dignity.

In spite of economic backwardness and other difficulties several African states have opted for socialism or have at least a socialist orientation. As Leonid Brezhnev said in the Report to the Twenty-Fourth Congress of the CPSU: 'There are already quite a few countries in Asia and Africa which have taken the non-capitalist way of development, that is, the path of building a socialist society in the long term. [...] Deep-going social changes, which are in the interests of the masses of people, and which lead to a strengthening of national independence, are being implemented in these countries, and the number of these changes has been growing as time goes on.'

Most recently, the Portuguese colonialists were defeated and Western circles reported gloomily on the trends developing in those former colonies. 'The Rise of Socialist Man in Africa', the London *Guardian* (3 February 1977) headlined its article on the Third Congress of FRELIMO of Mozambique.

'In classic Marxist-Leninist language, radio broadcasts have proclaimed the conquest of colonialism and the advent of the new age—the development of socialist man in Africa.' And further: 'The aim now is to build a party, politicize the people and plan for industrialization on the principles of Marxism.'

So it is not by accident that the enemy is stepping up his intrigues against progressive Africa at this time; now that the victorious revolutionary forces in the old Portuguese colonies, the latest free countries in Africa, have proclaimed socialism as their goal and have become an impressive force exerting steady influence on the destinies of the whole continent.

The Basis of Cooperation

For independent Africa on the whole, the presence of the Soviet Union has proved a boon. The anti-imperialist character of the foreign policy pursued by African countries creates the basis for cooperation and joint action with a great socialist state, the USSR, and other socialist countries in the UN and its agencies, apart from [connections] on many other levels.

In the General Assembly, African countries supported the resolutions on the non-use of force in international relations and banning the use of nuclear weapons, sponsored by the USSR. African countries know well the meaning of imperialist plunder. African countries also supported the convocation of the World Disarmament Conference.

At the same time, it should be noted that the anti-imperialist character of the foreign policy of African states has also come to have a bearing on the socioeconomic orientation of states.

As the national liberation movement develops in depth, some African countries concentrate on solving key socioeconomic problems and call, consequently, for the intensification of anti-imperialist struggle in the sphere of economic relations with the West. The anti-imperialist domestic and foreign policies also acquire an anti-capitalist character. This is a natural process for a consistent anti-imperialist policy inevitably leads to the rejection of capitalism.

Not only has the whole anti-imperialist world been strengthened from both sides, but in material development the African continent has also been able to take great strides forward, as the USSR extends its economic ties with states on this continent.

For example, the Soviet Union concluded agreements on economic and technical cooperation with more than 30 countries of Africa. The long-term loans granted under these agreements were invested in over 400 projects. Among them are electric stations, iron-and-steel works, machine-building and metalworking plants, chemical factories and oil refineries, factories in food and light industries, and a number of agricultural projects. Beginning in 1975, the USSR has signed agreements on economic, technical, scientific and cultural cooperation with newly independent African states. These agreements provide for Soviet assistance in the development of power, health care and education. Only recently, agreements and treaties of friendship and cooperation were signed between the Soviet Union and the People's Republic of Angola.

The emergence of the USSR on the world market spelt the end of the capitalist West's monopoly of deliveries to the Third World. This not only meant an alternative source of technology for the use of new states but also of equitable and mutually advantageous terms. Enterprises built with Soviet technology are placed under the full ownership and control of these countries. Other socialist states follow the same principle.

The socialist countries' aid is highly effective also because it is mainly directed at creating in the newly free countries their own infrastructure of science and education. Unlike the Western countries, the socialist states are building research and experimental centres in developing countries. In Africa, for example, there are technological institutions in Tunis, Conakry, Bahir Dar equipped with up-to-date laboratories. An Oil, Gas and Chemistry Institute has been commissioned in Algeria.

If all this, as the enemies of anti-imperialist Africa and of the Soviet Union would have it, constitutes 'the hand of Moscow' then it is a very friendly hand and we of Africa reach out to take it in friendship on this sixtieth anniversary of the October Revolution, as was done on the Nurek-Dushanbe road, on the collective farms of Central Asia, the Samotlor oil fields, the factories and workshops, where ordinary Soviet people had it in their own hearts to wish Africa victory.

CHAPTER SEVENTEEN

Apartheid Is Not Just a Regional Problem
(1979)

This short essay was part of a forum in Tricontinental. *The other three contributors included Josep Dubé, Juan Carlos Carullo and F. Gutiérrez. The title of the forum was 'Apartheid Is Not Just a Regional Problem', and this piece has often been given the provisional title 'To Give You a Brief Answer', drawn from the first line of La Guma's comments. I have used the forum's original title in this instance for its evocative quality. La Guma relocated to Cuba in 1978 to serve as the ANC's representative for the Caribbean and Latin America.*

To give you a brief answer, we can say that the whole world agrees that the ideological concept of racism—of apartheid—should be denounced. The world democratic movement is opposed to racism because it is a link in the world system of oppression. Even the imperialists oppose it, at least verbally, because they know they will alienate many of the people they seek to influence if they don't. Imperialist countries such as the United States have publicly denounced racism and apartheid, and Carter has even put forth a programme of human rights for everybody. He may not really mean it, but he uses it to try to recover some of the influence the United States has lost. Brazil, too, has denounced racism; but, when we look at what it does, we see that the words are hollow. When we hear a country denouncing racism, we have to ask ourselves how far it is prepared to go; how much Brazil or the United States, for example, hopes to gain from that denunciation. In any case, the real facts are that the United States, Brazil and other countries in the imperialist orbit continue to maintain their ties with the South African regime.

We understand there is no racial discrimination in Brazil, no racial barriers; in this sense, Brazil is a democratic country—which doesn't mean it is a free country, for millions of people are exploited there. To be against racism does not necessarily mean you end oppression and exploitation.

When a country denounces racism in the United Nations but continues its economic and political relations with South Africa, the denunciation really doesn't mean anything concrete. We are not at all impressed by President Carter's statements on human rights, because they haven't basically changed human rights in the United States. We can't be impressed when he talks about human rights in one breath and, in the next, permits the big US monopolies to continue operating in South Africa, so that the exploitation goes on because of the aid provided to this system of racial oppression. The same is true of Brazil. It can't be considered a positive step if these countries oppose racism verbally but still maintain their ties with South Africa.

When we speak of the struggle against racism, we don't mean removing a couple of signs banning integration in certain recreational or other types of facilities in South Africa—the fact that whites and blacks can now go to the zoo together, for example. We're not interested in drinking Coca-Cola at a counter with whites. That kind of thing is simply a cosmetic change that doesn't alter the basic situation in our country. When we talk about destroying racism, we're talking about destroying the system that allows black people to be exploited; we're talking about the basis of this exploitation and about reaching the point where black people have a right to be masters in their own country. That is why even the best-intentioned statements don't really alter the question of racism in South Africa.

As for the ideological struggle against racism, what I have just said is, naturally, related to it. We have made it our job to explain that the struggle against apartheid cannot be limited to superficial demonstrations against this phenomenon. The African National Congress, South Africa's liberation movement, is not simply a movement against the superficial aspects of apartheid. Ideologically, our work is oriented towards explaining to our people and to the whole world that the basic struggle against apartheid involves the seizure of power by the people. This liberation movement has been built and consolidated with the help of many people. The Indian movement in South Africa, which even antedates the African National Congress, was started by Mahatma Gandhi when he was working there at the beginning of this century. Later, Gandhi returned to his country and founded the all-India movement there.

We have come to the conclusion that the base for democracy in South Africa is government by the majority. The genuine support we receive comes to us out of the conviction that removing a few discriminatory signs does not end segregation, that you have to take into account the class origins of racism. We cannot overlook the basis, the roots, of racism in our country or anywhere else in the world. This is why our programme states that the source of South Africa's wealth will shift from the hands of the minority to the hands of the majority and that this action will ensure that, once our country is freed of the horrors and the misfortunes inflicted by racism, it will remain so.

CHAPTER EIGHTEEN

Caribbean Against Apartheid
(September 1979)

A transcript from a public address given by La Guma to a session of the UN Special Committee Against Apartheid held in Kingston, Jamaica, from 22 to 25 May 1979. It was originally published in Sechaba *along with extracts of the opening address by the Jamaican Prime Minister, Michael Manley (1924–97).*

Allow me on behalf of the African National Congress, the authentic representative of the oppressed people of South Africa, to greet all members of this august gathering, and to express our most profound enthusiasm for this important conference which we consider a significant milestone in the cause of international solidarity with our people who are today engaged in a decisive stage of the struggle to overthrow the bloody forces of racism and national oppression.

Our warmest gratitude goes to the government and authorities of Jamaica and Kingston, and to the UN Special Committee on Apartheid, who have made this conference possible, to all those Caribbean countries who are participating.

The struggle of progressive people and all democratic forces to bring about the final elimination of the pernicious system of colonial domination in Africa has entered a decisive stage. From the Zambezi to the Cape of Good Hope the people are engaged in acts of indescribable heroism.

What our people are demonstrating finally, and emphatically, is that they are no longer prepared to be ruled by the racists. They have demonstrated this by openly facing the state apparatus of fascist South Africa. In the same spirit as the people of Nicaragua and Latin America face the dictatorships, in the same spirit as the people of Iran showed when they brought about their democratic revolution, so our people are demonstrating their determination to be free.

The South African regime itself shows obvious signs of being unable to contain the situation indefinitely. The bloody acts of violence and terrorism against the people, the murder of political detainees, the incarceration of hundreds of militants, young and old, are all indications of the desperation of the regime.

A revolutionary situation is rapidly developing in South Africa—to the armed assaults and bloody force which the enemy uses against the people, the people have now to respond with armed force as well as political and economic mass action. The experience of these times in South Africa teaches us that the question of power and democratic rule in our country will only be resolved by the effective combination of mass action and armed support.

Faced with the prospect of mass uprising and revolt on the part of the people, the racist regime is doing its upmost to hold out, not only by forcible repression, but by seeking allies for its ignoble system from among the oppressed people themselves. The use of Bantustan puppet troops and police to reinforce white racist forces against ANC guerrillas, as was done in the so-called Bophuthatswana homeland, is in itself proof that the whole scheme of Bantustans is one designed to deny the black majority its true and democratic right to emancipation.

Disenfranchisement and dispossession remain at this moment the main objective of the Bantustan policy. Bantustans mean that every African becomes a foreigner in the land of his birth, without political, social, economic rights, prey to the exploiter, victim of servitude of a kind which boggles the imagination. Each Bantustan has become the dumping ground for thousands of unemployed, so-called surplus elements, and by forced removals are turned into a vast reserve of virtual slaves without option but to come when the master calls.

In order to disguise these nefarious objectives of the Bantustan policy, the racists speak of an independence which is spurious, a version of cultural advance which is a distortion, and a national pride which means nothing but a return to tribalism. By these means, the racists hope to divert the attention of the African people from the course of forging genuine nationhood, and so hope to destroy the national liberation movement, led by the ANC. By encouraging ethnic groupings, the regime hopes to turn African people against each other instead of against the real enemy, the racist system itself. The struggle to end apartheid, therefore, involves struggle against the whole Bantustan fraud and the black puppets who uphold this subterfuge.

This apartheid system is not upheld by the South African racists alone. We have warned the Western powers that unless they discontinue the short-sighted political, economic and military support for the Botha–Smith clique, they will gain nothing but the enmity of the free people of the future. We have warned the same powers who not only invest, but have helped, and continue to help, to bolster up the armoury of racist South Africa, ranging from the supply of conventional weapons to nuclear power. But the fanatical accumulation of wealth at the expense of the African masses seems to blind the multinational corporations to the inevitability of the end of apartheid and the rule of the fascist minority.

The initiative in South Africa has now passed into the hands of the struggling people led by the African National Congress. The support and solidarity of the international community will make our task easier and bring sooner an end to the apartheid regime which is not only a dire enemy of the South African people but which constitutes a threat to the peace of the entire African continent and the whole world. In the interests of solidarity with our struggle for a just society, for progress, peace and friendship among all peoples in and out of South Africa, we ask you to consider the following:

- That the Caribbean countries continue and intensify all efforts to complete the isolation of the racist regimes of southern Africa. All efforts should be made to extend the arms embargo to include economic sanctions and the cessation of all forms of support for the Botha–Smith regimes;
- that the campaigns for the release of political prisoners in southern Africa be intensified in the Caribbean region;
- that the demand be pressed for the treatment of captured freedom fighters as prisoners of war in terms of the Geneva Conventions;
- that Bantustan policies be isolated, and Bantustans be denied international recognition;
- that support for the liberation movements in southern Africa, the ANC, Patriotic Front and SWAPO be increased;
- that public opinion throughout the Caribbean be mobilized in support of these and similar initiatives.

The ANC pays tribute to the governments and people of the Caribbean who are with us in our just struggle. The final victory of the oppressed people of Southern Africa is in sight and the establishment of progressive and democratic peace-loving societies is assured. As the ANC programme, the Freedom Charter states: 'The people shall govern. No government can claim authority unless it is based on the will of the majority.'

CHAPTER NINETEEN

'This Is Our Vanguard, a Vanguard of Communists'
(1981)

A report of the Second Congress of the Communist Party of Cuba, held in Havana in December 1980. It was originally published in The African Communist. *The First Congress took place in 1975, and the Third in 1986, so this occasion was the first and only time La Guma was able to attend.*

On the morning of 17 December 1980, the population of Cuba was greeted by a red banner headline on the front page of *Granma*, organ of the Central Committee of the Communist Party of Cuba: '*Viva el comunismo!*' Under photographs of Marx, Engels and Lenin, the Cuban national heroes, Martí, Maceo, Gómez, Mella, Camilo and Che, it was announced that the Second Congress of the Communist Party was about to open that day.

So in the main hall of the Palace of Conventions, which was first used for the Sixth Summit of Non-Aligned Countries, 1,780 delegates assembled, elected at provincial assemblies, at Party conferences, in the armed forces and places of work. In addition, there were fraternal delegations from 142 sister Parties, revolutionary movements, national democratic and progressive organizations from all over the world—from the socialist countries, Latin America and the Caribbean, Western Europe, North America and Asia. Africa was represented by delegations from such as the MPLA Party of Labour, Ethiopia, FRELIMO, Algeria, Benin, Congo, Communist Party of Egypt, Mali, Polisario, São Tomé and Príncipe,

Senegal, Sudan, Guinea, Zimbabwe, Zambia and others. South Africa was represented by Alfred Nzo, secretary general of the ANC, and Dr Yusuf Dadoo and Moses Mabhida of the South African Communist Party.

As Fidel Castro himself said later, 'In fact there were times when it was hard to tell whether it was a Cuban congress or a congress of the world's revolutionary forces.'

At the time of the First Congress in 1975, Cuba was involved in helping Angola defend its territory from the north and south, above all, against the threat of South African racist troops on Angolan soil. Later a similar situation arose when Lt Col. Mengistu Haile Mariam requested aid to fight back the Somali invasion of the Ogaden. But it was not only in the form of military aid that Cuba's internationalism was being demonstrated. Above all, technical and scientific assistance and direct participation in constructive activities in friendly countries was the hallmark of Cuban solidarity. With the approach of the Second Congress, Cuba was collaborating in diverse ways with more than 37 countries and some 15,000 of her nationals were involved. Before, and since then, proletarian internationalism has been the banner of the Communist Party of Cuba.

It was in this spirit that the Second Congress of the Communist Party opened in Havana.

In the moving opening moments, the first Cuban cosmonaut, Colonel Arnaldo Tamayo, carried to the rostrum the national flag and the red flag of the Party which had gone with him into space. To the sound of the national anthem, amid stormy applause and jubilation, the Congress was opened. Making the formal announcement, Raúl Castro, second secretary of the Party, said: 'On the day that marks the 150th anniversary of the death of Simón Bolívar, Liberator of America, we now begin the Second Congress.'

Sacred Duty

The main report to the Congress was made by Comrade Fidel Castro. In the words of Marcelino dos Santos of Mozambique, the report was 'a vivid, impressive X-ray picture of Cuba, showing where we came from, who we are and where we're headed. It is an analysis of the role of the revolutionary party, of the role and place of a Communist Party in the country and for a people making a revolution, conducting the state and society.'

Introducing his report, Fidel said, 'The strength of a small country such as Cuba is neither military nor economic, but moral.' The last country to free itself from the Spanish, the first country to free itself from Yankee imperialist domination, and the first country in the Latin American continent to take the road to socialism, 'everything in our way of life is new, and it has not been easy. We had to confront the most powerful imperialist country in the world just 90 miles from our coast, and fight against reactionary ideas that have existed for hundreds and even thousands of years and the bitter hatred of the exploiting classes. We had to stand up against isolation, hostility, threats, libel and an implacable campaign launched by the monopolies that control a large part of the world's mass media.'

To continue advancing, Cuba had to defy attacks and even run the risk of being exterminated. 'Yet, here we stand, twenty-two years after 1 January 1959. We have not retreated or made any concessions to imperialism. We have not renounced a single one of our ideas or revolutionary principles.'

Not everything they did had been wise, Castro said. Not all their decisions had been correct. In no revolutionary process have all actions and decisions been the right ones. But the stock of experience and revolutionary ideas, which were inherited from Cuba's own history and that of mankind, was Cuba's most precious treasure. Through practice and example, this stock could be added to. This was a sacred duty of all revolutionaries, which demands the most rigorous criticism and self-criticism, and the most complete honesty.

Speaking, and referring, to all Communists everywhere, Fidel Castro said:

> Ever since the time of the Paris Commune, real Communists have been noted for their heroism. In all history, no one has excelled them in their capacity for self-sacrifice, spirit of solidarity, dedication, self-denial and readiness to give their lives for their cause. No other political idea in the course of development of human society has been taken up so strongly or elicited such selfless devotion as communism. The best and purest feelings of human beings have been expressed throughout the battles to do away with the age-old exploitation of man by man.
>
> Only the first Christians in the time of imperial and pagan Rome are comparable to Communists. Marx, Engels and Lenin were not bearers of mystical ideas, however, and their self-sacrificing followers did not seek their reward in another world. It is here on earth that man's future should be changed, and they were ready to face the cruellest repression and unhesitatingly give their lives to do this—that is, give everything in exchange for nothing themselves, but everything for others. [. . .]
>
> We cannot deny that anyone who struggles to obtain his homeland's independence from colonial or neocolonial power or for freedom from tyranny is a revolutionary, but there is only one higher way of being a revolutionary in today's world: that of being a Communist, because Communism embodies the idea of independence, freedom, true justice, equality among men, and, what is more, internationalism—that is, brotherhood, solidarity, cooperation among all peoples and nations of the world. When the ideas of independence, freedom, equality, justice and

fraternity among peoples and nations are combined, they are invincible.

This is what we want to be: Communists. This is what we want to keep on being: Communists. This is our vanguard, a vanguard of Communists. This is our Congress: a Congress of Communists, backed by the people, a people of Communists. There has never existed, nor can there exist, any force in the world that can prevent this.

Main Report

Fidel Castro, first secretary of the Party, proceeded to outline the record for the 1975–80 period, the goals and general guidelines for Cuba's future national and international policies.

It was pointed out that the 6 per cent annual growth rate proposed had not been achieved, but two-thirds of that goal had been realized. The admirable, heroic efforts that the working people and members of the Party had made, and their tremendous achievements in the hard and difficult years of the five mentioned, should not go unrecognized. Many capitalist countries—even developed ones with larger resources than those of Cuba—had been forced to retrench, cutting back production in some years, while their indices of inflation, unemployment and socioeconomic crises rocketed. 'Our socialist country, with an underdeveloped economy, advanced in the sphere of material production and registered important social progress during this five-year period.'

After surveying in detail developments in all branches of the economy and Cuban society in general, Fidel's report added:

> We are pleased to be able to state that, at the highest levels of the Party, the principles of collective leadership have been solidly applied. Both the Political Bureau and the Secretariat of our Party have met hundreds of times in the past few years, and the Central Committee has held its plenary sessions as scheduled. The most disparate international topics

of a state and party nature have been analysed collectively. No important questions were decided in any other way. The rigour with which this essential principle of Marxism–Leninism was applied in our leadership is truly exemplary and a source of pride. No manifestations of factionalism or exclusive groups appeared in our leadership, and the principles of Party democracy, democratic centralism and the most rigorous discipline govern all Party activities.

Speaking critically of signs of flagging in the social awareness and the spirit of austerity and modesty, which had been a characteristic of the revolutionary Cuban people, Fidel said that the worst enemy could not have done more damage. Was the Revolution beginning to degenerate on the imperialist enemy's doorstep, as a softening-up process became evident, in which some elements tended to let things slide? Perhaps it had been thought that with the institutionalization of the country, socialist legality, the creation of People's Power and the progressive implementation of economic programmes would in themselves perform miracles and that things were supposed to have got better automatically over the past Five-Year period, without the basic efforts of man.

These questions were discussed openly, measures were taken and the pernicious tendencies began to be surmounted. This, at the same time, involved consistent ideological struggle.

'Our people's unanimous support for the struggle to achieve higher standards and against all signs of softness and accommodation shows how thoroughly our masses have absorbed the moral principles of the Revolution and demonstrates that, far from degenerating, our revolutionary process is growing stronger all the time,' Castro asserted.

> Our people's communist and internationalist consciousness has undoubtedly been increased in recent years. [...] Throughout the country, attitudes towards work, organization, higher standards, combativity and revolutionary

firmness are all at a much higher level. This is especially evident in our working class and has been brilliantly manifested by our intellectual workers as well [...] and millions of our compatriots lead exemplary, genuinely proletarian, austere, collectivist, honest and disciplined lives.

This does not mean that we have always done the best possible political and ideological work or that we can cross our arms and say we have won the battle.

Special Situation

It was necessary, said Fidel, to understand the special situation in which Cuba has been waging for over 20 years its confrontation with imperialism in the realm of ideas.

The existence, just a few miles from our coast, of the richest, most aggressive capitalist country in the world, a paradise for individualism, gambling, drugs, prostitution and other alienating vices has forced us to respond courageously to this open and unending challenge.

The United States has always been the sworn enemy of our nation. [...] After the triumph of the Revolution, the United States opened its doors to Cuban war criminals, torturers, embezzlers of public funds, plantation owners, real-estate magnates, big businessmen and others of that ilk. At the same time, it went to great lengths to rob us of our engineers, doctors, administrators, technicians and skilled workers.

The US took advantage of its position as the world's richest, most developed country with its much higher standard of living than Cuba, to try to bleed the country of her skilled personnel and thus try to destroy the revolutionary process, linking this policy to economic blockade, threats of aggression of all kinds.

The Revolution valiantly took up the challenge and permitted everyone who wanted to leave to do so. [. . .] Millions of individuals, the vast majority of our people preferred to live here under economic blockade and the threat of annihilation rather than abandon their homeland. It was our socialist Revolution with its unselfish, heroic struggle that forged our Cuban patriotic national spirit, once and for all. A new generation of doctors, engineers, teachers and technicians has been trained in the years since the triumph of the Revolution, taking their place alongside the many intellectual workers who remained loyal to their homeland. [. . .] Imperialism, however, has never stopped attacking our Cuban national spirit, constantly putting it to the test. [. . .]

For these reasons, a bitter ideological struggle has been waged by our imperialist enemy and the Cuban revolution—a struggle that has been, and will continue to be, fought not only in the realm of revolutionary and political ideas, but in the sphere of our people's patriotic national feelings. Imperialism refuses to resign itself to a revolutionary, socialist Cuba; a Cuba that has held out and gained prestige in its struggle against the Yankee giant; a Cuba in which patriotic feelings are deeper, more solid and more lasting than ever.

Referring to the recent flight of lumpen and anti-social elements who were allowed to leave the country, Castro said, 'This time they got our scum.'

In spite of the tremendous efforts the Revolution had made to promote socioeconomic development—especially in education—some social disgrace from the past had still remained: a total lack of national feeling on the part of some, combined with the fact that the socioeconomic conditions in a developing country still produced some declassed, anti-social, lumpen elements that were receptive to imperialist enticements and ideas.

The people's marches—an outpouring in response to acts of provocation—will go down in history. Never before have there been such huge mobilizations in our homeland. Once again (the enemy) underestimated our people's level of consciousness. The Revolution and the masses decided, once and for all, to take up the challenge. [...] While Cuba made the cleanest sweep in its history, the masses were tempered and tremendously tempered in the struggle and their spirit of patriotism and the defence of the principles of socialism and proletarian internationalism were deepened. The struggle also boosted production and discipline and helped us find solutions for our internal weakness.

It was pointed out that the people's repudiation of the scum also meant that they repudiated undisciplined behaviour, sponging, accommodation, negligence and other negative attitudes.

Ideological Training

Mass ideological training, Fidel Castro told the Congress, especially the training of children and young people in the principles of socialist patriotism and proletarian internationalism, required systematic work.

> The principles of internationalism have been set forth broadly and consistently in our work of revolutionary orientation. We have made every effort to ensure that the true image of the Cuban revolution is projected abroad, explaining both our successes and shortcomings and difficulties and our socioeconomic advances in building socialism. Our people's political understanding is impressive, and they are kept informed about the main aspects of the world situation [...]
>
> Ideology is first of all consciousness; consciousness is revolutionary militant attitude, dignity, principles and morale. Ideology is also an effective weapon in opposing

misconduct, weakness, privileges, immorality. For all revolutionaries ideological struggle is today in the forefront, is the first revolutionary trench.

Socialism is a relatively new system in mankind's history, for it has only been in existence for a few decades. Right from the start it was opposed by imperialist threats, hostility, intervention and aggression. Fascism made a brutal effort to destroy the first socialist state only 24 years after it had been founded. The socialist camp was built on the rubble and ruins which the Nazi hordes left behind them in the most devastated parts of Europe, which were also the continent's least developed areas. It hasn't been easy, and circumstances have hardly been propitious for spreading socialist ideas.

Our enemy has used every means at its disposal to continue fighting socialism. On the military front, it has forced the socialist countries to invest huge sums of money in defence. Politically, it has made every effort to subvert, destabilize and discredit the socialist countries.

This reality should not be underrated [. . .] Only by consistently applying the principles of Marxism-Leninism can we be strong, invulnerable, invincible.

Ours is a state of workers who exercise revolutionary power. The Party and its members must always be solidly, closely and deeply linked to the masses. They must engage in rigorous criticism and self-criticism. They must not deviate from collective leadership, internal democracy, democratic centralism and the strictest discipline. They must lead a life of austerity and embody the spirit of self-sacrifice, unselfishness, selflessness, honesty, solidarity and heroism that should characterize every Communist.

Every Communist should be a staunch fighter, convinced of the absolute justice of his cause; he should be studious, hardworking, demanding and deeply committed to his people. The Party exists through and for the people. Bureaucratic and petty bourgeois attitudes are completely alien to its principles. The strongest, closest ties should exist between the Party cadres and members and the people, mainly based on the example set by revolutionaries and the confidence inspired by their commitment to the people.

We still have a long way to go and many problems to solve as we build socialism, but history has already shown that our ideas are far superior to, and infinitely more humane than those of, capitalism. The clock of history never turns back. Capitalism with all its egoism, crime and vice, will disappear, just as feudalism and slavery did; and even if one country should take a step backward, mankind never will.

A Friend of the Soviet Union

Dealing with Cuba's foreign policy, Fidel stated that while reviewing Cuba's attitude towards various international developments over the past five years and her relationship with the individual countries of the world, it was not possible to refer to each and every one of the situations the country and government had faced. But one thing was clear. 'Cuba is, and will continue being, socialist. Cuba is, and will continue being, a friend of the Soviet Union and of all the socialist states. Cuba is, and will continue being, an internationalist country. Principles cannot be negotiated.'

Cuba believed that for the world it was an historical necessity that normal relations exist among countries, based upon mutual respect, on the acknowledgement of the sovereign right of everyone and of non-intervention. Cuba considered that the normalization of its relations with the United States would improve the political climate in Latin America and the Caribbean and would contribute to world détente.

Events on the international scene confirmed the position taken at the First Congress—namely, that detente was what the people wanted, that it was an essential condition for mankind's survival and that it was being constantly threatened by the most reactionary sectors of imperialism, which simply would not accept it. But there was still a possibility of saving détente, even though it was in danger in the current difficult situation. That possibility was dependent, first of all, on the Soviet Union's firm and constant policy of peace, on the support the other socialist countries gave that policy and the backing it received from all other progressive forces. One essential element that no one could ignore was that the USSR was fully prepared to throw back any kind of attack aimed at its submission. A nuclear adventure against the Soviet Union would be suicidal for those who made the attempt. Even the most aggressive imperialists were aware of this.

Reagan Election

Sometime during the early days of Carter's administration, there seemed to be a certain inclination among the leaders of the US along the path of negotiations. Carter had made some gesture towards Cuba: at the beginning of his term, he cancelled spy flights, allowed US citizens to travel to Cuba and had proposed the creation of an Interests Section. Cuba had been receptive to these gestures, but in the end the reactionary ideas of some of his advisers prevailed over the less-aggressive trends in the State Department, and the relations became tense once again.

Reagan's election had introduced an element of uncertainty —rather of danger—in US–Cuban relations. 'The intentions they have expressed are extremely reactionary and dangerous,' Fidel told the Congress. 'There is no doubt that it (the election) has been a success for the extreme right in the politics of the United States. It is the duty of the peoples to be realistic, to have no illusions, and prepare themselves to staunchly oppose the policy announced by imperialism and by the reactionary group that has just come to power."

Reagan and his advisers were trying to attain military superiority and negotiate with the socialist camp from a position of strength, but this idea was simply absurd. This would lead to an unbridled arms race in the midst of the worst international economic crisis the world has recently had to suffer.

In our opinion, Reagan will be unable to solve any of the main problems affecting the United States: inflation, unemployment, energy crisis, economic recession, vice, drugs, violence, crimes, corruption, and his ideas on foreign policy can endanger world peace. [...]

Reagan and his advisers have announced that they intend to establish an alliance with the rightist, reactionary and fascist forces in this continent. But the peoples of our America will never submit themselves to this ignominious subjugation. The workers, the peasants, the intellectuals, the students will know how to resist such a cruel fate [...]

Reagan has said that in Vietnam the mistake was not making war but losing it. In Latin America, the mistake of making war might represent a greater defeat than that of Vietnam. Who has told Mr Reagan that making war means the right to win it? [...]

If Yankee marines or intervention forces land in Central America, the people of the United States will again witness the painful scene of their soldiers' coffins arriving home. Those who go to kill Latin Americans will also have to resign themselves to die. The blame will fall on those who refuse to acknowledge the lessons of history and the irreversible changes that have taken place in our world. No one is threatening life in the United States, but no one will accept without a determined and heroic struggle the threat of the United States against our lives.

Reagan and his advisers spoke of a military blockade of Cuba, under any pretext, even if, as they asserted, the Soviet Union were to carry out an action in any other part of the world. This was a cynical and repulsive thought, said Castro.

> Cuba will be ready to defend itself against any military blockade or imperialist Yankee invasion! In this country, the struggle will not cease as long as one single patriot remains capable of fighting, and there are millions ready to do so to their last drop of blood.

Party of the People

On the last day of the Second Congress of the Communist Party of Cuba, the citizens of the Havana provinces were again met with a red banner headline: 'Everybody to the Plaza at 5 p.m.' Everybody went. A sea of people overflowed from the *Plaza de la Revolution* into the surrounding boulevards. The little national flags of the Lone Star, waved aloft, rippled like the breakers of the nearby Mexican Gulf.

The report delivered by Fidel Castro to the Congress had been unanimously adopted; the working committees had completed their work, dealing with amendments to the party statutes, resolutions on the future five-year plan, and other matters pertaining to Party work. The Central Committee had been elected, the Political Bureau and Secretariat confirmed. In this connection, Fidel told the crowd, 'The leadership of our Party was given a strong dose of worker cadres, a strong dose of women and a strong dose of internationalist fighters.'

Addressing the tremendous crowd, Fidel, who had been unanimously re-elected First Secretary of the Party, said that they had demonstrated in practice what had been said at the Congress about the Party's solid, profound and indestructible ties with the masses. 'Thus the great truth that the Party is the Party of our people, and that the Party exists through the people and for the people is hereby confirmed.'

Speaking with emotion about the presence and solidarity of foreign delegations, Fidel referred to those from Grenada, Nicaragua, El Salvador and other Latin American revolutionaries; to 'our Angolan brothers and sisters, our Afghan brothers and sisters, our African brothers and sisters', those from Vietnam, Kampuchea, Laos, from the Communist Parties of Portugal and France, and, 'We had the pleasure to hear, in the words of that hero of the cause of communism, Henry Winston (of the US Communist Party), the message from the most pure and most honest of the North American people.'

Dealing with the work of the Congress and the opinions expressed, Fidel stated:

> There are two basic conclusions we can draw from the Congress. One, the work, the efforts to boost production and services [. . .] The first thing we have to do is to tackle our difficulties head-on and devote ourselves to work, to the services. We must redouble our efforts, work more efficiently and be more demanding in agriculture, in school, in the hospitals, everywhere. In short, we must work more and better than ever before.
>
> Second, we must prepare ourselves to defend the country. In other words, these are the two basic tasks: production and defence. We must prepare the people and the Party to fight under any circumstances.
>
> One thing must not clash with the other. Work in production must go hand in hand with combat training.

The Second Congress of the Communist Party of Cuba analysed and approved some basic ideas regarding the country's future development up to the year 2000. Cubans did not allow themselves to think only in terms of one year or of five years but also in terms of 20 years, basing themselves on real factors and the elements of security provided by their close economic relations and their coordinated plans for development with the Soviet Union and the rest of the socialist countries.

Thus, as far as Cuba's economic development is concerned, she can look towards the future with more confidence and assurance than ever before.

PATRIA O MUERTE!
VENCEREMOS!

CHAPTER TWENTY

Caribbean—Nobody's Backyard
(April 1982)

This piece comprises transcribed excerpts from a talk over Radio Freedom *by La Guma, in his capacity as the ANC's chief representative for the Caribbean and Latin America.* Radio Freedom *was the ANC's radio programme and was broadcast in Tanzania, Zambia, Angola and South Africa, among many countries. This composite transcript was originally published in* Dawn, *a monthly journal of Umkhonto we Sizwe.*

What is described as the Caribbean consists of a number of small islands, each one containing a very small population—and these islands are mostly ruled by conservative governments who have allegiances to the old British imperialist connection and who carry on the neocolonialist policy which is directed by big corporations in Europe.

One must of course add at the moment that these islands are also involved in opposition to these conservative governments on the part of the groups of democratic, progressive, revolutionary people who are determined to change the situation in this part of the Caribbean. At the moment, activities take the form of electioneering campaigns, agitational work and the creating of political organizations of the people. In countries like Trinidad, Tobago and Barbados, etc., at the moment, people are preparing for elections, and it is hoped from the point of view of the democratic organizations operating there that change will come about.

In Jamaica where the pro-US imperialist Labour party ousted Mr Manley's People's National Party in the last election, this latter party is active in regrouping itself to make a comeback.

Most of these small islands, which mostly are English-speaking, have taken the example from Grenada where people led by the New Jewel Movement, which in turn is headed by Maurice Bishop, seized power from the old Gairy regime and established a democratic regime in its place and is now engaged in social transformation which is directed at raising the standard of living of the people, extending democracy and creating new conditions for the masses [...]

In terms of what is taking place in the Caribbean and Central America, the US has adopted an attitude of its own which proves to be bellicose, warlike and threatening. In terms of the US strategy, it views the Caribbean as its so-called backyard, and Maurice Bishop replied to this by saying very firmly: 'We certainly, that is, people of Grenada, are in nobody's backyard.'

The Caribbean is also strategically vital to the US and its programme and policies; in that, as we all know from looking at the map, it describes the entrance between the Atlantic Ocean and the Central American area. It is sort of a gateway to the Panama Canal and it leads from Central America to the Pacific.

Cuban Example

Politically, the Cuban example has proved to Central America and the Caribbean in particular that no small people, no small country need hesitate in the fight for liberation [...] irrespective of the presence of vast US arsenals. Cuba proved to the people to be capable of continuing the struggle. As a result of this, the US has adopted this increasingly hostile attitude and, in particular, since the Reagan administration moved in, this attitude has become more and more harsh, more and more severe.

Recently, of course, the struggle in El Salvador has in particular reached a new impetus resulting from the tyrannical and murderous regime of Napoleón Duarte. Over the years, and up to now, guerrilla actions which have been carried out on a local basis, have now developed into a war on a national scale. The FMLN Front, we learn, at the moment controls about one-fifth of the national territory, and the population has already started a programme that should give encouragement to the rest of the population still under the heel of the fascist dictatorship. They have, for example, organized land to improvise food and supplies both for the population and guerrilla fighters. Medical aid is being organized and, at the same time, illiteracy is being dealt with and political schools have been opened and military training is taking place among the population. So that it is quite clear that the people of El Salvador have established a substantial base and also ensure that they will be able to advance from this base.

Local Reaction

Of course, all this has given the local reaction and US a really uncomfortable time and has resulted in the growing awareness, on their part, of the inevitability of the victory of the popular forces led by the FMLN. In order to counter this, of course, they have tried their best to project a picture of a democratic process reigning in the country, but all the dead bodies that pile up in El Salvador do not hide the fact that the regime is corrupt and only exists because the US props it up. Anyway, in order to project the so-called democratic image, the regime and Napoleón Duarte have been talking about holding elections, which is encouraged by the US, with the hope that the popular forces, given general participation in these elections, and the endorsement of the regime will be gained. However, the revolutionary forces have pointed out that while they are not against elections, it is of course impossible to hold elections on the conditions that prevail in El Salvador today.

First of all, there is a reign of terror by the government which results in thousands of people being killed, actually butchered by the fascist forces. The country is therefore being placed in a state of civil war. More than 2 million people have had to flee the country to escape the battle, the war and terror that have been the usual feature of the society. There are no proper electoral rolls by which voters can be organized the usual way, and all these factors contribute to a situation where nobody believes that an election in a normal way can take place. Hence, I said the indications are that the revolutionary forces led by FMLF are prepared to find a political solution to the terrible situation prevailing in the country.

At the same time, this can only be carried out if a normal situation prevails. They are prepared to negotiate for a peaceful settlement of the dispute between the democratic forces and those who stand in their way [. . .] This attitude has been supported by the reasonable forces, peoples internationally, but these conditions have been refused, and Duarte and the US hope that irrespective of the fighting that is going on, this election that is about to take place soon—the so-called election—will help to give them a sort of an aura of respectability and licence to carry on as they have done before.

Of course, the US is devoting hundreds of millions of dollars to arming the fascist junta in El Salvador and giving it economic aid in order to carry on boosting the country for as long as possible, under the pretext that the government there is upholding human rights and deserves to be assisted. In the neighbouring states of Guatemala in Central America, the people also suffer under a dictatorial regime. We know that, in 1954, the democratic government was overthrown by the reactionaries with the assistance of the CIA and, as a result, all freedoms have really disappeared in this country. There is no such thing like individual freedom, freedom of speech, freedom of political activity, etc. [. . .] In addition, of course, all revolutionary organizations are banned in Guatemala, and the people live under a barbarism carried out by the military, who have no compunction to kill off whole populations of villages, if they are found to be harbouring or engaging in helping the revolutionary forces and the democratic movement.

In Guatemala, some weeks ago [. . .] many popular organizations came together to form a united front to face the regime in an organized way and to advance towards a democratic state supported by the people. It has been reported last month that the revolutionary movement and guerrilla struggle have achieved certain victories that have shaken the regime. For example, at the moment the guerrilla movement controls certain localities in the country, and last month it was reported that they conducted two house raids at army barracks and police stations, and seized four radio stations in the capital and broadcast from them over a certain period. And so it is expected that the struggle in Guatemala will take on significant proportions and that the victory of the Guatemalan people is on the cards.

US Strategy

As I have said, in this whole area, Central America is important to US strategy, as well as for the economic resources which exist there, and as a result of this the US continues an offensive against the popular movement in this area. And, in the face, however, of obvious failure, Reagan is trying to now justify outright intervention in Central America by blaming the so-called assistance which countries like Nicaragua and Cuba are giving to El Salvador, for example.

These are, of course, lies and untruths about Nicaraguan–Cuban participation in El Salvador; no, there is no direct material aid nor troops of men in the guerrilla armies of Nicaragua or Cuba. Reagan is obviously lying to justify himself since he can't produce any evidence of this so-called intervention of Cuba and Nicaragua. Whether Reagan can actually intervene, sending troops into that area, that of course is another matter. In spite of all these things, Reagan is unable to convince his own friends or anybody else in the US. The US intervention of El Salvador, everybody feels, can only result in aggravating an all-out offensive by the entire democratic forces of Central America, which could possibly lead to another Vietnam-like situation which will involve the very broad strata of the Central American and Latin American people and of course, in addition, the entire democratic forces of the world are on the side of the Salvadoran people.

However, we believe that whatever attempts Reagan tries to make to undermine the successes of attempts of democratic forces in the Caribbean and Latin America are doomed to failure. The world balance of forces has changed in favour of independence, and people are in favour of progress and peace. In addition, these countries, Cuba, Nicaragua and Grenada, are ready to defend themselves and expose the hypocritical role of Reagan and his associates who profess to uphold human rights, who are still prepared to attack small peoples. The US foreign policy is based on seeking solutions to the profound crisis of its own economy and that of world capitalism as a whole. In old times, they could engage in world wars, today that is impossible because of the presence of the Soviet Union, the Socialist countries and international peace forces. War as it has always been known is not possible. No matter what threats are made, no matter how many nuclear weapons are brandished, any action on the part of the imperialists will meet with serious rebuffs for which they will pay very heavily. Nevertheless, the US continues to try with what it calls exporting counterrevolution to those countries which are daily exposing the violence, cynicism and hypocrisy of the US administration, and who are revealing the reactionary policies of the US which continues to support reactionary and counterrevolutionary movements everywhere.

Reports reveal the US government supports the fascist juntas of Central America, El Salvador, etc., in Guatemala and Paraguay and other places. Support for the military junta governments is inevitably reflected in other parts of the world as in Africa; the support for UNITA, for instance, in Angola, in order to strengthen counterrevolutionary movements to try and replace the revolutionary government by counterrevolutionaries led by Mr Savimbi. In addition, of course, it is also reflected by the Reagan administration's outright support for apartheid and the racists of South Africa, which Reagan has openly described as a faithful ally of the US. [...]

The US still hopes to act as a gendarme—a policeman who controls all countries of the world who try to move out of the grip of the reactionary role and out of the grip of imperialism. But this, in terms of the part of the reactionary on the pay of imperialism, only brings the democratic forces together in a solid united front, in the face of worldwide attempts by imperialist forces. For this reason, we see a growing solidarity between the people of the Caribbean and the people of South Africa, even though the Atlantic separates us geographically—on the level of our struggle we are together.

Seventieth Anniversary

Recently, with the commencement of the ANC's Seventieth Anniversary year, the Cuban mission of the ANC received many messages from organizations and movements in that area, e.g. Antigua, Tobago, Guyana, Barbados, Jamaica. In addition, from Latin America, from the Chilean anti-fascism movement, from Uruguay, from the Sandinista Front of Nicaragua, from the Socialist Party of Puerto Rico, etc.—all these view our struggle as part of the worldwide struggle against imperialism and against national oppression and independence, freedom and peace. And, for these reasons, they pledged their solidarity with the people of South Africa struggling against the fascist apartheid regime. This underlines our call for unity in action, and we are sure that thousands, millions of reliable allies of the ANC and the oppressed of South Africa, people in the Caribbean area and in Latin America, I believe also that the solidarity which we are experiencing can do a lot for the mobilization of sanctions against the racist regime of South

Africa, as have been called for by the United Nations. We know that governments and enterprises in that area have relations with South Africa, and the work that our friends in that area are doing in development of the liberation struggle is a demonstration of their solidarity, and their successes are sure to bring about the end of the connection between Central America, the Caribbean and Latin America as a whole with racist South Africa.

And for this reason, obviously, we of the ANC pledge to do what we can, on the one hand, to overthrow the regime inside our country, and are confident that the people of Latin America, Central America and the Caribbean are with us. For example, with relation to the mobilization of sanctions against the racist regime on the weekend of 8 March, which was the International Women's Day, the democratic women of Jamaica for instance called a conference and mass rally around the theme of sanctions against the South African regime so that these activities continue in that area, in spite of the fact that we are geographically divided. But we believe that our South African people, people of Namibia, the people of Angola will in the end see victory, progress, stability and independence with the aid from brothers and sisters in the Caribbean, Central and Southern America.

CHAPTER TWENTY-ONE

Israel and South Africa—Where the Vultures Perch
(1983)

This essay, which appeared in Lotus: Afro-Asian Writings, *describes the connections between apartheid South Africa and Israel in the wake of Israel's invasion of southern Lebanon in June 1982. La Guma's criticism not only reflects his experiences in Lebanon through the Afro-Asian Writers Association but also foreshadows the 'apartheid' analogy that has compared the present-day situation of Palestinians in the West Bank and Gaza with that of black South Africans during the apartheid era.*

In the newspaper *Rand Daily Mail*, it was reported on 10 July 1982, that twenty-two writers and academics protested to the Israeli Ambassador to South Africa against Israeli military action in Lebanon. The group said in a letter that it considered Israel's invasion as 'an act of genocide'. The signatories included Professor Ezekiel Mphahlele and Professor Chabani Manganyi from the University of the Witwatersrand, Mothobi Mutloatse, Stephen Gray, Mike Kirkwood and Jonathon Paton. Others who signed were Peter Wilhelm, Ahmed Essop, Jaki Seroke, Chris van Wyk, Farouk Asvat, Essop Patel, Shofa'ath-Ahmed Kahn, Dion Mattera, Cherry Clayton, Nape Motana, Jean Marquard, Achmat Dangor, Sipho Sepamla, Gcina Mhlophe, Makhulu Ledwaba and Matsemela Manaka.

As the whole world voiced their indignation and anger at the Zionist butchery in Lebanon and Beirut, its capital, it was inevitable that voices from the confined, military-and-police-dominated atmosphere of racist South Africa joined in protest in spite of the intimidating presence of the apartheid repressive machinery.

Ever since the racial-discriminatory and Zionist entities were engineered by the fine hand of Lord Balfour in the early part of this century, racism and Zionism have gone hand in hand. Recognition of their interdependence forms the basis of relations between Zionism and apartheid today. Created as the twin outposts of imperialism—one guarding the eastern Mediterranean and the northern entry into Africa, the other guarding the economic and strategic interests of the imperialist powers in southern Africa, the Indian Ocean and the South Atlantic—they act as economic and military agents of their masters in their respective regions.

'I cannot stress sufficiently how we in Israel cherish relations with South Africa,' said Itshak Unna, Israel's Ambassador to South Africa in 1979. 'South Africa has been consistent in her friendship towards us. South Africa must be seen as having special values for the free world [. . .] It would be a disaster if South Africa were lost as a constructive and active member of the free community of nations.'

Israel and South Africa cooperate not only with imperialism but also with each other: strengthening racism, cooperating in their aggressive manoeuvres against their neighbours and providing mutual military and financial support to ensure the survival of their regimes.

The economic cooperation between apartheid South Africa and Israel is mutually beneficial. Israel provides a channel for exports into African and non-aligned countries, which operate a trade boycott of South African goods, and allows South African goods to enter the EEC [European Economic Community] under Israel's free trade agreement. In return, Israel benefits from the financial and other aid provided by South Africa.

On another level, South African Zionists have been sending larger per capita donations to Israel than any other group, not excluding the US. There are regular fundraising drives in South Africa in which prominent Israeli political, military and commercial leaders participate. Despite its own foreign exchange shortages, the regime has permitted the regular transfer of these funds.

Israel obtains strategic goods and minerals from South Africa including chrome, platinum, titanium and uranium, and there is growing collaboration in various fields of energy. Joint research projects have been set up, and there is a regular exchange of information and technology, including research into solar energy.

Military cooperation between Israel and South Africa, like their economic links, is comprehensive. There are exchanges of personnel, information and technical know-how at all levels. Israelis have served alongside apartheid forces, and South Africans have fought Israel's wars of aggression.

According to a retired South African officer, Brigadier Penn, more than 1,000 racist South Africans had served in the 1948 war that dispossessed the Palestinians.

The importance of the contribution of these was that they supplied the core of medical assistance, special developments such as artillery, and the Israeli Air Force owes its birth to a former Western Desert pilot from Bothaville, Orange Free State Province, named Sid Cohen who founded the IAF with some old German ME-109 fighters, which were later replaced by Spitfires.

South African Mirages were used in the 1967 war of aggression. In addition to the provision of Mirages and spares, racist South Africans served with the Israeli forces. The South African Zionist Federation launched a fund which collected over R2.5 million. In all, over R21 million were transferred to Israel.

During the 1973 War, P. W. Botha was then Minister of Defence of South Africa and promised that South Africa would find ways and means of helping Israel without declaring war. 'There is a deep feeling on the part of thousands of South Africans for Israel in her battle against the forces supported by communistic militarism which also poses a threat to us,' Botha said.

Ninety-one doctors again flew to Israel; 1,500 South Africans served in the Israeli forces and 800 were among the troops that crossed the Suez Canal. At least one South African Mirage was shot down, and there were reports of a number of other South African planes being flown in the war.

A Canadian investigation, in November 1981, revealed that South Africa shipped 200 tanks to Israel by air to replace those Israel lost. This followed a promise by the US that it would help Israel replace those tanks after the war.

US nuclear technology has also reached South Africa directly and via Israel.

Israel has supplied technology, including information on its laser enrichment process, in exchange for uranium. Scientists of both countries have worked on the development of warheads and of the delivery system. The weapon that was tested in 1979, is generally considered to have been produced with Israeli assistance. Journalists who reported on the Israeli connection in this project had their permits to work in Israel withdrawn.

Israel is said to have cooperated with South Africa as well as Taiwan to build its nuclear capability. This information and other are contained in the book *Two Minutes Over Baghdad*, which purports to be the true story of the destruction by Israeli bombers of the Iraqi nuclear plant in 1980.

According to the American columnist Jack Anderson, Israel and South Africa have joined with Taiwan in further plans. In the framework of this triple-state cooperation, there are indications that a common effort is being made to develop a cruise missile with a 2,400-kilometre range. There are also signs that Israel and South Africa are managing to develop a neutron bomb and that they are working on the tactical arsenal no less than on the strategic one.

So the vultures of racism and Zionism perch at each end of the African continent waiting to devour the entrails of the freedom fighters of South Africa and the Middle East, SWAPO, the African National Congress and the Palestine Liberation Organization; to ensure that the liberation movements in these regions will not help to prevent the reconquest of once-colonized peoples in the interests of imperialism and to liberate those still beleaguered by oppressive regimes.

The writers of South Africa acted in the spirit of the national liberation movement when they protested against the barbaric invasion of Lebanon. The African National Congress stated at that time:

> The timing of this aggression against the Palestinian people and Lebanon is remarkable in that it takes place just as world imperialism led by the United States of America is on the rampage, initiating and creating pockets of conflict all over the world. This is done in an attempt to reverse the progress attained by people in their revolutionary struggles for national independence, democracy and peace.
>
> The ANC and the struggling people of South Africa express full support for the Palestine Liberation Organization, which is struggling against odds, making heavy sacrifices for the right of the Palestinian people to self-determination. Israel plays the part played by the racists of South Africa in the imperialist global strategy. It is the cause of tension, destabilization in the Middle East and a threat to world peace like racist South Africa is in southern Africa and Africa as a whole.
>
> We condemn the imperialist Zionist conspiracy against the Palestinian people. We call for the immediate unconditional withdrawal of the Zionist troops from Lebanon. We call for the international isolation of Israel.

CHAPTER TWENTY-TWO

Message to the People and the Government of the Socialist Republic of Vietnam
(1983)

This tribute, which appeared in Lotus, *marks the occasion of a meeting of the Afro-Asian Writers Association in Vietnam, as well as La Guma's continued interest in the country as a symbol against American foreign intervention.*

We, writers of Asia and Africa, have assembled here on the heroic and historic soil of Vietnam that has made enormous sacrifices and shed rivers of blood in defence of its national independence during the long years of the struggle against world imperialism headed by the US imperialists.

It is quite natural that this meeting of writers of the two great continents, and the meaningful and constructive dialogue has been crowned with success. Complete, mutual understanding has been reached concerning the extreme importance of the role played by the militant writer, his place in the struggle to secure a just peace and drain the quagmire of international tensions into which the peoples are being drawn by the forces of world imperialism, apartheid, racism, Zionism and reaction led by the US imperialists.

The writers of Asia and Africa assert that the goal of their literary work is to achieve an unshakable unity in order to strengthen the foundations of a just peace on our planet which is threatened with destruction by the dark forces of imperialist aggression. The struggle for a just peace, freedom and national independence is a foremost condition to ensure the development of culture and literature of all nations on our planet. Peace and détente must, under no circumstances, be left prey to the narrow minded and selfish politicians in the imperialist camp, but must be protected, fostered and consolidated.

To oppose the actions of the mindless forces acting against the worldwide liberation movement, against Asian and African peoples, the Afro-Asian writers must rally their ranks and redouble their efforts in the struggle against these forces hostile to the peoples. This would mean a triumph of human wisdom over dangerous and mindless aggressiveness.

We, writers of Asia and Africa, resolutely denounce the foreign policy of the United States of America and their racist reactionary allies' policy, the cornerstone of which has become a spiralling of the insane arms race and an attempt on the freedom of the Afro-Asian peoples.

We firmly believe that all forces of freedom, peace and justice on the earth, first and foremost the Soviet Union, the Socialist Republic of Vietnam and other states of the socialist community alongside the struggling forces of peace will strengthen evermore their unity in order to crush down the aggressive plans of world imperialism. We believe in such victory since we believe in man's reason.

The writers of Asia and Africa, having assembled on the beautiful and ancient soil of Vietnam, express their deepest gratitude and convey fraternal greetings to the people, the government of the Socialist Republic of Vietnam and the Writers Union of Vietnam for the hospitality rendered and the efforts made to provide a good organization and a successful holding of this meeting.

Honour and glory to the heroic people of Vietnam!

Honour and glory to the peaceful life, creative labour of the Socialist Republic of Vietnam and to its noble struggle for peace and détente!

On behalf of the Executive Council of the
Afro-Asian Writers Association,

Alex La Guma
Secretary General

CHAPTER TWENTY-THREE

Israel–South Africa
The Unholy Alliance
(1983)

Similar to Chapter Twenty-One (pp. 230–4 in this volume), this contribution to Tricontinental *outlines the connections between Israel and apartheid South Africa. La Guma discusses the economic and military collaboration between the two countries, and he captures an ANC perspective on how the anti-apartheid and Palestinian struggles fit into a broader pattern of activism against existing forms of imperialism and foreign aggression.*

The June 1982 invasion of Lebanon by Israel once again proved imperialism's contempt for world public opinion and its determination to destroy the struggle of the Palestinian people and the Lebanese progressive forces.

The affirmation by then US Secretary of State Alexander Haig that the Israelis could not be expected to leave Lebanon soon gave virtual carte blanche to the invaders to carry out their genocidal policy.

Similarly, in southern Africa, imperialism—led by the reactionary sector in the US—turns a blind eye on the aggression of the racists against neighbouring states. Among these, Angola bears a large share of the burden of South African arrogance and terrorism.

Thousands upon thousands of innocents have been massacred by the twin forces of Zionist-racist aggression and invasion as Israel and South Africa, lackeys of imperialism, set about the hopeless mission of putting an end to the liberation struggles of the peoples of the Middle East and southern Africa, led by the Palestine Liberation Organization, SWAPO and the African National Congress in their respective regions.

Recognition of their interdependence forms the basis of relations between Israel and racist South Africa, between Zionism and apartheid. Created by the fine hand of Lord Balfour in the early part of this century—one guarding the eastern Mediterranean and the northern gate to Africa, and the other the interests, both economic and strategic, of imperialism in Southern Africa, the Indian Ocean and South Atlantic—they act as the military and economic agents of their masters. They cooperate not only with imperialism but with each other, strengthening racism, joining in manoeuvres against their neighbours, and providing mutual military and financial support to ensure the survival of their regimes.

Economic Collaboration

Economic collaboration between apartheid South Africa and Israel is mutually beneficial. Israel provides a channel into African and non-aligned countries which operate a trade embargo against South Africa, and allows South African goods to enter the European Common Market under Israel's free-trade agreement. In return, Israel benefits from financial and other aid provided by South Africa.

Since 1976, cooperation on the state level has been through a Joint Ministerial Committee. The Committee was set up to discuss and implement the development of trade, scientific and technical cooperation and the 'joint utilization of South Africa's raw materials and Israeli manpower'.

At the end of 1980, an agreement was concluded providing for an aid package worth $250 million to Israel. It covers the extension of credits and permission for the further export of capital.

South African Zionists have been sending larger *per capita* donations to Israel than any other group, not excluding the US. In spite of its own foreign exchange shortages, the regime has permitted the regular transfer of these funds.

South African companies, including quasi-state organizations, are involved in joint ventures with Israel, often in industries which then export strategic goods to South Africa.

South African–Israeli trade has risen dramatically. The *Financial Mail* quoted the Chairman of the Israel Chamber of Commerce in September 1979: 'Until a few years ago we used to trade in figures of $15 to $20 million. But we are now dealing in hundreds of millions of dollars.' The same journal has estimated that by the end of last year South African sales to Israel would top one billion dollars.

Dramatic as these figures might be, they do not in themselves reveal the strategic importance of the trade nor its full extent. It is not insignificant that within one year of the 1967, war exports and imports increased by over 40 per cent. Similarly, immediately after the 1973 War, trade shot up, with Israel's exports rising from $9 million to $12 million, and South African exports from $11.6 million to $32 million.

The trade figures do not include the very large purchase of South African diamonds by Israel. Nor do they cover the very flourishing arms trade between the two countries.

Israel obtains strategic goods and minerals from South Africa including chrome, platinum, titanium, and there is growing collaboration in various fields of energy. Joint research projects have been set up, and there is a regular exchange of information and of technology, including research into solar energy.

Anxious to reduce its dependence on oil, Israel has been expanding its use of coal, and has found a ready source in South Africa. In January 1979, an agreement with the Transvaal Coal Owners Association provided for the import of 750,000 to

1,000,000 tonnes of coal annually for the Israeli Electric Corporation. By 1983, Israel hopes to import up to 3 million tonnes of coal from South Africa.

Military Collaboration

Military cooperation between Israel and South Africa, like their economic links, is comprehensive. Exchanges of personnel, information and technology take place at all levels. Israelis have served alongside apartheid forces, and South Africans have served in Israel's wars of aggression. In addition, South Africa has supplied strategic minerals to Israel, helped finance Israel's arms production and has received a variety of weapons from, and via, Israel in return.

The extent of South African support for Israel's wars of aggression was recently revealed by Brigadier Penn, a retired South African officer. According to him, more than 1,000 racist South Africans served in the 1948 War that dispossessed the Palestinians.

He said in the military affairs magazine *Armed Forces* that volunteers supplied medical assistance and special equipment such as artillery. The Israeli Air Force owes its birth to one Sid Cohen, former Western Squadron leader who founded the IAF with some old German-made ME-109 fighters which were later replaced by Spitfires.

Brig. Penn confirms earlier reports that South African Mirages were used in the 1967 War of aggression:

> General Dayan indicated to me that 100 Mirages ordered from France, and paid for, were not sent to Israel... South Africa also had Mirages and spare parts, and Dayan wondered whether he could get spares from South Africa.
>
> I told him I felt confident he would get cooperation, but it would be advisable for Mr Tekoah at the United Nations not to bark against South Africa louder than the

rest of the pack, and that his own advice on Russian equipment might be useful to the South African army. I need hardly tell you that both sides kept to this bargain.

During the 1973 War, P. W. Botha was South African Minister of Defence, and promised that South Africa would find ways of helping Israel 'within our means and without declaring war . . . There is a deep feeling on the part of thousands of South Africans against the forces supported by communistic militarism which also pose a threat to us'.

Fifteen thousand South Africans served in the Israeli forces and 800 crossed the Suez Canal. At least one South African Mirage was shot down, and there were reports of a number of other South African planes being flown in the war. The regulations on exchange controls were lifted and over $30 million was remitted to Israel at that time.

A Canadian investigation in 1981 revealed that South Africa shipped 200 tanks by air to Israel to replace those Israel lost. This followed a promise by the US that it would help Israel replace these tanks after the war.

In its turn Israel has become the source of weapons and military technology for the apartheid regime. Pretoria's entire armoured corps of Centurion tanks and Panhard armoured cars has been equipped with an Israel-developed armoured plate. Gunboats and fighter jets have been supplied as well as self-propelled artillery and anti-tank missiles, and air-to-air missiles.

Racist South Africa financed the new generation of Israeli ships, and South African engineers and technicians were trained in Haifa shipyards. Israeli technology has been used to fortify South African helicopter squadrons with electronic equipment.

Israel has also been the channel for the supply of other weapons to South Africa in violation of the UN mandatory embargo. Last year, Israeli Minister for Economic Coordination, Yaakov Meridor, publicly offered his country as proxy to those wishing to break the arms embargo. The US, Canada and the Federal Republic of (West) Germany were among those known to have used this route to supply South Africa.

US nuclear technology has also reached South Africa directly and via Israel.

Israel has supplied technology to South Africa, including information on its laser-enrichment process, in exchange for uranium. Scientists of both countries have worked on the development of warheads and of the delivery system. The weapon South Africa did not test in 1977 as well as the one that was detonated in 1979 are generally considered to have been produced with Israeli assistance. Journalists who reported on the Israeli connection had their permission to work in Israel withdrawn.

Israel and South Africa are now engaged in building a nuclear submarine. Preliminary work on the submarine base has begun at Simonstown, the South African naval base that is twinned with an Israeli town.

South African and Israeli collaboration grows by the day, and the unholy alliance which they form remains a threat to the peoples of Africa and the Middle East and a threat to the peace of the world. Each has committed aggression and stands in violation of the peace, yet remains protected against international action by the machinations of the imperialist powers. As they mutually link the survival of their vicious regimes, they more than double the threat to the peace of the world. Armed with nuclear weapons, they threaten the survival of all.

The struggle of the people of the Sahara, the Middle East and all progressive forces is threatened by this Israel–South Africa alliance. The Camp David Accord, the Reagan policies in the Middle East, the offensives against Libya, Algeria, Polisario and Lebanon are interlinked with this Israeli-South African conspiracy against the Non-Aligned Movement and the peoples of Asia and Africa.

CHAPTER TWENTY-FOUR

Cuba and Africa
(March 1984)

This article, which appeared in Sechaba, is notable for its criticism of the Reagan administration and its summarizing depiction of Cuba's engagements across Africa, especially its support of the anti-apartheid struggle.

The early days of November 1983 were brave ones for the Cuban people. At José Martí Airport of Havana, the planes were landing to disembark the 700-odd construction workers and cooperation personnel who had gone to Grenada to build the commercial airport at Point Salines, and who had taken up arms to defend their worksites when attacked by the Yankee invaders of that tiny island. Among them were their wounded, and with them came their 24 dead in flag-draped coffins. All of them were workers: bricklayers, painters, crane operators, mechanics, architects and so on. There were a handful of military personnel among them, giving the lie to Reagan and the US imperialists, who were stating that there were thousands of Cuban troops in Grenada.

Lie of a Cuban–Soviet Pact

It has been the policy of world imperialism, led by the United States, to advance the impression that Cuba is a military nation with thousands of soldiers ready to overrun the 'Third World'. Using the presence of internationalist Cuban troops in Angola or Ethiopia, imperialism has tried to spread the lie of a Cuban-Soviet plot to conquer Africa.

Time and again the government of the People's Republic of Angola has explained that, apart from the fact that Cuba and Angola are independent countries and can enter into whatever treaties and agreements they please, the presence of Cuban troops in that country is determined by the continued occupation of parts of Angola by South African racist forces and by the threat of further invasion by the apartheid regime.

It is well known that Cuban troops only arrived in Angola because that country was under attack from the racists' army. Obviously, the withdrawal of South Africa from the territory of Angola and the guarantee of Angolan security and no indication of invasion can be the basis for withdrawing the Cuban internationalist forces.

But it is not only with military support for certain countries that Cuba has shown its internationalist solidarity with Africa, apart from other developing countries.

Health Programmes

Angola inherited many terrible things from Portuguese colonialism, among these the deplorable state of medical and hygiene services. The Angolan authorities stress that Cuba plays a key role in improving medical care in their country by providing doctors, nurses, technicians and support personnel as part of bilateral health programmes.

By late 1975, the year of independence, a small group of Cuban health workers had already arrived in the northern province of Cabinda, and 1982 figures showed that by then 30 per cent of Cuban medical personnel on internationalist assignments were stationed in Angola.

In 1980, Cuban doctors in Angola saw 1,020,096 people in their surgeries, and, in the first half of 1981 alone, the number was 1,102,480. These figures do not include the tens of thousands of operations performed, vaccinations administered, babies delivered, laboratory tests and X-rays. In addition to clinical work done, there are also advisers at the international level in medicines, statistics and epidemiology, and teachers training nurses and intermediate technicians.

The Cuban medical personnel do not limit themselves to their specific work; rather they cooperate in all programmes outlined by the Angolan Ministry of Public Health and its agencies. Local officials say that Cuban participation in the drives against polio, leprosy and malaria has been especially significant, as well as their help in taking preventative measures against communicable diseases.

The importance of scholarships granted by the Cuban government to young Angolans to train in Cuba as doctors, dentists, physiotherapists, dental technicians and so forth has been repeatedly stressed.

All these examples of Cuban medical cooperation are in addition to the extensive building programmes which are being carried out by Cuban construction brigades in Angola.

Socialist Ethiopia

Similar medical assistance is given to Socialist Ethiopia, as well as assistance in combating the drought which affects that country. During the course of his visit to Ethiopia, Comrade Fidel Castro, accompanied by President Mengistu Haile Mariam, toured the area of Debre Zeyit, including the Centre for Recovery and Rehabilitation of Disabled War Heroes. Fidel suggested that agricultural projects could be established in the area as part of the rehabilitation of the patients, mostly young men who could work there, and this be useful to the revolution and to their country.

This was in 1978. The first Cuban technicians arrived a few weeks later, followed by heavy equipment, such as bulldozers, trucks, and so on. While this was going on in Debre Zeyit, the Cubans were also hard at work reviewing and adjusting the plans for the Birete Dam, which would provide water for the cement factory built with Cuban help at New Mugher in Shoa province, about 100 kilometres from the capital.

Also working with Cubans on these projects are Ethiopian technicians, along with thousands of people from near and far, who pitch in. Some are involved in construction, but the bulk of them work in agriculture. The waterworks and farms have provided employment for thousands of men and women.

Scores of Cubans work on these important tasks of aiding Ethiopia's hydrological development over the past years. As is the case with other Cuban cooperation programmes, every Cuban has an Ethiopian counterpart at his side. In this way, workers have been trained for similar projects all over this huge country, which covers an area of 1,235,000 square km.

People's Republic of Congo

Minister Mouabenga of the People's Republic of the Congo, when visiting Cuba, stated:

> One thing we should stress is the importance of our ties with Cuba. These ties in cooperation date back a number of years and will continue.

Among other things, Cuba gives assistance to the Congo in poultry and livestock raising and in agriculture generally. The Minister mentioned the work done at the Red Kilometre experimental farm located about 80 kilometres north of Brazzaville. Here, 9 Cubans are advising 21 Congolese professionals, technicians and workers who are engaged in the difficult task of providing this country with cattle that will be good milk and meat providers and that at the same time can adapt well to the climate.

Dr Ndouang Dambert-Rene, who heads the farm, said that in his opinion and that of the other Congolese staff members the Cuban advisers were 'dedicated workers and outstanding teachers'.

Another field of work in which the Cubans are engaged in the Congo is drilling for water in areas traditionally viewed by residents, and experts alike, as dry. The Minister remarked:

> It was believed there was no hope of finding water here. A serious social problem has been solved, since the people there never had water. Now that we've found it, they have water, thanks to the Cubans.

The Minister mentioned another very important aspect of cooperation, the training of cadres and skilled technicians.

> Many of our technicians and specialists study in Cuba, and now they are making a vital contribution to carrying out development programmes.

Education

Cuba continues to maintain friendly relations with many countries of Africa, including Mozambique, Cape Verde, Zimbabwe, Zambia and the Democratic Sahrawi Arab Republic.

One of the most important acts of solidarity with Africa and Asia and Latin America is the education of scholars and training of specialists in Cuba itself. More than 16,000 young people from 81 countries live and study in Cuba. Fidel said, 'By being internationalists we are repaying our debt to humanity.' A renowned centre of education for foreign and Cuban youth is the Isle of Youth (Isla de la Juventud), formerly the Isle of Pines. It is a sunny island, filled with orange groves and gently rolling hills, and dotted with dozens of modern junior high schools (ESBECs) in the countryside. A visiting foreign journalist remarked when visiting there, 'This must be the only place in the world where you can mistake a school for a first-class hotel.' African countries, who won liberation only a relatively short time ago and where illiteracy still rates an average of 90 per cent, still lack resources to tackle the major problem of education at all levels. After more than twenty years, Cuba is able to offer help to these countries in a field where she herself has scored many victories.

Visiting the Island of Youth, President Samora Machel addressed more than 2,000 Mozambican students studying there, saying:

> You are our ambassadors here. Your mission is to strengthen friendship between our peoples. You should return to Mozambique as men and women of science and culture carrying this people's values. We want to see what the Cuban people are like through you.

Many delegations from African countries, from the liberation movements, ANC and SWAPO, have borne testimony to the sterling internationalist work in education carried out by Cuba both on junior and higher levels.

The Hendrik Witbooi School, where Namibian scholars are situated, is well known. Many of the children there are survivors of the Cassinga Massacre and other terrorist acts of the South African racists. Bernard Kamwui, former principal of the Hendrik Witbooi Junior High School, said, 'Generally speaking, all our children have been directly affected by apartheid. The moment they arrive in Cuba they undergo a complete change; they're contented, happy, in their new surroundings.' On the higher level, students are educated in universities and institutes on the mainland. Ibrahim Konate, a hydraulic engineering student from Mali, said:

> I came to Cuba for many reasons. In the career I chose, Cuba is a wonderful example of what an underdeveloped country can achieve thanks to science and technology [...] The goal that we seek is to make the most of our stay in Cuba and return one day to our country as competent professionals; there's a lot for us to do here.

Speaking on behalf of ANC students in Cuba, a recently qualified medical doctor, Thabo Mnisi, said:

We feel profoundly grateful for having the experience of studying in Cuba, which has given generous internationalist help to many underdeveloped countries and to struggling people. ANC students manifest an eloquent and living testimony of this noble expression of solidarity. Indeed, this gesture of the Cuban people will live in the hearts and history of our people. We must now place our acquired skills and professional capabilities at the service of the just cause of our people.

We Are Latin-Africans

Touring Africa, Comrade Juan Almeida Bosque, vice president of Cuba, stated:

> It is important to draw attention to the fruitful relations of friendship and cooperation between Cuba (and Africa), relations that date back to the days when African men and women, victims of the colonialists' insane greed, were first taken to America to be placed under the odious yoke of slavery. From then on, criollo blood blended with the blood of the people of Africa and the Cuban nationality began to take shape [...]

'We are Latin-Africans', was the way Fidel Castro put it.

This is manifested in the character and cultural face of Cuba. Historically, Cuba received important cultural contributions, which constitute the foundation of Cuban culture. Thousands of African captives during the past centuries brought to Cuba elements of their civilization. Cuban ethnographer, Fernando Ortiz, has said that the Fantis, Minas, Ashantis and many other ethnic groups came to Cuba from Ghana. From Angola came Bacongos, Loandas and Benguelas, from Mozambique came the Macuas and Moçambiques. It was found that in the Volta region many understood the lyrics of Afro-Cuban songs when the Cuban National Folklore Group visited four African countries. Deep are the roots which are shared by Cuba and Africa.

No imperialist slander or bellicose threats will sever the bonds which bind our peoples and countries.

Patria o muerte!
Venceremos!

CHAPTER TWENTY-FIVE

Tribute to Indira Gandhi
(1985)

This brief letter, in which La Guma condoles the assassination of Indira Gandhi (1917–84), further indicates the wider political and literary world to which he belonged, as well as the duties he executed as the general secretary of the Afro-Asian Writers Association. It is somewhat surprising given the repressiveness of Gandhi's government, especially during the State of Emergency beginning in 1975. Nonetheless, India had vocally supported the ANC and the anti-apartheid struggle. Furthermore, Gandhi had fostered close ties between India and the USSR, while also promoting the Non-Aligned Movement, cofounded by her father, Jawaharlal Nehru (1889–1964). La Guma received the 1969 Lotus Prize in an award ceremony hosted by her in New Delhi in 1970. This letter reflects these different dimensions. It was published in Lotus.

Bhisham Sahni
Chairman of the Indian Afro-Asian Writers' Committee
Delhi
India

The Afro-Asian writers have heard with profound shock and sorrow of the tragic passing away of Mrs Indira Gandhi, prime minister of India, chairman of [the] Non-aligned Movement. The world anti-imperialist movement has lost an outstanding fighter and we recall with our own sense of loss the support given by Indira Gandhi to the cause of Afro-Asian writers during her lifetime.

Alex La Guma
General Secretary of the Afro-Asian Writers' Association

PART II

Cultural Scenes and Arguments

CHAPTER ONE

The Third Afro-Asian Writers' Conference
(April 1967)

This brief conference report was published in Cultural Events in Africa, *a journal affiliated with the Transcription Centre in London, where La Guma worked during his early years of exile. This conference marked the first occasion that La Guma attended an event hosted by the Afro-Asian Writers Association.*

The Third Afro-Asian Writers' Conference was held in Beirut from 25–30 March of this year and was attended by 146 delegates representing 43 countries of Africa and Asia. Writers from 11 European and American countries were present as guests and observers. Among the well-known writers and poets who participated in the conference were Mouloud Mammeri (Algeria), Mário de Andrade (Angola), Eustache Prudencio (Dahomey), Mulk Raj Anand (India), James Ngũgĩ (Kenya), Youssef El Sebai, Morse Saad Eddin (UAR), Raymond Kunene, Alex La Guma, Lewis Nkosi, Ruth First (South Africa), Eugene Yevtushenko (USSR), Shiro Hasegawa, Biken Kitamura (Japan).

The Conference was opened by the Prime Minister of Lebanon, Mr Rashid Karami. Throughout the conference the theme was the duty of the writer and poet towards mankind and his people. The speakers displayed a profound understanding of the social significance of literature and any believers in narrowly individualistic art and formalist canons would have been disappointed with the conference. The Beirut conference showed how closely related the writer's activity is to the struggle of the Afro-Asian people against imperialism and colonialism. Delegates spoke of the militant courage of the Angolan patriots, of the problems of the people of South Africa struggling against racialism, of the Arab people.

One of the intricate questions raised at Beirut was that of the interrelation of different cultures. Many of the speeches were direct replies to any attempts to place the culture of the West in opposition to that of the East. Many delegates spoke of the tragic pages of their history where the imperialists destroyed the national culture and literature of their countries. This, however, did not impel Afro-Asian writers to draw abstract lines between East and West. Western culture, the conference maintained, is rich in progressive, revolutionary, liberatory traditions, which can help the regeneration and development of the cultural values of countries oppressed by colonialism.

CHAPTER TWO

Culture and Apartheid in South Africa
(1968)

This article, first published in Tricontinental, *is an example of how La Guma was often assigned, especially during his early years of exile, to 'explain' apartheid to an international audience. It is also one of La Guma's initial interventions into the connections between culture and politics—the first of a provisional series as noted in the introduction of this volume. Though his novels and stories which preceded this piece clearly indicate his belief that art could engage with political questions and solutions, this essay describes in more explicit terms why cultural life and artistic creativity were indispensable aspects of the struggle, constituting an essential front against the apartheid regime.*

The democratic revolution in South Africa implies the process of upsetting the present structure of white supremacy bolstered by local exploiters and foreign imperialists, and erecting upon its ruins new institutions which will guarantee economic, political, social and cultural equality; a new life, dignity and humanity in the South African people. It implies a new community of people of all racial groups: African, White, Coloured and Asian, being given the opportunity of creating a single, unified nation.

To prevent this process from taking place, the present racist Nationalist Party government, led by Belshazzar Vorster, has erected a state machinery of repression comparable with the apparatus constructed under the leadership of Adolf Hitler. It must be pointed out, however, that colour oppression, race discrimination, *apartheid* as it is called today, is not the sole invention of the present rulers of South Africa. Political and economic power having always been in the hands of the white minority, successive governments controlled by the minority population have contributed to the construction of the monster which straddles the country.

Having achieved power, the present government set out to consolidate the racist structure of the country, penetrating all spheres of life: political, economic, social, residential, religious, educational and cultural; enforcing their policy by means of a vast Gestapo-like police force as well as the administrative machinery.

The notorious 'pass laws', regularly amended and 'improved' together with innumerable other regulations denying ordinary human rights and working-class activity, hold the African (Negro) population at the mercy of exploiters, who batten down on them as a source of cheap labour available through the administration of these laws. The Bantu Law Amendment Act of 1964 consolidates innumerable enactments and has had disastrous effects on African family life. Wives and other dependents of Africans working in the 'white' areas may not live with their husbands or fathers unless they have resided continuously in the same area previously. Visits between husbands and wives residing in separate districts (an African worker may have come from the countryside to work in the urban area) are limited to 72 hours without permission. A single African male can live in the urban area if he is born there or if he has been employed by one employer for at least 10 years. If he wants to marry from outside that area, the woman must have permission to enter it, and he must ensure that housing is available in the African residential area only. All these 'permissions' and 'allowances' are recorded in a pass book which is issued to the African on attaining the age of 16, and which he must be able to show on demand to any official or policeman, on pain of arrest and imprisonment or fine. The African working in the urban area ceases to work, loses his right to live there, and can be endorsed out of the area to the poverty-stricken countryside, even if he has no association there at all. Thus, the entire African working class, as well as other categories, is bound to the cheap labour system, as he has no alternative but to accept work even at starvation earnings—which proves convenient for the white-controlled economy.

Culture and social contacts between black and white are hampered by the rigorous application of the apartheid policy. Africans, Coloureds (mulatto) and Asians go to the 'white' areas only to work in industry and commerce, or as domestic servants, or to purchase goods. Non-Africans may not visit an African township or reservation without a special permit.

Apartheid permeates the entire country and governs the daily lives of all citizens, determining the location of each racial group, what kind of education they must receive, within what group they may marry, and the circumstances under which members of different communities may meet, what type of trade or profession they may adopt.

Consequently, it is not surprising that, due to the inability to advance politically and economically and in all other fields, 80 per cent of the non-white population live on or below the poverty line in South Africa. Crime and drunkenness, arising from frustration, increases with the publication of each table of statistics; the prison population grows from day to day. Under these conditions, the cultural level of the people remains at the lowest, and it is not only poverty which stands in their way.

The Group Areas Act divides the country into racially segregated districts, denying one group the right of 'occupying' the 'area' of another. As a result, whole non-white communities have been physically evicted from districts declared to be 'White Only'. Thus, schools, theatres, churches used by such communities have been lost to them. Where in the past non-whites might have had access to halls, theatres, open spaces for cultural activities, today most of these amenities are situated in 'white' areas and permission is required by non-whites to use them. In most cases, such permission is refused by the authorities, or it is stipulated that only an audience or artists of one racial group will be permitted use of an amenity.

Thus, the law allows no artists of various races to perform together, or no mixed audience to attend the segregated theatre. This state of affairs applies equally to sports in South Africa.

While it is difficult to prevent radio programmes being available to the general population, the South African Broadcasting Corporation has, however, established special 'Bantu' programmes and 'Coloured' programmes. The South African government, as a matter of policy, refuses to allow television in the country.

Schools in South Africa have always been segregated between white and non-white, meaning that while Coloured, African and Indian were allowed to attend one school, they could not attend a white school. Education was administered by the councils of the four respective provinces, and while facilities were varied as between races, syllabuses laid down by the respective Provincial administrations were the same for all groups at these schools.

In 1953, the Bantu Education Act was passed by Parliament. During the debate of this law in the House of Assembly, the late Prime Minister, Dr Verwoerd, who was then minister of Native Affairs, explained the proposed law:

> When I have control of native (Negro) education, I will reform it so that natives will be taught from childhood to realize that equality with Europeans is not for them . . . People who believe in equality are not desirable as teachers for natives . . . When my Department controls native education, it will know for what class of higher education a native is fitted and whether he will have a chance in life to use his knowledge.

This in a nutshell describes the object of separate education for the African child, but, continuing, Verwoerd, speaking from the assumption that South Africa is a white country, said further: 'There is no place for him [the African] in the European community above the level of certain forms of labour.'

The Bantu Education Act took African education out of the hands of the Provincial Council and placed it directly under the Minister of Bantu Education and Development and his Bantu Administration Department. It gives unrestricted power to the Minister to decide for himself vital matters such as teachers' conditions of service, the content of African education, the establishment of schools, etc. This law is one of the most vicious, for it prevents and curtails the educational and cultural advancement of the African child. Applying it to a poverty-stricken community, Verwoerd made it clear that parents, or communities of parents, too poor to afford equipment for their children other than primary readers may not send their children to school. 'Pupils in post-primary schools will have to buy all the school books they need. All other school requisites, including pens and exercise books, in both primary and secondary schools, must be provided either by the children, the Bantu authority, or the parents' association. Children without these school requisites will not be enrolled.' And as regards the purpose of this apartheid education: 'The economic structure of our country of course results in large numbers of natives having to earn their living in the service of Europeans'; therefore, 'it is essential that Bantu pupils should receive instruction in both official languages [English and Afrikaans] from the earliest stages, so that even in the lower primary school they would develop an ability to speak and understand them.' Equally, Eiselen, then secretary for Native Affairs, spoke of the necessity for the African child to be able to follow oral or written instructions and to carry on a simple conversation with whites about his work in English or Afrikaans.

Separate education for Coloureds and Indians has also been instituted under their respective ministerial departments' set up.

The proportion of funds expended by the government on the education of the different racial communities is of course compatible with its apartheid policy.

In 1953, when the Bantu Education Act was introduced, the expenditure on education was: whites, £63.18 (per pupil) and £13.9 (per head of population); Coloureds and Asians, £20.4 (per pupil) and £3.19 (per head of population); and Africans, £8.19 (per pupil) and £17 (per head of population). But from 1953 to 1962, for example, the figure per African pupil dropped from £8.54 to £6.15, and it is still dropping.

While the government attempts to whitewash its racist policy by claiming that it is assisting the African to develop his 'own culture' by also educating him in his own language, the facts show that actually less and less are achieving adequate education.

All teaching is done in the vernacular up to and including the First Form, and it is intended that this process should continue up to matriculation. But when the matriculant examination in one of the seven tribal vernaculars is taken, the student will automatically lose eligibility for entrance into any mixed university, and his 'Bantu' qualification will qualify him for entrance only into his appropriate 'tribal' university especially established for him, and for nowhere else. He will not even be able to leave the country and, on the basis of his 'Bantu' qualifications, proceed with his studies elsewhere. Instruction in the tribal language has been farcical and led to a startling decline in educational standards, for there are few or no advanced textbooks available in those languages. Likewise, at the moment, after education in the tribal language in the primary school, there is a sudden switch to the two official languages, English and Afrikaans, in the secondary school, and children having learnt only the simplest of English in particular, the standard of passes has dropped disastrously. Thus, achieving university standards is a frustrating process for the African scholar.

In 1959, 197 Africans obtained university degrees in South Africa, a great many of them actually through correspondence courses. In 1960, the number was 186; in 1962, 105; and in 1964, 103. In 1960, out of the non-white population of nearly 15 million, there were 130 non-white doctors in South Africa.

The government, of course, is extremely careful in providing the African schools with literature which conforms with its conception of cultural advancement. Thus, set books are screened by the Bantu Education authorities, and only those desirable in their eyes allowed into the schools. As a result, the quality of works published in the African languages are of a poor standard, and it is possible that large numbers of valuable manuscripts remain today unpublished since they do not meet the requirements of apartheid culture. At the same time, the general readership consists of a population many of whom have hardly had a secondary education and whose literary tastes are least formed.

The Suppression of Communism Act, among other things, debars Marxist literature, and any publication defined by the Minister as advancing the aims of communism, which usually means advocating equality of races, can be banned or prohibited. Thus, progressive newspapers and magazines have been closed down under this law. Under the same law, the Minister of Justice has also gazetted lists of South African writers and journalists whose works may not be read in that country, and, at the same time, anybody prohibited under the Act may not be quoted in the press or his statements circulated.

The English-language press in particular has come under regular attack from the government, and threats to introduce official censorship were countered by the press itself volunteering to impose self-censorship through a 'code of conduct'.

The Publications and Entertainments Act also controls literature, cinematographic and stage entertainment, gramophone records, etc., in South Africa. The Act makes it possible for the government, inter alia, to prohibit the circulation of any book imported or printed in South Africa; to close down any stage or film show; to prohibit the works of any South African artist, novelist, poet or sculptor—if it is deemed that such works and shows are 'undesirable'. Under this Act and the Customs Act, thousands of books have been prohibited from circulation in the country, ranging from the most advanced scientific writings to simple pornography.

The Group Areas Act also governs the use of public libraries, since it reserves public buildings in a particular area for the use of the population for which that area is reserved, and most adequate libraries are situated in 'white' areas. The Separate Amenities Act also governs the use of public libraries. In the city of Durban, in Natal Province, for example, 11 municipal libraries serve the white population, as against one for Coloureds and one branch library for Africans. In the Orange Free State Province there is no library service at all for Africans.

The examination of the cultural problems of the non-white population under the apartheid regime can reveal more and more inhuman aspects, and there can be little wonder at the fact that scores of artists, writers and other intellectuals, and hundreds of school teachers and students, have emigrated or fled the country to escape the stifling atmosphere of racialism. But the real alternative to racism is voiced by the great Freedom Charter, adopted in 1955 by representatives from all walks of life of South Africa's population, and which is now the programme of the Congress Movement headed by the African National Congress, which leads the resistance. The Freedom Charter states, inter alia:

> We, the people of South Africa, declare for all our country and the world to know: that South Africa belongs to all who live in it, black and white, and that no government can justly claim authority unless it is based on the will of the people . . . The doors of learning and culture shall be opened! . . . All the cultural treasures of mankind shall be open to all, by free exchange of books, ideas, and contacts with other lands . . . Education shall be free, compulsory, universal and equal for all children . . . The colour bar in cultural life, in sports, and in education shall be abolished.

For this, South African non-white workers have been shot down and clubbed; for this, thousands of political prisoners languish in the prisons of Vorster's white-supremacy republic; for this, thousands have demonstrated on the streets of South Africa; for this, the guerrilla forces of South Africa's liberation movement are fighting.

CHAPTER THREE

Culture and Revolution
(October 1969)

As part of an ANC delegation, La Guma attended the First Pan-African Cultural Festival held in Algiers from 21 July to 1 August 1969. This travel report was first published in Sechaba. *It indicates once again La Guma's efforts at cultural diplomacy to connect with other writers and artists from across the postcolonial world.*

Background to the First Pan-African Cultural Festival

For two weeks the theatres, public squares and sports stadiums of Algiers throbbed and pulsed to the music, songs and dances of Africa. The First Pan-African Cultural Festival sponsored by the Organisation of African Unity brought together in the capital of the Algerian People's Democratic Republic all the artistic achievements of Africa in all the diverse contributions which the people of our great continent have evolved over centuries.

From every state on the continent come troupes of dancers, singers, musicians. The opening parade through the streets of Algiers created a kaleidoscope of colour, changing from the brilliant robes and trappings of Arab horsemen to the ritualistic masks and panoply of tropical Africa.

The only states not represented on a governmental level were those of the racist South. These were represented by contingents from the liberation movements: the ANC (South Africa), MPLA (Angola), FRELIMO (Moçambique), PAIGC ('Portuguese' Guinea), ZAPU (Zimbabwe).

It is significant that these contingents received prolonged ovations from the massed crowds when they appeared in the streets of Algiers, for they represented those regions of Africa where indigenous culture is suppressed and the people's personality must be re-established by force of arms.

For from a mere stocktaking of African culture in all its aspects, the Algiers Festival was meant to confirm the self-awareness and expression of the African cultural phenomenon, to help in creating the outlines of a culture able to serve as an instrument of economic and social change. The symposium, attended by African and world personalities in the cultural field, met to discuss 'African culture, its reality, its role in the liberation struggle, in the consolidation of African unity and the economic and social development of Africa'.

Intrinsic Part of Struggle

Opening the Festival, President Houari Boumédiène of Algeria stated:

> This Festival, far from being on occasion for general festivities which might momentarily distract us from our daily tasks and problems, should rather be related to them and make a direct contribution to our vast effort of construction. It constitutes an intrinsic part of the struggle we are all pursuing in Africa—whether that of development, that of the struggle against racism or that of national liberation. Colonialism is an evil, which all of us have experienced and over its most insolent forms we have triumphed [...] For us culture is a beginning, which involves the best works of man in the stimulating task of development and social progress. What meaning, what role and what function could we give to culture if not to give our liberated peoples a better life and to continue the fight for our brothers still under the yoke of colonialism in one way or

another, to participate thus in the worldwide task of the rehabilitation of man by man?

Addressing the symposium the delegate from the Zimbabwe African People's Union (ZAPU) said:

> Culture is a dynamic expression. It becomes a way of expressing appreciation or rejection of a national event. In the circumstances of Zimbabwe, our songs now contain abhorrence of oppression and a good many raise the spirit of war against the oppressors. When culture takes this form it becomes the culture of resistance. A people's culture cannot be suppressed or oppressed without touching the heart of the people. Submission to oppression is abandonment of one's culture and effacement of one's personality. The Zimbabwe people today are engaged in a liberation struggle. The struggle is to reject foreign impositions in our systems and concepts of culture. The struggle in a positive sense is to salvage our culture, live by it and preserve the aspects we consider consistent with progress in this dynamic world.

Dynamism of Our Culture

Speaking on behalf of the South African delegation, Mazisi Kunene said that the Festival was an occasion to affirm those values which have kept our society intact:

> It is an occasion to not only perpetuate the memory of our great heroes but also, thereby, to assert the dynamism and continuity of our culture and history. It is an occasion to replenish old values with new experiences. The colonialists in their ignorance and/or arrogance, often as a matter of policy, sought to depersonalize Africa, and have created a cultural vacuum. They have poured scorn on the large number of festivals and sought to project us as happy ani-

mals [. . .] We are reasserting the continuity of achievements of our forefathers whose spectacular conquest of the physical challenges of this continent is a monument to their spirit of courage and adventure. We are here to continue in the heroic traditions and the directions which they conceived, perceived and explored. We are therefore instruments of our continental history, and as such we cannot assume the arrogance and myopia which claim the finality of its achievement. In this sense, our cultural festivities go beyond a day, a week or a month, and are thrust beyond it into the unknown in the name of a dynamic and a continuing African revolution. The struggle waged by us against the colonialists must be mobilized with even greater vehemence in the post-independence period of reconstruction against an imperialist elite. Our revolution in South Africa is based on the recovery of our social values defined not in airy-fairy attempts, but in concrete political, economic and social attempts. In short, we are fighting for a socialist state, and we are dedicated to this ideal and we shall not lay down our arms until these ideals have been achieved.

CHAPTER FOUR

African Culture and National Liberation
(1969)

This article was originally a speech delivered by La Guma at the First Pan-African Cultural Festival. It provides analysis of the event and its meanings for him and the South African liberation struggle. It was published in the Journal of the New African Literature and the Arts *in a special issue devoted to the festival.*

What we see on record here at the First Pan-African Festival is a vast manifestation of the spiritual and cultural achievements of the African continent. The Pan-African Cultural Festival gives the lie to the racist idea that Africa is a dark continent and that it has produced nothing to enhance the treasures of culture, which is the heritage of all mankind.

Now that the burdens of imperialism and colonialism have been eased from our shoulders in a great part of Africa, we are better able to venture across new frontiers of material welfare and cultural upliftment. We Africans are concerned with the development of this continent and with its future in relation to the rapid changes occurring in all aspects of African and world life. We look back at the past in order to uncover values, assess them from the point of view of modern times, and attempt to determine and understand their place and role in history and modern civilization.

The great problem facing new Africa today is that of ensuring that more and more of her people benefit from the successes over the forces which are responsible for the slowing down of African progress; which withhold scientific and technological development; which frustrated the development of our culture.

The end of the colonial period in liberated Africa left millions of illiterate people in its wake. We have to build a new life in our various independent states with the aid of those men and women who grew up under the colonial regimes. So our people are thirsting for knowledge because they need it in order to win. We know that knowledge is a weapon in the struggle for final emancipation, that many failures arise out of lack of education, and therefore it becomes a duty of the liberated countries to give everyone access to education. It takes knowledge to participate in the revolution with intelligence, purpose and success.

The main distinguishing feature of a true democratic cultural revolution is its mass, nationwide character. The strength and vitality of the revolution is derived from the awakened creative energy of the masses and their aspiration for a new life, enlightenment and culture. Real progress cannot be decreed from above; living creative progress is the product of the masses themselves. We must raise the lowest sections of the population to the state of making history.

Revolution in the people's minds is one of the most profound and most important manifestations of the cultural revolution. At the same time, the cultural revolution from which emerges a qualitatively new type of socially based culture must be seen as an integral part of the social revolution, as a far reaching upheaval in the spiritual life of society effected on the basis of radical political and economic transformations. With the political and economic changes which are taking place or are planned to take place in Africa, every individual must be given maximum opportunities to enjoy the benefits of past cultures and the opportunities directly to participate in creating new spiritual assets.

Under the colonial regimes and the rule of metropolitan capitalism, the brain of man created to give some the benefits of technology and culture and to deprive others of the bare necessities of life, education and development. Now we ask that all the marvels of science and the gains of culture belong to the nation as a whole, in order to introduce an all embracing and speedy elevation of the cultural level of the people, the cultivation of a new consciousness, morality and ethics.

While the material wealth and all the avenues of science and technology are not accessible to the people, cultural development will be impeded. Today, we know that man has walked on the moon. But in spite of this wonderful demonstration of mankind's prowess over nature, what does it matter to the people of Southern Africa if man can walk upright on the moon and he cannot walk upright in his own country? What does it matter that science has given rise to space exploration and in South Africa—52 out of every 100 African children die of malnutrition before the age of 5 years? What does it matter if we can plot the course to a star, and the brain size of South African children is already retarded at the age of 2 years because of malnutrition? Before we can truly appreciate these marvels, we must be truly free.

In Southern Africa, where cultural advancement or frustration depends on the whims of the racist oppressors, the people have taken up arms in order to exercise their right to reconstruct and rehabilitate the personality of the South African people; to open the doors of universal learning and culture; to gain access to the knowledge and science withheld by the white racists, knowing that in order to achieve this we must also control the material, social and political keys.

We have no doubt that the deliberations of the commissions of this symposium will have their eyes on the unliberated areas of Africa when the final word is said at the First Pan-African Cultural Festival.

CHAPTER FIVE

Paul Robeson and Africa
(1971)

La Guma delivered the following paper at a symposium entitled 'Paul Robeson and the Afro-American Struggle' held at the Academy of Arts in East Berlin on 13 and 14 April 1971. It was published in The African Communist. *This essay indicates La Guma's sense of affinity with fellow artist and communist, Paul Robeson (1898–1976), as well as his knowledge of and engagement with a broader trans-Atlantic Pan-Africanism. Notable also are his mention of Angela Davis, and his comparison of the assassinations of Martin Luther King, Jr, (1929–68) and Patrice Lumumba (1925–61).*

Honoured Chairman, friends, allow me to express my sincere thanks for the invitation to be present here to you and the organizers of this symposium on Paul Robeson and on the struggle of the Afro-American people.

We can well understand the sentiments which stimulated this gathering. The cause of Afro-Asian solidarity, solidarity with the Afro-American people, and in fact with all oppressed and persecuted people throughout the world is a characteristic of the German Democratic Republic. Since its inception, the GDR has done many things which have vindicated the honour of progressive Germany. Your people have risen like the phoenix from the ashes of Nazism; and you have shown time and again that the spirit of Thaelmann, Beimler, the Spartacists, Karl Marx and Frederick Engels did not die as a result of the Hitlerite depredations.

The present demonstration of your solidarity with the Afro-American people, whose suffering and heroism is today epitomized by Angela Davis, is certainly close to the hearts of the African people as well.

The forefathers of the Afro-American people were brought from my continent during the seventeenth century. The black people of the United States are there today because their ancestors were brought there against their will, chained and bound in the dark holds of slave ships. Since then, from free man to second-class citizen, the struggles of our peoples have always been towards the same objective: complete freedom.

The newly captured Africans who leaped from the slave ships to their deaths; the young Afro-Americans today facing the might of white supremacy on the streets of the United States; the heroism of Angela Davis are all common factors in the long and bloody history of the black man's constant efforts to free himself from the yoke of slavery.

Common Enemy

The struggle of the Afro-American parallels in many ways the struggles of colonial peoples all over the world to rid themselves of exploiters and slave masters. Dr Martin Luther King was murdered in Tennessee for the same reasons Patrice Lumumba was murdered in the Congo: and by the same forces. The African black man and the American black man are fighting the common enemy, international imperialism, whether in the form of Portuguese and South African racist troops in southern Africa or the police forces of the United States. In Vietnam and Indo-China, the same struggle goes on against the same enemy for the same reasons.

While we wage our present-day struggle, we must recall at some time or other the struggles of the past as well. We Africans who today confront the forces of fascism and racist oppression call all the time on the international progressive community for unity and support for our cause. The international alliance of solidarity with oppressed Africa has a history in which the contribution of progressive America has a place. Not only is Paul Robeson close to us because of his ancestral origins, but because he stands great in the long struggle of the American people, both black and white, for justice both in his homeland and outside.

Although of African descent, Paul Robeson did not come in contact with the cause of African freedom until the end of the 1920s. It was in 1928 that he placed the song 'Ol' Man River' on the musical map of the world. He had come to London then to appear in *Show Boat*. It is perhaps typical of a man from an oppressed community to feel more at home among others in the same plight, rather than in the company of the celebrities who feted him in London. So Paul Robeson felt much easier when in the company of British dockworkers and Welsh miners, and the many Africans whom he met. Many of the Africans in London then were students and political workers, and from these Paul Robeson found a revival of Africa within himself. Among the Africans he must have met in London then were several who were to become noteworthy afterwards—men like Jomo Kenyatta, Nkrumah and others.

Cheap Labour

It might be of interest to take a quick glance at what was happening in Africa at that time. It was a period when more and more efforts were being made by the colonialists to extract the maximum of wealth from Africa in order to bolster up their tottering economy. Law upon law, regulation on regulation were introduced in the regions of East and West Africa to ensure the maximum cheap labour and the highest production of raw materials and other wealth.

In Tanganyika, for example, an unwarranted departure from work was considered a criminal offence; in Uganda regulations enforced every adult African to work for 30 days a year without wages on road construction. Peasants were allowed to sell their crops only within a fixed time in restricted zones and for set prices. The policies of the imperialists transformed the countries of Africa into hell for the Africans and paradise for all foreign exploiters.

Increased exploitation coincided with social and political awareness among Africans and they were inevitably drawn into the anti-imperialist movement. In 1920, the Kikuyu of Kenya set up their first organization; in Tanganyika the establishment of mass peasants' and workers' organizations was a sign of the growing awareness of the working people; in Dahomey in West Africa railway workers launched a significant strike, the first of its kind; likewise workers took action in Senegal, Guinea and on the Ivory Coast. These were the first efforts of the modern working-class and political movements in Africa.

The Kikuyu Central Association sent their secretary general, Jomo Kenyatta, to Britain where he carried on intensive, work on behalf of the African population of Kenya. It is under these circumstances that Paul Robeson had the opportunity of coming in contact with the African situation. Through these contacts, through the inevitable discussions, Robeson became aware of the continent of his ancestors who had been taken from it in chains.

In what was then the Union of South Africa, a rapid consciousness of the importance of the national liberation struggle of the African people was also developing at that time. Together with the demands of the oppressed black people for emancipation, a class consciousness was also taking deep root. African workers saw themselves not only oppressed as black people but also exploited as workers. Inevitably the ideas of socialism caught the interest of more and more Africans.

The New Jerusalem

It is not coincidental that the visit to the USSR by Paul Robeson in 1934 had the same effect on him as it did on the South African leader Gumede. Paul Robeson on visiting the USSR said that he had seen whole nations of so-called primitive peoples now building highly developed socialist republics, working and building countless new factories, schools, universities, all within 20 years. To him this proved the falsity of the colonialist claim that black people would not be able to rule themselves for thousands of years.

Similarly, Gumede, a leader of the African National Congress, told a mass meeting of Africans when he returned from the USSR: 'I have seen the new world to come, where it has already begun. I have been to the new Jerusalem.' He claimed that he had brought the key which would unlock the door to freedom.

Paul Robeson the singer, since those days placed his voice and his talent at the service of the struggle for emancipation of the black oppressed and at the service of all progressive mankind. He was an artist who did not see art in isolation from the problems which beset society, the whole world, the whole of humanity. Becoming more and more aware of the problems of the Afro-American and African people, he was endowed with the wisdom to see the link between black oppression and the rest of the world's problems. It was therefore inevitable that he was drawn into the worldwide anti-fascist struggle of the 1930s and subsequent years.

Caught in the whirlpool of the fight to destroy fascism, a fight that was both dramatic and horrible, it was at this time that he saw clearly that he as an artist, a singer, a man of talent, could not possibly stand aloof from the furore of humanity. He saw that the artist who was honest could never belong in an ivory tower while mankind was engaged in one of the titanic struggles of its history.

I think that his outlook as an artist is significantly illustrated by a speech he made in Albert Hall, London, at a rally in support of the Spanish republic, and reported in the South African anti-imperialist magazine *The Liberator* in 1937. Paul Robeson said then:

Every artist, every scientist, must decide now where he stands. He has no alternative. There is no standing above the conflict on Olympian heights [. . .] The battlefield is everywhere, there is no sheltered rear [. . .] Fascism fights to destroy the culture which Society has created; created through pain and suffering, through desperate toil, but with unconquerable will and lofty vision [. . .] What matters, a man's profession or vocation? Fascism is no respecter of persons. It makes no distinction between combatants and non-combatants [. . .] The artist must take sides; he must elect to right for freedom or for slavery. I have made my choice. I have no alternative. The history of the capitalist era is characterized by the degradation of my people; despoiled of their lands, their women ravished, their culture destroyed [. . .] I say the true artist cannot hold himself aloof. The legacy of culture from our predecessors is in danger. It is the foundation upon which we build a still more lofty edifice. It belongs not only to us, not only to the present generation—it belongs to posterity and must be defended to the death.

These words of Paul Robeson hold good today as they did then.

Council on African Affairs

It was in 1937 that he also helped to found the Council for African Affairs of which he became chairman. This American organization had two main aims: to support the cause of African freedom, collecting funds for various African causes, and also to tell Americans the truth about affairs and events in Africa. Under the first of the Council's objectives, the people of South Africa remember the assistance provided during a severe famine in the eastern part of our country shortly after the Second World War. However, the other aims of the Council provided the opportunity for many Americans to learn the truth about our country. Until then, I believe that most

Americans thought in terms of Edgar Rice Burroughs' stories of Tarzan of the Apes, whenever they heard the continent of Africa mentioned.

The South African people also remember, with appreciation and affection, Paul Robeson's first task when he was released from the United States after the McCarthy persecutions. In 1958, just arrived in Europe from the US, he sang in a special service in St Paul's Cathedral, London, in aid of the fund for the defence of South African political prisoners.

As a South African, I believe I can say with truth that Paul Robeson had a special spot within himself for my country. We recall that in 1950 when workers were shot down by the fascist police at a May Day demonstration, Paul Robeson addressed a meeting of the National Labour Conference for Negro Rights, telling his audience:

> Twelve South African workers now lie dead, shot in a peaceful demonstration by Malan's fascist police; as silent testimony to the fact that [. . .] it is later than they (the oppressors) think in the procession of history, and that rich land must one day return to Africans on whose backs the proud skyscrapers of the Johannesburg rich were built [. . .]

Today the South African people stand on the threshold of the final struggle for the liberation of the black majority and the other oppressed communities. In 1961, the armed struggle for the overthrow of fascism in South Africa was begun; for the overthrow of white supremacy, of injustice, of racial hatred and the exploitation of our hard pressed people. In 1967, the first battalions of our partisan fighters met the racist troops of South Africa and Rhodesia. Our people have died there in the beautiful Zambesi valley, since they have said that they no longer wish to lay down their lives defencelessly. I do not think that the South African movement today claims wholesale success or that victory will come soon. But we have reached the turning point in our history, and we have no doubt that victory will be ours.

Nixon's Lie

Very recently Nixon, president of the United States, in his so-called World Report, claimed that he and his government are against apartheid and racism in South Africa. This is a lie. In the first place, the ruling class of the US cannot be against racism in South Africa and at the same time condone and encourage it in the US. Secondly, the United States of America is the second biggest foreign investor in South Africa and millions of dollars in profits are being sucked from the marrow and blood of African exploitation in South Africa.

We South Africans know full well who are our friends and allies in the United States. They are people like Paul Robeson who has raised his voice in song and worked in the interest of solidarity with the South African people. They are people like the late Martin Luther King, W. E. B. Du Bois, and today, Angela Davis and all the Afro-Americans and genuine democrats fighting for the cause of justice, freedom and humanity in their country.

CHAPTER SIX

The Condition of Culture in South Africa
(1971)

This essay appeared in Présence Africaine, *in a special symposium entitled 'Cultural Days on South Africa'. The other four contributors were Arthur Maimane (1932–2005), Edward Ngaloshe, Lionel Ngakane (1920–2003) and Gerard Sekoto (1913–93). La Guma's piece was the lead article. Though his historical discussion draws from preceding essays, this article marks a deepening critical engagement with the limits of South African culture under apartheid and the concurrent possibilities of a cultural rebirth through the liberation struggle. It is the second in a provisional series of essays on these issues.*

It is perhaps possible, within the environment of developed societies, to create with a certain amount of confidence the impression that art, culture, the level of civilization of a people, have nothing or little to do with socioeconomic and political forces within these societies; that culture has nothing to do with politics. In South Africa, this is not possible.

The proposition of art for the sake of art finds no foothold in the atmosphere of racism, violence and crude exploitation, which is the day-to-day experience of the South African people. We assume that in societies of' advanced technological, scientific and industrial organization, citizens have a greater cultural freedom. South Africa is a country of advanced technology and economic and scientific development. Surgeons have arrived at transplanting the heart from one person to another yet, in many areas of our country, 52 out of every 100 black children born each year die of dietary deficiency diseases before they reach the age of five. Eighty per cent of the population lives at starvation level. We are the greatest producers of gold, but our miners receive $68 per year in wages.

The usurpation of wealth by the ruling white minority has made a mockery of the accumulation of the positive achievements, both material and spiritual, made by mankind.

It is apt to recall an incident surrounding the Beethoven Bicentenary of last year. In South Africa, four African and Asiatic children applied to enter the Beethoven recital competition for young people, arranged by the South African Broadcasting Corporation. Their applications were refused on the grounds that non-white people should concentrate on their 'own' music. Beethoven having been a white man, his music, in the eyes of the South African official purveyors of culture, holds no meaning for black people.

This illustration could well serve as a microcosm of the 'South African way of life'.

The ideology of racism, which postulates the inherent inequality of races, has its roots in the history of man's exploitation by man. Throughout human history these two have developed side by side. At different times and in different countries, racism has assumed different guises, but these various guises always had a common denominator, namely, that there was a superior race. The Herrenvolk was the repository of power, the creator and custodian of civilization and all the noble achievements of humanity, while the so-called inferior race was unintelligent, lazy, subhuman and devoid of all feeling and morality. The inferior race is only human in form, its members are fit only to be servants, slaves, hewers of wood and drawers of water, and to minister to the desires and requirements of the master.

At bottom, racism is the extension of a myth that rationalizes the position of the master, his power and wealth, at the expense of the servant who passes his life in toil to produce that wealth. Slavery, feudalism, the caste system, all these were based on the theory of the superiority of the owners of wealth. With the development of capitalism, the idea of a superior stratum and an inferior stratum was applied as between capitalist and worker. The children of the capitalists inherit all the powers and wealth amassed by their fathers, while the children of the workers inherit poverty, ignorance and disease.

Not satisfied with the robbery of their own people, the industrialists, traders and capitalists of Europe sought new sources of plunder in other parts of the world. In the course of this piracy, whole populations of countries have been decimated. In America the Red Indians and in South Africa the Khoisan people were virtually exterminated, while millions of blacks were transported as slaves. Not only were our forefathers robbed of their land and the right to rule themselves, but their labour mercilessly exploited and their cultural development stifled.

Racism in South Africa, the ideology of white supremacy and black inferiority, was born with the invasion of our country by white settlers in the seventeenth century. Jan van Riebeeck, leader of the first Dutch to settle there, referred to the aboriginals of the Cape as 'a stinking nation'. These first white settlers were later reinforced by the British and by French Huguenots, and the descendants of these are today still being reinforced by Europe.

During the seventeenth, eighteenth and nineteenth centuries, the whites carried out their policy of theft, fraud and aggression against the African people in our country. They were naturally met with resistance. In the Cape alone, nine wars of resistance were waged against the encroaching whites by the Africans.

With the colonial occupation of South Africa came a steady breakdown of African social organization and the almost total alienation of the people from their cultural activities.

* * *

The legal foundation of South African racism was laid when the British betrayed the African people by vesting political power in the hands of the white minority in 1910. The first assault by the all-white parliament on the rights of the African people was the Land Act of 1913. This prohibited Africans from owning land outside the 'reserves' which constitute approximately 13 per cent of the area of South Africa. The remaining 87 per cent was appropriated by the whites. One of the effects arising out of the application of this law was to deprive the African people of the opportunity to publish their thoughts through the printed word.

The earlier conquest by the colonialists had produced new techniques and forms such as the Latin alphabet and the introduction of European literature. By pawning their land, the intellectual elite had been able to set up printing presses and small publishing houses, believing that the white man could be beaten at his own game. Numerous volumes of political and historical treatises, broadsheets and translations were issued. The Land Act and laws controlling Africans in urban areas spelt doom for these efforts and left the Africans to the mercies of the presses of the white overlords. Other laws were passed to prevent publication which might 'rouse hostility'.

We might add that as far back as 1840, articles and verses by Xhosas were appearing in the missionary press and the missionary newspapers like *Isigidimi samaXhosa* in the 1860s and 1870s. They were directed against the colonialist atrocities and very well written.

The first African sociopolitical newspaper, *Imvo Zabantsundu*, under the editorship of John Tengo Jabavu began to appear in 1884, and in the early part of this century newspapers sprang up in different areas.

Intellectual and cultural development has been drastically frustrated by the further extension of separate racial education.

The introduction of 'Bantu Education', at a later stage, brought all African education under the direct authority of a government department and made it a criminal offence to educate children outside the official structure.

Education in many countries reflects the social and economic system and responds to the needs arising out of this. In South Africa, education is part of the grand *apartheid* design. While education in South Africa has always been segregated and had its inequalities, the present system is planned to remould the population's character in terms of white supremacy. The idea that all children are the inheritors of world culture runs completely counter to the educational system imposed on the people of the Republic of South Africa.

Insofar as the African is concerned, there is no better description of the intent of 'Bantu Education' than the one given by Verwoerd himself, when Minister of Native Affairs. Addressing the House of Assembly in 1953, he stated:

> When I have control of native education, I will reform it so that natives will be taught from childhood to realize that equality with Europeans is not for them. People who believe in equality with Europeans are not desirable as teachers for natives [. . .]. When my Department controls native education it will know for what class of higher education a native is fitted and whether he will have a chance in life to use his knowledge.

He stated further: 'There is no place for him (the African) in the European community above the level of certain forms of labour.' And, 'What is the use of teaching a Bantu child mathematics when it cannot use it in practice?'

J. N. Le Roux, who later became Minister of Agriculture, asked: 'Who will do the manual work if you give the natives an academic education? I am in thorough agreement with the view that we should conduct our schools in such a way that the native who attends those schools will know that to a great extent, he must be the labourer in the country.'

Practically enunciating the principles of education in Nazi Germany, Verwoerd said also: 'Why should girls bother with Higher Mathematics, or Art, or Drama or Literature? They could have babies without that sort of knowledge.'

Separate education for Coloureds (mixed blood) and Asiatics is also a feature of the educational system. The proportion of funds expended by the government on the education of the different racial communities is, of course, in accordance with *apartheid* policy.

The total allocation to African education for the financial year 1969–1970 was less than 0.4 per cent of South Africa's Gross National Product of about R10,000 million. South Africa spends about 4.5 per cent of its national income on education and training at all levels. In 1965, when the Gross National Product was R774 million, R326 million were applied to education. Of this, 77 per cent was spent on whites, 9 per cent on Coloureds, 4 per cent on Asians and 8.9 per cent on Africans. In terms of per head of population, this meant R74 for each white child per year, R17 for each Coloured, R26 for each Asian and R2.39 for each African child.

It must also be added that the national income of the white population is more than 10 times that of the other three races combined.

* * *

'University Colleges' have been established for Africans on a tribal basis, and there is one for Coloureds and another for Asiatics. While there is compulsory education for white children between the age of 7 and 16 years, and for Coloured and Asiatics between 7 and 14 'where there is a demand for it and accommodation permits', there is no compulsory education for African children. In addition, Africans have to contribute large sums of money towards the cost of education over and above taxation. They must pay for their own books except lower primary readers, for all stationery, for handwork materials, school and examination fees, uniforms, transport and meals. African parents and school committees raise money to pay additional teachers' salaries. School boards must also raise half the cost of erecting schools for classes from higher primary onwards, and must pay for their maintenance.

While the government attempts to whitewash its racist policy by claiming that it is assisting the African to develop his 'own culture' by educating him in his own language, the facts show that actually less and less Africans are achieving adequate education.

All teaching is done in the vernacular, up to and including the First Form, and it is intended that this process should continue up to matriculation. But when the matriculation examination in one of the tribal languages is taken, the student will automatically lose eligibility for entrance into any mixed university (for which he must have a permit) and his 'Bantu' qualification will qualify him only for entrance into his 'tribal' university. Education in the tribal language has been farcical and has led to a startling decline in educational standards, for there are few or no advanced textbooks available in those languages. Likewise, the sudden switch from the vernacular in primary school to English and Afrikaans, the official State languages in secondary schools, has resulted in the standard of attendance and passes to drop disastrously.

In 1959, 197 Africans obtained university degrees in South Africa, a great many of them actually through correspondence courses. In 1960, the number was 186; in 1962, 105; in 1964, 103. In 1960, out of a non-white population of nearly 15 million, there were only 130 non-white doctors in South Africa. Recently, it was decreed that the qualifications obtained overseas (e.g. Glasgow and Bombay) by doctors would not be accepted in South Africa.

The government is of course extremely careful in providing the African schools with literature which conforms with its conception of cultural advancement. Thus, set books are screened by the Bantu Education authorities, and only those desirable in their eyes are allowed into the schools. As a result, the quality of works published in the African languages is poor, and it is possible that a large number of valuable manuscripts remain today unpublished.

Inevitably, the white community itself must suffer as a result of this cultural bias. Within the environment of the racial structure, the white child grows up to despise the African. This mentality is fortified by the concept of 'Christian National Education'. In a book, *The Power of Prejudice in South African Education*, the educationist F. E. Auerbach remarked on differences in presentation of history to Afrikaans- and English-speaking children:

> This trend has been influenced by the philosophy of Christian National Education. It is characterized by much emphasis on the history of Europeans in South Africa, and of the forbears of the Afrikaans-speaking community especially [. . .]. White children who learn history and related subjects with this emphasis [. . .] are likely to be imbued with the erroneous belief that Africans are permanently tribal and inherently inferior to Whites, and that Western civilization and Christianity are racially linked with people of white or Caucasian stock.

The writer also quoted from a First Form textbook: 'When the Lord planted a new nation at the tip of Africa [. . .] this people was to stand on the verge of being wiped out, and yet was to be saved in a wonderful manner.'

* * *

The mentality of the *laager* permeates white society. The laager gives the impression of a defensive position, but in fact the whites are rallied into the laager for the most brutal aggression against non-whites. The 'black menace' has been waved like a rallying flag, but it is really the black flag of piracy. Far from the tribal mentality succeeding with Africans, it has actually permeated the minds of the whites. The art and literature of this minority community continues to be bound within the narrow confines of their exclusiveness. A commentator writing in a London newspaper some time ago remarked that, after so many years of ascendancy, the white community of South Africa has produced no musical composition of lasting value, not a single opera, not a painting of note. Its literature bears the stamp of the tribal ethos, and any of its authors who might break out in a spirit of liberalism, like Paton, Gordimer or Fugard, is considered with suspicion and liable for persecution.

Still more recently, it was suggested that the proposed opera house in Cape Town would become a white elephant since there was no white interest in that form of entertainment and that the building be given over to the Coloured community whose amateur opera company has gained exceptional praise both from locals and visitors from abroad. In fact, a Coloured singer from South Africa is now contracted to the Metropolitan Opera in New York.

The purveyors of *apartheid* culture seem determined to reduce the entire population to their own limited standards. Laws are consistently enacted to prevent any advancement towards a non-racial outlook. Under the Suppression of Communism Act, the Publications and Entertainments Act, for example, thousands of books and other publications have been prohibited from importation and circulation. Progressive newspapers and magazines have been closed down. The Minister of Justice has gazetted lists of South African writers and journalists whose works may not be read. According to UNESCO statistics, 13,000 titles were banned in South Africa by 1969.

The Group Areas Act divides the country into racially segregated districts, denying one group the right of 'occupying' the 'area' of another. As a result, whole non-white communities have been evicted from districts declared 'white only'. Thus schools, theatres and churches used by such communities have been lost to them, or physically destroyed. Where in the past non-whites might have had access to halls, theatres, open spaces, etc. for cultural activities, today most of these amenities are situated in 'white' areas and permission is required by non-whites to use them. Usually this permission is withheld. The law allows no artists of different races to perform together or for mixed audiences. This law applies equally to sporting facilities.

While it is difficult to prevent radio programmes from being available to the general population, the South African Broadcasting Corporation has, however, established special 'Bantu' and 'Coloured' programmes. At the moment, the introduction of television to South Africa for the first time is under consideration. It has been observed that television in South Africa would inevitably be a boring experience in view of the plethora of regulations conditioning entertainment and culture.

* * *

The foregoing is a general account of the burdens placed upon the cultural development of the South African people, and of the African population particularly.

To doubt that this state of affairs will ever come to an end would be to doubt also the inevitable progress of humanity and that the patience of the African people is limited. Already the democratic spirit that is present in every true culture is showing its restlessness to emerge in our country. Juxtaposed with oppression, it has developed the democratic movement whose voice is heard in the songs, the writings and poetry, the militant literature of resistance. As long as racism and oppression last in Southern Africa, culture will take this form. When the oppressed have freed themselves from the shackles of economic, social and political limitations, flowers will bloom anew in an environment of happiness in a life lived in dignity, a life of freedom and comradeship among our peoples.

Perhaps it is a manifestation of the untiringly progressive spirit of humanity that within the atmosphere of racism, and in spite of the atrocious handicaps placed upon them, the oppressed African people and other non-white communities have thrust to the fore their intellectual members of note. We might be accused of boasting if it is pointed out that more African intellectuals have emerged in our country than in most African countries. These have longstanding traditions and include prominent authors, painters, educationists and public leaders known all over the world, such as the late Chief Luthuli, the first African to be awarded the Nobel Prize.

In conditions of appalling racial hatred they have been able to overcome racial and nationalistic exclusiveness and egotism, paying great service to the spirit of democracy, which is struggling to emerge in South Africa. The influence of South African democratic forces has been spread to other parts of the African continent in many ways.

First of all, this influence is still being spread by the thousands of migrant workers who come to the mines from nearby countries as contract labourers under conventions signed between their white masters many years ago. Returning to their countries, these workers have spread South African experience, ever since the early part of this century when the Portuguese government signed the first convention to send Mozambique labour to the Transvaal province.

Southern Rhodesian plantation owners had noted the concrete manifestations of this influence way back in the early 1920s when they became incensed by the fact that seasonal workers, after their stay in South Africa, became 'troublemakers', held rallies and meetings and tried to set up organizations on the pattern of those in South Africa.

Many statesmen and party leaders of the African States have gone through the school of political struggle in our country, and they admit the profound lessons learnt from these experiences.

In the face of tremendous odds, in the face of the pressure put upon us, we do not fear the future, confident of the final emergence of the true ideals of humanity, culture and progress in our country. Although many of us have been forced into exile, to live as refugees in strange countries, I do not believe we have become so demoralized as to doubt the final victory. But finding ourselves in this new environment, we are compelled to turn our eyes away from our African continent now and then, and ask the question: 'How is it that these people around us could allow the predatory excursions of their rulers to bring such misery to our people?' This is the France of Villon, of Danton, Robespierre, Voltaire; of Zola, Hugo and other great cultural giants. It is also the France of the Paris Commune whose hundredth anniversary we celebrate this year.

Yet our people are at the mercy of Mirage jet fighters and Mystère bombers, Alouette helicopters, among other things.

We hope that this small appeal we make for the spirit of 1789, to touch our people, will go out from here and be heard by the people of France.

CHAPTER SEVEN

GDR Opera Supports Liberation Struggle
(1974)

This short review for Sechaba *further demonstrates La Guma's commitment to minor genres of writing—in this instance, a report of an opera production in East Germany. These occasional pieces reveal his profound interest in promoting cultural life and literacy within the liberation struggle. Like many other contributions, they also provide a makeshift diary of where he travelled and what he witnessed while in exile.*

The German State Opera of the GDR launched its latest production on November 17. It was *Reiter der Nacht,* an opera based upon the South African Peter Abrahams' novel *Path of Thunder.* The novel concerned the love of a white landowner's daughter for Lanny, the Coloured schoolteacher, in the little country town on the South African highveld. This somewhat improbable, nevertheless tragic, affair is, however, adequately dealt with by the libretto of Gunther Deicke who manages to present a topically political production on the stage of this early work of Abrahams, considering all the emotionalism and humanitarianism involved. The composer Prof. Ernst Hermann Meyer uses a modern form for his score for the opera and so avoids much of the sugary sentimentality with which much operatic music is associated, especially tragic love stories.

So good is the production that South Africans attending the premiere felt as if they were transported into the midst of a typically Coloured rural community in their motherland. Unfortunately, the few white characters were however costumed throughout in the neat bush jackets and riding breeches with which colonialists are usually caricatured so that those who have seen the real Afrikaner farmers are apt to smile at this portrayal of the 'Baas'. However, this is a detail.

The opera as a whole does much to focus on the inhumanity of apartheid, and one is happy to see that the pessimistic and negative ending of the original story is replaced by a more inspiring climax when the people rise to disarm the tyrants and avenge the murdered lovers.

It is hoped that the opera will be translated and performed outside the GDR. This would be a useful contribution to the movement of solidarity with the South African liberation struggle.

CHAPTER EIGHT

Culture and Liberation
(1976)

This piece first appeared in Sechaba. *It is the third in a provisional series of articles by La Guma on the role of culture in South Africa and the liberation struggle. It is notable for demonstrating the influence of Amílcar Cabral (1924–73) on his thinking. This essay was later republished in* World Literature Written in English *in 1979.*

The topic being presented here has been the subject of so many conferences, seminars and workshops that one's immediate reaction on being asked to reintroduce it is that there is little new to say, and that all the old ideas can conveniently be repeated. It is therefore difficult to avoid the risk of repetition, but since the cause of art and the cause of liberation is centuries old, the inevitability of reiterating the finest principles of both is unavoidable, and in this turbulent age, their emphasis is essential.

One may ask what has art, culture, literature got to do with the liberation? The question is usually asked by those who wish to separate culture or art from politics, for when we talk of liberation we are talking of it in its political sense, otherwise we would not be present here.

But life is the criterion through and by which the artist's imagery and literary observations are evaluated. When we talk of the relationship between art and life, we mean that unity between what is reflected and the manner in which it is reflected, and this is the quintessence of art.

What we respond to when we read a poem or a novel is not only life but also its artistic merit. But life does not merely mean breathing in and out but involves also man's struggle to reach higher levels of civilization, of social, economic and cultural status, the mighty struggle to conquer his own disabilities and the forces of nature. So then life must include men's struggle for liberation from all that hinders his development, and as we have said that life is the stimulation of artistic endeavour, art cannot be separated from this desire for liberation.

The struggle of the peoples of what we sometimes call the Third World for national liberation and independence has become a titanic force for man's progress and is without doubt one of the most dynamic and most important features of our time.

Perhaps we might even say that for the first time man has come to realize the totality of his planet Earth; that all Earth is inhabited by man and that the principles which seemed once to be the monopoly of apparently learned metropolitan countries now apply equally to those once looked upon as lesser beings. We by no means defend imperialist rule by recognizing that, by reducing the world's dimensions, it gave it greater horizons; that it revealed new phases in the development of human societies and, in spite of or as a result of prejudices, discriminations and crimes it perpetrated, helped to impart a deeper knowledge of man as a whole, as a unit in the complex and diverse character of his development.

Indeed paying all respect to Europe, I believe that at the pass of Thermopylae where certain Spartans died for independence centuries ago, there was erected an inscription, which says: All the world is the grave of heroes.

Unfortunately, through historical circumstances the Philistines of Europe—ignoring the lofty principles which had risen around them, since the times of ancient philosophers, the words of 'La Marseillaise'; the works of Heine and Goethe; the ideals of Byron—set out to plunder and subject other peoples.

Royal Hunt of the Sun

This was described as a civilizing mission. It is hardly a matter of question as to who were the more 'civilized': those naively friendly Indians who welcomed Columbus, the people of the Cape who met van Riebeeck; or their European visitors who returned these greetings quickly with firepower and 'The Royal Hunt of the Sun'.

'A clash of cultures' it is designated: these burnings for accumulation of gold by the Inquisition, this description in van Riebeeck's diary of the massacred and plundered local people as 'a stinking nation'; this blowing from a cannon of Sepoy 'mutineers' and the 'civilizing' war cry—'The only good Indian is a dead one'—as the prairies were seized from their owners.

In Europe herself, the common people groaned under the yokes of her own slavery and feudalism. The example of the Russian Revolution released the energies of millions of people, gave them confidence in the ultimate success of their own aspirations. The period after the Second World War in particular saw the development and success of anti-imperialist struggles, particularly in Africa and Asia. The degrees of independence might vary from country to country, but certainly major advances have been made in destroying the old colonial empires governed from Europe.

The peoples of these countries are reaching towards modern forms of civilization and culture, working to end the heritage of the colonial past, to catch up what they missed during centuries of foreign oppression and to take their rightful place alongside advanced countries.

On a subject people, colonial domination may be imposed by way of suppressing traditional ways of living and thinking, together with the introduction of alien ideas and values, since the essential feature of colonization is the destruction of a people's identity. This may be done through various agencies of the colonial power.

The Kenyan writer, Ngũgĩ wa Thiong'o, in a university paper, says:

A Chinese, a Frenchman, a German or an Englishman first imbibes his national literature before attempting to take in other words. That the central taproot of his cultural nourishment should lie deep in his native soil is taken for granted. This a-b-c of education is followed in most societies because it is demanded by the practice and the experience of living and growing. Not so in Africa, the West Indies, the colonized world as a whole, despite the crucial role of the twin fields of literature and culture in making a child aware of and rediscover his environment.

[. . .]

The other day I found my own son trying to memorize a poem by William Wordsworth. I asked him: What are daffodils? He looked in the book: Oh, they are just little fishes in a lake! [. . .] (At another school) they told us about a poem of fourteen lines called a sonnet written by one William Shakespeare comparing old age to winter!

As I once tried to explain in another talk, if many Africans become alienated from their cultural background, if they are so uprooted that they dare not assert it openly any longer, this background never dies completely. It survives the death of tribal economic structures and remains hidden, ready to be used as a basis for future development.

The late Amílcar Cabral said: 'The exercise of imperialist domination demands cultural oppression, but the people are able to create and develop a liberation movement because it keeps its culture alive in the teeth of organized repression of cultural life—because its politico-military resistance being destroyed, it continues to resist culturally.' (UNESCO Paper)

The colonial power cannot impose a complete cultural occupation. The majority of the people retains their identity and are the one entity really able to preserve and create it—that is, they can make history.

A people's cultural manifestations, including their literature, oral and written, their songs and poetry, reflect this resistance, reflect the various stages of development of the anti-imperialist movement.

At a certain time, political resistance may take on various forms, politically passive or active, economic or armed; as it develops, it adopts other political methods, including violence, to end imperialist violence.

Perhaps the best examples of this cultural-plus-political manifestations are contained in the poetry of the former Portuguese colonies. Investigation shows that the history of poetry of the people of these territories for centuries under the Portuguese is also the history of their revolution.

We Are One People

The liberation struggle is the most complex expression of the people's cultural energy, of their identity, of their dignity. Liberation opens up new avenues, helps to enrich art and culture, and in the course of the anti-imperialist struggle finds new forms of expression. These manifestations also become a powerful instrument for political information and training, not only for independence but also in the great battle for progress.

What should be taken into consideration is that the anti-imperialist struggle involves that of national liberation, a struggle for the consolidation of a cultural community, for national statehood, national territory, a national economy. Colonialism and its attendant manifestations prevent this process.

In addition, the anti-imperialist struggle has united millions of people across borders and across continents. Out of the artistic manifestations of this struggle can also be traced a common desire, ambition, aspiration, that of international friendship and indeed a brotherhood, based upon equality, which includes the fusion of all that is good in all cultures into the basis of an eventual common world culture.

We have talked of this struggle for national liberation, of anti-imperialism. This implies, of course, that imperialism and its colonial system is not yet dead.

Only recently the people of Angola entered victoriously the final stages of their battle to set up an independent state. To the south of them the white minority regimes still menace and frustrate the ambitions of the peoples of Namibia, Zimbabwe and South Africa, who are engaged in heroic resistance to these regimes. A quotation from *A Short History of the African National Congress* illustrates concisely the cultural basis for the national struggle of the African majority:

> The most astonishing feature of that conference (1912) was the number of tribes who sent representatives. There were Zulus, Xhosas, Tswana, Sothos, Vendas, Shangaans, Tsongas and others. These tribes, some of them only recently locked in feuds, had looked upon each other with suspicion; each was proud and could only, with difficulty, look upon others as equals. For two years before they had seen the bitter fruits of their disunion and division when, at the formation of the Union (of South Africa), they had all been ignored when Boer and Briton met to form the so-called Union of South Africa.

As Dr Pixley ka Isaka Seme, prominent leader and lawyer, stated at the Conference: 'We are one people. These divisions, these jealousies, are the cause of all our woes and of all our backwardness and ignorance today.' And further: 'The ANC realized from the outset that the problems of forging unity among Africans was the KEY to our freedom struggle.' The formation of the ANC, therefore, marked the birth of a nation whose foundation was laid in a stirring call by Dr P. I. Seme, later to become its treasurer general, when in an article written in 1911 he declared: 'The demon of racialism, the aberrations of Xhosa–Fingo feuds, the animosity that exists between Zulus and the Tsongas, between the Basuto and every other Native, must be buried and forgotten. We are one people.'

To appreciate what culture means in the pre-liberation movement needs a distinction between culture and cultural manifestation. Cabral said that culture is the dynamic synthesis, at the level of individual or community consciousness, of the material and historical reality of a society or a human group, of the relations existing between man and nature, as well as among men and among social categories. Clearly a multiplicity of social categories and particularly of ethnic groups makes the role of culture in the liberation movement more difficult to define, but this complexity cannot and must not lessen the importance to the movement, most of all to recognize and define the contradictory data so as to maintain the positive values and channel them in the direction of the struggle, with an added dimension: *the national dimension.*

Within the indigenous society the action of the liberation movement on the cultural plain entails cultural unity, corresponding to the moral and political unity necessary for the dynamics of the struggle. With the opening up of closed groups, tribal or ethnic, racist aggressiveness tends to disappear and give way to understanding, solidarity and mutual respect, a unity in struggle and in a common destiny in the face of foreign rule. These are sentiments which the mass of the people adopt readily if the process is not hindered by political opportunism. South African white domination moved away from a policy of elimination or enslavement of the immediate local population to an advanced stage of capitalism and imperialism, within which the black population serves as colonial serfs and a major part of the industrial working class, all within one geographical boundary. It must be observed that the attitude of the ruling power is hopelessly contradictory. On the one hand, the white ruling class has to maintain divisions, a system of apparent conservation conditioned by confinement of the indigenous society to geographic zones, or reserves called homelands or Bantustans, to destroy the cultural unity of the African people; on the other hand, to maintain in its industrial enterprises a working class contrary to ethnic or tribal divisions. The late Dr Verwoerd conveniently equated 'tribe' with 'nation' and claimed that the so-called Bantu homelands established the rights of the different 'nations'.

Mr John E. Fobes, deputy director-general of UNESCO, stated in Paris in April 1975:

> South Africa has made much of her protection of separate cultures.
>
> What does this amount to? Does this mean restoring the economic and political bases on which independent African civilizations were built? Certainly not. These were broken in a series of wars of conquest, in the introduction of wage labour and in the alienation of the land. Does this mean restoring the trade routes, the cultural exchanges which archaeologists now tell us existed before European conquest? Certainly not, for in the place of so-called tribes absorbing each other, constructing as did the Zulus, a coherent kingdom, we have tribal separation. Does the South African protection of separate cultures mean what UNESCO means by the diversity of cultures?
>
> Certainly not. For the diversity of cultures also implies a relative equality of power relations and the right of groups to maintain, to change, to borrow. It is for the culture groups themselves to decide the direction of evolution of their cultures. On the other hand, we have in South Africa a government-imposed 'traditionalism'—in fact, the use of traditional culture to maintain the legitimacy of a culture of domination.[1]

---

1 John E. Fobes, 'Seminar on South Africa', UN Special Committee Against Apartheid (Paris, April 1975).

Mr Fobes further put the matter in a nutshell: 'The Republic's protection of cultures means for Africans the external trappings of once great cultures reduced to the folkloric and the caricature.'

'To maintain the legitimacy of a culture of domination'—these words explain the white supremacists' rationalization of their fear of being culturally drowned in the sea of liberated black cultural development. 'Our culture will be obliterated' or 'We shall be swamped.' This, direct economics and politics apart, is the rallying cry of the white laager.

It is an old pretext. Forgetting that Europe gained from mathematics, the compass and a multitude of cultural and scientific contributions made by those outside Europe, the racist insists that the blacks or Asiatics have nothing to offer but a return to barbarism. A variation of 'East is East and West is West, and never the twain shall meet.'

Old Clichés

It is not a digression to point out that Japan, constituting a people who prefer chopsticks to knives and forks, is today one of the great industrial nations of the world. Nearer to our home, we might point out that the impoverished and 'barbaric' black working-class man, the most advanced industrial enterprises, so-called manifestations of 'Western' culture in modern South Africa. The preservation of 'our culture', the 'clash' of cultures are old clichés which, consciously or unconsciously, racists have mouthed for latter centuries in order to preserve a system of economic exploitation and deliberate subjugation of so-called inferior peoples. We say 'latter centuries' because contrary to the belief that racial prejudice always existed, racism is a phenomenon of capitalism and did not exist as a social phenomenon before the advent of that system. The slaves of ancient Greece and Rome knew of no difference in their master's attitude to them dictated by their outward appearance. The white gladiator Spartacus received the same treatment, took the same risks as the gladiator from Africa. Moslems were received into the Christian or Jewish religions in the Middle Ages, and vice versa without consideration for racial origin; religious differences were the main ideological reasons for overrunning alien lands in the epoch of feudalism.

The development of the plantation system and production for profit gave rise to the slave trade. Africa became the main source of supply. At first, the plantation owners and traders were content to claim that slavery was essential for the nation's economic prosperity. Later, when the opponents of slavery stepped up their opposition, the idea was propagated that blacks were inferior beings with no sense of morality, they were apes, they had no souls. Racism became a characteristic in the ideology of exploitation since these times.

Thus, it is doubly easy 'for the embattled White minority, defending their "culture" from the majority Black hordes seeking liberation, to free themselves from the oppressing White nation, to fulfil a God-given mission on the tip of Africa, defending civilization against barbarism.'

It is in the name of these so-called principles that many innocent people of western Europe have been led into supporting or passively acquiescing to the racist regime of South Africa. We will say nothing here of the support of big business, international monopolies, multinationals for South African racism. They do it for the blatant purpose of reaping super-profits from the exploitation of the blacks. Compelled to make gestures in favour of assisting black economic backwardness, some of their few hypocritical contributions have made no difference to the dire plight of the African majority.

Arms are supplied to the racist South Africans in the same old name of 'Western' civilization, culture and anti-Communism. We will not deal in detail with these matters here, nor with the questions of apartheid in its details. No doubt these will come out in open discussion. What we are rather confronted with is the question of whether those here are content to let this matter go by the board. All men of letters have always been interested in the question of the peoples' freedom. No doubt you will be able to point out numerous Netherlands examples of the artist's identification with progress, justice and the true development of culture.

Authors, playwrights have condemned apartheid in South Africa, withheld their plays from segregated audiences. Inside South Africa, censorship in the name of a minority government curtails publication. Long lists of names of writers banned in South Africa have been published. Local white writers have also started fretting over the claustrophobic cultural atmosphere prevailing. This is dealt with in a separate brochure.

Whither the Dutch?

We ask the question: Are the Dutch men of letters, Dutch intellectuals, the public of the Netherlands going to stand aside from the worldwide support of the South African people and the black majority in particular in their struggle against white domination?

In terms of the ordinary citizen, it may be to the credit of the Netherlands that figures for immigration to South Africa placed this country fifth on the list with 9,434 immigrants between 1966 and November 1972. From 1971, there has been a decrease in immigration to South Africa.

Mr Edwin Ogbu of Nigeria, former head of the UN Special Committee Against Apartheid, declared last year: 'Let us make it clear that every white migrant is, in effect, a usurper of the inalienable rights of millions of black people of the country to land, employment opportunities and freedom [...] Every white migrant is a violator of the United Nations Charter and the Universal

Declaration of Human Rights, as well as the principle of trade unionism.'[2]

In June 1972, there were three South African Immigration Department offices in The Hague, which I am afraid might be construed as the Netherland's government's disregard for the Declaration of Human Rights and the UN Charter. But we mention immigration also because of its direct bearing on the South African racist's bigoted and intolerant attitude towards cultures even among their own race. The study for the UN Unit on Apartheid (White Immigration to Southern Africa) from which Mr Ogbu was quoted above also points out: 'Intending immigrants are asked to state their religion . . . (towards the end) of the 1960s when there were many Afrikaner protests about numbers of people arriving from Southern Europe—Portugal, Spain, Italy, Greece [. . .] Thus the Nasionale Jeugbond (Nationalist Youth) expressed fear that the large number of immigrants threatened the identity of the Afrikaner', calling for a policy of immigration 'which will not endanger the future of the Afrikaner nation'. One no longer need quote Adolf Hitler on the dubious question of 'racial purity'.

A delegate to a Transvaal Nationalist Party Congress protested, 'Coloured people cannot marry my daughter, but when she is 21, a Portuguese can'. There is also the 1820 Memorial Settlers Association for English-speaking immigrants.

The Immigrants Selection Board, established in terms of the Aliens Act 1937, grants permanent residence only to those who are 'likely to become readily assimilated with the European inhabitants and to become a desirable inhabitant of the Republic within a reasonable period'.[3] It needs no explanation that 'a desirable inhabitant of the Republic' means one who quickly accepts the status quo—white supremacy.

---

[2] United Nations Unit on Apartheid, 'White Immigration to Southern Africa', Notes and Documents No. 3/75.

[3] United Nations Unit on Apartheid, 'Paper by the Christian Institute of South Africa', n.d.

It has been argued inter alia that immigrants from Europe 'will leaven the white society, bringing new attitudes and insights, and that this will eventually erode the racist attitudes of white South Africans'. But empirical research has shown this to be a false expectation. Professor John Stone has found that 'British immigrants drifted rapidly into the structure of South African society and were rapidly acculturated into South Africa's racial norms and dominant values.'[4]

For those cultural workers who suffer from the same illusion that their humanistic and progressive works might help to influence progressively the attitudes of the white South Africans, let us point out that for generations they have had the benefit of the humanistic literature and drama of Europe: Ibsen, Shakespeare, Whitman and a host of others. The effect has been like pouring water on a duck's back. Year after year, white theatregoers have complacently lived out their lives made comfortable by the exploitation of their black servants. Each election sees the white political parties, all of which uphold racism and inequality in one form or another, returned to Parliament.

Psychological Cripple

The Dutch public might be interested in a theatre advertisement appearing in one of the South African dailies a little while ago. 'This is a moving play,' said the notices. 'A poignant and sincere play.' It was *The Diary of Anne Frank* performed at a theatre for white people only.

If there are white artists and writers in South Africa itself who are concerned with apartheid, we may look on them with some degree of regard, but we who are engaged in the struggle to destroy once and for all the very basis of racism, apartheid and national oppression are not impressed by the obscurantist emphasis on

---

[4] United Nations Unit on Apartheid, 'Paper by the Christian Institute of South Africa'.

black–white sexual gymnastics, the negative elusion of the pass laws, the psychological cripples who may engage in revealing fruitless dialogues and never dare, in the words of Athol Fugard himself, 'like the revolutionary, to break eggs in order to make an omelette'. This literature glosses over injustice and oppression and does not inspire the resistance to oppression.

The dynamic of the South African people will always be represented by the militant poetry and songs, by the writings of those who do not fear to reflect in real struggle, that is, to overthrow white supremacy, not merely nibble at the fringes, lagging behind the inevitable advance. If, as we have said, life is the criterion for artistic creation, then the dynamism of the developing revolutionary situation in South Africa will inspire the artistic manifestations of our people, their artists, writers, poets, black and white. Our art and culture, as somebody stated elsewhere, will be warmed by the fires of the battle for liberty. As this struggle develops the people's art, as we have pointed out in the case of the former Portuguese territories, will reflect our struggle. Revolutionary poetry is used in evidence today against students arrested for opposing the South African state; academics, black and white, are being arrested for identifying themselves with the struggle for liberation.

Drawn by the lodestone of the people's struggle, those who unhappily have had to accept the ruling power's cultural colonization in segregated universities, fed on the crumbs of so-called Bantu education, are forming part of the people's wide movement for national liberation.

Southern Africa today is rapidly developing a revolutionary situation, which can turn the tide once and for all in favour of genuine democracy and progress. The heroic examples of Mozambique and Angola have raised the hopes and spirits of millions still ruled by the barbarian vandals represented by the white racist minorities. But changes are wrought by the active participation of people.

Pariah of the World

As we have tried to point out earlier, the anti-colonialist struggle has drawn millions of people together from all parts of the world. The colonized countries, the newly independent countries, the progressive, enlightened people of the metropolitan countries, all form this mighty force, reinforcing each other, in the struggle for the progress of all mankind. South Africa has no longer become a localized issue.

As Mr Dramane Ouattara, executive secretary OAU, stated to the United Nations:

> The oppressed people of South Africa . . . have committed themselves to the struggle to recover their legitimate rights in accordance with the Universal Declaration of Human Rights . . . the entire world, the international community and all international gatherings have recognized that . . . it was vital to help the liberation movements in this duty of liberation. Today more than in the past, this assistance has become a necessity. It must be multifaceted: political, diplomatic, cultural, economic and material.

The result has been that these forces, guided by the strategy and tactics of the struggling African people, have made South African racism the pariah of the world. Attacked in the United Nations, expelled from many international agencies, harassed from all sides, support for the white supremacy regime and its policies in all degrees has become the hallmark of reaction in our world. We ask how much more the Dutch people, the intellectuals and cultural workers of the Netherlands will contribute to helping in the universal cause of solidarity with the oppressed people of South Africa.

What must be borne in mind is that while the success of the national liberation movement unites all sections and ethnic groups of a people under the banner of nationalism, and it accelerates the process of nationhood; while cultural manifestations will reflect this fusion in terms of national art, national literature and so on, the influence of the international character of the struggle at the same time gives the national form an international content.

Other things apart, this depends also on whether the liberation movement establishes the precise objectives to be achieved on the way to regaining the right of the people it represents and whom it is assisting to make its own history, to control freely the disposal of its productive forces, with an end to the eventual development of a richer culture—popular, national, scientific and universal.

Highest Aspiration

The South African racists wish to maintain the African people, and indeed the whites themselves, within the narrow confines of a 'traditionalist' past. But the advances of the twentieth century cannot entertain the anachronisms of stultifying tribalism and 'laagerism', inevitable as their doom may be. Culture is closely linked with economic and social reality, with the level of productive forces and the methods of production in the society in which it struggles or flourishes. Thus, it is obvious that the oppressed once liberated must make use of the advances made within society in order to advance itself.

The main concept of the struggle in South Africa today is the liberation of the African majority. At the same time, its programme states that South Africa belongs to all who live in it, black and white, these include the other oppressed minorities—Coloured and Asiatic; that the wealth and the development of such resources shall not be manipulated by any one group or individual. The revolutionary programme of the African National Congress, with whom the writer identifies, states: 'A democratic government of the people shall ensure that all national groups have equal rights, as such, to achieve their destiny in a united South Africa.'

Given equality, the universal and inevitable cultural exchanges with mutual respect will lead eventually to the fusion of everything worthy in the cultures of all peoples, leading eventually to the aforementioned development of a richer, popular and universal character of the South African people.

In conclusion, let us hear again the words of Nelson Mandela at the Rivonia Trial, which resulted in his imprisonment for life:

> In their relationship with us, South African Whites regard it as fair and just to pursue policies which have outraged the conscience of mankind and of honest and upright men throughout the civilized world. They suppress our aspirations, bar our way to freedom, and deny us opportunities to promote our moral and material progress, to secure ourselves from fear and want. All the good things of life are reserved for the White folk and we Blacks are expected to be content to nourish our bodies with such pieces of food as drop from the tables of men with white skins. This is the White man's standard of justice and fairness. Herein lies his conception of ethics. Whatever he himself may say in his defence, the White man's moral standards in this country must be judged by the extent to which he has condemned the vast majority of its inhabitants to serfdom and inferiority.
>
> We, on the other hand, regard the struggle against colour discrimination and for the pursuit of freedom and happiness as the highest aspiration of all men.

CHAPTER NINE

Has Art Failed South Africa?
(1977)

This article first appeared in The African Communist *under the pseudonym of Gala. It is the fourth in a series of essays that argued for the inseparability of art from politics, writing from revolution.*

The rolling veld, the karoo in spring, still lifes of wild flowers and the majesty of the Drakensberg Mountains, these are the subjects chosen by many South African painters, and they decorate the houses of the well-to-do or are lined up in various art galleries.

It is concentration on this aspect of the South African scene which has compelled the painter Cecil Skotnes to comment (*Rand Daily Mail*, 3 November 1976) on 'a singular lack of guts' in South African art. 'Since the high days of the little Bushman who set down a complete document of his lifestyle, no school of art or period has ever attempted to come to terms with what we call "South African",' he says.

Skotnes observes that South Africa at present is embroiled in 'a classic revolutionary situation' and that the stimulation arising from this situation should affect all the elements of the creative society and in particular the artist.

> In South Africa there is a small bright light pointing the direction we must travel. The main artistic contribution of that direction has been made by our writers [...] they have written without fear and sometimes at great personal

discomfort. From Plaatje to Gordimer and Fugard, from Eglington to Grey, the accent has always been man and his living in our sun-kissed land. Not so in painting and sculpture.

Putting aside censorship and the practice of apartheid, reading is of course among the most popular cultural pursuits of the people. They can go to libraries, buy from second-hand stalls and bookshops, but it is only the rich who can afford to purchase individual works of fine art, and the ruling minority prefers not to have its walls hung with reminders of the oppressive society it perpetrates. In addition to the ideological influence of the ruling clique, the painter and sculptor are also bound to consider the home market while the writer often has the chance of selling his work abroad.

In more open class societies, art for the general populace has to a certain extent gained ground. One can, for instance, name places like Mexico where the gigantic public murals of Rivera and Orozco are on view. In the socialist countries a point is made of orientating art towards the political and cultural upliftment of the common folk.

Certainly over the years South Africa has produced individual artists who have demonstrated various degrees of social consciousness, and we are reminded of such as Peter Clark, Lesley, Gerard Sekoto, Feinberg, Dumile Feni, but Cecil Skotnes is commenting on the sum of fine art in South Africa.

Cultural Poverty

It was once remarked by an overseas observer that white South Africa had not produced one painter of international repute, no singer, opera or ballet company. Neither, one can say, had Nazi Germany. It is not necessary to dwell on the cultural poverty of racist and fascist minorities, but these are phenomena of capitalism, a class society, and it is in this type of society that we find the emergence of two cultural expressions: that of the upper class, and that of the oppressed.

Mr Skotnes laments that 'since the British decided to do away with the last vestige of the Zulu empire in 1879 to further the aims of the great imperial family, the systematic application of Western culture has destroyed those tribal forms which might have created a folk art of consequence.'

For us 'the systematic application of Western culture' also means the development of capitalism in South Africa, but far from attempting to turn the clock back or mourning the destruction of tribal forms, it should be realized that the process, together with the emergence of the national movement of the blacks, also welded the various ethnic groups into a vast working-class and a united African people. The cultural expression of this force in South African society, in spite of attempts to divide it, consequently transcends the more ethnic or folkloric.

Here we must also question Mr Skotnes' knowledge of the history of the African people when he asserts that there is 'on the black front the lack of a strong artistic tradition'. If, as Cecil Skotnes goes on to say, 'the almost total disregard for the visual arts by the indigenous people is perhaps the greatest loss', it is not their fault but that of a system which has little regard for culture and denies a population the stability and security in which such as the plastic arts can flourish. For this reason, among others, the oppressed people have concentrated on other art forms: songs, poetry and writing. While Cecil Skotnes might claim that the 'vast urban complexes such as Soweto develop without any consideration for the artistic potential of the black man' we need not agree that it 'weakens the artistic power of the white nation' for the people continue to manifest a cultural life.

What should be expected from the present revolutionary situation, Skotnes states, is a 'meaningful artistic upsurge and an intensification of output although it must be realized that what finally emerges might well be mediocre in quality.' Again we do not agree that mediocrity is the result of artistic commitment to, or involvement with, a revolutionary upsurge. Mr Skotnes' view is perhaps echoed by the poet, Uys Krige (who, incidentally, we understand supported the Spanish Republic in the Civil War) who said in the Johannesburg *Star* (9 November 1976): 'The poet's job is to express what is lasting and abiding, what is common to all people. The closer you get to the politics of your times, the more insignificant you become.'

Revolutionary situations and revolutions themselves unleash the vast cultural potential of the common people, and great works of art and literature by individual artists have been inspired by such upheavals in society. We do not wish to repeat all the discussions on this theme, which have appeared before in this journal, but it is worthwhile reiterating that for the artist to ignore social realities is no guarantee that he will produce works of merit.

Mr Skotnes nevertheless longs for 'effective contact' between the various fragments of the 'art world' which he rightly says 'has been blocked not only by government decree but more so by the vast difference in living standards between the overfed whites and the underfed blacks. This applies to intellectual pursuits as well as food,' and acknowledges that 'the blacks, after all, control the final outcome of the present confrontation of ideas.'

His complaint is that the divisions which exist in South Africa, and the destruction of 'tribal forms' and 'folk art' did away with 'a foundation on which to build an identifiable expression', perhaps a unified art. This is also ignored by artists who go on demonstrating the 'lack of guts' by producing '"good" pictures' that have 'little to do with humanity and [the] atmosphere of Africa and in any particular shape or form of our part of that spirit or atmosphere.' This also includes the few blacks who, he points out, are also isolated from their white fellows, while both sections are being influenced by 'European ideas' consolidated by the influx of the international print and the marvellous magazines and art books.

Likewise, 'in the mid-Sixties, a small group of professional black artists began to express their reactions to township life in a strong "German Expressionist" manner, using conte chalk as a medium,' while, on the theoretical and ideological level we assume, the 'application of international ideas to our situation has clouded our artistic insight.' All these, he says, have contributed to the 'spiritual bankruptcy that seems to be establishing itself in our art.'

But 'European ideas' need not necessarily detract from the merit of artistic creation or its national character, and certainly the success of the revolution does not mean the jettisoning of worthwhile cultural acquirements, theoretical or material, in order to return to 'a folk art of consequence' which Mr Skotnes longs for.

The Dilemma of Isolation

The absence of stimulation among artists might not be mainly historical, as Cecil Skotnes claims, and it need not be 'international ideas' which cloud artistic insight, although he does not identify these ideas; nor need it mean that these artists are necessarily oblivious of or unaffected by the revolutionary situation referred to. Certainly the oppressed black majority are far from pessimistic, both in their political and artistic resistance. But believing that all artists, plastic and literary alike, must entertain a broadminded outlook, albeit on varying levels, it is not difficult to imagine the dilemma of those who belong to the ruling racial minority in South Africa.

The black artist in South Africa is not averse to mixing his work with 'politics'; he cannot but accept that as one of the victims of the oppressive society, his work almost automatically becomes involved, even if merely to 'record our times' as Mr Skotnes wants art to do.

For us or the conscious artist, man is not made for the Sabbath, but the Sabbath for man—society is not made for the artist, but the artist for society. The function of art is to assist the development of man's consciousness, to help improve society.

Others of course emphatically reject this standpoint. They maintain art is an *aim* in itself and to convert it into a *means* of achieving any extraneous aim, even the most noble, is to lower the dignity of creative production.

Those who have been raised in the school of the bourgeoisie easily cling to such conceptions. On the other hand, considering that it is impossible for everybody to be of like mind, it is not difficult to imagine that there are artists in South Africa who are by no means in agreement with the course taken by their society and are embarrassed by it. The artist's relations with the ruling sphere may be a source of great vexation to him. But unable to accept the so-called utilitarian view of art, that is, the tendency to attach to artistic productions the function of judging the phenomena of life, he chooses to ignore life, society, altogether. At best this might mean 'art for art's sake', and adopting this theory is an easy way out; the ivory tower is a refuge from the slings and arrows of an outrageous society.

For any intelligent and sensitive person, life in the South African racist atmosphere might be a distressing experience. The general callousness of his community and the forbidding stare of the oppressed must frighten the sensitive white artist in particular. Rather than paint the ugly face of his racist community, he turns to the natural beauty of the land; rather than eulogize the luxurious life of his people, he prefers still lifes and wild flowers. Under these circumstances, emphasis on 'art for the sake of art' might have its merits.

But we have seen that even the most tightly fortified white laager cannot ignore the effects of the upsurge of the revolutionary black people forever, if at all. The life of the black people can never be separated from the social environment as a whole, and so the artist inside the laager too must take cognizance of this upsurge.

Meaning of Revolution

The development of the revolutionary struggle is a most important characteristic of the South African scene today, and not even the practice of apartheid or the police state can separate experiences which can be shared, however difficult, across the barriers. Skotnes says that through 'limited confrontation between a few artists and the reality of our time some anger has resulted, but here again it is the writer who has led'. Then it is the writers who are more in touch with reality, and this is demonstrated by their general concern with social and political problems.

It must mean that all the complaints and observations made by Cecil Skotnes about the failure of painters and sculptors being unaffected by developments in South Africa must hinge largely on their ignorance or lack of awareness of reality. Sensitivity is one thing, but to demonstrate this sensitivity positively is another. 'Art for art's sake' arises essentially where the artist is out of harmony with his social environment, but the millions of black people are also part of the South African picture, and the beauty of the African landscape is no substitute for the dynamism of their life and struggles.

Undoubtedly the momentum of the revolutionary struggle will drag many more artists from their ivory towers to force them to come out on one side or the other. Though he himself queries 'what events will check the spiritual bankruptcy', Cecil Skotnes passes his own judgement on his guilty colleagues:

> The key to a meaningful art that will record our time lies in the spirit of the artist—in his humanity and his intellectual honesty. And if the times have little influence on an artist's work, especially such momentous times, he should seek a new profession.

CHAPTER TEN

To Alternate Member of the Politbureau, CPSU CC, First Secretary of the Communist Party of Uzbekistan, Comrade Sharaf R. Rashidov
(1978)

This letter was part of a series of documents from the Afro-Asian Writers' Meeting held in Tashkent, Uzbekistan, in October 1978 to mark the twentieth anniversary of the first conference held in Tashkent, which established the organization. These documents formed a special section of Lotus: Afro-Asian Writings.

Dear Friend,

The Executive Committee of the Afro-Asian Writers' Association which met in your beautiful and sunny country from 9th to 14th October, and which at the same time participated in a literary symposium around the high sentiments of which bind together all the peoples of Africa and Asia, wish to extend our sincerest and warmest thanks to you, the representative of the dear and generous Uzbek people, for their abundant hospitality.

We ask you to extend to the General Secretary of the CPSU, President of the Presidium of the USSR Supreme Soviet, Leonid Brezhnev, our profound thanks for the warm greetings sent to our anniversary meeting. Let us assure the people of the Soviet Union that the writers of Africa and Asia remain dedicated to the cause of progress, peace and friendship among all peoples, and that the words written by us, writers, will forever reflect the sentiments of all our people, indeed all mankind—peace, happiness, progress, and the end of falsehood, oppression, racism and colonialism in all its forms which are the hallmarks of imperialism.

We wish the people of the Soviet Union success in all their endeavours, in their noble struggle to ensure that all mankind lives free from the scourge of war; free to develop their lives and cultures in a spirit of mutual friendship and common happiness.

Yours sincerely,
Alex La Guma
Acting Secretary General
of the Afro-Asian Writers' Association

CHAPTER ELEVEN

Report of the Acting Secretary General
(1979)

This speech was delivered at the Sixth Conference of Afro-Asian Writers held in Luanda, Angola, in July 1979—the first time the association met in sub-Saharan Africa. It was published in a special section of documents on the meeting in Lotus: Afro-Asian Writings. *This document is important for its overview of the association's activities, particularly following the assassination of Youssef El Sebai (1917–78), an Egyptian writer who had edited* Lotus *and led the organization for years.*

Our Sixth Conference of Afro-Asian Writers is meeting here as a result of a resolution taken at the previous conference held in Alma-Ata. The resolution called for this conference to be held on the soil of Africa. It is being held in Luanda, capital of the Popular Republic of Angola, revolutionary Angola, as a result of the generous invitation from His Excellency, Comrade Agostinho Neto, president of this dynamic country; from the MPLA-Party of Labour, the government of Angola, and the Angolan Writers Union.

We rejoice, then, that our resolution has been carried out, and that Angola is the venue of this august gathering of writers from our two continents, together with our colleagues from the socialist countries of Asia, Europe and Cuba, from the democratic literary community and supporters from Western Europe, North America and Latin America. We believe that, as progressive writers committed to the struggle of our various peoples for peace, social progress, and an end to suffering, exploitation and cultural domination by reactionary influences, it is only natural that we should be guests of one of the newest independent and revolutionary states on this continent, and a country in the frontline of the struggle against imperialism, colonialism and racism.

The contribution made to Afro-Asian literature by former Portuguese colonies, especially in the genre of poetry, has been like a cascade of jewels poured into the treasure chest of literature. The literature which arose out of the struggle for independence of the peoples once ruled by Portugal has consistently demonstrated to the world the dynamic unity between artistic ability and social reality, and for this example of the purpose of Afro-Asian literature, the literature which our movement manifests, we are indebted to such great names as Agostinho Neto, Ribeiro, Craveirinha, dos Santos. Let us not forget the profound and important contributions made to the exploration of the relation between culture and society by the late Amílcar Cabral.

Arising out of the identification and involvement of writers with the profound changes taking place in their societies, the democratic and revolutionary content of their works has linked together people all over the world fighting against injustice and has stimulated the character not only of African literature, but that of all continents.

As an independent country, Angola continues to brave the aggression of world imperialism which is shamelessly using racist regimes of southern Africa as its spearhead. Armed aggression by these racist regimes continues against Angola and what are known as the frontline states in a desperate attempt to destroy democratic societies as well as the national liberation movements which together spell the doom of reaction and oppression in this region, the most important stronghold of imperialism on this continent.

In Africa and Asia, the claw marks of colonialism are still imprinted on many places, on economy, on social, political and cultural life. The socioeconomic and technical backwardness of the people is the consequence of imperialist plunder and pillage. The dire results of colonial rule have yet to be completely overcome. International imperialism, wielding the bludgeon composed of its multinational corporations, continues to impede the progress of the colonial and postcolonial peoples.

One consequence of the cultural invasion by colonialism is the destruction of native languages, or their supplantation by the languages of the colonizing people. We might find that some independent countries are therefore faced with the problem of deciding which is the best way of utilizing the unfortunate facts of life for the purpose of cultural advancement; whether the revived indigenous languages should replace adopted or absorbed languages; or whether the adopted languages can be guaranteed equality with others, maintained as the common media of communication without hindering the utilization of the indigenous tongues.*

Likewise, writers, cultural workers and society as a whole must discover the best ways of integrating traditional forms with modern experience—for example, the transfer of the oral tradition to the written form of communication. Then we are also concerned with the utilization in the most beneficial way of other cultural media (radio, cinema, television, etc.) as a means of expressing genuinely the culture of the populations.

Writers are also expected to explore ways and means of enhancing their work undertaken for the purpose of raising educational levels, to bring these into line with new developments.

Taking all aspects into account, we must acknowledge that the imperialists still have at their disposal great reserves of power and resources which they use to reverse the process of progress in our world. Their intensified machinations and open activities are carried

---

* I have corrected part of this sentence. The original read: 'or whether the revived languages can be guaranteed equality with others, maintained as the common media of communication without hindering the utilization of the indigenous tongues.' [Ed.]

on in the context of a changed balance of forces now in favour of national liberation, genuine progress and peace, and the failure of the local henchmen of imperialism to stabilize the neocolonialist system.

There has been launched what may be described as a new type of cold war. In this new move, conspiracies are being hatched against the national liberation movements and increasingly ludicrous lies are being manufactured about the socialist countries, in particular the Soviet Union, GDR and Cuba, in order to justify the frantic arms build-up and the interference of imperialism in Africa. This deliberate engendering of tension, for which the imperialists are solely responsible, is of course contrary to the interests of all peoples pursuing a new and better life.

In order to keep countries and people in bondage, the imperialists are using now all forms of neocolonialism, economic, political, ideological and armed aggression.

The importance of a consistent, principled struggle against imperialism and its allies on the basis of a broad anti-imperialist united front was the major theme of the International Conference of Solidarity with the Struggle of African and Arab Peoples Against Imperialism and Reaction held in Addis Ababa in September 1978. That conference adopted several resolutions and a General Declaration, which expressed support for the Ethiopian Revolution and the people fighting against racism, colonialism, Zionism, apartheid, imperialism and local reaction in Africa, the Middle East and Latin America.

Our conference is meeting at a time of great historic achievements and revolutionary changes. Let us not hesitate to say that the international influence of the socialist community has become the decisive factor of present-day development. Over all continents, the pressure of the progressive forces is mounting. The abolition of the last vestiges of colonialism is near. The peoples are relentlessly fighting to consolidate freedom and independence. They are resolutely defending their options and repulsing the interference of imperialism in the internal affairs of their countries.

The collapse of colonial empires, the gaining of political independence and the creation of independent nation-states is one of the great historic achievements of the peoples. This was made possible by the changes in the international correlation of forces due to the defeat of Hitlerism and Japanese militarism, the weakening of international imperialism, the emergence of socialism on a world scale, the great upsurge of the national liberation movements and the unfailing support given to them by the socialist states and the international democratic movements.

Important victories have lately been achieved by the peoples of Asia in Afghanistan, Iran and Kampuchea. These have been major advances along the path towards just societies, the end of man's inhumanity to man. But in Asia and in the Middle East, imperialism and its lackeys have also been active.

Thus, in the Middle East, the so-called peace of Camp David has appalled and affronted the democratic forces of the world. Not only was the Camp David treaty worked out with the assistance and participation of the United States, the leader of world imperialism, but it is, in fact, a direct outcome of US' Middle East policy and a product of the persistent efforts to secure the imperialist interests of the US and its ally, Israel. The democratic world has been unanimous in its opinion that the Camp David treaty contributes in no way towards cancelling the efforts of Zionist aggression or resolving the Palestinian question, which the Arab peoples, supported by the peace-loving, democratic, anti-imperialist forces, have for many years been struggling to settle.

The object of US policy after the October 1973 War was to nullify its effects, which were extremely disadvantageous for Israel and for her imperialist supporters, and to move to a settlement on conditions that would satisfy the US and its ally, Israel. This was an essential feature of Kissinger's shuttle diplomacy.

In broad outline, the Camp David deal can be described as an act best suited to the interests of Israel's expansionist policy; in fact, a gift to Israel, which has committed many acts of aggression against Arab countries and wants to keep what has been seized.

But, perhaps, it is enough to reiterate here the words of the leader of the Palestine Liberation Organization, Yasser Arafat, on the occasion of the anniversary of the Palestine Revolution, on the eve of 1 January this year:

> There can be no peace, no security, no solution, and no stability in this region through the neglect of the essence and the basis of the problem, i.e. the inalienable national rights of our Palestinian people, including their right to return, to self-determination and to establish their independent state over their national soil. [. . .] Together with our brothers, allies and friends, we are building our road towards a just and lasting peace in the Middle East, and not the peace imposed by the strong over the weak; not the peace dictated by the conditions of surrender and by the imposition of domination and control through the dreams of empire and dreams of colonial control [. . .] Let it be clear that our revolution will not be defeated by the Zionist enemy, nor by the imperialist war machine [. . .] Our inevitable victory will come sooner or later, whether our enemies wish it or not; for this is the will of history, the will of blood and of Palestine and Arab fists, the will of all that is great in this Arab nation; and the will of all who are honest, brave and just in the whole of progressive humanity.

Asia and the Middle East, like Africa, are still the objects of world imperialist intrigues and local treachery. No honest supporter of the cause of national independence, no upholder of the cause of humanism and social progress, whether from the standpoint of decent democratic sentiment or of proletarian internationalism, could condone the aggression of the People's Republic of

China against Socialist Vietnam. On behalf of the Afro-Asian Writers Association, the Temporary Secretariat, meeting in Addis Ababa in March of this year, issued a statement indignantly protesting against the barbaric invasion by China's ruling circles of the independent and sovereign Vietnam, and reaffirmed our full solidarity with the people of Vietnam in their just cause, demanding the immediate and unconditional withdrawal of all Chinese troops from the territory of Vietnam.

Whether it is about the aftermath of flood, drought and devastation in our continents, the problem of illiteracy in Bangladesh or India, or the question of the militarization of Japan, today and tomorrow these questions will touch the hearts of the Afro-Asian writers and make them take up their pens as well as join in the general struggle of all people for human dignity and progress, to help cure the ills left with them as part of the legacy of colonialism.

We give our support to the brave fighters for freedom in Nicaragua; we express our anger at the massacre of protesters on the cathedral steps in El Salvador; our continued solidarity goes to the anti-fascist forces in Chile, to all those fighting for democracy and justice in Latin America, to the people and government of revolutionary Cuba, still burdened with the imperialist presence on its soil and the imperialist economic blockade.

But, most of all, we Afro-Asian writers hail with joy the victories, small and great, of the people of Africa, Asia, Latin America, the socialist countries and the democratic forces of other regions.

II

This situation, which affects our two continents in the main, has been but briefly summarized. In addition, it has pertained generally to the period since our Fifth Conference in Alma-Ata, Kazakhstan, USSR. Developments on the international scene resulting in various effects on our work have forced the Afro-Asian Writers Association drastically to amend its organizational tasks, and we have been able to carry on up to this time in accordance with the decisions taken.

The Lotus Prize for 1977–78 was awarded to the following: Abu Salma (Palestine), Yoshie Hotta (Japan), Meja Mwangi (Kenya), Kamil Yashen (USSR), Nguyen Ngoc (SRV) and Sami al-Droubi (Syria).

Immediately following the Alma-Ata Conference, our Association took part in a poetry symposium organized by the Writers' Union of Armenia, as well as in a festival in Baku.

A meeting of young writers of Africa and Asia was entertained by the Uzbek Writers' Union in Tashkent in 1976, and a symposium was attended by editors of literary magazines in Beirut. In addition, we were hosted at literary events in Manila by the Philippines Writers' Union. At all these functions, the Permanent Bureau was able to discuss and carry on the work of the Association.

The Association also took up the matter of the imprisonment in Kenya of Ngũgĩ wa Thiong'o, the famous African writer. Constituent members also joined in the international campaign for his release. We must concentrate all efforts on gaining the release of the poet Kim Chi Ha, who is still imprisoned in South Korea.

A very successful celebration of the Association's twentieth anniversary was held in Tashkent, Uzbekistan, the birthplace of our movement.

There are still matters outstanding, such as a proposed drama symposium to take place in Damascus. It was also suggested that the hundredth anniversary of the Pakistani poet, Iqbal, be celebrated by the Association. We are happy to mention the fiftieth anniversary of the Mongolian Writers' Union, which took place recently and at which our Association was represented by Subhas Mukherjee. At the moment, preparations for the Conference of the Bangladesh Writers' Union are under way. The tenth anniversary of the Sri Lanka Writers' Front will also take place in September.

Report of the Acting Secretary General • 329

As circumstances would have it, the continuity of the Association's work was interrupted by the untimely and tragic death of the Secretary General, Youssef El Sebai. It was with profound regret and sorrow that the Association learnt of this. The tragedy left a gap in the work of the Association, as Mr Sebai had been carrying out his functions as secretary general in Cairo, where the Permanent Bureau Office was situated. The leadership of the Association had to be taken up by the two honorary officials, the Deputy Secretaries General, Mr Alex La Guma and Mr Subhas Mukherjee. With equally deep feeling we must record the passing of several other colleagues, including Sajjad Zaheer (India), Mirzo Tursun-Zadeh, N. Tikhonov (USSR), Yuri Rumiantsev, Vladlen Chesnokov (USSR) and Hamid al-Amin (Sudan).

Following the death of Mr Sebai, a meeting of the Permanent Bureau was called in Berlin, GDR, where it was decided to summon the Executive Committee to make arrangements for the future functioning of the Association until the organizational problems could be solved. The Executive Committee thus met in Tashkent in October 1978, which coincided with the twentieth anniversary of the Association.

At the meeting of the Executive, it was decided to defer the election of the new Secretary General to the Sixth Conference. One of the Deputy Secretaries General, Alex La Guma, was appointed Acting Secretary General until the Sixth Conference. The meeting also elected a temporary secretariat to act in the place of the Permanent Bureau and to handle the affairs of the Association.

It is yet to be decided whether the centre of the Association will continue to be based in Cairo. In any event, it is felt that the election of the Secretary General and the choice of a permanent centre are matters which must involve retaining the unity of the Association and its principled anti-imperialist political character. Together with this must go the functioning of the Association. It is felt that a Secretariat, effectively composed, would be less cumbersome than a Permanent Bureau and its members should be able to devote themselves to stimulating the activities of local literary organizations as well as the affairs of the Association on the principle of the division of labour. The Sixth Conference must therefore give careful consideration to this aspect of organization. Likewise, it would be in keeping with the character of the movement, if the main base for all its literary and cultural activities was its central organ, *Lotus* magazine.

The Executive meeting, with the improved organizational structure in mind, elected a Constitution Committee to go into the matter of amending or redrafting the Constitution. The Constitution Committee will report to the Sixth Conference.

The Lotus Prize jury was also discussed and fresh criteria for awarding the Lotus Prize were recommended.

The Association received an invitation from the Ethiopian Writers' Union to hold the meeting of the Temporary Secretariat and the Working Group of the International Preparatory Committee (IPC) in Addis Ababa, where the Union would hold a literary event. The invitation was gratefully accepted, and the meetings were held in Addis Ababa in March.

The IPC continued its discussion of the preparations for the Sixth Conference. The temporary Secretariat and the IPC jointly also went into the question of the *Lotus* Editorial Board. In view of the death of the former chief editor, it was decided to appoint a new chief editor assisted by deputy editors to take over the running of the *Lotus* magazine. Faiz Ahmed Faiz of Pakistan was appointed Chief Editor, with Subhas Mukherjee to handle the English edition and Mouin Beseisso the Arabic edition. The position of the deputy editor of the French edition is yet to be filled. Anatoly Sofronov (USSR) was appointed Soviet Liaison Officer. It is felt that this is the best way to ensure the efficient editorship of our magazine, and it is recommended that this arrangement should stand.

There is, of course, the urgent matter of the editorial office, which was formerly in Cairo.

All the arrangements made by the Temporary Secretariat appointed by the Executive Committee were in the best interests of the Association following the dislocation caused by the absence of a permanent Secretary General and an administrative apparatus. We must commend the Soviet Liaison Committee for invaluable assistance in keeping lines of communication open between interim officials and the membership up to the time of this Sixth Conference.

III

The Sixth Conference of Afro-Asian Writers meets under the general theme of the national renaissance of the African and Asian peoples and the continued struggle against imperialism, colonialism, racism and apartheid; the participation of writers in resolving the problems of newly independent countries relating to, among others, the questions of national integrity, the re-understanding of national self-awareness, the problems of self-integration in multilingual and polylingual societies. In addition, the matter of literary communication among the Afro-Asian community for international understanding and solidarity.

These generalities involve a number of particular elements, which the delegates will deal with. One thing is clear, now that the greater part of our continents is in the process of developing new societies—the problems of material and cultural life will be confronting the people in times to come, especially where the yoke of colonialism has only recently been thrown off.

We should see clearly that at the moment of time in which we live and write, it is impossible to overcome the political, economic and social crisis in our countries without the social system that draws in the widest participation of the masses; that age-old backwardness cannot be abolished and no fundamental cultural or socioeconomic progress is possible unless society is securely based on the people. For example, working together in a spirit of genuine democracy, all progressive forces are able to solve the important ethnic problems in an internationalist spirit. As we have said, imperialism and local reaction are using certain ethnic differences to undermine and disrupt countries. The forces of national and international reaction exploit anti-communism, chauvinism, tribalism and religious fanaticism in order to sow confusion among the broad masses and to halt, or even reverse, progressive and unified development. It is therefore necessary for Afro-Asian and all progressive writers to contribute to the confounding of imperialist sabotage by upholding an internationalist spirit, which is consistent with the principles of genuine humanism. All progressive forces, in which writers play an important role, must defend these principles, which unite men as human beings and equals, against those who seek to divide us. All the progressive writers within the democratic and revolutionary alliance should be dependable allies in the common struggle against imperialism, neocolonialism, Zionism and racism; in the struggle to consolidate independence for the peace and security of nations and for their social progress.

CHAPTER TWELVE

Final Speech, Secretary General of the Afro-Asian Writers Association
(1979)

This speech was delivered at the Sixth Conference of Afro-Asian Writers held in Luanda, Angola, in July 1979. La Guma had become secretary general of the organization by the end of the meeting. It was published in a special section of documents on the meeting in Lotus: Afro-Asian Writings.

The Sixth Conference of the Afro-Asian Writers Association is about to close. Thanks to the generosity of the Angolan government and people, the MPLA-Party of Labour and the Angolan Writers Union we have met here in Luanda.

The first important fact to acknowledge is that we have been able to meet in spite of problems and setbacks, and our discussions have laid the way open for further advancement of the Association. We have been able to meet successfully because the strength of the anti-imperialist forces in the world today is such that there is little room for doubt that any unit of the progressive movement, like ourselves the Writers Association of Africa and Asia, will receive the wholehearted support of those forces. Our contribution to Afro-Asian solidarity, to the world anti-imperialist struggle, is one which is important, in that we have among our objectives the hearts and minds of millions of potential readers whose political consciousness and revolutionary determination we are able to strengthen through our progressive writings.

In the course of our conference, we have discussed the role and purpose of writers in the reconstruction of societies once under colonialist rule. We have also talked about ways and means of facilitating communication between peoples and countries. We have demonstrated our determination to help complete the revolutionary process that will finally liberate Africa and Asia and indeed the whole world from the forces of oppression, injustice, militarism and reaction.

Once again we have added something to the wealth of strategy and tactics in the field of cultural struggle for justice and international understanding of world peace.

In addition, our conference has made new strides in the search for writer solidarity among progressive writers. Our newly amended Charter and Constitution allows four categories of membership, which will welcome into the Association many friends in the world cultural movement who support the Afro-Asian writers' cause. Who knows that our Association might one day become the cornerstone of a broad movement uniting men of letters from every continent and country who are determined to add their efforts to the just cause of human progress and lasting peace.

We have met here in Africa, writers from all continents have gathered here under the auspices of the Afro-Asian Writers Association. All of us have been affected by the revolutionary fervour of the Angolan people. We have met in the frontline where the struggle for the social liberation of southern Africa and indeed the whole continent is taking place.

Looking here, the enemy can see the doom of colonialism, racism, apartheid in Africa, for Angola is one of those countries which have demonstrated to the oppressed people that the enemy can be defeated. As the heroic people of Vietnam showed that the armed fight of US imperialism can be beaten, so did the people of Angola, Guinea, S. Tomé and Mozambique shown that colonialism can be defeated in Africa.

Mother Africa is returning to her children. We will gather around her skirts again, a family, a continent. We will welcome our friends to share our bread and our joy at being free. Mother Africa will spread her arms to welcome all who share her love for peace, happiness and well-being.

Comrade President, on behalf of the Afro-Asian Writers, may I extend through you warmest greetings and thanks to the Angolan people. The writers of Africa and Asia and their friends leave these shores with feelings of pleasure at having met your people and witnessed their efforts.

This short visit will become a long memory.

I thank you.

CHAPTER THIRTEEN

'Walk Among the Multitudes'
(1981)

This essay, first published in Tricontinental, *is notable for La Guma's discussion of Amílcar Cabral (1924–73), Chinua Achebe (1930–2013) and Frantz Fanon (1925–61) and the role of the writer within broader cultures of anti-colonialism.*

For the people of Africa, whose oppression under colonialism, white supremacy and racism has lasted beyond the memory of our youth, the expression of their pain, fear, hopes and determination through music, poetry, dance and literature has always been important, a feature of their daily lives. With the harsh hand of colonialism preventing advancement in many fields, culture has been a steady vehicle of struggle accessible to the people.

I introduce colonialism because it is obviously impossible to talk about any aspect of African life without mentioning this horrendous phenomenon, which for generations smothered the continent in a stifling blanket of ignorance, poverty and stagnation. Moreover, it is difficult to mention literature in Africa without this reference.

Certainly, African literature existed long before colonialists shot their way onto our soil and seized and ravaged our continent. The language and writing, folktales and religious scriptures of ancient Africa have been studied for centuries. The myths and legends of ancient Egypt are known all over. Evidence demonstrates that an indigenous alphabet of Semitic origin was in use in Axum or ancient Ethiopia as early as the fourth century AD. The Arab language and culture had a profound influence on the northern, north-eastern and north-western peoples. Below the Sahara, the literary manifestations of the tropical African people were, in the main, of the oral tradition, tracing the origins of the people far back into the mists of ancestry.

With the coming of the colonialists into black Africa especially, the development of the people and their social and economic life—and, consequently, their cultural life—was drastically interrupted.

Frantz Fanon, in *Black Skin, White Masks*, says the black man has not only been oppressed by the white colonizers, but he has also been murdered culturally.

That great leader, statesman and writer Amílcar Cabral pointed out that if under colonialism many Africans became alienated from their cultural background, even if they were so uprooted that many could not assert it, this background did not die completely. He said:

> The exercise of imperialist domination demands cultural oppression, but the people are able to create and develop a liberation movement because they keep culture alive in the teeth of organized repression of cultural life—other resistance being destroyed, they continue to resist culturally. The colonial power cannot impose a complete cultural occupation. The majority of the people retains their identity and are the one entity really able to preserve and create it—that is, they can make history.

Of course the study of culture involves all aspects of a people's character, such as music, dance, architecture, painting, sculpture, cuisine, philosophy and religion. One should also preferably be competent in these fields, but, since the concept of culture is such a broad one, we can only devote ourselves to some remarks about African writing.

The cultural resistance of the African people to colonialism has inspired the best of her writers and indeed gave rise to the fame of these artists, brought to the world knowledge of their great talent. The African writer—indeed, any worthy writer—is always inspired by the dynamic character of the masses.

In the field of writing, perhaps the best example of this inspiration is found in the poetry of the former Portuguese colonies. One can actually trace the various stages of the colonial presence and its effects on the life and attitudes of the people. Here we find the concrete identification of the writer with social life. Similarly, writers of the Caribbean, black America and southern Africa give expression to their peoples' struggles to overthrow oppression.

As José Martí himself learnt, there exists a need for the artist to integrate his life with his compatriots, so Martí's own consciousness was filled with the agony of his people. As Martí said, 'Poetry is durable when it is the work of all. Those who understand it are as much the authors as those who make it. To thrill all hearts by the vibrations of your own, you must have the germs and inspirations of humanity.'

All that is worthy in African literature engages, in one way or another, in resistance to colonialism, past and present. With the physical retreat of colonialism from Africa, new tasks faced African writers. Where independence had been gained, the examination of this independence holds the attention of many writers. Such authors as Achebe, Ngũgĩ, Beti, Oyono and Sembène are concerned with the new African man emerging from the colonial darkness. Naturally, not all writers are satisfied with independence as they find it; they pose themselves against various aspects of their society, question many things and attack many as well.

The debate over Africa's future and her association with the past involves various stances and interpretations. In terms of Francophone and Anglophone, the former produced Négritude and the latter, the African personality. According to the Kenyan scholar Christopher Wanjala, those who, such as Padmore and Nkrumah, represented the African personality wrote political articles against their colonizers—unlike the followers of Négritude, who used verse to romanticize the African image, determined to impress on all that Africans have their own history and culture.

From serving as a rallying cry for African nationalism, Négritude attempted to become a philosophy, but philosophy implies a world outlook and cannot be confined within the narrow limits of nationalism.

Nevertheless, African writers continue to wrestle with the problems of their societies, identifying with the problems of their peoples. Chinua Achebe stated at a conference on British Commonwealth literature in 1964 that part of his business as a novelist was to teach, to re-educate his society out of its acceptance of racial inferiority, 'to help my society regain its belief in itself and put away the complexes of denigration and self-denigration'.

Though each may interpret African reality according to his individual viewpoint, African writers have one common task. That is to help remove the debris of colonialism and to bring forth the African past from where its progress was halted and relate it to the present, with the view of creating for the future, using innovation, technique and modern technology, all for the purpose of reaching the hearts of the African masses on the progressive road to a new life.

Like his fellow man the ordinary member of society, the African writer is of course faced with all the problems of postcolonial, underdeveloped society. Illiteracy, multiethnic societies, language, printing and publishing—all these considerations face and affect the African writer. These problems obviously cannot be solved by the writer alone. They involve profound political and socio-economic changes, which must take place in Africa.

The imperialist presence still exists, hoping that Africa is not entirely lost to it. Some African states are working to shed the imperialist burden once and for all; others remain in its clutches in one form or another.

The Kenyan writer Ngũgĩ wa Thiong'o says, 'It was capitalism and its external manifestations, imperialism, colonialism and neo-colonialism, that had disfigured the African past. Capitalism even at its most efficient has failed to create equality and balanced human relationships in Europe and America. Why do we think it can work in Africa?'

Africa, its culture and its literature cannot be viewed in isolation from the total human course of events. Africa will change with the world. Already the dynamic revolutionary struggles of Ethiopia, the former Portuguese colonies, the Congo and Algeria have had a profound effect on the peoples of other countries. This effect will be revealed more and more in the literature of Africa in the future, and a start has already been made.

In the final analysis, the writer, whether African or not, belongs with the majority of the people. He should, as José Martí also said, 'walk among the multitudes who suffer, with love in [his] heart'.

CHAPTER FOURTEEN

To Yuri Andropov, General Secretary of the CPSU CC, President of the USSR Supreme Soviet
(1983)

This short statement appeared in the press bulletin for the Seventh Conference of the Writers of Asia and Africa held in Tashkent from 26 September to 2 October 1983.

We, the participants in the Seventh Conference of the Writers of Asia and Africa, assembled in the city of Tashkent on the occasion of the Organization's twenty-fifth anniversary express our sincere gratitude for the high assessment of its activity, expressed in your message of greetings. We take this opportunity to cordially thank the Soviet government and the Writers' Unions of the USSR and Uzbekistan for making it possible for us to meet here in Tashkent where the tradition of representative forums of progressive writers of our two continents was born.

We set great store by your support of the noble aims of the writers of Asia and Africa to contribute to the sacred struggle for peace and mutual understanding among nations, to preventing nuclear war, to curbing the arms race, for the bright ideals of humanity, against imperialism and racism, Zionism and neocolonialism. We resolutely support your confidence that by common effort people of goodwill can uphold peace and redirect the resources of modern civilization to meeting the vital needs of millions, to eliminating the disgraceful aftermaths of the colonial past.

We have read with great attention your statement, which convincingly exposes the militarist course of the present US administration in posing a serious threat to our planet. The confident voice of reason has once again come from Moscow: to stop the forces of reaction, to prevent the world from slipping into the abyss of war.

We the writers of Asia and Africa will carry on the battle for peace in our works. We will uphold humanism and goodness, love and mutual understanding among people. We will always and everywhere fight against hatred and hostility, against imperialism and racism, which run like a sinister crack through the heart of the single world created for brotherhood and freedom.

Long live peace and fraternal unity of the people of goodwill.

Alex La Guma
Secretary-General
of the Afro-Asian Writers' Association
Tashkent, 1 October 1983.

CHAPTER FIFTEEN

Is There a South African National Culture?
(1985)

This article first appeared in The African Communist *under the pseudonym of Gala. Among his final essays, it offers a critique of cultural apartheid in South Africa and the hope that a new, unified South African national culture would be born through struggle to replace it.*

A considerable amount of literary work continues to come from South Africa. Since the decades of the 1950s and '60s in particular, the scene of creative writing has been illuminated to varying degrees by such names as Can Themba, Mphahlele, Maimane, Modisane, Rive, Matthews, Nakana, Gordimer, Brink, Fugard, Coetzee, Serote, Mtshali and others. The emergence of the new generation of writers stimulated wide interest in our country's literary past and thus research and thousands of words of commentary, analysis and review brought once more to light such [writers] as Sol Plaatje, Olive Schreiner, Mofolo, Dube, Abrahams, etc.

All these writers have in one way or another concerned themselves with the realities of our country in its varying aspects and influences, and so their works are included under the collective heading of 'South African Writing'. Writers of course approach their subject matter from their individual points of view, yet writers in societies the least bedevilled by social and economic divisions, which might influence their ideas, have been able to gain the distinction of contributing to their 'national' literature.

In socialist countries, writers have a greater opportunity of producing works reflecting the oneness of their people's lives and characteristics in spite of certain barriers, which still might have to be overcome.

What can we say of South Africa benighted not only by class divisions but also by apartheid, racism, national oppression, minority superiority, ethnic and community differences?

The founding fathers of the national movement of the African people of our country said:

> The demon of racialism, the aberrations of Khosa–Fingo feuds, the animosity that exists between Zulus and Tsongas, between the Basuto and every other Native must be buried and forgotten. We are one people. (*Short History of the ANC*)

Later the Freedom Charter proclaimed:

> All national groups shall have equal rights. All people shall have equal right to use their own languages, and to develop their own folk culture and customs: all national groups shall be protected by law against insults to their race and national pride.

This recognizes that South Africa is inhabited by peoples with distinct historical and cultural backgrounds and characteristics, customs, etc. We need not here go into the question as to which one of them constitutes a nation or not. Let us agree that our population consists of these various communities or groups.

The Right to Equality

There are indeed those who argue that to place any emphasis on this 'multinational' or 'multiracial' character of South Africa is to deny the unitary or 'non-racial' objectives of our struggle. But this counterposing of multinationalism to non-racialism can only arise out of some mistaken view of the battle to overthrow the rule of apartheid. From our point of view, 'non-racialism' refers to the right of all people to equal citizenship, to political, social and economic rights, irrespective of their race or *'national' features, history, culture, customs, languages, etc.* which will not automatically disappear under a unitary and democratic regime.

The success of the struggle to overthrow apartheid, national oppression, racism, group privilege, guarantees the groundwork for the future unification of all our different peoples into a single South African nation. This amalgamation, we stress, can only happen under conditions of freedom and equality of all groups, but this equality also includes that of their various cultural identities, which of course rules out the racist criteria formulated by the apartheid state.

The Road to South African Freedom: Programme of the South African Communist Party (1963) says: 'The state should encourage in particular the unity of the African people and foster the spirit of unity of all South Africans. It should encourage and stimulate the development of healthy, non-antagonistic national consciousness [. . .] It should encourage the development of national cultures, art and literature.' This is in line with Marxist-Leninist theory: 'The elimination of national oppression [. . .] is possible only under a consistently democratic republican system and state administration that guarantee complete equality for all nations and languages',[1] and international cooperation 'is possible only between *equals*'.[2]

These citations are from the original text. Corrections and additions have been made when possible. [Ed.]

1 V. I. Lenin, 'The Seventh (April) All Russia Conference of the R.S.D.L.P.(B)', *Collected Works*, 4th EDN, VOL. 24 (Bernard Isaacs ed. and trans.) (Moscow: Progress Publishers, 1964).

2 Karl Marx and Friedrich Engels, *Werke* (Berlin: Dietz Verlag, 1967).

In the meantime, the struggle to achieve this condition will be reflected not only in our political activity but in artistic efforts as well, and the ravages of apartheid as a reality will continue to be a feature of art and literature from South Africa, even though this feature might reveal individual 'ideological' attitudes of which some 'purists' might complain. The Kenyan author Ngũgĩ wa Thiong'o has written: 'Literature does not grow or develop in a vacuum; it is given impetus, shape, direction and even areas of concern by social, political and economic factors in a particular society.'[3] These 'areas of concern' are reflected in most works coming out of South Africa: everyday experiences; the armed struggle; the political movement; psychological effects, life, love and hate in the racist society. South African writers are stuck with it, and there is little they can do but expose it, unless produce innocuous products about moonlight on the veld, or not even write at all until Liberation Day as some gloomily contend.

Forms of Stimulation

Without racism in the US we might not have had Richard Wright's *Native Son*, or the horrors of the First World War might have been ignored had Remarque not given us *All Quiet on the Western Front*. Racism, apartheid or imperialist and colonialist aggression are certainly not encouragers of art and culture, yet on the other hand they have stimulated works of considerable artistic merit and progressive content.

The South African Kenneth Parker observes that 'in the area of creativity no less than in other spheres we are confronted with a strange paradox: on the one hand, the existence of an abundance of conflicts (personal as well as environmental) which potentially give rise to art; on the other, the absence of those minimum condi-

---

3 Ngũgĩ wa Thiong'o, *Homecoming: Essays on African and Caribbean Literature, Culture and Politics* (London: Heinemann, 1972).

tions of freedom which permit the growth of that art.'[4] Dealing with 'creative writing by black South Africans', Cecil Abrahams says:

> It is imperative that the critic and reader of this literature be aware of the following standpoints: first, that South African black writing forms a separate segment of African literature; second, that the fabric of racial discrimination dominates the thematic structure of the writing, they go beyond the generalized attempts at portraying the evils of racism [. . .] fourth, that because the writers have been brought up in particular segments or pockets of racism, they are inclined to search out their line of differences within the special expression of their group [. . .][5]

These standpoints must of course apply to concerned white South African writers as well. For example, in an interview, Nadine Gordimer says: 'When I write about people, about their private selves [. . .] I am aware that they are what they are because their lives are regulated and their mores formed by the political situation [. . .]'[6] But while it is the movement against apartheid which seeks the unity of our peoples, so literature has a duty to reflect that search irrespective of the restrictions placed upon it. For do not these restrictions represent those placed on the people? Writing in South Africa should not intend only to show the struggle of the people in their various 'segments or pockets of racism'.

The struggle has given rise to unprecedented demonstrations of solidarity among the communities and groups of our country, and the growth of a united front against the racist regime has become a most important feature of the struggle, crossing the

---

4 Kenneth Parker (ed.), *The South African Novel in English* (New York: Africana Publishing Company, 1978).
5 Cecil Abrahams, 'The Context of Black South African Literature', *World Literature Written in English* 18(1) (1979).
6 Nadine Gordimer, 'A Writer in South Africa', *The London Magazine* 5(2) (May 1965).

barriers of race and cultural differences. So must the writer through every stretch of imagination and talent aspire to the oneness of the democratic and revolutionary principle; to surmount those hindrances which Ezekiel Mphahlele, for example, describes meeting in the course of his career: 'I don't know how white people behave in the home when a family member is dead [. . .] I have no way of knowing at first-hand how a white child in South Africa grows up.'[7]

Segmented as our people might be, the universality of their aspirations must be a consistent theme in progressive and democratic writing.

The Drama of Struggle

We have no doubt that great writers have through their foresight and talent already supplied important examples of what our literature should be aiming at. Of Olive Schreiner, writing at the end of the last century, it has been said: 'What she has done in *The Story of an African Farm* is to create a lasting symbol of South Africa [. . .] where everyday life becomes a drama played out in a tense multiracial society; where the individual must conform or engage in bitter struggles against sometimes overwhelming odds.'[8] As with present-day literature, Olive Schreiner wrote against the background of the divided society of her time. Progressive literature from South Africa with its base in the universality of man's aspirations in general and those of our own people in particular must transcend the group divisions which apartheid tries to force upon society via separate development, Bantu education, Bantustans and the like. Literature should be able to examine our society as a whole. In short, by doing so, writing today will contribute to the founding of the nation of the future.

---

7 Ezekiel Mphahlele, *The African Image* (New York: Praeger, 1974).
8 Ursula Edmands, 'Olive Schreiner' in *South African Novel in English*.

Stalin observed:

> A nation is primarily a community, a definite community of people. This community is not racial, nor is it tribal. The modern Italian nation was formed from Romans, Teutons, Etruscans, Greeks, Arabs and so forth. The French nation was formed from Gauls, Romans, Britons, Teutons and so on [. . .] Thus a nation is not racial or tribal, but a historically constituted community of people [. . .] a stable community of people.[9]

Lenin came forward with a more precise definition: 'The nation is a lasting historical community of people constituting a form of social development based on the community of economic life in a combination with language, territory, culture, consciousness and psychology.'[10]

Can we not look into the future and see the barriers fallen away under the hammer blows of progress as our people, having emerged victorious over racist tyranny, national oppression, ethnic or community divisions, commence to build a new life? Can we not dare to bring within the boundaries of our community Marx and Engels' even longer-term view of the world of the future?

> In place of the old local and national seclusion and self-sufficiency, we have intercourse in every direction, universal interdependence of nations. And as in material, so also in intellectual production. The intellectual creations of individual nations become common property. National one-sidedness and narrow-mindedness become more and more impossible, and from the numerous national and local literatures there arises a world literature.[11]

---

9 J. V. Stalin, *Marxism and the National Question*, 1913.
10 Institute of Marxism–Leninism, CC CPSU, *Lenin and the National Question* (Moscow, Progress Publishers, 1977).
11 Karl Marx and Friedrich Engels, *The Communist Manifesto*, 1848.

Flourishing under the warm sun of the equality of all peoples, our culture, art and literature will intermingle as our liberated peoples will do, blossoming into a South African culture; we shall then read a South African literature, not what is described today as merely literature 'from' South Africa or 'South African Writing'.

PART III

Literary Criticism and the Writing Life

CHAPTER ONE

Literature and Life
(1970)

This essay first appeared in Lotus: Afro-Asian Writings. *It is significant in its invocation of Maxim Gorky (1868–1936) and the influential role Soviet literature had on La Guma and the emergence of Afro-Asian literature more generally.*

While we meet on the occasion of the Tenth Anniversary of the Afro-Asian Writers' Conference, it is appropriate to mention that this year marks also the centenary of Maxim Gorky. When we talk of literature in its true sense, we cannot exclude the contributions of Gorky. Maxim Gorky wrote a vast amount about literature, but perhaps these words of his are significant at this time:

> Literature is the heart of the world; all the joys and sorrows, dreams and hopes, despairs and wraths of it, all the emotions of man as he faces the beauties of nature, all his terrors as he faces nature's secrets, lend it wings. This heart of the world palpitates indomitably and immortally with the desire of self-knowledge; as though in it all matter, all the forces of nature, having created in man the highest expression of their own intricacy and rationality, were trying to discover the essence and object of their own being . . .
>
> One might call literature also the all-seeing eye of the world, an eye whose glance pierces the deepest secrets of the human spirit . . .

There is as yet no united world literature because there is as yet no language common to us all; but all literary creation in prose or in verse shares the unity of the emotions, thoughts and ideas common to all men, the unity of the sacred striving of man towards happiness and freedom of the spirit, the unanimous hope for better forms of life, and finally the desire common to all men of something beyond the reach of word and thought, something that even the emotions can barely apprehend, something mysterious to which we give the pale name of beauty and which flourishes in the world and in our hearts evermore brightly.

The writers who mean anything in what is called the 'Third World' today are devoting themselves to the cause of the 'sacred striving of man towards happiness and freedom of the spirit, the unanimous detestation of the misfortunes of life, the unanimous hope for better forms of life'.

When in Scandinavia at a conference early last year, somebody introduced a lengthy debate on whether writers should only write or also help to 'raid radio stations and run guns' for the liberation struggles, it is answer enough to say that in Vietnam writers, poets and artists are today doing both!

When I write in a book that somewhere in South Africa poor people who have no water must buy it by the bucketful from some local exploiter, then I also entertain the secret hope that when somebody reads it he will be moved to do something about those robbers who have turned my country into a material and cultural wasteland for the majority of the inhabitants. But this is already being done in South Africa, and I would be satisfied to know that I had something to do with it.

The writers of Vietnam are in the frontline of the struggle against the destroyers of both material and cultural life in their homeland—the barbarian US Army and its puppets. Vietnamese writers and the people who inspire them will win! All writers worth their salt are among the ranks of those struggling for human happiness and progress in all parts of the world.

One cannot separate literature from life, from human experience and human aspirations. We may not be able to explain exactly how man came into existence on this planet, but scientists agree on one fundamental point and that is that man is distinguishable from animals in two respects: his use of tools and his ability to speak. Monkeys can handle sticks and stones, but only human hands can fashion them into tools. By using tools, early man was able to safeguard his existence. We learn that in its early stages, production was a collective labour. Many hands worked together, and in these conditions tools inspired a new method of communication. The first utterances of man had to be meaningful, articulate, and then elaborated and used as a means of coordinating their activities. So in inventing tools man also invented speech.

In its development, speech grew in direct accompaniment with the use of tools into a fully articulate method of communication between individuals, a language. Further, if we study the folklore and myths of early man, we learn that all his superstitions, his religious myths, his magical incantations were related to life around him: birth, death, hunting, fighting, the seasons and so on. His gods and goddesses took human form and indulged in activities of a human nature; their fictitious lives were closely interwoven with the realities of the lives of their worshippers. Ancient man's spoken literature and folklore is full of examples of this relationship.

In a Kono myth from Guinea, *Sa*, Death, created an immense sea of mud in order to live somewhere. One day the God, Alatangana, appeared and visited Sa in his dirty encampment. Shocked by this state of affairs, Alatangana reproached Sa, saying he had created an uninhabitable place, without plants, without living things, without light. To remedy the situation, Alatangana set out first to solidify the dirt. He thus created the earth and because it was sterile, he created vegetation and animals of all kinds.

In the Lozi legend from Zambia, the Creator, Nyambe, carved things from wood, he forged iron and he hunted the elephant. In Greek, Asiatic and Aztec folk legends, similar associations between the deities and human activity are found.

Likewise, man's incantations before his various deities were the beginnings of poetry as ordinary language gave rise to special effects and images. Even today, to the African railway worker in South Africa, an ordinary train is not merely a steam engine on wheels but also a symbol of destruction, for this train takes his sons to the mines or his womenfolk to the brothels. So on seeing the locomotive, the worker chants:

The one who roars in the distance,
The one who crushes the young men and smashes them,
The one who debauches our wives ...

Similar illustrations are found among all nations and in all languages.

One of the greatest values of literature is that by deepening our consciousness, widening our feeling for life, it reminds us that all ideas and all actions derive from realism and experience within social realities. Fundamentally, all men and all languages are concerned with the same basic requirements, of themselves and of their own fate.

The murders perpetrated by the imperialists and colonialist plunderers are just as abhorrent in Vietnam as they are in South Africa; and those who cherish freedom, humanity and progress are hailed with joy equally in all parts of the world. We all come from various countries, we speak various languages, and we are travelling along various paths, but all towards a single goal.

Literature, art, culture, civilization, these are not abstract conceptions as some would imagine. They define the direction and basis of our actions at a particular time. They must therefore be understood and interpreted on their revolutionary paths as the ethos which drives man forward or retards his progress according to the dynamism of that civilization.

Imperialism and colonialism in all their forms are the very negation of the cultures and civilizations of their victims, if one means by culture and civilization the unity of all material and spiritual values acquired by people over centuries and placed at the service of mankind, for the elevation of man's life, for the advancement of all nations and peoples.

Every true culture promotes national independence. Imperialists know this only too well. Being enemies of the people, they cannot help but be the enemies of culture. 'We have heard the word "culture", I reach for my gun.'

Thus imperialism and colonialism, in their attempts to uproot national cultures, have shamelessly falsified the histories of the peoples of Asia and Africa, suppressed their national languages both as official languages and as vehicles of culture, and systematically frustrated the cultural and artistic aspirations of their victims.

The people of Vietnam, the people of the Portuguese colonies, of Namibia, Zimbabwe, South Africa who are today waging an armed struggle for national liberation and independence simultaneously struggle for the rebirth of their national cultures.

In these parts of the imperialist dominated world, the armed struggle helps solve the contradiction between imperialism and the aspirations of our peoples to national rejuvenation. Deprived of the right to live according to their own values, our peoples are engaged in a struggle that will lead them to full expression in terms of their own history and culture.

It is not by accident that the best writers and artists have identified themselves with the peoples' movements, and their art and their writing have found a new and dynamic content while identifying themselves with their people's struggle for a new life.

In the words of the poet Aldo do Espirito Santo of São Tomé Island:

> It is the flame of humanity
> singing of hope
> in a world without bonds
> where liberty
> is the fatherland of men.

This new force which is rising in the literature of the oppressed people will continue and will acquire new character when we have attained victory, and the flowers and fruit of our nations will rise again from the dung heaps of colonialism.

In conclusion, allow us on behalf of the liberation forces of our country to thank you all for giving us the opportunity to address these words to you. Since we are meeting in Uzbekistan, it is fitting that I end with a few lines from 'The Gardener' by the Uzbek poet Maksud Sheikhzadeh, for his lines reflect our mood:

> Reach out to the sun, now spread deeper your roots,
> And though I may never enjoy your sweet fruits
> My grandsons will pluck them from your bough one day,
> Recalling their grandsire who laboured today.

CHAPTER TWO

Address by the Lotus Award Winner
(October 1971)

La Guma received the Lotus Prize for Afro-Asian literature in 1969 along with Mahmoud Darwish (1941–2008) of Palestine and Tô Hoài (1920–2014) of North Vietnam. This occasion was the first for the prize, and it was La Guma's first major international award. This lecture was subsequently published in Lotus: Afro-Asian Writings.

The presentation of an award to a writer places him in somewhat of a dilemma: he is not sure whether it is given as an acknowledgement that he has contributed something worthwhile and positive to the vast storehouse of literature which is humanity's heritage, or whether it is given in order to get rid of him with the broad hint that he has written enough!

But we are here because the Afro-Asian movement, which represents millions of people of our continents, takes a serious view of its work both in matters social and political, and in cultural.

It is an enormous privilege and honour to be here in India among the first to be awarded the Afro-Asian Prize for Literature. This is the India of long culture and literature. India is the motherland of the Ramayana and the Mahabharata, those epic poems of ancient times. It is the motherland of *Pather Panchali* of later date, of Tagore and of Mulk Raj Anand's work, to mention only these. Moreover, India is the motherland of Mahatma Gandhi.

The Lotus Prize for Literature that has caused me to be here points at several considerations. It is a tribute to my own humble contribution to the store of Afro-Asian literature. It is also a declaration of solidarity with the people of South Africa who are fighting the worst forms of oppression.

If this award should go to anyone, it should really go the South African people. For in truth, without the people of South Africa, I could not be a writer. Who has inspired me to set down those thousands of words in the books published with my name on their covers? The lives of the people, their love, their hates, their sorrows and joy, their hopes and aspirations, all these things stand behind all worthy works of art and culture. Without the background and inspiration of the people, art, literature would degenerate into meaningless scribblings.

There are, of course, those who contend that a writer, an artist, stands above the times and events, that he is only an onlooker on the sidelines who should not be involved in the conflict of human aspirations, classes, ideas.

But the history of the peoples involves the actions of human beings, their efforts, their trials and achievements. It is often written in blood; often with guns and explosives and rockets, as is being done in South Africa, in the Portuguese colonies, in Vietnam and in the Arab world.

A real writer can never divorce himself from the life of the people, from the struggle for human happiness, freedom and social justice.

Much is being said at this time about the individual freedom of the writer; that writers have an individual talent and viewpoint, which must be respected above all things. Certainly a writer is free to write reams and reams of paper expressing his viewpoint. But one man's freedom ends where another's begins.

So when the writer submits his work for publication, he finds that the publisher also has a viewpoint. If he expresses the view of the establishment, which publishers represent, the writer is of course welcome.

In the world alignment of imperialism and anti-imperialism, for instance, a writer who assists the imperialists one way or another through his work is welcomed by them. His viewpoint helps the imperialists at a certain time, and he is free to have his work published. The same writer would not be welcomed by anti-imperialists, or will be criticized.

So writers, in spite of the vague slogans of freedom so popular today, find themselves bound up with the forces which contend for the achievement of certain values. On the one hand, there is stagnation and reaction; on the other, progress.

The writers cannot escape their destinies because they are bound up with the destinies of whole societies of people.

In South Africa, manuscripts are gathering dust on their shelves because the authors do not conform to the standards of the racist publishing houses, or the Bantu education authorities, the Publications and Entertainments Board or the Minister of Justice. In South Africa, the authorities go to the extreme of prohibiting an author from putting pen to paper even before he has even considered submitting work to a publisher. By June 1969, the racist regime had banned 13,000 books from importation and circulation. Genuine authors who aspire to see their work in print have had to leave the country and write in exile.

Even in the so-called free world, authors are not as free as some might suppose.

The commentator, Milton Schulman, writing in the London *Evening Standard* some time ago observed that 'the average professional author—men who have published three or more books—earns from his books less than a dustman and about half as much as a doctor. Almost half of them make less than £5 a week from their books—below the level of an old-age pensioner.'

This commentator also quotes a George Jeger, member of the British Parliament, who wrote to the same newspaper, saying, 'If writers don't like their rewards why don't they do something else?'

Maxim Gorky said: 'The writer is the eyes and ears of the era.' To be able to project a whole era one has to have good eye-lenses and a proper point of view. In other words, the position which corresponds the most to our understanding of the world and its ideals.

Literature can be important in assisting to determine the specific goals of advancing people. Unfortunately, where the revolution has not yet taken place we are handicapped because we might only reach a small part of the audience.

But we have an important task to play in shaping the aspirations and hatreds of the audience to the task of wiping out the causes of their misery in the world of concrete life; cause emotional reorganization in those who read our work.

We Afro-Asian writers are involved in this work. The writers of the Portuguese colonies, Vietnam, the Arab world and South Africa, have specific tasks, which differ from those who write in the countries where the revolution has triumphed.

Because it has been felt that we here today have done something positive in fulfilling this work, we are being honoured by our colleagues and comrades.

For my part, this award, this honour, the Lotus Prize for Literature does not come to me only. It goes to all those writers, suppressed and unpublished in South Africa, who might be more worthy of the prize.

On their behalf, I accept it with humility and pride.

The prize goes also to the whole oppressed people of South Africa for it is they who inspired whatever I have written.

It is not necessary for me to speak at length about racism in South Africa; its policies and politics have forced themselves on to the world stage.

In the words of the late Chief Luthuli: 'It is a museum piece in our time, a hangover from the dark past of mankind, a relic of an age which everywhere else is dead or dying.'

Under the leadership of the African National Congress, head of the national liberation movement, a new spirit is sweeping South Africa.

What could have been settled in the past by a few, through calm and peaceful discussion, must now be resolved by the oppressed masses in widespread armed conflict.

No one imagines that the defeat of imperialism in southern Africa will be quick and easy. The reality is awesome, not ecstatic.

All that can be confidently said is that the final phase in the struggle against white supremacy and imperialist domination in southern Africa has begun in earnest.

A people's culture cannot be suppressed without wrenching the heart of that people. To submit to oppression is to abandon one's culture and to reduce one's personality. The people of southern Africa are therefore engaged in a liberation struggle. The struggle is to reject negative impositions on our cultural development, to salvage that which is lost or obscured and to embrace new and meaningful additions. Through our war of liberation we are reasserting the continuity of the achievements of our forefathers and to recover values in progressive political, social and economic organization.

Therefore we do not fight and struggle alone, but with all other peoples who have the same ideals, the peoples of Vietnam, the Arab world, in Latin America, of Asia, knowing that through our efforts and the solidarity of the liberated states and the socialist community and all progressive mankind, we shall triumph.

Victory to the anti-imperialist struggle!

Power to the people!

CHAPTER THREE

A Poet Is Born
(1972)

A book review regarding the poetry of Oswald Joseph (Mbuyiseni) Mtshali, which appeared in The African Communist *under the pseudonym Gala. It is notable for La Guma's enthusiasm and promotion of black South African writing, as well as his engagement with poetry, which he did not write or publish himself.*

Sounds of a Cowhide Drum by Oswald Joseph Mtshali (Renoster Books, Johannesburg).

The heedful owl hooted hilariously
the birth of a new bard,
'Hail! a poet is born.'

The words are his own and the poet is Oswald Joseph Mtshali. And although these words are written with irony typical of Mtshali, South Africa can indeed hail him as among the most important voices of our country in the poetic field. Indeed it is difficult to point out anybody else in our poetry who can be said to surpass effectively this 30-year-old messenger from Soweto. Here is the poetic voice of urban black South Africa in the English language. Here is the bitter life of our people spun in the magic of words, of rhythm, of realism and fantasy, of passion and wry humour.

We find in language two kinds of speech: common speech, the normal everyday means which people use to communicate; and poetical speech, a medium more intense, preserving in a higher degree the qualities of rhythm, melody, imagery. Mtshali has succeeded in blending everyday communication with the medium of poetry. The resentment of the oppressed people's subconscious being finds a voice in his work:

> I shuffle in the queue
> with feet that patter
> on the station platform,
> and stumble into the coach
> that squeezes me like a lemon
> of all the juice of my life.

or,

> I show him
> the document of my existence
> to be scrutinized and given the nod.

Perhaps because he is a black South African, his poems are laced with irony, the barbed spear directed at the life created out of the oppression of the black people:

> Glorious is this world,
> the world that sustains man
> like a maggot in a carcass.

and:

> 'My child! Dear child,' she heard,
> 'Suffer for those who live in gilded sin.
> Toil for those who swim in a bowl of pink gin.'

But his work is also full of the pride of the African waiting for that time when he will be treated once more with the dignity he had known in the past:

> 'Where I'm a man
> amongst men,
> not John or Jim
> but Makhubalo Magudulela.'

and not:

> a faceless man
> who lives in the backyard
> of your house.

Mtshali's talent ranges from the near-classical style of pastoral descriptions:

> The rays of the sun
> are like a pair of scissors
> cutting the blanket
> of dawn from the sky.

to hard and sharp-edged modernism:

> The sun spun like
> a tossed coin.
> It whirled on the azure sky,
> it clattered into the horizon,
> it clicked in the slot,
> and neon lights popped
> and blinked, 'Time expired',
> as on a parking meter.

Where here and there somewhat academic, yet evocative, imagery tries to emerge—'as unruffled as a duck in a pond', or 'pale and taut like a glove on a doctor's hand'—it is overridden by the power of that imagery drawn out of the grim experiences of South African life, like 'bones protruding as if chiselled by a sculptor's hand of Famine', and

> Handcuffs
> have steel fangs
> whose bite is more painful
> than a whole battalion
> of fleas.

Here then are the African masses, the detribalized urbanites, the countryman just arrived from the reserves, the reapers in the rural areas, the road workers and night watchmen, the gangsters dead in the alleys of the townships, the washerwomen, the domestics, the drunks, the miners, the inevitable victims of pass laws and police raids, the children of the streets—all brought alive in the short, crisp lines of Mtshali's exciting talent. According to the editors of this volume, he is claimed to be 'the first sustained voice in the English poetry of this country for at least twenty years. It is emphatically the voice of our day.' It is hoped that *Sounds of a Cowhide Drum* will not be the last we shall hear of this fine poet. If it is at all necessary to prove that the oppressed African people have no need to import humanistic or revolutionary literature and art to inspire them; that they have the power and talent to thrust forth their own—then we need simply to point at Oswald Joseph Mtshali. It is hoped that this collection of 60 poems will continue to circulate in South Africa.

CHAPTER FOUR

On Short Stories
(July 1973)

This editorial by La Guma provides an overview of the working mandate of Lotus: Afro-Asian Writings, *with which he was involved throughout the 1970s, serving on its editorial committee at different times. As such, it offers a glimpse of his personal tastes and the importance of the short story as shared form among African and Asian writers—a situation that has resulted, at times, in the critical neglect of Afro-Asian writers who did not publish novels or other longer works.*

Our magazine has published a total of 56 short stories in its Numbers 1 to 10. This figure covers the vast geographical area of the African and Asian continents, and it is indeed a tribute to the administrators of *Lotus* and to the seriousness of our movement in carrying out the resolution of the Conference which established our magazine. It is widely representative in the genre of the short story from Africa and Asia.

Your reporter will roughly enumerate each individual country represented in this field: so, for purposes of information, of the 56 stories, the Arab Republic of Egypt supplied 5; South Africa 5; Tunisia 2; Palestine 3; USSR 6; Mongolia 3; Japan 4; Algeria 2; Lebanon 2; Kenya 2; Zambia 2 and other countries, including the US, 1 each. Regionally, the short stories can be divided as follows: black Africa 16; Arab countries and Middle East 21; Asia and the USSR 10; Southeast Asia and Japan 7; Pacific and the US 2.

As is usually the case, each story might make a different impression on the individual reader from the point of view of presentation, impact, style and form. Without going into the technical merits or otherwise of each story published, it must be stated that in general the material published reflects the writers as human beings most sensitive, conscious and capable of expression; moreover they are committed to the problems of human beings, irrespective of the stage of development of their countries in the context of the great changes taking place in our Afro-Asian world.

The stories published in *Lotus* magazine under review here are full of contempt for colonialism in all forms, also for social injustice, poverty, human degradation and racial arrogance. Above all, they are full of the driving spirit of humanity.

At this stage, your reporter must be allowed to point out at random to certain of the works which manifest varied forms and constructions, yet which embrace the common attitude.

Perhaps, every aspiration of the peoples who are portrayed in all the stories in our collection are epitomized in the fable-like story 'New Year and Bitter Tears' by the Mongolian writer, D. Nachagdorj (Issue No. 4). In this tale the longings of the oppressed girl Tserima for happiness, and her final salvation from exploitation and persecution on a New Year's Day by her young lover Tsoultoum, expresses the aspirations of all peoples.

In the same Number, the Palestinian Y. Shorourou presents a directly political script dealing without allegorical style with the problems of the Arab people vis-à-vis Zionist persecution.

In Issue No. 6, Kemal Bilbasar writes a touching love story centred around apparently traditional wooing in the Turkish countryside. This story is 'Sale of Saltanat'. Like that of Nachagdorj it is a plain tale with a folk background, and both their colours harmonize to produce a single picture.

In the very first issue of our magazine, 'Okolo; or, The Voice' from Gabriel Okara of Nigeria is concerned with the bringing of new light to the so-called knowing-nothing; and Dazai Osamu's 'Osan' (Japan) could well serve those women who struggle for emancipation.

Again the fable-like atmosphere appears in Issue No. 5 with Efua Theodora Sutherland's story, 'New Life at Kyerefaso' (Ghana), and contrasts in presentation with Abioseh Nicol (Sierra Leone) who writes 'The Judge's Son', with its condemnation of lust and violence.

As has been stated, we do not wish to go into detail over each and every short story published, but wish only to give random illustrations of the diversity of styles and form presenting a common theme. In a more exact examination it would behove us to deal with a wider scale like that ranging from the impressionistic works, such as 'Dreams of a Tired Sailor' by El-Assouad of Tunisia, to the almost photographic technique of other writers, and the brilliant glimpses, like looking into a kaleidoscope, of Idrus of Indonesia (Oh . . . Oh . . . Oh!), and the connection between literature and national events as in 'Rains in the Jungle' by Thao Boun Lin of Laos.

However, we do not wish to conclude this survey without mentioning other stories, like El-Sharkawy's 'The Scorpion' from the UAR, Fazil Iskander's 'Old Crooked Arm' from the USSR, and from the Philippines, Wilfredo Dayo Nolledo's 'Guernica and the Blue Star'.

It was not possible to establish when each of the stories on which we report were written, but some of them are familiar and have been published elsewhere. While their appearance in *Lotus* does no damage to our magazine, we should however attempt to become the first on the list with Afro-Asian authors. Perhaps, now that we are offering fees to contributors, it will be possible to urge writers to give *Lotus* first option on their short stories and so become a fountainhead, as it were, of Afro-Asian publication in this genre. Nevertheless, we should now be in a position to consider a substantial single volume of short stories.

We must commend the several translators for their efforts in representing the works from various areas into the English language, considering all the problems of recreating atmosphere and style. It must be assumed that translations in the French and Arabic editions are of a similar standard. The artists who decorated the pages of *Lotus* also deserve commendation.

It is quite possible that more negative aspects of the work could have been searched for and examined in this report. But your reporter, being an inveterate optimist, may be forgiven if he quotes one of the characters from the Japanese writer Dazai Osamu: 'Revolutions are to make people happy. I do not trust the revolutionary with the tragic face.' Besides, the more positive aspects of the works under review far outshine the negative, which are of such a nature that they do not detract from the value of the works.

Having read 56 short stories from all over the Afro-Asian world appearing in our magazine, one is tempted to ask the question: 'Is *Lotus* fulfilling its duty?' We have set out upon a road, and we are still far from its end, and there is still a lot which can be done, but maintaining the present standard as a basis, great things can still arise through our publication. What we have started to do is to provide a valuable service, not only to students of Afro-Asian literature, and in this case of short stories, but to bringing the literature of our continents into the arena of world literature. We have established the wherewithal for the preservation of writings which might otherwise have gone astray instead of being passed from eye to eye, from mind to mind, across the world. The writer Mohamed Dib said, 'The memory of a people is their national library.' Your reporter believes that we are on the way to establishing such a library, in terms of Afro-Asia.

CHAPTER FIVE

In Memory of Hutch
Alfred Hutchinson
(July 1973)

This obituary of the Coloured South African writer Alfred Hutchinson (1924–72) appeared in Lotus: Afro-Asian Writings. *Hutchinson left for exile in Ghana, London, and eventually Nigeria, following a period of activism in South Africa during the 1950s. He is the author of the memoir,* Road to Ghana *(1960).*

The South African exile community, the Anti-Apartheid Movement and all his friends heard with deep sorrow of the death of Alfred Hutchinson who died suddenly in Nigeria in mid-October. Alfred Hutchinson, known to all his associates simply as 'Hutch' had gone to Nigeria earlier this year to join the education department there after having worked as a teacher in England for several years.

Born in 1924 in the Transvaal, Hutch graduated from Fort Hare University College and worked as a teacher in South Africa. During the 1950s he took part in the Campaign for the Defiance of Unjust Laws and served a term of imprisonment, as a result of which he was victimized by the Transvaal education authorities. He then joined the staff of the Johannesburg Indian School established as a community protest against the Group Areas Act. In 1956, he was one of the 156 accused in the famous Treason Trial.

During the period of the State of Emergency declared at the time of the Sharpeville Massacre in 1960, Hutchinson escaped from South Africa and made his way to Ghana and after a period in

Africa came to England where he worked in Brighton and then in London as a teacher.

However, Alfred Hutchinson was best known as a writer and many of his short stories appeared in South Africa in such magazines as *Fighting Talk* and the newspaper *New Age*, banned in 1962 by the South African government. As a writer, his short stories were full of the life of the oppressed African people of his country, dealt with great compassion and brilliant imagery. His work was published in collections outside his own country, and his major work was *Road to Ghana* published shortly after he left to go into exile, which, apart from being an account of his escape from South Africa, was also in a way a personal testament.

Unfortunately for the South African literary scene, Hutchinson did not pursue his literary career as fully as would have been hoped while in Europe, and it was anticipated that his return to Africa would stimulate further writing. Alfred Hutchinson's passing has therefore left a lasting gap in South African literary life, and for all who knew him the absence of his tall, powerful and jovial personality will always be remembered with sadness.

CHAPTER SIX

Lust without Passion
(1973)

A review of a poetry collection by the South African writer Dennis Brutus (1924–2009), which appeared in The African Communist *under the pseudonym Gala. It is surprisingly critical in tone, though it is characteristic of La Guma's strong opinions—and commitment to realism—which personal friendship did not always mitigate.*

A Simple Lust (Collected Poems of South African Jail and Exile) by Dennis Brutus, published by Heinemann Educational Books. £1.75.

Heinemann Books in London recently published a collection of poems by the South African poet Dennis Brutus. The collection includes his earlier works, namely, *Sirens, Knuckles, Boots; Letters to Martha; Poems from Algiers; Thoughts Abroad*. All these and others are now published under the title, *A Simple Lust*.

A victim of apartheid oppression and police persecution, one who served a sentence on the notorious Robben Island, Dennis Brutus has also been active in the campaign to isolate South Africa from world sport and in campaigns for the release of political prisoners. The reader of these 'poems of South African jail and exile' would therefore look forward to an experience of poetry rooted in the realities of South African life and the poet's identification with his country and his people's experiences, inside jail and out. But the reader with this expectation is disappointed, for Brutus seems to be concerned only with his own personal relationships and reactions to the world about him. 'A troubadour, I traverse all my land / exploring all her wide-flung parts with zest...'

For the African people, poetry has little to do with books. It lives in their speech, in their songs, it reflects their attitudes towards life about them, it is common property. Poets, like Oswald Mtshali for example, who have written, have succeeded in transferring common experiences to paper and have still retained their own personalities as poets. But for Brutus, everything, jail, exile, oppression, happiness, despair, happens to himself, the poet, only. '... The iron monster of the world ingests me in its grinding maw.' 'What wonder such gingerly menacing claws, they would rend me if they could ... but I accept their leashed-in power...' Even when he turns outward or pays tribute to somebody else, like Luthuli, one has the feeling that it is more a gesture than identification.

It can be argued of course that Brutus comes from a more individualized section of South African society and carries with him the poetic traditions included in the education of that community. Perhaps modern poetry is the product of a more individualized society, and Brutus is a modern poet. But the world is common to the poet and his fellow man, the poetry in which he formulates his experience of it must still evoke a general reaction, touch a chord in every heart, expressing what others feel but cannot express themselves, drawing all into closer communion. The poet, thanks to his talent and inspiration, can at least express what others feel, and when he expresses himself they recognize his longings as their own. It is difficult to find this with Dennis Brutus. He is more the poet's poet. His imagery satisfies himself and the cognoscenti perhaps, but hardly anybody else. Who but the initiated among us can explain 'an ordinary girl' surveying the poet 'with Stanislav disdain', or 'the diurnal reminders excoriate their souls'?

Then again he is more concerned with geography and the physical world than with people. Robben Island is a 'barred existence' and 'Cement-grey floors and walls, cement-grey days, cement-grey time . . .' The poet is alone there, and only half hears 'the weary tramp of feet as the men came shuffling from the quarry.' In fact this is the only line in 'On the Island' that is concerned with his fellow prisoners, out of four verses. Outside of prison, under house arrest, in exile, travelling, everything seems to be happening to the poet only and to nobody else.

Brutus is also the intellectual poet and words in ink mean more in his book than any that could have been written in human blood. While much of his imagery is derived from the sexual experience, which in itself could profoundly evoke the human spirit, Brutus' simple lust is unfortunately without a simple passion.

CHAPTER SEVEN

Alexander Solzhenitsyn
'Life through a Crooked Eye'
(1974)

Published in The African Communist, *this essay is one of the more controversial pieces of criticism that La Guma wrote given its strident critique of Soviet dissident writer and Nobel Laureate Alexander Solzhenitsyn (1918–2008). La Guma takes an orthodox Soviet view, though his reproach can also be understood as emerging from personal frustration with the hypocrisy of Western critics: Why should Soviet dissidents be celebrated in Western Europe and the United States while exiled South African dissidents fighting against apartheid be ignored?*

For a long time now those in the West interested in literature, as well as those with an eye on Soviet affairs generally, have been assailed through the anti-communist mass media with the virtues of writers and intellectuals who are defectors from and 'dissenters' within the Soviet Union, among them Alexander Solzhenitsyn. I am not sure whether any writers of the 'Third World' have taken the time to take issue with this aspect of the anti-communist, anti-Soviet campaign—we have our hands full with the problem of literature in the struggle of our people for survival. But looking through a copy of *South African Outlook* (September 1972) we discover that Solzhenitsyn has actually passed the South African censors, and that his Nobel Lecture is reprinted there.

Alexander Solzhenitsyn has the distinction then of being the only writer in the Soviet Union, as far as we can remember, to pass

South Africa's racist and anti-communist censorship examination. While the works of progressive authors have been banned in our country, we are told by *South African Outlook* that 'readers of this journal need no introduction to the author of *Cancer Ward* and *The First Circle*.'

Apart from this, *South African Outlook* describes itself as a 'journal dealing with ecumenical (and racial) affairs' and gives information 'according to what it believes to be Christian standards'. Well, Solzhenitsyn did convert to Christianity; and any non-Christian ideas about art, literature and 'The Role of Writers in Society'—the title of his Nobel Prize Lecture—might not then make much appeal to him or his protagonists. However, seeing that his work is allowed circulation in South Africa, we have some cause to enter the lists over these ideas.

For Solzhenitsyn, art is something that is above, separate, from people. We hold 'Art in our hands' (he gives it the capital letter) and ask ourselves: 'As the savage, confronted with a strange object asks ... did it fall from the sky?' 'Art is not sullied by our efforts... and however applied it grants us a share of its own secret, inner light.' He tells us that 'in the pre-dawn twilight of mankind we received it from Hands we were unable to see.' Therefore we must conclude that even if there was no humanity, no mankind, no people on earth, Art could still be there. 'It is we who will die; art will remain.' Art is some mystical phenomenon, 'its dazzling convolutions, its unpredictable discoveries, its shattering influence on people, are too magical to be plumbed by the artist's philosophy or scheme, or by the labour of his unworthy fingers.'

But Solzhenitsyn himself would never have been able to produce his works if he had not put his hand to a pen and the pen to paper. If he had not been born his friends would never have been able to say this is 'the world-celebrated author whose works are banned in the Soviet Union' (*Times*, London, 29 August 1973).

Primitive man might have sat in a cave after a good meal of roasted auroch and idly scratched with his toasting stick on the dirt floor, in reverie tracing the events of the hunt. He might have then discovered that he could reproduce a natural occurrence and later he transferred this reproduction to the wall of his cave.

Everything that we call works of art came and comes from human endeavour. One person may be able to represent life better through one or other medium than another. This we call talent. But if talent was not *exercised* we would not have art.

So we may say that art is a representation of life. As Maxim Gorky put it: 'What the imagination creates is prompted by the facts of real life, and it is governed not by baseless fantasy, divorced from life, but by very real causes . . .'

Art and Life

But, further, art is a representation of life also modified by the personality of the artist; for the artist has a character, an outlook on life, the world around him. And through his art he hopes to modify the personality of others. Man's ideas all stem from the real world about him, and from his experience of that real world he has been able to form opinions, take up attitudes. Moreover, man is a social being, and the society in which he lives helps to influence the artist's attitude to work and life as well as those of anyone else. In short, being determines consciousness.

While the idea that 'social being determines consciousness' does not necessarily constitute a complete aesthetic, Plekhanov helps us by explaining that the mode of production in society—i.e. the material means of production, technique and organization—and the relations of production determines men's mode of life or their condition; their condition in turn determines their psychology—their forms of thought and their emotional makeup; and their psychology determines their works of art. To quote Gorky again: 'It has turned out that people cannot be grasped apart from real life, which is steeped in politics through and through. It has turned out that man . . . still remains a social unit, and not a cosmic one like the planets.'

But Alexander Solzhenitsyn's 'Art' is above all this. For 'Mankind as a whole is squeezed into a single lump, lack of mutual understanding threatens to bring a rapid and stormy end'. Mankind is not divided into opposing political and economic forces. It is merely a 'lack of mutual understanding' and if this goes on 'we shall not survive on the Earth, just as a man with two hearts is not long for this world.' But 'who will create for mankind a single system of evaluation? Propaganda, compulsion and scientific proof are all powerless here. But fortunately the means to convey all this to us does exist in the world. It is art. It is literature.'

Solzhenitsyn's 'art and literature' is a sort of djinn out of a bottle that appears to solve the problems of mankind. 'Art can straighten the path of man's history', and he would 'insistently remind you of this great and blessed property of Art'.

The Class Struggle

Solzhenitsyn's conception of the world is not one of contending classes, of working class against capitalist exploiter, or imperialism against anti-imperialism, man struggling to create a better life in which his 'Art' will have to take sides. No, for him social contradictions stem from the Freudian conception that living beings have an aggressive instinct whose manifestation is natural and inevitable. 'The old same primitive urges rend and sunder our world—greed, envy, licence, mutual malevolence, though they now adopt euphemistic pseudonyms as they go, such as "class struggle", "racial struggle", "the struggle of the masses", "the struggle of organized labour".'

Note that he does not include the exploitation of workers by the bourgeoisie or the national oppression of millions of non-white people among these 'euphemistic pseudonyms'. This puts

Solzhenitsyn in solid with his friends in the West and with the South African censors. In any case, if all mankind is a victim of 'the old same primitive urges' then the exploiter can't really be blamed for what he's up to. Solzhenitsyn goes even further, to insult the working class directly: 'Whenever any group of workers sees a chance to grab something extra—never mind if they don't deserve it, never mind if it's more than they need—they up and grab it and ruin takes society.' Thus quoting the scurrilous remarks of all capitalist politicians word for word!

For Solzhenitsyn 'this twentieth century of ours has proved crueller than the preceding ones... the spirit of Munich is the dominant one in the twentieth century.' Not the spirit of the Socialist Revolution, not the spread of socialism over one-third of the world, nor the emergence of independent peoples in Africa and Asia, nor the heroic struggles of oppressed peoples for liberation. No, Solzhenitsyn sees that 'violence strides bold and victorious through the world.' But violence in his eyes is confined to hijackers, the youth and Chinese Red Guards; it never includes the imperialists who rain death and destruction on millions of innocents.

Nevertheless, somewhere among a hotchpotch of platitudes and generalizations about the separation of art from the artist, and about 'World literature as a single great heart', Solzhenitsyn must concede that 'Man is built in such a way that his experience of life, both as an individual and as a member of a group, determines his world outlook, his motivations and his scale of values, his actions and his attentions.' But he is not satisfied, and adds his personal formula: 'As the Russian saying goes: "Trust not your own brother; trust your own eye, even crooked." That is the soundest basis for understanding one's environment and for determining one's behaviour within that environment.' Then Solzhenitsyn finds himself, in all modesty, specifying that 'Russian literature has tended away from self-admiration and frivolity for decades now. Nor am I ashamed to continue in this tradition.'

What has Solzhenitsyn to say of Russian literature? 'I have mounted this platform from which the Nobel Lecture is delivered ... while others perhaps more gifted than I perished ... in the Gulag Archipelago.' It is explained that Gulag stands for 'State Prison Camp Administration'. 'A whole national literature has been left there! Buried without a coffin, without even any underclothes, naked, just a name-tag tied around one toe.'

One can hardly comment upon such a gross exaggeration. But Alexander Solzhenitsyn is obsessed with prison camps. Any socially conscious writer is naturally concerned with the problems of his country, the society in which he lives. For us, social consciousness is the sum total of the political and legal theories, the moral, religious, philosophical views of a given society, and in addition includes the social sciences, art and social psychology (social attitudes, moods, customs, etc.).

Soviet Life

A writer might not be able to deal with all individual problems of his fellow men, so he tries to learn from the average experience. Thus, conscious writers in South Africa, for example, are concerned with racism and apartheid. But to give the impression that prison camps form the general experience of the Soviet people is, to say the least, a gross distortion of the realities of Soviet life. No honest person who has visited the Soviet Union can claim that he experienced the atmosphere of oppression, concentration camps and secret police present, as Solzhenitsyn would have it. The common problems of the Soviet people today are those concerned with the transition from socialism to communism, and that is what most writers in the USSR also are concerned with.

Literature and art not only reflect the life of the people, but they also help to mould the human mind. The idea of the indivisible link of literature and art with the interests and struggle of social classes and, in socialist society, with the life of the entire people was theoretically substantiated by Lenin who propounded the principle of the partisanship of literature.

Bourgeois propagandists attack this principle, trying to prove that to serve the interests of a definite class is incompatible with artistic creation. But we need, for example, only point to the clutter of innocuous and trivial reading matter produced in the West, which helps to divert the masses from more serious aspects of life, and ask whose interest the writers of such material serve. Artistic creation cannot remain outside the struggle of classes, outside politics; for each writer, whether he likes to or not, expresses in his work the interest of some one class.

> An artist can be really inspired only by what is capable of facilitating intercourse among men. The possible limits of such intercourse are not determined by the artist, but by the level of culture attained by the social entity to which he belongs. But in a society divided into classes, they are also determined by the mutual relations of these classes...

(G. Plekhanov, *Art and Social Life*)

Socialism is the first social system which freed culture from the influence of the moneybags. It affords the artist a chance to create not in order to pander to the tastes of a small coterie of 'cultured', but for the masses. Does this infringe the freedom of the artist? Each real artist searches for the truth, seeks to depict the truth. But this is what socialist society is also interested in. The main demand of socialist realism is to portray life truthfully, in its progressive development.

Three novels and a play by Solzhenitsyn translated in the West are all concerned with prison camps. His Nobel Prize Lecture is concerned with prison camps. Admittedly he might well have had unpleasant experiences in the past, while a prisoner. But one cannot be expected to accept the aftereffects of those experiences as examples of the author's genius, or of the common experiences of all his people.

We have learnt that Solzhenitsyn spent eight years at hard labour from 1945 to 1953 and afterwards a period of exile. He was rehabilitated in 1956–57. Solzhenitsyn may have been innocent of the charges against him, as may have been others imprisoned. The Soviet Union openly admitted that mistakes were made during the period of Stalin's leadership. Alexei Surkov, once first secretary of the USSR Writers' Union, said of Solzhenitsyn's *First Circle*: 'There is no denying this novel contains much bitter truth—but it represents our society as a society of prisoners, and this is tendentious lying' (*Financial Times*, London, 7 April 1970).

Solzhenitsyn of course has the right to make his point about his experiences as a prisoner. He wrote *One Day in the Life of Ivan Denisovich*, which was published in the magazine *Novi Mir* in 1962. But from thereon he persisted with 'prison camp' books. 'The Soviet people are portrayed as a misled herd, which the war has proved it is not' (ibid.). Apart from this, many of his stories are concerned with death. For example, of his *Stories and Prose Poems*, the reviewer Gabriel Pearson says: 'The dead are Solzhenitsyn's theme and what drives him is the urgency of their cause as though they were in his keeping' (*Guardian*, London, 10 July 1973).

From the standpoint of Western reviewers all this must have contributed to the 'unprecedented consensus that Solzhenitsyn is a great writer in the grand Russian tradition of ethical urgency and openness of life' (ibid.). But his Soviet colleagues did not think so. According to them, in his work 'life is reflected in a distorting mirror, and moreover with an obvious anti-Soviet slant' as Soviet writer Nikolai Gribachev put it (*Soviet Weekly*, 17 January 1970). The poet Sergei Mikhalov said, 'Anyone is free to choose his own way of life. But one cannot remain in the ranks of those who are heading in a different direction. We Soviet writers have no intention of going Solzhenitsyn's way, and Solzhenitsyn is not heading our way. The best way out is to part' (ibid.). Even the anti-Soviet émigré paper, *Russkaya Misl*, said bluntly that the novel *First Circle* was fully and completely directed against Soviet reality.

Solzhenitsyn declined the offered assistance of his colleagues to make ideological corrections to his work: including *Cancer Ward*; *First Circle*; *The Banquet of Victors*; *Stories and Sketches and Sad Stories*. He preferred to have them published in the West, where as he later said in his Nobel Prize Lecture, they 'rapidly acquired a responsible world readership, in spite of hasty and often defective translations.' These works were advertised as ones in which the author 'boldly' and 'in a talented way' came out against the ideas of socialism, against the Soviet system. Such claims by Solzhenitsyn's backers are not baseless: that *is* exactly the outlook they show. The reason why these works are published in the West is clear. The aim is to further anti-Soviet sentiments. As the late Ilya Ehrenburg said back in 1954 (the Second Congress of Soviet Writers): 'A book is the heart of a writer and one cannot separate the author from his work.' Soviet publishers and his colleagues, as well as public opinion, all found that Solzhenitsyn and his work did not coincide with their requirements of conduct, social activities and creative work.

Is This Silence?

Solzhenitsyn's expulsion from the Writers' Union in 1969 was of course seen in the anti-Soviet West as an attempt to silence him. He still lives near Moscow and still gives interviews to Western correspondents. He has not been deprived of pen and paper. (In South Africa, authors are prohibited from writing even before they have thought of a publisher.) South Africa aside, whether in the bourgeois democratic West or in the Soviet Union, a writer may be able to write up as many reams of paper as he wishes. But when he takes his work to a publisher he discovers that the latter also has a say in the matter of what is produced. How many writers in the 'free' West have not had their works rejected because they do not conform to the standards of publishers? How many writers have not been asked to alter or modify their manuscripts to suit the publisher? If a Western publisher has this right, why not a socialist publisher?

How many unions in the West have not expelled members for contravening their programme, or the rules and duties imposed on members? Nikolai Gribachev quoted elsewhere here said also, 'Besides, we are not just a writers' union, but a union of *Soviet* writers.' Solzhenitsyn's works show that he is far from concerned with the realities of Soviet life. 'Trust not your brother; trust your own eye, even crooked.' Seeing Soviet life through a crooked eye got him the Nobel Prize [in Literature] for 1970. No one will deny that in the eyes of millions of people the Nobel Prize is a halo. Its prestige is enhanced by the fact that associated with it are leading names in the field of science, such as Einstein, Joliot-Curie, Pavlov, as well as outstanding scientists of our day, including Soviet ones.

It is a different thing with fiction, about which every literate person can pass his judgment. While we might accept that scientists awarded the Nobel Prize are authorities in their specific field, it does not follow that the prize awarded to somebody in any other field elevates him to an authority. It is in the sphere of fiction that we are able to see the class and political sympathies and antipathies of the Nobel award committee.

The Nobel Committee traditionally has had its own specific view of Russian literature and its representatives. While in the West several periodicals describe Solzhenitsyn as a spiritual successor of Chekhov and Tolstoy (neither of whom ever won a Nobel Prize!). Maxim Gorky and Vladimir Mayakovsky, without whom one cannot imagine the prose and poetry of our century, did not suit the tastes of the Nobel Committee. It took that committee several decades to name its first Russian author. Its choice fell on Ivan Bunin. It 'discovered' Bunin not at the height of his talent but only when he emigrated from his country and adopted an openly hostile attitude to the young Soviet state.

It was then that awarding a Nobel Prize began to be used as an act in the 'cold war' leading to the award of a Nobel Prize to Boris Pasternak for *Doctor Zhivago*. That talented poet and translator—

who in fact in his time was awarded the USSR's highest prize for literature—drew the attention of the Nobel Committee only after he had published abroad this indifferent but anti-socialist novel. The award of the prize to Alexander Solzhenitsyn in 1970 came only as a logical conclusion of the Nobel Committee's policy not so much on the merits of the literature, as on its attitude to the Soviet Union, to the ideas of socialism.

It is true there was an occasion when it was thought that honesty and objectivity prevailed over political sympathies. The outstanding Soviet author, Mikhail Sholokhov, was awarded the Nobel Prize some seven years ago. But now, examining the facts, one must perceive even in this a programmed calculation, an attempt to create an alibi for subsequent large-scale anti-Soviet assaults. Many Western newspapers and periodicals have openly expressed the opinion that Solzhenitsyn deserves the prize if only because he 'fights courageously' against the society in which he lives. Even the conservative press admits openly that the decision to award him the prize was influenced not by his literary talents but by his anti-Soviet rhetoric. In the distorted mirror, through the crooked eye, an ordinary slanderer can be seen as a 'champion of truth'.

It is perhaps significant that not as much hullabaloo was raised in the West over *August 1914* as was over such openly anti-Soviet works as *One Day*, *The Cancer Ward* and *The First Circle*. One need not accept that the 'experts' who praise Solzhenitsyn necessarily believe their own words. If Solzhenitsyn were not available they would find someone else. Having accepted his award, Alexander Solzhenitsyn has been seeking kudos for his friends of like persuasion. The Western praise-singers have become enthused over the new Nobel Prize winner's attempts to rehabilitate a man, Vlasov, who fought against his country in the ranks of the Nazi army, and to suggest the Nobel Prize for Academician Andrei Sakharov. While the democratic and progressive world condemned the putsch in Chile, the 'scientist' Sakharov called on the dictatorship to protect the poet Pablo Neruda in the name of the military junta's 'epoch of renaissance and consolidation announced by your Government'.

But we have not heard the last of the so-modest Alexander Solzhenitsyn. The West is still to inherit a legacy of 'the main part of my work' (*Times*, 29 August 1973). This will come to us after his death. But a natural death is not good enough for Solzhenitsyn. It is after 'I am killed or suddenly mysteriously dead' that these main works will be published. Anti-Soviet Western publishers must therefore impatiently chew their fingernails while they wait for the day when his 'literary last will and testament will irrevocably come into force.' They might have consolation in the knowledge that when that day comes, they will be able to publish some more of Solzhenitsyn's obsessions and distortions, seen through his crooked eye.

CHAPTER EIGHT

Hello or Goodbye, Athol Fugard?
(1974)

This essay is an assessment of the work of South African playwright Athol Fugard, first published in The African Communist *under the pseudonym Gala. In contrast to his assessment of Brutus, La Guma is critical of Fugard not for his lack of realism but for his consent to certain dictates of the apartheid government and not becoming part of the liberation struggle.*

'Athol Fugard's play broke the dead-weight of precedence which decreed that Black men and White could not appear on the same stage, and his two characters in *The Blood Knot* are the ideal ones to have done so.' With these words the now-banned magazine *Fighting Talk* introduced Fugard and his unique play to South African audiences back in 1962. 'This thin, bearded man with the intense flashing eyes is modest, self-effacing, direct and unsentimental; talks staccato as he writes and simply doesn't see colour—in persons.'

Now twelve years after, Athol Fugard is still considered a phenomenon in South African theatre and has become an established international name. His plays have travelled outside of our country and at the time of writing he is receiving acclaim in London with his newest productions: *The Island*; *Sizwe Bansi Is Dead*; *Statements After an Arrest Under the Immorality Act*.

Fugard can be looked at as an example of the contradictions within white South African society. As a force for social change the white community as such must be viewed negatively. The

Programme of the South African Communist Party (1963), *The Road to South African Freedom* stated:

> The relatively high standards of life and wages enjoyed by White workers represent, in reality, a share in the super profits made by the capitalists out of the gross exploitation of the non-Whites. Systematically indoctrinated with the creed of White superiority, the White worker imagines himself to be a part of the ruling class and willingly acts as a tool and an accomplice in the maintenance of colonialism and capitalism.

Similarly the African National Congress states in its *Strategy, Tactic and Programme*:

> The material well-being of the White group and its political, social and economic privileges are, we know, rooted in its racial domination of the indigenous majority ... By economic bribes and legal artifices, which preserve for him the top layers of the skills and wage incomes, the White worker is successfully mobilized as racialism's most reliable contingent.

In spite of this, white South Africa has not been without its inevitable contradictions and inevitably it has produced from within its ranks numerous opponents. Thus we have seen the emergence of such outstanding revolutionary figures as Bram Fischer, as well as authors and artists of various degrees of philosophical outlook, many wrestling with themselves, but opposed to apartheid and the perpetuation of racism. Among the latter, Athol Fugard appeared as a noteworthy figure on the South African stage.

It is not our intention to discuss here the relationship of Fugard's work to the history and development of South African theatre. Likewise in the absence of appropriate studies, it is difficult to trace the historical sequence of playwriting in the English language only in South Africa. According to Alan Lennox-Short (editor, *English and South Africa*, 1973), various productions have appeared since the 1890s; the year 1911 started the twentieth-century theatre with a production in the Pretoria Opera House, but 'the depressed Thirties were unpropitious to any form of drama'. Those who have tried to follow the growth of English-language theatre might recall the postwar works like *Kimberley Train* (Lewis Sowden) and *Try for White* (Basil Warner).

It was *The Blood Knot* (1961, published in 1963) which established Athol Fugard's reputation in South Africa, the US and Britain. Before that he had written and produced *No-Good Friday* (1958) and *Nongogo* (1959), both naturalistic tragedies set in Johannesburg black townships and staged with African casts. Of these earlier works the writer Lionel Abrahams said, 'Fugard already displays distinctive imaginative vigour and a new ease with his dramatic medium that had not been obvious in the efforts of other South African playwrights.'

Athol Fugard was born in Middleburg, Cape Province, on 11 June 1932, his father the son of Scandinavian Manchester immigrants and his mother a descendant of Afrikaner Voortrekkers. Colin Smith in the *Observer* (6 January 1974) puts it: 'The result was a university bantam-weight boxer, merchant seaman, journalist, magistrate's clerk, actor, director, who at the age of 41 has become South Africa's most successful dramatist.' He is married and has a 12-year-old daughter.

Fugard the playwright is never divorced from Fugard the actor-producer, the theatrical explorer. He usually participates in the staging of his own plays, and his own acting has much to do with their impact. In Port Elizabeth, he brought into being an African theatre workshop, The Serpent Players. He worked with Cape Town actors in 1971 to create an almost wordless presentation of *Orestes*, which technically emerged largely from the actors' improvisations. In 1972, he engaged in experimental theatre at The Space, a new venue in Cape Town, and the first work to be produced there was his own *Statement After an Arrest Under the Immorality Act*.

Fugard's works are not plays in the accepted sense of the word, but consist in the main of dialogues between two characters. There is an ever-present concentration on experimentation and technical innovations, and the influence of Samuel Beckett is clearly present.

But it is the content of Fugard's work which must certainly reveal the real man. *The Blood Knot* is a play in seven scenes, with two characters. It is an episode in the life of two lonely brothers, one fair-skinned, the other dark, who begin a pen-pal friendship with a woman. The pen-pal venture boomerangs when the girl turns out to be white, and what started almost as a lark turns to torment as the two men act out their dilemma—they are brothers but separated by the gulf of colour. The fair-skinned brother, Morris, forces Zachariah to probe his blackness, first to cringe from it, debase himself before it, then to glory and triumph in it. In the climax of the play, the brothers act out the story across the colour line: subservience, cringing humility, then a creeping apprehension, a growing awareness, fear, terror, the falling darkness while Zachariah—and South Africa—stand in wait.

When the curtain rose on this play in the early 1960s, it was the time of the Treason Trial, Sharpeville, the State of Emergency, of high ferment on the political scene in South Africa. Among the whites, liberal consciences were being stirred. Perhaps for this reason a group of white authors called themselves 'Die Sestigers' (Men of the Sixties). *The Blood Knot* itself was a sign of the times for white liberal intellectuals in particular, and it was acclaimed with enthusiasm by all who saw it. Fugard is a liberal and at this time displayed all the emotional fervour of the liberal for the freedom of the individual, abhorrence for colour discrimination and the nightmare life of the blacks under apartheid. He was, like many, captured by the new spirit of rejection of racism.

International reaction against apartheid was mounting as racism became more and more intensified. Overseas playwrights were beginning to follow the call to isolate South Africa on all fronts. Athol Fugard himself felt the restricting confines of laws preventing mixed audiences and actors in halls, and saw justification in the decision of non-South African authors to refuse to allow their works to be performed before segregated audiences, and went on to encourage them in this action. Segregated theatre in South Africa began to enter a critical period.

The South African security police naturally took an interest in this rebellious Afrikaner playwright. Yet he appears to have accommodated them in typically liberal fashion. 'They're all great fishermen. I gave them one of my best interviews sitting on a rock with a rod in my hand and the waves washing over our feet' (*Observer*, 6 January 1974). He continued to write and produce, but the pressures on him did not fail to leave their influence.

It must be significant that his next play, *People Are Living There* [1968], his first one about whites only, had less richness than the previous work, but proved popular nevertheless. *Hello And Goodbye* (1966) followed *The Blood Knot* in confining its cast to two related characters, a white brother and sister, devoured by the memories of their parents. Now the characters were a cripple and a prostitute. The deteriorated symbolism in these two deformed beings cannot go unnoticed. At the end of the play one of them chooses to revert to a lonely continuation while the other takes up a bizarre existence.

Segregated theatre still continued in a state of crisis. There were acts of copyright piracy by theatre companies desperate for plays and unconcerned with the anti-apartheid struggle. In 1967, the government withdrew Athol Fugard's passport. Four years later, a petition with 4,000 white South African signatures persuaded them to return it, so that Fugard could direct *Boesman and Lena* [1969] in London. The chastened Fugard had by this time abandoned his support for the international cultural boycott. His new work received praise in the press in South Africa. *Boesman and Lena* received an official South African subsidy and was acclaimed in the

Nationalist newspaper *Die Burger*. The play has been filmed in South Africa, though not yet released.

Lena is a hag, a Coloured hag. A hard-drinking Coloured woman, knocked about by her man, Boesman, treated as rubbish by those in authority. Life's crumbs for Lena are bitter. These characters might still be Fugard's concern for the downtrodden, but Boesman and Lena are the kind of characters the 'white madam' laughs at, tolerates; they are demoralized people who accept their lot, hoping to survive, doing no harm, finding solace in the bottle. So once more Fugard's cripples dominate the scene.

Miss Yvonne Bryceland, the actress who played Lena, has claimed that this play has done 'tremendous good' for South Africa overseas (*Star*, Johannesburg, 14 September 1971). The government's decision to grant Athol Fugard a passport had turned out to be 'incredibly wise'. Now he would have no difficulty in getting the rights to virtually any play for production in South Africa. He would be able to break through the cultural boycott, she said.

Athol Fugard is now the playwright first. It is now enough for him to portray various aspects of life through his skill and dramatic talent. He has suffered the fate of South African liberals with their absence of any scientific or consistent attitude towards the society in which they live and work. The relationship between the artist and what is essential to his social environment has been conveniently bypassed.

It is not enough for South African art merely to idealize the negation of the racist way of life. Art must also be warmed by the fires of the struggle for liberty. The South African delegation to the Fifth Afro-Asian Writers' Conference in Alma-Ata last year stated in a paper:

> Some writers are still writing as if they were talking to a third party in that party's terms, and not in terms of the masses, for, from and to the masses. Many poems exploit

the tragedy of the situation without offering positive inspiration. Much reportage is saying, 'Look how bad it is', and achieves nothing more than a liberal plea for a liberal conscience.

Sizwe Bansi Is Dead [1972] shows what it means to be a black man in South Africa. It is a savage and, at times, hilariously funny account of the workings of apartheid and particularly of the pass laws. *The Island* has, like Fugard's other plays, been acclaimed by audiences and critics in London. It is centred upon the life of two convicts in a prison cell. Much of the play is very funny, too, and the comedy arises out of their struggle to stay alive, to retain their humanity.

Of *The Island*, the *Observer* (6 January 1974) reports: 'There is some mention of a "liberation movement", but to go any further into that territory would have meant treading on dangerous ground inhabited by banned political parties. "The idea is to get plays performed, not banned," he (Fugard) says.' Or is it to get the author not banned? After all, plays are already banned in South Africa through apartheid and the lack of facilities for blacks.

Unlike Shakespeare's soldier, Athol Fugard no longer dares 'seeking the bubble reputation, even in the cannon's mouth'. For Fugard now 'the play's the thing' and no doubt his work will continue to receive the admiration of all who abhor apartheid, even in the absence of a more concrete response to the realities of the South African scene. He admits entertaining a doubt about 'the revolutionary's crude policy of breaking eggs to make an omelette . . . "I would feel more entitled to support that argument if I was an African, but I don't think a white man has the right to say it."'

As we have said, while we do not believe that it will be the white people who will bring about the revolution, the revolution nevertheless has no colour bar, as others have shown. Athol Fugard need not only be an observer of his country's condition, or as he puts it merely 'bear witness', and be 'a classic example of the guilt-ridden impotent white liberal of South Africa'. An admission of guilt is in itself a step towards personal re-evaluation, and a more profound understanding of his function as an artist.

CHAPTER NINE

Against Literary Apartheid
(1974)

This essay appeared in The African Communist *under the pseudonym Gala. It is notable for its harsh critique of Nadine Gordimer (1923–2014), who would later receive the Nobel Prize for Literature in 1991, and what La Guma sees as her 'separate development' model of literature.*

The rich literary tradition of the African peoples played an important part in the national liberation movement as an artistic and political factor. It was, and continues to be, a source of inspiration, a background and basis for popularity for many works of modern authors. It was that sphere of intellectual and artistic life which was relatively free from colonial deformations, and whose renaissance since the beginning of this century has helped in the spirit of enlightenment and strengthened the ideological background of liberation movements. In short, its renaissance formed the intellectual basis for the preparation of the African masses and became therefore an aspect of that movement.

This emergence of a cultural revolution on our continent has given rise to manifold investigations of our art and literature arising from the universal interest it has stimulated. In her introduction to A. C. Jordan's *Towards an African Literature* [1957], Mrs L. N. Jordan remarks:

> This outpouring of writings on African literature, and other things African, began in the late 1950s and early 1960s. By no mere coincidence, this is the period in which

most of Africa became independent. [. . .] However, most of the books on Africa by American and European Academicians are far too superficial, because most of these scholars have only a superficial knowledge and understanding of Africa.

The South African writer Nadine Gordimer should by no means be regarded as a foreigner to Africa, and her attempts at an examination of literature may be welcomed as coming from someone at least permanently on the scene. Study Project on Christianity in Apartheid Society (SPROCAS) in collaboration with Ravan Press, Johannesburg, recently produced her investigation of African literature in the English language under the title *The Black Interpreters: Notes on African Writing*, the first section of which deals with 'Modern African Fiction in English'.

An examination of literature in one language need not necessarily mean a restricted vision of the subject and should not prevent the examiner from relating it to the whole panorama of writing. The facet is part of the whole diamond, and it is difficult to do justice to a part without taking into account its relation to the whole. This requires a wider effort, and we must admire the work done by such as Ezekiel Mphahlele, whose *African Image*, first published in 1962, has recently been updated by him and the new edition appearing this year, which of course does not concern itself with the English language only. Nevertheless, Miss Gordimer has chosen to present her subject from her own point of view, and her effort warrants inclusion in any comments to be made on the question of African writing.

Before dealing with modern writing in English, Miss Gordimer must of necessity define where modern African writing as a whole started. She claims that modern African writing has its beginnings in the 'Négritude' movement 'because it was motivated by a deep need in which black people everywhere were at one'. This movement originated with the Caribbean's search 'to create a lost identity' which was to be found in Africa. 'The impetus of reaffirmation was brought by the Négritude movement, came across seas and language barriers and filtered down through the thinly-spread African intelligentsia . . . So it was a movement from outside Africa yet it could be the beginning of modern African writing.'

This, however, sounds as if one must accept, according to Nadine Gordimer, that modern literature is divorced from old or traditional literature and that it is really a sort of artificial transplant. Surely 'modern' literature must have something to do with the development of Africa itself from old into new, and that must for the writer also mean the development of his milieu. In South Africa, the new forms of economic, political and social structure of society at the beginning of this century produced new attitudes and reactions towards their surroundings from among the people, which were reflected in the development of new forms of their own economic, political and social organization, as well in their cultural expression. On the continental scene, the change from colonialism to independence must also have inevitably had an influence on the writing, among other things, from those parts. So 'modern' literature must have some relation to its time, a new historical situation, and not merely to an idea, which might have 'filtered down'.

Miss Gordimer explains Négritude as the 'need to stop hanging about outside the White man's door . . . to present oneself, in full self-acceptance, in the opposing dignity of one's own house'. One wonders if this is necessarily a 'modern' idea, or whether it is not a convenient generalization which does not take into consideration that the assertion of 'Négritude', or the 'African personality' as it is also called, might mean different things under different circumstances, since African aspirations have different priorities from area to area, level to level, and cannot be casually lumped under one general heading.

The African Personality

On one level, as Mphahlele states in *The African Image*: 'The personality that Nkrumah talked about was a beacon on the battlefield, a thrust, an assertion of the African's presence.'

The theory of the African personality evolved over long years of the African peoples' struggle, is a positive and fruitful concept stimulating the solution of urgent problems in modern Africa. It is based on the creative idea whose realization helps to rebuild a completely independent and spiritually rich Africa on new heights.

On the cultural level, the nascent new forms of art in Africa, the development of the theatre, the film industry and the opera, parallel with the traditional forms of art, show that the African personality seeks new means of expression to go with the old. To refuse these new means would impoverish language, culture, psychology and degenerate the African personality.

The literary heritage of the African peoples became a forming element of the new social consciousness, because of its subjects, its content of reality and humanism and last but not least—through the representation of the African cultural tradition—because of its mission of enlightenment. This heritage has been integrated in the modern arts and literature and was one of their starting points. This process marks in its literary aspects the beginning of a comprehensive cultural revolution. Before political independence it meant mainly the fight for the cultural emancipation from colonial deformation. Now the main task seems to be the further development of national cultures, deeply concerned with the progress of the African peoples.

While concerned with the development of our national cultures, in the expression of our own art forms we inevitably select and digest all that is best in the cultural heritage of East and West in order to strengthen ourselves, which means that in progressive development it becomes impossible to remain 'in the opposing dignity of one's own house', which would be rather like accepting a sort of cultural 'Bantustan'.

Mphahlele says that in its literal meaning: 'Négritude as an artistic programme is unworkable for modern Africa. It pegs an emotion, a thought, a wish. I am not a Christian or a Muslim. But I would still appreciate a poem whose motivation was Christian or Muslim or whatever if it did not trap me there . . .'

So, what are modern Africans writing about? Miss Gordimer asks. Certainly not what modern Europe is writing about, she replies. 'If one compares (African) themes with those that have preoccupied Europe and America over roughly the same period, one is struck by the differences between them.'

'The differences' which she discovers arise out of a rather superficial view, nor does she adequately explore the reasons for them to vary, concentrating more on academic and somewhat cursory comparisons between works from Europe and America on one hand, and Africa on the other 'over roughly the same period'. But since none of these areas have developed equally over any period, one cannot expect to see identical pictures of these areas, and so one is surprised that the comparison should arise in the form in which it does.

> The angry young man of European novels of the Fifties and early Sixties does not exist in African literature. Neither does . . . the man and woman, often an academic, in whom the fruits of mass culture and/or intellectual privilege have produced sour fermentation of disillusion with the material satisfaction offered by an affluent industrial society . . . . Another European theme that has no place in African literature is that of the problem of communication itself . . . European and American writers find themselves on the very edge of being. More and more novels written by them deal with gross abnormalities, both physical and mental. One could say that sickened by the madness of this world,

the appalling logic of deformity and insanity attracts their exploration.

It is of course possible that we are at divergence with Nadine Gordimer as to what is to be classed as good literature and bad literature, and it is difficult to compare chalk with cheese. If we accept for our purpose that general interest in life is the content of art, then we must agree that different *priorities* does not exclude the common interest in the problems of life. Miss Gordimer assumes, or that is the impression she gives, that writing in Europe or America has taken one road and in Africa another.

All examples of good literature must have something in common, irrespective of their language, country and the level of development of the society in which they originate. Otherwise we are liable to accept a form of 'separate development' of literature, or, as we have indicated before, a sort of apartheid in literature. As Miss Gordimer puts it: 'What are the most striking features of the way Africa sees itself and its relation to the rest of the world? Well, to begin with, some attitudes that are likely to be surprising to the world.'

The African writer might be as interested in 'life', in the problems of his own society as the European or American is in his, but they will not produce identical works, since their experiences and priorities are different. But while creative work is an individual act, the sum total of these acts is the artistic chronicle. The writer's participation in the development of life is measured *by the ideological artistic level of his work, the depth of his depiction of events and problems*. The writer must find the epicentre of events and determine his place in them, his point of view. Then he will find application for his talent and personal experience and will worthily serve the cause of aesthetic and social progress.

There are writers who work in a kind of vacuum, who stand apart from events, who do not maintain close ties with the truth of their ethos, their source of inspiration. An atmosphere of vacuum cannot stimulate works that contribute towards the common progressive character of life and literature. If we are concerned with this characteristic of literature, then we must distinguish between the wood and the trees and so discover that what African literature reveals need not 'be surprising to the world'.

We are witnessing how the cultural heritage of Africa is transformed into modern, socially and politically orientated literatures and arts. This is one of the most important tasks of the mentioned cultural revolution and a stirring event in modern and progressive world culture. Perhaps, above all, it includes a message of humanism to all mankind.

Theme and Content

But Miss Gordimer distinguishes between 'testifiers' and 'writers who are creating an African literature', going on to say that the former 'like their counterparts, lesser writers all over the world, they take stock-in-trade abstractions of human behaviour and look about for a dummy to dress them in'.

The African writer's choice of theme and plot is viewed as an entirely subjective matter. Giving 'some examples' we are told that:

> [T]he would-be writer says to himself: all over Africa village boys have become Prime Ministers and Presidents; I will write a book about a village boy who, like them, leaves home, struggles for an education, forms a political party, resists the colonial authorities, wins over the people and moves into Government House . . . Another would-be writer says to herself . . . it is one of the customs of my country for the husband of a childless woman to take another wife; I will write about a childless woman whose husband takes another wife.

If this is what is a characteristic of bad writers all over, one must ask why she should then make it an issue in the case of African writers, and why her criticism of 'overlong and clumsy novels' should be confined to African writers particularly.

It would appear that Nadine Gordimer's contention is that shortcomings and defects in the 'testifiers' are due to these authors giving too much attention to social issues. But softening the social impact has never guaranteed success for any work of art. It is also true that refusal to raise questions of import to all society, or substitution of real problems by ones of imaginary importance and the author's self-absorption, diminishes a work to the extent that the reader loses interest because of the writer's feelings becoming too subjective. But then we have to distinguish between good and bad writing, not between 'testifiers' and 'writers who are creating an African literature'.

Mphahlele says, 'There will always be stubborn and insoluble tensions between the workings of the imagination and the social forces and imperatives it "criticizes"—more stubborn than we are often prepared to admit; almost as if social reality and the imagination were rejecting each other, like mother and child. There will also be moments of reconciliation between the two realities.'

In an open letter (*West Africa*, August 1962) to an American critic, Martin Tucker, Nigerian writers said: 'Writing does not grow on air but is the result of social and other pressures and the desire for self-expression. The American Negro of the deep South wrote his novels because of the way he was treated by the Whites, just as Dickens wrote his novels because of the social injustices of his time.'

Quoting another American critic, Irving Howe, in that 'where freedom is absent, politics is fate', Miss Gordimer points out that 'in African literature politics does not occur as a vulgar interruption of the more exalted pursuits of life'. She does not explain how politics is distinguishable from, or has no relation to, 'the more exalted pursuits of life' although even this is not identified but tells us that 'novels of political action' are a category of African literature to be considered separately. We are not sure that she infers that such novels are not a feature of writing from other areas, but she makes no comparisons with English-language literature from other areas at this level although such works certainly exist.

On the whole, Miss Gordimer has locked herself in by her own restricted viewpoint. While her attempt to give us some insight into African literature in the English language may be admirable, unfortunately she also gives us the uncomfortable feeling of being a student in the presence of some pompous schoolmistress who knows all about it and defies us to go beyond the limited bounds of her assessments.

Nowhere can we find any view of the historical situation from which English literature emerged in Africa. It is simply there and that's that. One gets the added impression that she has studiously confined her examination to black writers so as not to involve white writers from Africa (there are such) in the English language, as if it is less complicated to compare black writers with European and American writers, even though she defines African writing as 'writing done in any language by Africans themselves and by others whatever skin colour who have shared with Africans the experience of having been shaped, mentally and spiritually, by Africa rather than anywhere else in the world.'

So we cannot be blamed if we get the feeling that her study is one from the viewpoint of exclusiveness, albeit wholly unconscious or unintentional; as though she and others of her race have nothing to do with the future of Africa and African literature.

After an examination of the themes of several writers, mainly Nigerian, she asks what main trends African English literature shows in its development. This question itself isolates the language literature from the trends of African literature as a whole in its historical development, as if it is the language that determines its trend. But even this question Miss Gordimer cannot answer in terms of African reality. Instead, she borrows from Georg Lukács a formula which asserts 'critical realism as not only the link with the great literature of the past, but also the literature that points to the future'. And so she concludes with amazing aplomb:

> [T]here seems to me little doubt that African English literature's best writers are critical realists, and that this is the direction in which literature is developing.
> [. . .]
> In these novels, as in those others in which politics is fate—'environment, fetter and goal'—there is little to indicate that that fate seeks to determine itself in terms of profound social change.

But African development and African literature have not come to a full stop. As Nadine Gordimer herself says: 'The theme of "Let My People Go" has not come near to its ultimate expression yet.' African life, saturated with turbulent political events, is exerting an ever-increasing influence over writers. One can confidently say that writers will continue to take subjects from life and that reviewers will have to take facts as they are.

Each writer is able to choose a theme according to his task and artistic leaning, and he is free to do so. But no matter what language he reads in, the reader looks forward to one thing—the truthful living word that can assist him a step higher, to find his place in life and to glimpse the future.

We still live in a complex, exceedingly heterogeneous time. On the one hand, we have created a state of affairs under which the agony of simply surviving has become obsolete; on the other hand, there are millions of people entirely concerned with making ends meet. The exploitation of man by man and colonialism is guilty of this state of affairs concerning a major part of humanity. Deliverance from the consequences of colonialism is the cause of all mankind, and the problem facing all of world literature.

We all have to understand these consequences in order to deliver man from centuries of inferiority, to revive the human in the human being, to make the spirit of fraternity natural to him.

Our common interest lies in the development of genuine internationalism in all the spheres of life, in all manifestations of the human spirit and action. There is no task more insistent, more cardinal, more humane for literature than to strengthen in every man faith in himself and faith in life. For this man must be freed from the vestiges of colonialism that humiliate his psychology, his way of thinking, his idea of himself and the world surrounding him. Up till now the world's culture has been divided into the culture of the East and the culture of the West. The time has come to unite our spiritual resources for the single purpose of serving humanity.

CHAPTER TEN

Sounds of a Cowhide Drum
by Oswald Joseph Mtshali
(1974)

This book review from Lotus: Afro-Asian Writings *revisits La Guma's earlier appraisal of Mtshali from 1972, published in* The African Communist. *As before, it is an enthusiastic review, demonstrating La Guma's promotion of younger, lesser-known writers and black South African voices more generally.*

Oswald Joseph Mtshali is claimed to be the first sustained African voice in the English-language poetry of South Africa for at least 20 years. Perhaps due to the word-size of the volume, or to a cynical presumption of the authorities that poetry is only read by an insignificant elite, this volume of poems has avoided censorship. In South Africa, some 13,000 titles had been banned by June 1969, and in that year, the South African Publications Control Board had prohibited 63 local publications. It is therefore with some relief that the poetry of Mtshali can be read (at the moment) in his own country.

But censorship apart, it is difficult to point at anybody else in the English poetry of South Africa who has surpassed this 30-year-old messenger who lives in Soweto, the vast black township near Johannesburg. Here is the poetic voice of urban black South Africa.

> I trudge the city pavements
> side by side with 'madam'
> who shifts her handbag
> from my side to the other . . .

Sounds of a Cowhide Drum *by Oswald Joseph Mtshali*

Oswald Joseph Mtshali was born in 1940 at Vryheid in Natal Province, where he matriculated. His special interest in poetry began when a teacher made him aware of the living connection between his classical English-set books and the stuff of daily experience. At 18, he came to Johannesburg where he had a variety of jobs. In 1967, he began submitting poetry for publication, and his sharp, ironical work, vigorously rooted in life, incisively observant, soon attracted attention.

In his work, the bitter life of the black people of South Africa is presented in the magic of words, of rhythm, of realism and fantasy, of passion and humour.

We find in language two kinds of speech: common speech, the normal everyday means which people use to communicate; and poetical speech, a medium more intense, preserving in a high degree the qualities of rhythm, melody, imagery. Mtshali succeeds in blending the everyday communication with the medium of poetry. The resentment of the oppressed people's subconscious being finds a voice in his work.

> I shuffle in the queue
> with feet that patter on the station platform,
> and stumble into the coach
> that squeezes me like a lemon
> of all the juice of my life.

Inevitably, because he is a black South African, his poems are laced with irony, the barbed spear directed at the life created out of the oppression of the black people:

> Glorious is this world,
> the world that sustains man
> like a maggot in a carcass.

and:

> 'My child! Dear child,' she heard,
> 'Suffer for those who live in gilded sin,
> Toil for those who swim in a bowl of pink gin.'

But it is also full of the pride of the African waiting for that time when he will be treated once more with the dignity he had known in the past:

> 'Where I'm a man
> amongst men,
> not John or Jim
> but Makhubalo Magudulela.'

and not:

> a faceless man
> who lives in the backyard
> of your house.

The colloquial tone, ironic humour, the liberation of imagination, imagery created out of keen observance of the world about him, all these go to form the style and outlook of the poet. His relationship with his immediate world is married successfully with his style. The most striking poems are often those where verbal magic—the creation of mood and sense of place—contains also a sting, which leaves a somewhat bitter observation behind.

The near-classical pastoral atmosphere which begins 'The Shepherd and His Flock':

> The rays of the sun
> are like a pair of scissors
> cutting the blanket
> of dawn from the sky.

ends with the sudden realization of the shepherd boy as he greets the white farmer's children as they go to school:

> 'O! Wise sun above,
> will you ever guide
> me into school?'

Questions such as this, asked in totally different categories in the poems, fuse together in the context of black-township life, and so tells us much we need to know about that life. Mtshali is one of the millions of Africans who inhabit the so-called white areas, the vast pool of cheap labour for the mines and industries, bound by contract the breaking of which amounts to a criminal offence, living where they do under sufferance of permits, denied the recognition of their trade unions, living below the poverty line, victims of police raids and harassment for documents in the streets:

> I show him
> the document of my existence
> to be scrutinized and given the nod.

All the squalor and humiliation, the poverty and violence which is the life of the black proletariat of South Africa ('Caesar's empire'), here in the crisp lines of Mtshali's exciting talent.

Here is 'The Miner':

> With gnarled hands
> Daubed with gold-tinted ochre [. . .]
> armpits mouldy with sweat . . .

and the gangsters dead in the township alleyways, the drunks, the washerwomen and the domestics, the road gangs, the teeming population of the city streets and the slums, like that:

> . . . itchy-footed man:
> reeking from a beerhall
> shuffling to jail
> swaying to hospital.

Neither has Mtshali forgotten anything of the black man's rural past or the scenes of the South African countryside, the so-called tribal homelands from which millions of his people have been indentured to become the black working class. But Oswald Mtshali, ironist, is essentially the voice of:

> a thousand black bodies
> encased in eleven coaches

that hurtle through stations
into the red ribbon of dawn
crowning the city skyscrapers.

The world you will enter through these poems is that world of the black man created by the white oppressor. The daily circumstances of Mtshali's life remain those of the majority of the population of South Africa. If the poet Mtshali belongs automatically to an elite in this world, it is a dead-end elite into which black artists and intellectuals are thrust by a racist society. He is married and works as a messenger, and that is a situation which the white supremacist in South Africa believes that all blacks should remain in. But Mtshali sees, albeit ironically:

a banner billowing in the sky, emblazoned,
'Have hope, brother,
despair is for the defeated.'

Look back to the rolling fields
waving gold-topped wheat stalks
mowed by the reaper's scythe,
bundled into sheaves
carted to the mill
and ground into flour.

> Kneaded into mountains of dough
> to be churned by rollers
> and spat into pans as red hot
> as Satan's cauldron.

Brought to the cafe,
warmly wrapped in cellophane,
by 'Eat Fresh Bread' bakery van;
for the waiting cook
to slice and toast
to butter and to marmalade
for the food-bedecked breakfast table.

Whilst the labourer
with fingers caked with
wet cement of a builder's scaffold
mauls a hunk and a cold drink
and licks his lips and laughs
'Man can live on bread alone.'

Look at her hands
raw, knobbly and calloused.
Look at her face
Like a bean skin soaked in brine.

For countless years she has toiled
to wash her master's clothes
Soiled by a lord's luxuries.

In frost-freckled mornings,
In sun-scorched afternoons,
She has drudged murmurless.

One day she fell and fainted
With weariness.
Her mouth a foaming spout
Gushing a gibberish.

'Good Lord! Dear Lord!' she shouted
'Why am I so tormented?
How long have I lamented?
Tell me Lord, tell me O Lord.'

'My child! Dear child', she heard,
'Suffer for those who live in gilded sin,
Toil for those who swim in a bowl of pink gin.'

'Thank you Lord! Thank you Lord.
Never again will I ask
Why must I carry this task.'

The train stopped
at a country station,

Through sleep curtained eyes
I peered through the frosty window,
and saw six men:
men shorn
of all human honour
like sheep after shearing,
bleating at the blistering wind,
'Go away! Cold wind! Go away!
Can't you see we are naked?'

They hobbled into the train
on bare feet,
wrists handcuffed,
ankles manacled
with steel rings like cattle at the abbatoirs
shying away from the trapdoor.

One man with a head
shaven clean as a potato
whispered to the rising sun,
a red eye wiped by a tattered
handkerchief of clouds,
'Oh! Dear Sun!
Won't you warm my heart
with hope?'
The train went on its way to nowhere.

It lies shimmering on the pavement
like a drop of molten lead.

Pedestrians
blind like bats in the sunshine
flit past.

An urchin
rummaging for cigarette stubs
scoops it up,
and rushes to a Greek cafe—
bread for life?
sweet for joy?—
a chocolate slab
of 'Happiness'
to be swallowed in a gulp
into an empty tummy,
and come out as sweet nothingness
in an alley toilet.

I get up in the morning
and dress up like a gentleman—
A white shirt a tie and a suit.

I walk into the street
to be met by a man
who tells me 'to produce'.

I show him
the document of my existence
to be scrutinized and given the nod.

Then I enter the foyer of a building
to have my way barred by a commissionaire
'What do you want?'

I trudge the city pavements
side by side with 'madam'
who shifts her handbag
from my side to the other,
and looks at me with eyes that say
'Ha! Ha! I know who you are;

beneath those fine clothes
ticks the heart of a thief.'

At the strike of the noon bell
he pops out of the shaft
like a pea shot from the muzzle of a bazooka.

He plods on iron-spiked boots
to stretch limbs on a coir-mattress bed in the compound,

With gnarled hands
Daubed with gold-tinted ochre
to wash a face
and armpits mouldy with sweat of pushing a cocopan
down the rails into the ore crushing mill.

He shakes a plastic 'skal' in a noisy beerhall
and gulps down the beer
and strikes his chest,
a victor over a day's work:
'Hurray I'm the brawn—
And you're the brain.'

I counted ribs on his concertina chest:
bones protruding as if chiselled
by a sculptor's hand of Famine.

He looked with glazed pupils
seeing only a bun on some sky-high shelf.

The skin was pale and taut
like a glove on a doctor's hand.

His tongue darted in and out
like a chameleon's
snatching a confetti of flies.

Sounds of a Cowhide Drum by Oswald Joseph Mtshali

O! child,
Your stomach is a den of lions
roaring day and night.

Master, I am a stranger to you,
but will you hear my confession?

I am a faceless man
who lives in the backyard
of your house.

I share your table
so heavily heaped with
bread, meat and fruit
it huffs like a horse
drawing a coal cart.

As the rich man's to Lazarus,
the crumbs are swept to my lap
by my Lizzie:
'Sweetie! Eat and be satisfied now,
Tomorrow we shall be gone.'

So nightly I run the gauntlet,
wrestle with your mastiff, Caesar,
for the bone pregnant with meat
and wash it down with Pussy's milk.

I am the nocturnal animal
that steals through the fenced lair
to meet my mate,
and flees at the break of dawn
before the hunter and the hounds
run me to ground.

Handcuffs
have steel fangs
whose bite is more painful
than a whole battalion
of fleas.

Though the itch in my heart
grows deeper and deeper
I cannot scratch.

How can I?
my wrists
are manacled.
My mind
is caged.
My soul
is shackled.

I can only grimace at the ethereal cloud,
a banner billowing in the sky, emblazoned,
'Have hope, brother,
despair is for the defeated.'

CHAPTER ELEVEN

I Came Here to Sing
A Tribute to Pablo Neruda
(1974)

This tribute to fellow writer and communist Pablo Neruda (1904–73) appeared in Lotus: Afro-Asian Writings. *In addition to his influence on La Guma, this short commemoration further indicates the expansive literary geography claimed by the Afro-Asian Writers Association.*

While the fascist tanks and guns blasted the Moneda Palace in Santiago de Chile on 11 September 1973, and President Salvador Allende died, the embattled Chilean people's greatest poet lay gravely ill in a nearby hospital. Perhaps he heard the rattle of gunfire and remembered another time when many of his people had given their lives in the struggle against tyranny.

> All along the ramparts of our fatherland,
> bright at the edge of the blank glass-glitter of snow,
> hidden behind the maze of the green-branched river,
> under the nitrate, under the fuse of bursting seed,
> I found thick-strewn the drops of my people's blood.
> And each drop burned like fire.
> ('The Dead in the Square')

Pablo Neruda died of cancer a short time after his friend and President passed at the hands of the military junta. 'Grave death, bird of harsh plumage' claimed the life of Chile's, and indeed all progressive mankind's, greatest poetic talents. Neruda is the most circulated poet in history, and in his own country the number of Chileans who do know his strongest poetry by heart, the number of Latin Americans who identify with him and to whom he gave heart, will outlast the tyranny of the junta.

Neruda was a poet of the twentieth century, one who was rich in the experience of our times. A great patriot, when he was awarded the Nobel Prize in 1971, the Chilean government of Salvador Allende declared a national holiday.

Born in 1904, the son of a railroad worker and a schoolteacher, Neruda produced his first book of verse, *Crepusculario*, when he was seventeen. After publishing several other volumes, including the neo-romantic *Twenty Love Poems and a Desperate Song*, which appeared when he was twenty, and which won him renown, Neruda was appointed Chilean consul in Rangoon. He remained in the Far East from 1927 to 1932, visiting China, India, Japan, Indonesia. During 1934, he served in a diplomatic post in Spain, and when the fascists rose against the Republican government, he enlisted as a soldier, fighting side by side with the patriotic writers of Spain. A collection of his Spanish Civil War poems, *Spain in the Heart*, published in Chile in 1938, forcefully expressed his identification with the heroic anti-Franco struggle in such lines as:

> Let them know, the ones who killed you, that they will pay with blood.
> Let them know, those who tortured you, that they will face me one day.

('To Miguel Hernandez, Murdered in the Prisons of Spain')

This period produced a great change in the poet who returned to his country resolved to serve the people as artist and as citizen. He served as Chilean consul in Mexico in the early 1940s, during which period he visited the United States of America. Upon his return to Chile he threw himself into the political life of his country, was elected senator by the saltpetre miners and shortly afterwards joined the Communist Party. When the people's front government was betrayed, Neruda took a leading role in the underground struggle to liberate Chile. He was also active in the world peace movement.

During those crowded years, Neruda's evolution as a poet was significant. Addressing the Continental Peace Conference in Mexico City in 1949, he said:

> We must give our American lands the strength, the joy and the youth they do not have. We shall not stand idly by while our treasures are shattered by the warmongers and while those philistines rob us of joy. We must overcome our sorrows and rise above destruction. We must teach the road and travel that road in the full view of our peoples. We must cleanse that road and make it resplendent so that tomorrow other human beings may travel over it.

He had found much of his earlier work 'bore the marks of bitterness of a dead epoch... So I renounced them'. His actual experience as a Chilean patriot and fighter in the world anti-fascist struggle impelled him to renounce the bourgeois aesthetic influences of his earlier period. He had begun as a brilliant innovator, somewhat given to pessimism and subjective fantasies. But his thought moved from almost exclusive concentration on form to a primary concern with social content; from a sort of detached contemplation to revolutionary partisanship.

In the 1950s, he started his *Elemental Odes*. These embodied a deliberate move to bring the language of poetry away from the exotic and closer to the ordinary. Neruda was the true people's poet. In spite of the fascist terror at the time of his death, thousands of Chileans turned out for his funeral. The bourgeois aesthetes who had once been entranced with his earlier work had come to ignore Pablo Neruda who nevertheless grew immeasurably, and a worthier audience multiplied all over the world.

There is in his poetry such a depth of emotion, sincerity and truth that many who had regarded themselves deaf to the persuasion of poetry were kindled to a new understanding and enthusiasm. Whoever touches this poetry touches a man of vast sympathy, a heroic figure who was able to encompass the deepest striving of millions. He was above all the poet of the undefeated.

For Pablo Neruda, humanity was living at the most inspiring hour. The poetic testament of that inspiration is Neruda's immense *Canto General*, a work awesome in vision, begun in 1937 and published in Mexico City in 1950. This work embraced the life of his country and his continent in a variety of verse forms, which set out to contain and celebrate the miraculous vastness of the Latin American continent historically, geographically, zoologically and politically. It is certain to remain the greatest poem of Latin America yet. Its spirit is expressed in Neruda's usual simplicity: 'My people shall win. All people shall win.'

This is the heart of his poetry and the heart of our time.

The fascist followers of Chile's junta demonstrated the characteristic barbarism of their kind by sacking Neruda's house in Isla Negra, a little village on the Pacific coast. But for the Chilean people his words written years ago will remain a beacon:

O fallen brothers, out of the silence
your voices will rise in the mighty shout of freedom
when the hope of the people flames into paeans of joy.

('The Dead in the Square')

This was the heart of a man whose greatness remains reflected in a simple ambition as stated in his 'Let the Rail Splitter Awake':

I did not come to solve anything.
I came here to sing
and for you to sing with me.

CHAPTER TWELVE

South African Freedom Poetry
(1975)

This short book review appeared in The African Communist *under the pseudonym Gala.*

Poets to the People, edited by Barry Feinberg. George Allen and Unwin, £2.95, paperback, 85 pp.

Barry Feinberg, the South African artist and poet living in London, has brought together a collection of poems by ten poets of our country who project through their work the rising voice of protest and rebellion of the oppressed people. Entitled *Poets to the People*, the editor has managed to choose the most significant of the works of those compatriots who reinforce the fact that the South African scene has been stimulated by the eruption of black socially and politically conscious poetry not seen for many years in our country.

It was in the nineteenth century, the golden age of African literature, that the disturbances in the continent of Africa produced major heroic epics which recorded the great era of resistance against the colonial aggressor. Today the oppressed people are entering an intense period in struggles of this century, and it is fitting that the passion of the people for freedom be manifested in their songs and poetry.

Moreover, in the words of the editor of this collection: 'This is the first anthology of poems projecting the alternative revolutionary voice of South Africa. These ten poets have all been fired by their national realities, realities which are not only daily dominated by the brutalities of Apartheid, but are also witness to the gathering forces which must inevitably destroy that system.'

'We shall be avenged'
and the people take up the shout
'Our heroes shall be avenged.'

These are the words of one of the contributors, A. N. C. Kumalo, and the spirit is maintained throughout. The importance of this collection of such poetry is also that it serves to illustrate that in times of severe repression poetry serves to express the feelings of the people and can also point towards their political goals. Rising above the well-worn slogan of 'art for art's sake' only, poets of Palestine, Vietnam, Latin America, the Portuguese colonies have demonstrated against all argument that literature must reflect the feelings of the people and their time if it is to serve their cause and become popular. Similarly, the recent flow of militancy from South Africa's black oppressed, workers and students, after a period of ebb due to severe pressures and setbacks, has given rise to this poetic expression reflecting the upsurge before which the barriers of national oppression and apartheid which frustrate the spirit and deny cultural identity must finally sunder.

Certainly not all the poetry appearing today shows a combination of both social or political consciousness and artistic merit, but Barry Feinberg has been able to extract some of the best examples for his collection. Ranging from the technical craftsmanship and symbolism of such [writers] as Kunene, Nortje and Brutus, through the social protest of Mtshali and Serotse to the politically committed like Kumalo and Scarlet Whitman, the compiler (who is himself also a contributor) has given us a collection of the most representative examples of South African revolutionary poetic expression, while the promise of even better is sure to be fulfilled as our people advance towards new heights of struggle and the final goal.

In an introduction to the collection, the eminent British poet Hugh MacDiarmid says, 'There can be no greater mistake than to criticize these poems for not answering the requirements of what reactionary academics regard as "high poetry" . . . The greatest poets have written neither to extrovert their personalities nor to comply with the demands of taste, but to voice the common thought of masses of men'. This is the atmosphere of *Poets to the People*, but nevertheless none of the works contained in the volume lacks the imagery and skill which characterise fine verse.

The collection is dedicated to South Africa's political prisoners and the African National Congress. All royalties from sales will go to the International Defence and Aid Fund.

CHAPTER THIRTEEN

South African Writing under Apartheid
(1975)

This extended analysis of South African literature first appeared in Lotus: Afro-Asian Writings. *It is notable for its discerning of an indigenous literary tradition before European settler colonialism, thus linking South African literary production to the ideas of the Afro-Asian movement, which promoted local cultural forms and traditions. This essay is also critical of white writers, such as Nadine Gordimer and Alan Paton (1903–88), while expressive in its admiration of black writers, particularly those in exile like Lewis Nkosi (1936–2010), Bloke Modisane (1923–86) and Mazisi Kunene (1930–2006). La Guma ultimately argues for 'liberation' in two interrelated senses—political and aesthetic.*

South African literature is a vast subject covering not only the stylistics of literature in four major languages—Nguni, Sotho, English and Afrikaans—but also the very content of the history of national groups that today make up the peoples of South Africa. To understand contemporary writing in our country and particularly 'resistance' writing, one must know the background of traditional literature, which can be understood only in context of the historical processes that shaped the destinies of the people of this part of Africa. That this very literature and history remains suppressed and almost unknown to the rest of the world is one of the great tragedies of colonial occupation.

The recorded literature dates from the late fifteenth century. This is, of course, misleading because like everything in Africa, few civilizations are 'discovered' until a day after independence. We can, therefore, accurately predict that the day of liberation will see the discovery of our literary tradition.

Imperialism is fond of referring to African civilization as no more than a disorganized entity having no value and no relevance to the civilization of the world. That very imperialism has destroyed our creative instruments and products. It is for this reason that the period of the nineteenth century has particular significance not only as a refutation of these claims but also in itself as an achievement of great excellence. This was our golden age of literature. The disturbances in the continent of Africa produced major heroic epics, which recorded the great era of resistance against the colonial aggressor. In the Cape alone, nine major wars were fought against the invaders; whilst these wars were going on the Zulus in the north were creating a military machinery as had never been known before in this part of the world. Because of the closeness between life and literature in African societies, these factors in themselves produced a feverish flowering of not only epic poetry but also satirical, lyrical and dramatic. The poets and story tellers not only told tales and recited poetry but also extended the scope of literature which ceased merely to comment on everyday social events, but became the true vehicle of social, political and historical analysis. Individuals ceased to project their own personal excellence but became symbols of resistance. In the case of the Zulu empire, individuals came to symbolize courage, fearlessness and prowess.

Going through this whole nineteenth century period we come across numerous examples of the same epic quality. In the Cape, for instance, the literary idiom assumes not only this epic quality but also, true to all resistance literature, uses a highly symbolic language. Its ultimate intention is not only to create a strong central authority but also to convey meanings that evoke the identity of those who constitute the resistance force.

The heights of literary genius are also reached by the Sotho people during the reign of their able monarch King Moshoeshoe I.

Not only are the people called upon to resist the invader but also to sink their differences.

The unification of the white front in 1910 resulted in the creation of a unified oppressive machinery. The literature of this period is significant for its pathos and a sense of despair mixed with a nostalgia for the days of old. The temporary defeat of the African people stimulated a philosophy of deprivation. But this was only more apparent than real. A new intellectual elite was emerging whose belief was that the white man would be beaten on his own ground with the combined forces of all the African people. Thus we find one of the most outstanding political documents given by Dr Seme in 1908, stressing the absolute necessity of the unity of the African people against the oppressor. The unity was not only of a local kind but encompassing the whole continent of Africa. The significance of the document, or rather the political views contained therein, lies not only in the dimensions of political interpretation of resistance but also because such views became part of the literary mood of the period. This was reflected in the numerous volumes of literature—translations, historical and political treatises—defining the African intellectual resistance movement. That these corporate works sought to interpret African political and historical thought is seen from the very titles: *The Origin of the African Peoples* by Soga, *Shaka's Page Boy* by Dube, *African Political Organizations* by Dladla, etc.

To define exactly this movement one must study the political and social factors operating in this period. The formation of the union of South Africa signified, as stated, the unification of the oppressive forces. The immediate task of these forces was to drive the African people from the land so that they became a landless, mobile labour pool available for the newly established industries. To ensure the total and universal implementation of this programme, a tax was imposed so that every able-bodied man should be forced to seek employment in the white man's cities. The 1913 Land Act not only deprived the African of the right of ownership of land but under the Urban Areas Act the Africans were prohibited from owning any interest in land except with the express authority of the Governor General. The immediate result was the restriction of the African population, which outnumbered the whites four to one, to only 12.5 per cent of the land area of South Africa. The position remains unchanged except for one half per cent added later as a compensation for the loss of voting rights. In spite of all this, it took some time before the law took effect. What is then the significance of this Act to literature? Hitherto the African intelligentsia and others had been able to pawn their lands and buy printing presses and locate them on their land. Thus J. L. Dube, one of the early leaders of African intellectual resisters and first president of the African National Congress, was able to establish Ilanga Lase Natal Press. Through this press he published a newspaper, which was one of the mouthpieces of the intellectual resistance movement. In the Cape and Natal, a more united and a more vocal group of intellectuals established an African press. They, at once, mobilized African opinion and exposed the most brutal forms of oppression perpetuated by the regime. It was not only through this that political resistance of the African people was kept alive but also through literature produced from African-owned printing presses. It is to the credit of these intellectuals that they not only saw their destinies invariably tied up with those of their own people—in spite of endless attempts by the regime and missionaries to isolate them—but also affected their beliefs by publishing in African languages. This meant that all literary productions were available to the general African populace.

The immediate effect, then, of the Land Act was that it deprived the Africans of the control of publication and left them at the mercy of the mission-owned printing presses. It also deprived the small landowning group of the capacity to produce literature without too much dependence on the meagre earnings from white men's industries and schools. The result was a decline not only in literary output, which had been impressive, but also a decline in content. The novelettes produced failed to deal with social and political drama and remained soulless material, which neither challenged the regime nor depicted the African situation. Instead the literature became no more than sentimental reportage of love situations between frozen and fleshless characters.

In all this, traditional African literature itself suffered a significant blow. The destruction of the African social and political units by colonialism meant that the very basis of our traditional literary productions was broken up. Nevertheless, amidst all this decay, there were signs of an awakening, an attempt at creating an idiom that bypassed the censorship. The whole picture cannot be fully known until liberation, since literally thousands of manuscripts lie buried in shelves, rejected by schools. Some principled writers refused to alter their manuscripts to suit the whims of a cruel regime and thus remain unpublished to this day. Also on the traditional literary side the resistance is shown in the works already quoted. All there were harbingers of the great literary works of Dlomo, Mghayi, Vilakazi, Mofolo, etc. These writers produced not only historical novels but also poetry of resistance. To evade censorship they used literary nuances, which could only be understood by those who knew African languages well. Mghayi, for instance, the great Xhosa poet not only revised the traditional literary idiom but developed the structure to accommodate new literary ideas. By using double meanings he managed to compose virulent satires on the regime and the British Empire. Vilakazi, the great Zulu poet, viciously attacks the cruel system of migrant labour in the mines whilst appearing to be concerned with the muscular beauty of the former soldiers of the Zulu empire. Using a symbolic language, he draws attention to rusting qualities of mine bells, which, in fact, are representations of the miners who are discarded soon after contacting silicosis. H. I. E. Dlomo similarly writes of the Valley of a Thousand Hills whilst, in fact, writing about the political denudations of African liberties. It is in this period when we see the re-emergence of nationally orientated literature. As yet the literature is concerned with protest but does not call the population to revolt. All the same this is in itself an achievement of great significance. For the very art of protest meant that the writers of this period were redefining once more the very ethos of the African nation.

Since 1927, in particular, numerous laws have been enacted to suppress publication of works expressing the genuine life and thoughts of the black majority essentially. Likewise the Bantu Education Act by bringing all schools under the direct authority of a government department gave authority to the same department to prescribe set books for schools in all the provinces. This, in practice, has meant that books prescribed were those written by government-sponsored writers who wrote ideological tracts orientating the African child towards acceptance of his inferior status in society. Side by side with this development was the taking over of book publication by semi-government presses. All literature currently being published in South Africa for the African public and African schools is the most poisonous and trite, or else the innocent mutterings of a politically unsophisticated romantic, except perhaps very few exceptions, which have a negligible circulation.

To come to fruition, the artistic spirit needs a combination of conditions which are seldom found together—the time and opportunity to compose, the stimulus to communicate and achieve an objective, an interrelationship between the artist and society which makes communication meaningful, the possibility of publication, and so on—not to mention the requirement of artistry or genius on the part of the producer.

The apartheid laws deliberately place barriers in the way of communication, and these barriers are so obstructive that it is a tribute to the human spirit that anything gets through at all. The very word 'apartheid' means the condition of separateness, and in terms of the apartheid laws there is no South African people but only a number of separate racial groups whose contact with one another must be reduced to the minimum.

Under the Population Registration Act of 1950, the population is divided into three main categories—Whites, Africans and Coloureds, and the government is given the power to proclaim sub-categories within the African and Coloured categories. The Africans, again, are classified into ten ethnic sub-groups—Xhosa, Zulu, Northern Sotho, Tswana, Tsonga, Swazi, Venda, Southern Ndebele and Northern Ndebele. By law the racial identity of every person is entered in a population register, and every South African citizen must carry an identity card stating his racial classification. The purpose of these racial classifications is to make communications between the various groups more difficult, so that white racists may continue in power on the well-worn basis of 'divide and rule'.

Under the Group Areas Act separate areas are set aside for residential occupation by the various groups, and it is illegal for a white to enter an African area without a special permit from a government official. White and Black cannot sit down together in a restaurant to have a meal. Cohabitation between Black and White is a criminal offence punishable by up to seven years imprisonment. Marriage between Black and White is legally impossible. Black and white actors cannot appear together on the stage. Black and White cannot be members of the same audience at a play or concert. Black and white sportsmen cannot belong to the same team, or even compete against one another in separate racial teams. Qualified black nurses cannot attend white hospital patients.

Nor does the separation stop at the black–white barrier. Even the whites are separated (although not by law) with Afrikaans- and English-speaking whites belonging in separate institutions from one end of their lives to the other. At school, Afrikaans–English separation is enforced by law, which lays down that children must be educated in their mother tongue. Outside of school, separation is enforced by social and politically encouraged custom whereby there are parallel institutions for the two groups in every sphere of life—separate chambers of commerce, teachers and students' organizations, youth organizations and the like. The purpose of this separation between the two white groups is to establish the hegemony of the Afrikaners in every sphere of life, and to ensure that Afrikaans culture is not submerged by the stronger worldwide English culture.

Describing South Africa as a collective white dictatorship, a Cape Town university professor, Jan Loubser, in a speech on 9 October 1972, said that within the white group there was a dictatorship of the Afrikaner over the English-speaking South African. 'Over the past 24 years (since the first Nationalist Party government came to power in 1948), an Afrikaans imperialism has developed over the English speakers,' he said. This imperialism is evident in the police, and armed forces, in the radio service and in many other institutions, all of which are dominated by Afrikaners. Were it not for the economic power the English-speaking section wielded, said Professor Loubser, their position today would have been very much the same as that of the Africans.

What does all this mean for the creative artist in South Africa? In the most obvious sense, the cultural facilities available to the black majority are far inferior to those of the whites—and in some cases simply non-existent. In the giant African township of Soweto, from which Johannesburg draws most of its labour force, there is only one cinema for a population of nearly one million, and the number of films which may be seen by audiences at that cinema is grossly restricted by a censorship which places all Africans on the same level as white children under 16. The best libraries in the country are barred to blacks. Very few blacks have ever seen the inside of a theatre or a concert hall.

But there is an even deeper sense in which cultural deprivation cripples the artistic spirit. Nobody—literally nobody—knows life in South Africa well enough to describe it adequately, let alone tell the truth about it, the whole truth and nothing but the truth, as is expected from the artistic as well as the legal witness. The artistic vision is restricted by apartheid barriers, and even the most vivid imagination is no substitute for experience.

In the Western capitalist countries, there are true class barriers which divide the nation. But a writer or a painter can cross these barriers. He can merge himself with any section of the community, and live their day-to-day life just as they do. The educated middle-class writer can go 'slumming' for his raw material.

But in South Africa the wall is impenetrable. No white can live in a black township, eat, drink and sleep there, make love and marry there, bring up a family there, starve and die there. He may observe a little from outside the fence, but he can never get inside a black skin and feel in his bones what it is like to be black. He may imagine hunger in a certain milieu to describe the way in which hungry children, having eaten their portions but remained unsatisfied, continue to scrape their spoons round the bottom of their porridge bowls in the hope that somehow the metal may be transformed into a further quantity of food . . . an image captured in all its pathos and simplicity in one of the early short stories of the African writer Alfred Hutchinson, who died recently in Nigeria at the tragically early age of 48.

No writer in South Africa can see life steady and see it whole. Out of his own experience he can only tell what he has seen and known, and this is inevitably only part of the total picture. No white writer has yet managed to create a real and convincing black character, and vice versa. Nor has any writer, white or black, been able to describe the relations between white and black, which are accurate and valid for both parties.

A Nadine Gordimer can tell the reader in delicate and precise prose how a white liberal looks at a black world, she can even portray accurately how a black appears in the eyes of a white observer, but she cannot get inside the black body and look outwards.

Similarly, the white characters in the novels of Peter Abrahams are caricatures, stiff and unreal. They speak and act abruptly, crudely, like puppets lacking flesh and blood. Alan Paton's black priest in *Cry, the Beloved Country* is a sentimentalized white do-gooder with a black habit, a sort of religious Black-and-White minstrel. Such creative failures are inevitable in a divided society.

A subsidiary problem for the South African writer is—for whom does he write? What is the market for his work? To whom does he address himself? This is partly a question of language. The African who writes in his mother tongue, even the Afrikaner, starts with a tremendous handicap by comparison with the English-speaking South African who has a world language at his disposal. It is partly a question of economics. Book production for a tiny market is unprofitable.

But above all it is a question of attitudes. The political and literary lingua franca of black South Africa is English, which enables all Africans to communicate with one another across the ethnic border, and also to address whites in their own country and abroad. Paradoxically, the group which suffers most from apartheid in culture is the Afrikaner tribe, who are the most isolated in their own homeland in which they enjoy political hegemony. Afrikaans as the language of the conqueror, the administrator, the policeman, soldier, location superintendent and pass officer is detested by the non-Afrikaans majority in South Africa.

The newspapers which are directed towards the African market—even those owned by supporters of the Nationalist government—are written in English. So are most of the books produced by non-Afrikaans writers.

Today, we notice a new phenomenon: a section of the Afrikaans intelligentsia are finding it more difficult to speak to their own people because they find themselves out of sympathy with its objectives. Moral conflict has almost destroyed a writer like Uys Krige, who loves his language and its heritage, but finds himself not only unable but possibly also unwilling any longer to communicate with fellow Afrikaners who are moving in a direction where he cannot follow. The poet Breyten Breytenbach, because he has married a Vietnamese woman, is unable to live in South Africa where his marriage would not be recognized, and so is today in exile in Paris though acknowledged as the greatest Afrikaans poet of his generation. On 2 April 1971, it was announced in Johannesburg that Breyten Breytenbach had been awarded the Central News Agency (CNA) Literary Prize for his book of poetry *Lotus*. This was the third time in the last four years that Breytenbach has won the Afrikaans Section of the CNA literary awards.

Breytenbach did not go to South Africa to receive the award. On previous occasions, Breytenbach has received the award at a special presentation ceremony in Paris. This year, it was accepted on his behalf by his father, as Breytenbach refuses to return to South Africa until his wife is able to accompany him freely and without hindrance of any kind.

'Obviously, I cannot return alone,' he told a correspondent of the *Rand Daily Mail*, 'Because this would signify my acceptance of laws which are reactionary, inhuman and completely stupid.'

Many Afrikaans novelists have achieved publication with parables and fantasies because to handle the truth is too difficult or too dangerous. And many are reduced to silence.

The Johannesburg *Sunday Times* wrote, on 22 October 1972: 'The completed manuscripts of several prominent Afrikaans authors are being preserved until South Africa's censorship laws are abolished or sufficiently relaxed to permit their publication. In this way a treasure house of Afrikaans literature is being built up for the enjoyment of future generations.'

Many South African writers are in jail because of their opposition to apartheid—like Govan Mbeki, winner of the 1970 I. O. J. Prize and author of *South Africa: The Peasants Revolt*, now serving a life sentence for 'sabotage' on the notorious Robben Island. Others are living under savage restrictions, which cripple their relationships with their fellow men, outlaw them from society and even make it an offence to write or prepare any material for publication.

Under most banning orders imposed in South Africa today—and there are hundreds and hundreds of them—to have even a page of manuscript or a sheet of paper in a typewriter can constitute a criminal offence, punishable by a minimum of one year and up to ten years imprisonment—or even the death penalty if the subject can be construed as encouragement to 'sabotage' or 'terrorism'. Little wonder that in these circumstances the creative spirit is often crushed.

Many of those who live abroad have found in exile opportunities to create and communicate with their fellow men, which were denied them at home. Some have enlarged on reputations already established.

Lewis Nkosi, for example, was well known in South Africa as a journalist of the magazines *Drum* and *Post*, financed by white capital but directed at the black market. In London, today, he is established as a freelance writer and has also made frequent appearances on television.

Another is Bloke Modisane, also formerly of *Drum* magazine and well known for his autobiographical *Blame Me on History*. Modisane has spread his talent wide in exile. He has taken part as an actor in the production of Jean Genet's *The Blacks*. His play *The Quarter Million Boys* was broadcast over the BBC. Set in Johannesburg, the play deals with a group of Africans who, after holding up a bank, visit a shebeen and get involved in an argument with the regulars which reveals that the boundary between crime and political rebellion is often hard to define.

The African poet Mazisi Kunene recently published *Zulu Poems*, an outstanding collection which expresses the fierce surge of national spirit always running through the consciousness of the exiled patriot, the nostalgia, pride and longing for the return to the motherland.

Dennis Brutus, best known to some as an international campaigner against apartheid in sport, is also the author of four volumes of poetry. A number of Brutus' poems are included in the anthology *Seven South African Poets*, edited by Cosmo Pieterse. Pieterse devotes himself largely to the task of collecting and annotating the works of his fellow South African writers, and has had a number of essays published in various journals. In addition to Brutus, *Seven South African Poets* features the work of Arthur Nortje, Dollar Brand, Jonty Driver, Timothy Holmes, Ismail Choonara and Keorapetse Kgositsile, some of whose writings owe their publication to the pioneering efforts of Pieterse. Two volumes of poetry, *For Melba* and *Unchained* also stand to Pieterse's credit.

Other writers working in exile are Ezekiel Mphahlele also in the US, author of *Down Second Avenue*, *The African Image* and other works, and Ronald Segal, internationally known commentator and publicist.

And so the list could continue, almost interminably. Many of the names which have appeared in this article could be replaced by others equally deserving, but pressure on space forbids.

It is a list revealing a talent of which any country would be proud. And, truth be told, the people of South Africa are truly proud of them. But the unrepresentative South African government, which speaks in the name only of the racist minority, is terrified to let their voice be heard. All of those who have been mentioned in this article are against the government's apartheid policies. In reprisal, most of them have been placed on the government's banned list, with the result that their works may not be circulated in South Africa, and it is an offence for any journal to publish anything they write or say.

The South African government is cutting people off from their own culture. This is a most appalling crime against the human spirit, and one for which it will never be forgiven, either by the South Africans themselves or the rest of the world.

The South African government is spending hundreds of millions of rand every year in its bid to keep the South African people apart from one another, but stronger forces, both political and economic, are forcing them together in a common mould. In the ranks of the South African liberation movement, it has been demonstrated that South Africans of all races, creeds and colours can work together as equals to achieve their common objective—freedom. When the apartheid walls have finally been broken down, the tremendous creative forces of the peoples of South Africa will be unleashed, not only to create a better material world but also a richer and more profound culture than ever dreamt of in the past.

CHAPTER FOURTEEN

What I Learned from Maxim Gorky
(October–December 1977)

This autobiographical essay is an essential piece for understanding the literary origins and motivations of La Guma, specifically the influence that Russian and Soviet literature had on him from an early age. Gorky and socialist realism had a decisive effect, both enabling La Guma's ambitions and pointing to how art and politics could go hand in hand. Of particular interest in this piece is La Guma's mention of Gorky's short story 'A Christmas Story'. La Guma's first published short story in 1956 shares the same title, suggesting a direct homage to Gorky. This essay appeared in Lotus: Afro-Asian Writings.

When I was a lad I was given approximately 10 cents each week as pocket money. With this handsome amount in my fist I went into the city each Friday and purchased a book at my favourite bookstore. I bought the works of Dumas, Fenimore Cooper, Robert Louis Stevenson, Mark Twain, Walter Scott and many similar authors. When I did not have the full amount to pay for a volume, the 10 cents served as a deposit, and I collected my book the following week.

I enjoyed tremendously the heroes who filled the pages of these books with their adventures. They were all strong, brave, honest, upright men who performed deeds of remarkable gallantry and always overcame the villains. Having read a story, I used to gather my friends about me, and sitting on the edge of the sidewalk recounted the exciting adventures of my heroes to them. Very often I added more and more incidents from my own imagination for these heroes to perform, and we all thrilled to the escapades of this romantic world.

Then one Saturday morning, I found myself in the central second-hand market in Cape Town. I was irresistibly drawn by the stall of old books. Browsing through the rows of battered volumes, my eyes caught a title. The lettering on the spine of the small fat volume said, *Selected Stories by Maxim Gorky*. I had not heard of this author before. Inside the cover it said, 'Translated from the Russian'. This sounded very interesting. So I exchanged the few coins I happened to have, for this book.

Here was a new experience in reading. I read what was translated as 'A Christmas Story'. This was very strange. It was not at all like the Christmas stories I had read before. There were no carols, no plum puddings, no tinsel and holly leaves. Instead there were two ragged urchins with dirty faces, barefooted and probably with running noses, begging for pennies from passers-by in the shivering streets of a city at Christmas time.

But the strangest thing was that I seemed to know these children. They were the same children who begged for money along the main street of the slum quarter where I lived. I saw them in the gutters along Hanover Street, tugging at the sleeves of shoppers, or snatching an apple from a barrow and tearing off into the Saturday morning crowd. But surely such people could not be put into books and made into heroes? Well, they were there in Gorky's pages, were they not?

I read further. There was a story of a ruffian fleeing from the police having committed some crime. Through the grimy streets he dodged, keeping to the darkness, avoiding everybody, with the police searching for him. Then. on the way, he comes across a baby abandoned on the roadside, wrapped in rags and wailing with cold and hunger. The hunted man could have passed on to safety, but instead he stopped to pick up the baby, thinking not of his own safety but of the survival of this mite. His humanity and generosity cost him his freedom, but saved the life of the infant.

Again I realized that there were just such ruffians hanging around District Six where I lived. They stood on street corners or in doorways, rough, ragged, often brutal, often fleeing from the police. But they were kind, too. They had concern for children and protected them from bullies. But they had never been put into books to my knowledge. But here Maxim Gorky had done just that.

So a hero did not necessarily have to carry a sword and wear a plume in his hat. A hero could be an ordinary, simple, poor person. Thinking about it, I realized that there were more such heroes in the world than those who thronged the pages of romance. It meant that my Aunt Maggie who drank too much but who once fought blacklegs outside the garment factory when she was on strike was a heroine. Ragamuffins, street Arabs, starvelings, tramps could be heroes.

Gorky explained it in my later reading:

> Young people have asked me why I wrote about tramps. Because living among the lower middle class and seeing around me people whose only object was to exploit other people by hook or by crook, to turn other people's blood and sweat into kopeks and turn the kopeks into roubles, I came to hate fiercely the parasitic life of these commonplace people who resembled each other like copper coins from the same mint.
>
> Tramps for me were 'uncommon' people, they were uncommon because they were 'declassed', men who had cut loose from their class or who had been repudiated by it and had lost the most characteristic traits of their class [...] In Kazan, in the 'glass factory' I came across another lot of about twenty people of divergent origin [...] Most of these people were diseased and drunkards; fights between them

were frequent, but ties of comradely mutual assistance were well developed among them, and everything that they managed to earn or to steal they ate and drank in common. I saw that although their living conditions were worse than those of ordinary people, they considered themselves better and indeed they felt better than ordinary people because they were not greedy, they did not try to get the better of each other, they did not hoard money . . .

(*How I Learned to Write*, 1928)

But apart from the 'lower depths' he found a place also for the products of the imagination, such as 'The Sons of the Falcon', 'The Legend of the Burning Heart' and 'Stormy Petrel'. He distinguished between active romanticism and passive romanticism. Active romanticism, he said, attempts to strengthen man's will to live, to rouse him to rebellion against reality with all its tyranny.

Later in life, I read that great novel *Mother*. To me personally it was not only a picture of revolutionary activity in Russia of that time but also a picture of the efforts of my own people in South Africa, struggling against injustice. I saw Coloured factory workers and African labourers organizing against economic exploitation; I saw women standing firm when their menfolk were hauled off to prison for 'sedition'; I saw the cynicism and cold-heartedness of the South African police; I saw both the wavering elements and the courageous among my own people.

But what was important in *Mother* was that Gorky had found a new relationship between the individual and society. Here the conflicts were no longer clashes between individuals driven by their own limited interests, but they were struggles of communities for the basic aims and ideals of life. There was no longer a single person revolting against society, but the spirit of social consciousness and collective effort pulses through this book in which the individual, freed from narrow, self-centred concerns, is absorbed by the collective and finds inspiration therein. Furthermore, the characters of *Mother* are not just inventions or abstract romantics but are modelled in concrete, historical lines reflecting actual life and activities of progressive men and women in Russian society of the earlier part of this century. Not only an epic story of social struggle, *Mother* is also a novel about the education of the 'new man'. It describes the transformation of the oppressed, the determination of common people to rise up and purge themselves of centuries of degradation, of all things which suppressed and distorted their true selves.

Addressing the First Congress of Soviet Writers in 1934, Gorky stated, inter alia: 'It is one of the most essential duties of literature to develop the revolutionary self-consciousness of the proletariat . . .' This is a concept of course rejected by bourgeois writers of the capitalist world. As Gorky himself explained:

> In a state founded on the senseless and humiliating sufferings of the vast majority of the people, it is fitting that the creed of irresponsible self-will in word and action should be the guiding and vindicating principle. Such ideas as only this self-will will bring him (man) his 'greatest advantage' and 'let the whole world perish as long as I can drink my tea'—such are the ideas capitalism has inculcated and upheld through thick and thin.

but,

> [W]e must grasp the fact that it is the struggle of the masses which forms the fundamental organizer of culture and the creator of all ideas, both those which in the course of centuries have minimized the decisive significance of labour—the source of our knowledge—and those ideas of Marx and Lenin which in our time are fostering a revolutionary sense of justice among the proletarians of all countries . . .

('Gorky on Soviet Literature'. First Soviet Writers' Congress, 1934. Co-Op Publishing Society.)

Gorky's propositions on the purpose and function of literature arose out of a profound knowledge of the basis and origin of literature. His theories are of a stature no open-minded honest writer could ignore. These theories cannot of course be reproduced here in entirety, but no student of literature can avoid the deepest interest provoked by Gorky's work on aesthetics and cultural history, while his challenging assertions cannot but provoke the closest attention:

> The people is not only the force that creates all material values, it is also the sole and inexhaustible source of all spiritual values, first of all poets and philosophers, unsurpassed in creative genius, author of all great poems, all the tragedies ever written and also of the greatest of them all: the history of human culture.
> (*The Destruction of Personality*, 1909)

> Do away with the class struggle which keeps the brute instincts of greed, fear and hate alive in men, do away with social inequality and then the transformation of physical energy into mental energy will be easier, and hence the available intellectual forces in the world will increase in quantity and improve in quality.
> (*From Afar*, 1912)

Living in a country like South Africa with its atmosphere and all the evils of racism, economic exploitation, social inequality, its enormous frustrations and cruelty, the contentions of Gorky came to me like a spear of light through the cloying darkness of an oppressive society. If a man must write, then surely there is abounding material in the lives of millions of Africans, Coloured, Indians, whites living from day to day in this monstrous environment; surely their struggles, their ignorance, their wretchedness, their hopes are fountains of inspiration? And if a man must write, surely his pen can contribute towards destroying those conditions, which 'keep the brute instincts of greed, fear and hate alive in men'?

Apart from the specific attitude towards life and literature, which Gorky helped to instil, there are invaluable writings on the techniques of the craft. 'A writer,' he said:

> should know everything, or at least as much as possible. He should be able to pick out of the chaos of impressions, out of the variegated tangle of emotions, the things that are of universal significance and typical; he must be able to discard the narrow, personal, subjective, impermanent things that are in constant flux and soon disappear without leaving a trace. If he can accomplish the first, his work will be artistic and socially significant; but if he cannot accomplish the second, he will write anecdotes devoid of all social and educational substance. The purpose of all art, consciously or unconsciously, is to rouse certain feelings in men, to develop in them a certain attitude towards certain phenomena of life. The adherents of the so-called free 'art for art's sake' also profess this to be their purpose, although their attitude towards social tendencies is negative and even hostile.
>
> The writer's work is extremely difficult; writing stories about people doesn't mean simply to 'spin a yarn'; it means depicting people by means of words as one draws them by means of a pencil or paints them by means of a brush. In order to do this, one must discover the essential traits of one's subject, understand the deepest meanings of his actions, and describe all this with words so vivid and accurate that on the pages of the book [. . .] the reader sees the living face of a man, the connection between whose actions and feelings appears self-evident.
>
> True art arises where complete confidence is established between writer and reader. The writer's job is to pour out into the world all that fills that receptacle for impressions which men call the soul. When a writer speaks of the

joys and sorrows of our life, of things evil or good, ridiculous or vile, if he speaks from his soul as if he is speaking to his best friend, he will be understood by the reader and accepted as a friend.

(Preface to *An Anthology of Proletarian Writers*, 1914)

So the words of Gorky, whether on the philosophy of literature or the craft of the writer, need very little commentary. His ideas are as simple, stirring and straightforward as his stories, and as profound. It needs only for the broadminded to read and examine them. Having written numbers of short stories and three novels myself, far be it from me to compare myself with this great master, but I must say that out of all the criticisms and surveys of my work, the words which gave me the greatest pride were those expressed by a reader: 'It is a little like Gorky.'

Such a remark should be enough to stimulate a writer to greater effort.

PART IV

Five Stories and One Play

CHAPTER ONE

Come Back to Tashkent
(1970)

This short story, written in Moscow and Tashkent in 1968, first appeared in Lotus: Afro-Asian Writings. Though a vignette, it demonstrates how La Guma's extensive travelling began to inform his fiction writing and his experimentation in depicting situations and contexts beyond South Africa, thus contributing to an internationalist Afro-Asian literature.

You came downstairs into the sunlight that lay bright as cellophane in the street and the first person you saw was a man in a *tubiteka* and breeches going by. There were other people too passing, but you weren't looking at them, and only saw the man in the tubiteka by chance, because you were really looking for somebody else. Then seeing her you felt your heart expand, feeling the joy of seeing her again because you identified yourself with this city through her. You hated being alone and now you became part of the Tashkent street with the tree-strung square across the way and the women in multicoloured silk walking past the sparkling fountains.

You said, 'Hullo, Devochka.'

'Harry.'

'I don't like to go.'

'No.'

'It's been good here.'

You had packed your bag upstairs in the room with the moths against the ceiling, their movements rustling like dry leaves. While packing you had thought of the times you had eaten *pilaf* together, and the *pirojok* at the kiosks in the street, enjoying the taste of the spiced meat inside the dough, and once there had been crumbs and grease on her chin and you had giggled foolishly at it while a child in a headscarf stared curiously. Across the way from the kiosk, the tan plaster walls of an old house were still cracked from the earthquake but beyond it the great blocks of flats were going up and a crane like a giant stork swung its load determinedly across the sky, bringing another birth, while the aroma of grilling *shashlik* from the long trays over the fires on the sidewalk lay heavily on the air.

Now she asked smiling, 'Are you feeling good?'

And you said, 'I'm a little hung over. Those people at the collective farm really laid it on thick.'

You'd been together to the Hamrakul Tursunkulov Kolkoz in the Yangiyul district beyond Tashkent, driving along the road through the brown and green cultivated land and the cotton rows, past the parked metal harvesters that crouched like great mechanical insects. In the farm square the horns were blowing and the farm girls danced with the sun on their veils and headdresses. Later on you sat cross-legged on a stillage by the drinking platform, sipping green tea in the shade with some old men tough as barbed wire and gnarled like oak and brown as earth—old men who had bright piercing eyes, sharp as plough blades, and wispy grey beards below their turbans.

And now you had to get ready to say goodbye. You were going to say goodbye to her at the station. You had said goodbye in London, Oslo, in Dar es Salaam and Leningrad and in a lot of other places to many friends and now you were going to do it again.

So you were sad, too, inside. You lighted a cigarette and looking through the blue smoke you saw her eyes, brown like shashlik, and the hair dark and awry as the cinders of a gipsy's old fire.

'Why the hell must people always be saying goodbye?', you asked.

'Maybe so they can say hullo when they meet again.'

'Will we meet again?'

'I don't know, Harry. It's such a big world.'

'Yes, and I liked it being here with you and having to say goodbye isn't going to be the same as the other times.'

'Are you sure, Harry?'

'I don't know what I'm sure of, but I'm sure it's not going to be the same.'

She wasn't wearing the usual silk *khanatlas*, the Uzbek dress, but a red frock, the colour of love, and looking at her you thought, Oh, damn and blast it. Why must it be like this?

She said, 'I have to do something at the office, but I'll be at the station to see you off.'

You said, 'OK, but be sure to be on time.'

'I'll be there, Harry, don't worry.'

'Don't get lost the way you almost did in Samarkand.'

In Samarkand, it was sacred, a public holiday, a festival for the poet Navoï and the streets were packed. The Uzbeks and Russians jostled each other along the sidewalks, overflowing into the roads. All along the streets they were selling fruit, groundnuts, piled melons and food. In Registan Square and the marketplace, the clamour of voices was solid around the stalls and at the foot of the mighty tile-and-mosaic-work buildings with their skyscraping columns and blue minarets. These were centuries-old monuments to a cruel power, the excitement and beauty of them, which left you awestruck. This was Timurlane's capital, Timur the Lame, Timur the Cruel, Timur the Conqueror and the scourge of Allah. You could see the hordes, eyes sharp and hard as arrowheads, riding out across the dusty beige and olive green land, the fur hats and long robes and high boots, the chain mail and the round iron shields, the scimitars curved and cruel and the lances piercing the sky, the horsetails and manes blowing in the wind. The horns blew and the drums throbbed, another city to burn.

But it wasn't Timur's folk any more, but a merry party on a wagon going by blowing and jingling, laughing at the crowds, surrounded by happy horsemen. And now you had to say goodbye. At the railway station they'd loaded your bag and you waited outside the carriage. There was the usual bustle you saw at railway stations all over the world. People were climbing aboard and you looked anxiously along the platform for her. You only learnt afterwards that some official at her office had insisted that she did some job, and had adamantly refused to let her off in spite of the explanations, the protests, the pleas. The bloody authorities, you called them.

So she didn't come after all and you were alone again on the emptying platform, feeling lonely and alone. The conductor with a brown face urged you aboard but you stayed till the very last, hoping she'd somehow make it. But she didn't. For a hopeful moment you thought you saw her and your heart said, 'Devochka!' But it wasn't her after all, but somebody else. So you climbed half-heartedly aboard. The conductor slammed the door and you stood in the corridor while the whistles blew. The train lurched like a frightened heart and the station slid slowly by, taking you out of her life. The wheels clicked across the joints in the lines and you listened sadly to their rhythm and tried to think of the things you had meant to tell her, like wanting to be kind to her, forever hoping you'd get the chance to do so someday because the wheels were saying, 'Come back again, come back again, come back again.'

Tashkent/Moscow, 1968

CHAPTER TWO

The Man in the Tree
(1971)

This playscript was published in The Literary Review, *a literary journal based at Fairleigh Dickinson University, New Jersey. It is reproduced here with permission. Though its performance history is unknown, La Guma did produce a number of radio plays while working at the Transcription Centre in London in 1967 and 1968. This play may be a remnant of those years. Though about forced removals, it should be mentioned that the subject matter also relates to a situation described in 'The Time Has Come: S. A. Coloured People's Social and Economic Deterioration' (see p. 66 in this volume), thus demonstrating how La Guma's journalism flowed into his creative work.*

CAST

MR MILES: an estate agent
PETER GESLER: a house hunter
WINIFRED GESLER: Peter Gesler's wife
ABRAHAM: an old Coloured man

(*Footsteps on a veranda.*)

MILES. Well, here we are. You will notice the size of the veranda? It runs the whole width of the house.

WINI. Hmm. It looks a nice place. Lovely view of the mountain, too.

MILES. It is rather. It's lovely in the summer, Mrs Gesler. Now just let me find the key. (*Door is unlocked.*) There. I think I'd better lead the way, if you don't mind. We'll take a look inside first, and then at the grounds. Leave the door open to let some air in, shall we?

WINI. It does look quite nice and big, doesn't it, Pete?

PETE. Yes, it does. Quite nice, Winifred.

MILES. I think you're going to like this place. As I pointed out, the property is also near the local transport and a stone's throw from the shops. Well, this is the entrance hall, as you can see. Quite spacious. You could fit in a clothes cupboard—there's enough room.

PETE. Did you people do the painting?

MILES. Oh, yes, we had the whole place cleaned up after the last owners left. It was in a very good state of repair, but we renovated the entire house, fresh coat of paint and so on, new electrical wiring installed. Of course we did it so it wouldn't interfere with the plans of the new owner. You can make minor additions here and there . . . Now here's the sitting room. Through here, please.

PETE. Lead on, Mr Miles.

WINI. They were Coloured people, weren't they?

MILES. I beg your pardon?

WINI. The previous owners. They were Coloured people.

MILES. Er—oh, yes. But quite respectable types. They had to give up the place. You see, the law made them move. Group Areas Act makes it compulsory after the district has been proclaimed for—er—another race, but as you see, we did have the whole place redecorated.

PETE. Oh, it's all right. I mean, they've all gone now. That's so, isn't it, hey?

MILES. You mean from the street? Oh, yes, they all had to move. Actually, this is the last house up for sale. Everything else has been taken. You really don't have to worry, Mr Gesler.

WINI. Well, they did keep this place in a nice state, it looks. Hmmm, a lovely big room.

MILES. Yes, some of these people do keep their places in good order. As you will notice, this room looks out on to the veranda. Steel-frame windows—they open on two sides.

PETE. Yes, quite a decent-sized room. Quite airy. What d'you think, hey, Win?

WINI. We can make it the living room. I saw some lovely curtains—just the right thing.

MILES (*chuckling*). There you are, Mr Gesler. Looks as if the good lady has already made up her mind.

PETE. Ha, ha... How are the ceilings?

MILES. Oh, perfect condition. The fellow who owned the property did a bit of building work himself.

PETE. Could we have an architect go over the place? Just to satisfy ourselves?

MILES. Architect? Of course, any time, Mr Gesler. Now if you would just come this way. Here we have the main bedroom. There are two others. This one looks out into the back garden ... (*fade*) ... And this is the kitchen.

WINI. Oh, lovely.

MILES. Yes. Everything for the housewife, Mrs Gesler. Modern kitchen unit, hot and cold water, built-in cupboards, big window looking into the back garden. You can see it from here as well as the main bedroom. With a little bit of development you could have a splendid garden. Your own homemade scenery. Can't beat South Africa for scenery, eh?

PETE. Wouldn't exchange it for any other place in the world.

WINI. Ah, Pete, I'd be able to watch you cutting the grass from here. It really looks like a lovely job for you.

PETE. You can say that again—all that undergrowth.

MILES. It is a bit overgrown with weeds, but quite a big piece of ground. Fifty thousand square feet at the back, and a tool shed thrown in. Ha, ha.

WINI. Oh, look, there's a full-grown tree and all.

MILES. Oh, yes, an apple tree. You can see it from the main bedroom window also.

WINI. Does it bear fruit? Apples?

MILES (*chuckling*). I'm afraid that's one of the things I don't know, Mrs Gesler.

WINI. I'm sure we'll be able to have a lovely lawn at the back, after you've cleared it up, Pete. Of course, you'll have to get somebody to help, dear.

PETE. Wini, if you think I'm going to clear up that jungle on my own, you've got another thing coming.

MILES (*chuckling*). Well, I'm sure Mrs Gesler won't make you work too hard, Sir.

WINI. You talk to Mr Miles, Pete. I'm going to take a look around outside. I'm really a country girl, you know. Is the back door unlocked?

MILES. Here, let me draw the bolt for you, Mrs Gesler. (*Bolt is drawn, door opened.*)

PETE. Careful on the step, Wini. Don't break an ankle, hey.

WINI. Don't fuss, dear, I'll be careful. (*Footsteps as Wini goes onto the back porch and down steps. Sound of movement through wild grass.*) Hmmm. With all this grass and weeds cleared away we could have a lovely lawn. Here's a good place for a kitchen garden. I could put in potatoes, carrots, beans and things. My word, all these weeds. Ah, the old apple tree. Old and gnarled already, and nothing but leaves. If Papa was alive he'd have been able to do something with this tree, I'm sure. He had a real hand for trees and plants, he did. Not a bad place this at all. The area ought to be all right now the Coloureds have moved out.

I wonder if Pete will make up his mind. Don't you worry, Winifred Gesler, you'll make it up for him, if necessary. Ah, that tool shed or outhouse or whatever it is, over there. Let's take a look. It could be useful.

(*Abraham's voice is heard, growing louder as Winifred approaches the shed.*)

ABRAHAM. It's going to be awright, Mr Edwards. It's going to be awright, you'll see. You and me, Mr Edwards, we'll be here all the time, no matter what. Yes, Sir, Mr Edwards, you just go on staying up in the tree long as you likes, hey. Nobody going to chuck you out . . .

WINI. My heavens, there's somebody in the shed.

ABRAHAM.—and even if the family all went, I'm still here to see to you, Mr Edwards. Don't you bother about nothing, because why Old Abraham is right here. You just stay in the old tree long as you like, Sir. There's nobody going to chase you away . . .

WINI. Who's there? You in that shed, come out at once. I'm going to call the boss.

ABRAHAM. Mr Edwards, nobody going to chase . . . What? Who is that in the yard? (*Shed door creaks open.*) Oh, excuse me, Madam, excuse me, please. Good afternoon, Madam.

WINI. It gave me a bit of a start, hearing your voice, old man. Who are you? What are you doing here? You've no right to be here.

ABRAHAM. Excuse me, Madam. I was just sort of, sort of . . .

WINI. Who are you? What is your name?

ABRAHAM. They just calls me old Abraham, Madam.

WINI. This is private property—for white people now. Have you been living in this old shed?

ABRAHAM. Oh, Madam, I been staying there, sort of. Just looking after the place, like. You won't get me into trouble?

WINI. Looking after the place?

ABRAHAM. Children comes over the fence and they throw stones at the windows.

WINI. Are you the caretaker then? Mr Miles, the agent, said nothing about a caretaker.

ABRAHAM. Well, Missus, it's like this. I use to be with the folks what lived here, doing odd jobs, sort of. They give me food and clothes and some money on Fridays. I was with them for many years—and then they all went away.

WINI. Yes, I know, they all had to move. But you had no right to stay, you hear?

ABRAHAM. Oh, Missus, I just couldn't leave here—leave old Mr Edwards on his own. They all went away and left him.

WINI. Mr Edwards? Ah, I heard you talking to somebody in there. Tell him to come out at once, hey.

ABRAHAM. In here? Oh, no, Madam, there's nobody in here.

WINI. What in heaven's name are you jabbering about? A moment ago I heard you talking to somebody in that shed, and you've just now told me there's a Mr Edwards.

ABRAHAM. Oh, Madam, that was only me, only old Abraham. I gets lonely like, and I talks to myself sometimes. But there isn't nobody in there, Madam.

WINI. You're lying, you rascal. Here, let me take a look. Stand aside. (*Door creaks.*) Why, it's empty. There's nobody here. Just an old mattress, a bundle of clothes and things. (*To Abraham*) What's the matter with you? Are you daft?

ABRAHAM. I'm sorry, Madam. Like I told you, I gets lonely. A man gets lonely here.

WINI. Well, why don't you go off somewhere else then, if you're lonely. You'll only get in trouble here.

ABRAHAM. I don't hope not, Madam.

WINI. Talking to yourself. I heard you, as if you were talking to somebody. Who is this Edwards, anyway?

ABRAHAM. Mr Edwards? Oh, madam, he was the boss of this house.

WINI. You mean the last owner?

ABRAHAM. Yes, Madam, that's right.

WINI. Well, why didn't you go off with him, then? They all had to move. Government orders, wasn't it?

ABRAHAM. Go with him? No, Madam, I couldn't go with Mr Edwards. Begging your pardon, Madam, Mr Edwards, he never went away.

WINI. Never went away? What do you mean, you old fool? He isn't anywhere here. He's not in the shed and he's not in the house.

ABRAHAM. Yes, Madam. I mean, No, Madam. What I mean, Madam, is Mr Edwards, he died here.

WINI. Died here?

ABRAHAM. Yes, Madam. It was in the newspapers, too. Mr Edwards, Madam, he hanged himself.

WINI. Hanged himself?

ABRAHAM. Yes, Madam. In that tree.

WINI. You mean that apple tree over there?

ABRAHAM. Yes, Madam.

WINI. Lord, whatever for?

ABRAHAM. Well, madam, Mr Edwards he lived here all his life and his mother and father for many years before him. And then, Madam, when the government came and said this street was for white people only—begging pardon, Madam—and no more for Coloured people, well Mr Edwards, Madam, he couldn't bring himself to go. He couldn't leave his old home. So one morning, just before everybody had to move, he came out here and hanged himself in that tree.

WINI. Just because he had to move?

ABRAHAM. I reckon so, Madam. Oh, it was a terrible time, Madam. There was Mrs Edwards and three children and everything.

WINI. But why? What good did it do? Just because he had to move? It sounds so—so silly. He must have been out of his mind, hey?

ABRAHAM. Maybe, Madam. Me and Mr Edwards, we was very close, Madam. Very close, we was. He did it, some people say, because he was kind of protesting.

WINI. Protesting? What do you know about such things? It's a strong and dangerous word—protest.

ABRAHAM. Yes, Madam, like they say. But Mr Edwards, he was sort of protesting with his life. He said, when the family got the notice, how can the government just come along and take a man's home away from him? Just like that? Broken-hearted he was, and him near sixty years old.

WINI. Well, we've got to obey the government, no matter what. But this Mr Edwards or whatever his name was, he hanged himself in that apple tree there? How horrid.

ABRAHAM. Yes, madam, right there.

WINI. But why did you say—when I heard you talking to yourself like the idiot you are—why did you say that he's to stay in the tree as long as he liked? All that crazy talk, that he never went away?

ABRAHAM. Oh, Madam, it's just a manner of speaking. A man gets lonely, and then sometimes I think I see him still hanging there in the tree.

WINI. You're out of your mind, too. Still hanging there, what nonsense. You can see there's nobody there, no man in the tree. Why, everybody imagines he sees things now and then. Even I. I once saw great horses running across the veld, and they were only the shadows of clouds. My Ma used to laugh at me, the things I thought I saw.

ABRAHAM. Yes, Madam, but like I says, a man gets lonely and maybe things come into his mind, I reckon. But me and Mr Edwards was close, very close, so then sometimes I think I see him still hanging up there in the tree. Maybe because we was so close.

WINI. How silly. Well, you better go, you hear me? If the master finds you here you'll be in trouble.

ABRAHAM. Yes, madam. Especially last day of the month.

WINI. What?

ABRAHAM. I said especially on the last day of each month, that's when I reckon I see poor Mr Edwards in the tree.

WINI. What rubbish. Once I saw a church on a mountain, but it was just the way the rocks were formed. But why the last day of each month? When you're drunk, I suppose.

ABRAHAM. No, Madam. You see, it was at the end of that month everybody had to be out. Everybody in the street had already gone, but only poor Mr Edwards wouldn't go. His family, they talks to him, but no, he wouldn't listen. Then the last day of the month is near and if they not out the police is going to come to put them out. The family, they makes all the arrangements, but poor Mr Edwards just sits there, thinking like. And then on that last morning, when they was all going to move, poor Mr Edwards does it. He comes out here while they all still sleeping, and he does it.

WINI. And so on the last day of each month you think you see him hanging there? (*Laughs.*) I think that's the time you're very much in your cups, hey? Having a good time with a bottle of cheap wine.

ABRAHAM. Well, no, Madam, I . . .

PETE (*in the distance*). Winifred. Are you there? We're about ready now—Hey! Who's that there with you?

MILES. What's that man doing here? Is he interfering with you, Mrs Gesler? (*Their voices draw near. Undergrowth rustling.*)

PETE. Who's this? Who's this old ruffian?

MILES. What are you doing on this property? You have no right to be here. It's trouble for you, boy.

ABRAHAM. I'm sorry, Masters. I'll go now. I was just talking to the Madam.

WINI (*laughing*). He's been telling me ghost stories. I found him here in this shed.

PETE. Winifred, you must be more careful!

WINI. Oh, he's harmless.

MILES. Ghost stories? Here, what have you been up to, rascal?

ABRAHAM. Excuse me, Sirs.

MILES. You keep quiet. I hope he hasn't harmed you, Mrs Gesler. I had no idea . . .

WINI. Oh, it's all right. It was quite mysterious also.

PETE. Mysterious?

WINI. It seems he was working for the people who used to live here—the Coloured people. He was a kind of handyman or houseboy—do they have houseboys?

MILES. Er—some of them do, I think.

WINI. Well, this old beggar worked here on the place, and he says when the people had to move, the owner—a Mr Edwards—came out here and committed suicide. Hanged himself in this tree. Couldn't face up to having to leave the old home, it seems.

PETE. He must have been off his rocker, killing himself just because he had to move. There are other places the government set aside for these people. Do you know anything about it, Mr Miles?

MILES. Er—oh, yes. Come to think of it there was something in the papers. But it's got nothing to do with us, of course. I believe the inquest showed something about 'while mentally unbalanced'.

PETE. Hanging himself because he had to move. Well, we didn't make the Group Areas law, did we?

MILES. Of course not. The government declared this area for whites only and that's that. Those Coloureds just had to get out, that's all.

WINI. What's more, this old uncle says he actually sees—or I should say, thinks he sees—the man hanging in the tree on the last day of every month. That's when it happened, he says. (*Laughs.*) Ghosts on the last day every month.

MILES. Last day? Hanging? What the devil—here, you, I think I've had enough of you. Making trouble on private property. I've a good mind to call the police.

WINI. Oh, let him go, Mr Miles.

MILES. Very well then, Mrs Gesler. You, boy, you clear out. Trek, do you hear?

ABRAHAM. Awright, Master, awright. Old Abraham will go then. Let me get my things, Sir.

MILES. Hurry up then.

(*Shed door creaks as Abraham goes in to collect his belongings. His voice is heard inside.*)

ABRAHAM. Old Abe got to leave this place, Mr Edwards. Sorry, Mr Edwards, old Abraham, he got to go now.

MILES. Is there anybody else in there?

WINI. No, I looked. It appears he gets lonely and talks to the dead man. Imagines he's still here, I think. He's been staying on here in this shed ever since everybody else moved.

PETE. Bloody cheek.

WINI (*laughing*). So you've got a ghost in the back garden, Mr Miles. At the end of every month.

MILES. But it's too ridiculous for words, Mrs Gesler. It's all a plot, that's what it is. The things these people get up to. I shouldn't be surprised if it was all planned by some mischief makers.

PETE. I shouldn't be surprised either. These people are starting to get out of hand altogether.

MILES. I do hope this nonsense won't influence you in any way, Mrs Gesler. Your husband and I came to an arrangement.

WINI. Oh dear, no. I was quite amused by the poor old thing's chatter. He must be a little queer. Besides, Pete, you remember how you and the others used to make fun of me? I used to see things, too.

ABRAHAM. Goodbye then, Mr Edwards. Don't you worry about nothing. Everything is going to be awright, you'll see. (*To the others as he emerges from the shed.*) Please excuse me if I was any trouble.

WINI. Couldn't we keep him on to do the garden?

PETE. No, Sir. I'm not having any barmy darkies on the place. We'll get a proper servant.

MILES. I wouldn't advise you to encourage this one, Mrs Gesler.

ABRAHAM. Goodbye, Madam. Goodbye, Sirs.

MILES. Get along. Off with you.

ABRAHAM (*his voice fading*). Us poor people, we always chased . . .

PETE. Well, that's the end of that.

MILES. I hope you haven't been put off by this. These people—one never knows with them. So hard to keep them in their place. Now, Mr Gesler, about the property . . .

PETE. What do you say, Winifred? I think it's what we want.

WINI. Yes, I think so, Pete. It's big enough and I suppose reasonably priced. With two extra bedrooms, Ma could come and visit us sometimes.

PETE. Oh Lord. Well, that's it then, Mr Miles.

MILES. Marvellous. Now, if you don't mind, I'll lock up and we can drive over to my office. I'll just lead the way again . . .

(*Fade*)

WINI. Morning darling. It's seven o'clock. There, I've brought you your coffee. Here's the paper, too.

PETE (*yawning*). Morning, sweet. How are you today?

WINI. Oh, recovered from yesterday's bustle. It takes ages to get a house organized, doesn't it? I suppose we'll get everything straightened out, one day.

PETE. Thanks. Well, we've done all right so far. Soon we'll have settled down proper, then we'll advertise for a girl and you won't have to slave so hard, dear.

WINI. Hurrah. I wonder how the other new arrivals in the street are doing? The people two doors away seem quite nice.

PETE. The folks with the station wagon? Beyers their name is. Yes, I spoke to the husband. He's a foreman at some sheet metal works.

WINI. Oh. And that Mrs Carlson had some good ideas about curtaining—I spoke to her.

PETE. What's wrong with the stuff you've put up? By the way, open the curtains, will you? Let's take a look at the paper.

WINI. Here you are. (*Rustle of newspaper being opened. Footsteps as Wini goes to open the curtains. Curtains are opened.*)

PETE. Ah, that's some light on the subject. Let's see, what have we this morning? Hmm. Houses for sale.

WINI (*laughing*). Pete, what on earth for are you looking at houses for sale? We've got a house.

PETE (*laughing*). Of course. Just absent-minded, darling. Those long weeks of house hunting are still with me. That reminds me, you know what day this is?

WINI. What? Not your birthday?

PETE. Of course not. No, it's the end of the month today. We owe that blighter of an estate agent the first instalment.

WINI. Why, of course.

PETE. Oh, well . . . What's the weather like?

WINI. Lovely morning outside. One day when we've got the ground laid out it will be beautiful there at the back of the house.

PETE. You bet. Have to get somebody to clear it up. Now what bad news do we have today? (*Newspaper rustles.*) Hmmmm.

WINI. (*Catching her breath.*) Pete.

PETE. Hmmmm?

WINI. Pete . . . out there in the old garden.

PETE. Garden? What's up?

WINI (*her voice rising*). Pete! Out there—in the apple tree!

PETE. Darling, whatever's the matter?

WINI. IN THE TREE, PETE! THERE, PETE! THERE'S A MAN HANGING IN THE TREE!

CHAPTER THREE

The Exile
(January 1972)

This story marks a return to South Africa and presages some of La Guma's concerns for rural politics later addressed in Time of the Butcherbird (1979). *It also reconsiders notions of exile—more specifically, being an exile in one's own country—while equally conveying a longing for South Africa, which he had been away from since 1966. This story appeared in* Lotus: Afro-Asian Writings.

That afternoon when McPherson unlocked the trading store after the lunch-hour break, he was feeling in a good mood. He had had a good meal, prepared by the African cook, and he had drunk two whiskies. So that when he opened the front door and stepped out on to the veranda, he smiled at the group of Africans who waited in the dust below the steps.

There were the usual women and the naked children, and in addition, two horses were tethered to the corner post, their riders seated on the edge of the veranda, smoking long pipes. They wore the usual ragged clothes under bright blankets, and shabby hats. One of them sported a tuft of beard. They slid off the veranda as the door was opened, and came around to follow the women into the store. McPherson smiled at them as they passed him and they nodded with the dignity of these people.

He hadn't seen these two before, or perhaps he had—these buggers all looked the same, he thought. And there were always horsemen around, coming down from the hills where they had their little villages and scraps of land. There was trouble further south, in the Transkei proper, and a state of emergency; police patrols and roadblocks. It had been rumoured that some of these horsemen and others were armed and were getting ready to kill all the whites. But McPherson had never been bothered, and he never bothered with politics, anyway. Once there had also been rumours that this crossing was a place where guns were being run through into the Transkei, and a police patrol had been sent from Aliwal, which had stayed on for a few days searching people and causing concern among the few black farmers and labourers in the district. But nothing had come of it, and they had gone away again.

Beyond the veranda, the sun glared like a basilisk on the land, and dust rose in small brown clouds as the horses moved. Chickens scrabbled and several dogs, lean and scruffy, circled suspiciously. Two women came up, one of them old, carrying empty four-gallon cans, and stopped to talk with another in the area in front of the trading store. An old man dozed in the shade of a ruined wall.

Across from the store, the river slowed down between low banks and crept idly over the shallows. It was low here, so you could see the white stones, worn smooth as marbles, in the bed. The sun brightened the surface of the water with a sheen of quivering quicksilver. To the west of the crossing, a good way off, was Aliwal and the Orange River; east were the first heights of the Drakensberg, the high mountains like the splintered, sawtooth back of a vast and petrified dragon sprawled across the horizon, with Basutoland beyond.

Inside the store, the women and the two horsemen were engaged in alternate debate with Sam, McPherson's 'boy'. McPherson leant against the doorframe in the shade and stuffed his pipe. Looking south, he could see the gap in the Stormberg, with its backdrop of flat blue sky. Beyond was the Eastern Cape Province and the Transkei territory.

The three women chattered and laughed in the sunlight. Against the wall the old man dozed in the shade, oblivious of the flies and dogs and chickens. Always old ones, McPherson thought; and almost always women. The younger men went into the cities and to the mines to earn a little money to augment the few coins that came from scratch farming and raising lean and bony cattle.

McPherson blew heavy blue smoke and dispersed it with a flick of his big, red hand. The horses twitched at flies with their coarse-haired tails, and children searched the dust with their toes, and the old man slept in the shade under the ruined wall. McPherson wondered idly what the devil these women were talking about. It crossed his mind that the old man looked like a stranger, but then, he thought again, you could never tell one from the other at a distance. The same black, the same ragged clothes. He wondered what the old man was dreaming of, there against the wall . . .

The old man was dreaming about his dog. He was dreaming that the dog, an old hound of mysterious ancestry, but which bore most of the physical characteristics of a shepherd, was licking his face. In his sleep, the old man felt the harsh, warm tongue against his wrinkled cheek, and he smiled in his sleep, murmuring.

If he could have dreamt many days into the future, the old man would have dreamt that he lay under a bare and withered thorn tree on a dusty, stone-rough hillock in the twilight, peering out across an eroded meadow towards the ridge where his house stood. The ground would be hard and uncomfortable through his tattered clothing, and he would watch the house waiting for the darkness to fall.

There were three houses along the ridge, rough but sturdy affairs built of stone and mud, and thatched with dry grass. In one of the huts, next to his, lived the headman of the village, a servile man and a betrayer. So the old man would wait for the darkness, listening to the bleating of sheep in the pens beyond the houses.

While he waited, he would see the boy come out of his house into the dooryard, and his heart would leap with excitement and love. The boy would collect firewood onto an arm and carry it inside. While the old man waited, he would hear suddenly the barking of a dog, and then the crashing through the undergrowth, and then the dog would be there. It would bark and snuffle, flinging itself joyfully at its old master, and it would be then that he would feel the harsh, hot tongue against his cheek and smell the scent of the dog.

He would say, laughing softly, 'Ah, old friend, it is you. It is you.' He would reach out and pat the head and run his fingers through the coarse dusty hair of the hackles, hearing the hoarse panting in the animal's throat. The dog would leap happily at him, circling, whining with pleasure.

Then, when the darkness came crawling over the hills and the stars brightened, the old man would listen for a while, holding the dog, his strong, gnarled fingers in the loose skin of the dog's neck, until he was sure that it would be safe to go forward. Then he would rise quietly, and they would cross the parched meadow in the darkness and the sounds of the crickets, circling so as to avoid the headman's house, and come up to the side of the old man's house.

Then there would be the amazement, the shock, as the eldest boy opened the door to his knocking and the dog's yelping, and saw the old man there in the doorway in the half-light of the flames in the fireplace. The amazement would turn to joy and the boy would cry out and jump up and down as the old man entered, ducking his head under the low lintel. The woman at the fireplace would turn, and the younger boy would look up from the rough table where the evening meal was set.

The eldest son would shut the door quickly, knowing the danger, while the old man would stand there, a hand, hard and at the same time gentle, on the boy's head, smiling at the woman. There would be tears in his eyes, too, as he watched the wonder on the woman's face in the dimness of the house.

She would say in wonder and gladness: 'You? You?'

'It is I,' he would say.

'But—'

'Yes, I know, woman. It has been a long time—three years. But it was bad there, and cold and lonely. So I left.'

'Left? But sit down, first. We greet you. You are back, Father.'

The old man would sit down by the table, turning to warm his hands over the fire. 'Yes, I left. And how is my young one? Ai, he's grown up. It is a joy to see these children. And you, woman? Is everything well? Has there been enough rain?'

The boys would close up on him, smiling, their eyes big in wonderment, while his hands patted their ragged shoulders.

The woman would say, clasping her hands, brown and hard, like bundles of twigs: 'But, how, father—?'

'I decided to leave that place. There was nothing there, only loneliness and hunger. So I left one night, walking all the way.'

'Walking?'

'Yes. But sometimes some kind people gave me a ride on a wagon or a lorry. But most of the time it was walking.'

The woman would start. 'But, the police will take you if you are found.' She turned to the eldest boy. 'Go outside, stand and watch. If somebody is seen, come quickly.' The boy ducked his head and went out quickly.

'How are things here?' the old man would ask again, as the woman laid a plate of roasted meat and boiled meal before him. 'The boy has grown up.'

'Yes. Everything depends on him now. He tends the field and the little one looks after the sheep.'

'Ah. They are good children.'

'There has been little rain, and the earth is dry. But you—what will you do? The police. Will you stay here?'

The old man would sigh sadly, pausing in his hungry eating. 'No. I would gladly and happily. But I cannot. I must go again. But what of the one next door? I made up my mind to go into Basutoland. There are friends there, at least. It is the only place.'

'Basutoland? But that is far away, through the mountains.'

'Yes. But no farther than where they sent me.'

'It is true. How will you go, then?'

'As I came. Walking. It should be better there. And perhaps one day you and the boys will come, too.'

'Ai. But we have roots here. It will be hard to go, as it was hard for you. We will stay until there is nothing else to do.'

'Yes. It is a hard thing, and a sad thing. But what of the one next door? The betrayer. I will not even say his name, because it is bitter in my mouth.'

'He went into town on business with the white magistrate. He has much business with the magistrate. Things are bad here. There are people taken and sent to prison now with this emergency. He laughs at those they call troublemakers, who are arrested.'

The old man would shake his head sadly. Then he would say with more pleasure: 'It is good to be home again, to see you and the children. I told myself, I will leave this place and go where there are friends, but first I will see my wife and my sons.'

'Three years. It has been a long time. But I remember as yesterday, the day the police came with the paper saying that you were banished from this place.'

'Yes. The parting was bitter, but I returned to see you.'

The woman would say, 'But to walk all this way!'

'Well, you know I cannot write.'

The old man would sigh as he ate, and they would talk in quiet tones of what had happened since he had left; of the land, of the few sheep, of the people, while the youngest son would sit drowsily by them at the table, his chin resting upon his small hands.

Once, long ago, the old man had lived at this place with his wife and sons, until times had grown from bad to worse, and people had started talking out against the government. There had been things like the government's 'Bantu education' and 'Bantu authorities' which the people did not like and did not want. Some of the headmen like the one of this village went along with the authorities and were given more power over the people. Then the people muttered among themselves at first, and then called meetings to talk about things, and to say what they wanted and what they did not want.

So the old man had spoken out against the government, and because he was an old man and respected among the villagers, the headman had complained. Then, a few days later, had come police with a long document couched in wordy terms, which he could hardly understand. But the gist of it was that under the Native Administration Act he had been exiled to one of the government's trust farms in the north of the Transvaal province and was not permitted to leave it except with permission of the Secretary of Native Affairs, on pain of arrest.

This trust farm had been an empty and windy place, swept by winds and inhabited by strangers who had been kind enough, but who were not of those nearest to him. How far away was this place? The old man did not quite know. A thousand miles? Two thousand? Across two provinces, far away near the no-return border of the country. So he had sat there for three years, eking out an existence, and always thinking, thinking, thinking. Until he had gathered together his meagre belongings and had set out one night, to cross the two provinces again, in order to see the woman and his sons once more, before slipping across into Basutoland.

Now, sleeping in the shade of the ruined wall by the river crossing, where he had come to rest, he dreamt, and if he could have dreamt ahead, he would have dreamt that he said to the woman, his wife:

'One day things will be better. The world changes.'

'We should pray,' the woman would say, quietly.

'Perhaps,' the old man would reply, a small smile on his wrinkled face. 'Perhaps praying helps. I am not altogether sure any longer, woman.'

But they would bow their heads in the flickering half-light of the fireplace, and the outside sounds of the crickets and the snuffling of cattle in the pen would be heard, the woman's body rocking gently.

Then, the door would be thrust open and the elder boy would cut through the old man's murmuring, saying in his excited child's voice, 'There is a light coming along the path from the road.'

The old man looked up. 'Would it be the one next door returning?'

'It might well be,' the woman would say, a ring of fear in her voice.

The boy would say, excitedly, 'He left with two others, and I think there are three coming back now. It is dark, and I am not certain.'

'It is best that I go now.' And the old man would gather pieces of meat and lumps of meal into the bundle, which he had brought with him.

The woman would begin to wail softly, and the old man would place a gnarled hand on the cloth-covered head. 'The ancestors watch you and our sons.' The woman wailed softly and tears slid softly from her closed eyes, gleaming like diamonds on her starved face.

Outside the night would be chill, and the sounds of the crickets much louder. The stars would be like scattered jewels on the velvet cupola of the sky.

The old man would say to the youngest son, 'Hold the dog. I do not want him following me.' His fingers would stroke the boy's short wiry hair for a brief moment, before he set out to walk through the mountains.

'I will walk a little way with you, Papa,' the other boy would say.

'Good. But we must go quickly, Son.'

The dog would whine and tug in the grip of the youngest boy who would be crying softly, while his brother and the old man would be shadows moving off into the darkness under the infinite sky . . .

The darkness had not yet come to the crossing at the river, and the sky was a pale lavender diluted with pink. McPherson came out of the store again after he had checked up on the 'boy' and had taken another glass of whisky.

He thought that it was bloody lonely out here sometimes, and wondered whether he should take the truck and drive into Aliwal for a little recreation. All one saw were these native boys and girls and the mountains.

Across the river, a herdsman was driving a few cattle, heading for the ford, and the dust from the hooves was yellow-brown against the evening light. The chickens had disappeared from the yard in front of the store, and the two women had left a long time ago. As had the horsemen.

McPherson scratched an armpit and leant against a veranda post. He noticed idly that the old man who had been sleeping under the ruined wall was no longer there, but he was really thinking about going into Aliwal. He remembered that from Aliwal North the train lines went southwest and then south at Dreunsberg and Burgersdorp, thrusting through the mountain country and heading towards the gap in the frowning Stormberg, through to Sterkstroom on the other side of the mountains and then spearing down out of the highlands towards Queenstown. From Queenstown you could go on down towards Amabele and east towards Butterworth, crossing the Great Kei again, passing the hills and the sunburnt land and the scattered villages with mealies struggling against the slopes of the stingy hillsides, and on into Umtata. Through all these places the railway twisted and curled and climbed, like silver string dropped on to crumpled, coloured gift-wrapping.

But McPherson decided that he would not go into Aliwal after all. He looked towards the horizon while he lit his pipe. The sky beyond the high purple hills was changing from lavender to a darker blue. He could not see, far up the darkening valley, the old man trudging towards the gap in the mountains.

CHAPTER FOUR

Late Edition
(April 1972)

In this story set in South Africa, within the urban environs of Cape Town, La Guma employs an Afrikaans-inflected, working-class dialect—kaapse taal—which is common among Coloured South Africans. The attention to the dialogue of the characters conforms to a broader concern in the Afro-Asian Writers Association for local languages, cultures and indigenous artistic forms. 'Late Edition' first appeared in Lotus: Afro-Asian Writings.

Around that corner the great trolleybuses hissed and rumbled, swaying towards the terminus, the passengers packed inside and overflowing onto the platform. The vast yellow sides of the buses, bright with advertisements, towered for a second over him and then passed on. The knock-off-time crowds coming in from the city and the railway station converged on that corner, too, and unreeled in a single thread up Main Street, so that it was a good site for hawking the evening papers.

Above the grumble and hum of late afternoon noise, his voice rose high pitched and immature, 'Late. Late. City Late.'

Under one ragged elbow, the dead in an air crash froze in the snow of a mountainside, their refrigerated bodies sprawled at grotesque half-tone angles. His grimy fingers smudged and blurred the ink of the black headlines, which announced a dramatic sea chase by the British Navy, and past the ebony forearm, the anonymous face of a man missing from home for the last week, peered vacantly. Silver Queen was the favourite for the main race on

Saturday, near his chest, and beside the disaster dead, the mayor announced a vigorous campaign against traffic offenders.

'Late! Late! Sorry, Late!'

The bundle of newsprint under his arm dwindled rapidly as the crowd streamed past. He gave change expertly and quickly from the sagging pocket of his out-down trousers. His dark, bitten fingers sorted out the variety of coins with the skill of a bank teller. The bundle disappeared but there was another on the pavement at his feet. The aircraft dead, the missing men, Silver Queen, all vanished, folded under the arms or into the side pockets of customers, to reappear again over the supper table, read to the smell of stewed beans, fried meat, onions or yesterday's leftovers.

The last of the late edition he sold to a coal-dusted docker who smelt of cheap muscatel and tobacco, and then he turned from the site and headed for the rendezvous with the agent who contracted with the publishers for the sale of the paper.

From the gutter at the roadside, an eye winked at him. He stooped quickly and experienced fingers skimmed the glistening thing from the accumulated detritus of the street. It was a glass-eye marble, brand new and untouched by dust and grime. Peering excitedly into it, he saw inside the glass sphere the convolution of colours forming a pattern that seemed to squirm and change form. 'Hey, good luck,' he thought. 'This will bring good luck. I bet it's a real lucky charm glass-eye marble, this.' He polished it against his ragged shirt, peered into it again, knuckled it between thumb and forefinger, smiling happily. Then he tucked it into a pocket of his trousers and started off again. Every now and then he reached into the pocket and caressed the marble. 'Lucky charm,' he thought. 'Good luck cat's-eye.' It would bring good luck.

At another corner, the agent was surrounded by other newsboys. The agent was a skinny man in a suit too big for his body, flopping and hanging from his frame like the second-hand clothes you saw in Old Solly's shop in Caledon Street. The agent had one gold tooth, too, and he showed it each time he grinned.

He had a little black book, dog-eared and battered and greasy, in which he recorded the names of his sellers and the number of papers issued to them.

'Hullo, Mister Frikkie,' the gold tooth grinned down. 'And what did Mister Frikkie do today? Hey?'

'All sold.'

'All sold, hey, Mister Frikkie?'

'Hey,' said another boy, 'We came first.'

'You came first? Gwan.' The agent's arm swung out, backhanded, and cuffed the dirty ear. 'You came first, awright. But Mister Frikkie here is just a small little man, and I think you boggers can wait, hey?'[1]

The cuffed ear sniffed and grumbled. The boy touched his lucky marble expectantly.

'Now then, Mister Frik.' A fingernail, long as a talon and rimmed with black, wandered over a greasy page in the record book. 'That's a honnered and forty-four, hey? Let's see. That makes two and eighty-eight cents. Honnered and forty-four as two cents, mos.'[2]

The boy was already stacking the coins in neat cylinders on the kerbside, and the agent towered over him, grinning. When the stacking was done, he sat on the kerb himself, to check.

'OK, Mister Frikkie. All cooreck. You's a wake-up johnny, Mister Frikkie. Now, honnered and forty-four ha pennies is seventy-two cents. That's commission, and twenty-two for the Chris'mas party. That's five bob left.'

[All notes in this chapter are by the editor.]

1 The expression 'small little' is repetitious slang, and 'boggers' is slang for 'buggers'.

2 The word 'mos' is inserted for emphasis, like 'man'.

He counted off five ten-cent pieces and held them up, grinning with the gold tooth.

'Whatter Chris'mas party?'

'Whatter Chris'mas party?' The gold tooth looked surprised. 'You ask whatter Chris'mas party?' The agent clucked with mock consternation. 'Don't you know about the Chris'mas party I give for my boys every year? I'll tell you, man. Everybody pays me something a week from their commission, and I give a big party for youse boys at the end of the year. Each one gets a bottle of ginger beer and a cake. Everyone of youse eleven pikkies.[3] Hell, it happens every year. Everybody pays something a week and gets a bottle of ginger beer and bun come Chris'mas. Don't I say?' He grinned around at the pinched faces.

'Was these men at the party last year, Mister?'

'These? Hell, no. Youse all new boys. Other was a lot of lazy boggers. Worked until the party come and got their ginger beer and cake, and never come back to sell papers again. Lot of lazy lighties.[4] But youse lighties is going to have a real wake-up party. You'll see.'

The agent grinned around at all of them, patted sundry heads and returned to business. 'Now, like I said. Five bob is your commission, Mister Frikkie. After twenty-two off for the bun and ginger beer.'

'I rather want the lot and leave the party, Mister.'

'Leave the party? Garn.' The agent scowled now, the gold tooth taking on an ominous aspect. 'Garn. All the boys is paying in their bobs. There, you take your fifty cents, Mister Frik. OK?'

The agent's right hand closed casually into a knobby fist, and it dug playfully into the small, meagre ribs, hurting just a little.

He backed away from the fist, his mouth sulky, and said sullenly, 'Awright. Give my five bob, in change, then.'

---

3 A 'pikkie' is a child or youth.
4 The word 'lighties' also refers to young men or boys.

'Change, Mister Frikkie? Naturally, man. Ten one-cents, two five-cents and three ten-cents. That OK? Now let's see what you other boggers have done. Same time tomorrow, Mister Frik. So long, old man.'

He was walking past the rows of windows crowded with clothes, pyramids of fruit, musical instruments, gaudy with placards and posters announcing 'Sale Now On', and price tickets and cigarette advertisements. He was jostled and pushed and scolded out of the way.

Fifty cents in small change hung in his pocket, and the grubby fingers turned over the coins. He could keep his usual five and hand over the rest to the Old Woman. On the other hand, he could tell her he had only made four bob and give her thirty-five. That meant he would have fifteen cents to spend. It also meant bioscope on Saturday afternoon, with a parcel of fish-and-chips thrown in, and a frozen sucker. Or maybe he'd just keep the five and perhaps the Old Woman, his mother, would give him something extra. He caressed his lucky glass-eye marble.

The brilliant window of a toyshop attracted his attention, and he hopped over and stood against the great pane, staring at the array of dolls, tin motorcars and big humming tops. Long barrelled, gleaming silver six-shooters with wonderful red and white and black handles hung in rows. Hey, that's guns just like John Wayne carries, mos. How much?

He stared at the beautiful guns and the stubby, battered encrusted toes of one foot gently caressed the other leg. His running nose made a wet mark on the window. Wow! What beautiful guns.

A fat, pink man lumbered out of the shop and cried: 'Go away, you skolly-boy.[5] You dirty the window. Go away.' A plump hand seized a shoulder of the ragged jersey and bounced him roughly.

---

5 A 'skolly' is a gangster or criminal.

He skipped a little distance, then turned and shouted back: 'Yah, old fatty. Yah, you big fat fatty.'

The pink man waggled a plump finger at him and advanced a step, red-faced, but he thumbed his nose and scampered off among the legs of passers-by.

Fat old man, fat old man, fat rich old man, he thought as he went up the street, one foot in the kerb and the other in the gutter, so that he walked with an exaggerated limp.

On the pavement, an old man in a dirty and greasy apron and a grimy turban was turning the handle of a battered candyfloss machine, while children gathered around, their eyes following the spinning wheel that produced the fluffy, pink, sugary strands inside the brass drum. The handle went whirr-whirr as the old man turned it.

Pennies appeared and bunches of sticky fluff squeezed into anxious mouths. He presented a five-cent piece and the pink candy passed through the bony forest of upstretched arms.

'Where's my change, bubby?'

He was licking at the dyed and cottoned sugar, his free hand held out, the small, dirty palm open. The cotton tasted wonderful, and it stuck to his lips and around his mouth.

'Whatter change?' The wrinkled brown face, with its wispy beard like that of the djini in a fairy tale, peered at the tiny, nondescript urchin face. 'Whatter change? You give me a penny. Whatter change?'

'I did give sixpence, bubby.'

'Loop. Go, joing: Blerry skolly, you. Whatter change?'[6]

The aproned figure advanced upon him through the scattered debris of stunted childhood. Arms like stripped branches flapping

---

6 The word 'loop' means 'walk'. 'Joing' literally means 'young', referring to a 'mate' or 'young man'. 'Blerry' is slang for 'bloody'.

as if he was driving chickens before him. 'Voetsek.[7] Go. Blerry little skolly. Whatter change you want?'

He backed away with the laughter of the other children around him. When he was at safe distance from the sweet vendor he stood scowling for a moment, forcing back the tears, and then yelled suddenly: 'Skelm. Cheat. You old skelm man.'[8] Then he was off again up the street, leaving the laughter and the whirr-whirr behind him.

Up and down the street the shops were being locked and the burglar-proof bars fastened over the plate-glass windows. The trolleybuses were no longer packed now, and the stream of grown-ups on the pavements had dwindled. Over Signal Hill, on the other side of the city, the sun hung beribboned with cloud, for the last few minutes before going down.

The last of the candyfloss had melted away on his tongue, leaving a lingering taste of sugar behind. Making his way up the street, he thought, I did give him a sixpence, mos, the old skelm. And the Old Woman is going to skel, scold me, and maybe give me the strap. Oh, la, la, la. He felt the sting of the strap in his mind. Tears came again, and there was a lump in his throat, and a tiny growth of fear down inside his body. But perhaps she'd understand. He hoped so. The glass eye lay in his pocket.

He jingled the coins in his pockets, calculating the amount he had already lost. But, awright, the Christmas party was going to be a wakeup. With ginger beer and buns. Maybe the agent could get some cocoanut balls, too. He would tell the agent tomorrow. He jingled the remaining coins again, the tears receding with the prospect of ginger beer and buns, and perhaps those cocoanut balls, rising within his imagination.

At the tall iron trelliswork of the cinema gates, he pulled up. The massive coloured faces of film stars smiled down on him from the posters on the boards above the gates. A huge woman with

---

7 'Voetsek' is an Afrikaans expression for saying 'get lost'.
8 'Skelm' means 'sly' and is often slang for 'criminal'.

yellow hair and a red mouth and beautiful teeth seemed to be laughing at him. She was wearing a bathing costume and the enormous thighs and legs looked ready to engulf him. He thrust his face between the bars of the gate and stared at the black-and-white stills on the easels in the dusty foyer.

A cowboy film star wearing a beautiful white hat and ivory-handled guns, frowned at a fat, moustached crook who looked obviously afraid of the hero. He had to come and see the play on Saturday. Nobody could beat The Durango Kid the way he shot down those crooks and fought them in the bars with the furniture smashing to matchwood and his beautiful white hat never falling from his head through all the riding and the rough-and-tumble. And that's his horse, who could outrun anything the crooks rode.

He turned from the gate at last, and his eyes were confronted by two shiny brass-belt buckles and two pairs of navy-blue serge trousers, which they held up carelessly. The belt buckles and the trousers hemmed him in, and he raised his cropped head to stare up at two faces, which seemed a long way above him, and the tears began to form again. His nose was running, too, and he wiped it on one ragged sleeve, smearing the vestiges of pink candyfloss with mucous.

'Hullo, ou man,' one of the faces said.[9] 'I hear you got chink in that pocket, mos, man.'

'Give us a bob, man,' the other face laughed.

He tried to slip around the navy-blue clad legs, but they turned with him, trapping him skilfully.

'I got to go home,' he whined, very near tears again. 'My ma is waiting for me.'

'Awright, man,' the first face said.

'You can go now, now, man. Just turn out that pocket, man.'

---

9 The expression 'ou man' refers to 'old man'.

'Hell, shake the lighty,' the second face said and seized one stick-like arm. 'Come on, pikkie. Let's have the chink.'

He began to cry, struggling to get away from the crushing, hurting grip on his arms. He cried out while they emptied the pocket, the tears cutting lines through the grime of his face and his nose running into his mouth. The glass-eye marble was hurled into the distance.

They let him go, at last, with a cuff across the cheek, sending him spinning. He sat on the pavement with the pain, and wept, while the two faces laughed and receded.

A stout woman stormed out of the alleyway next to the cinema, shouting at the two faces, scolding and shaking a fist. But the faces went on laughing.

'Gwarm, Aunty. Go to hell. Mind your own blerry business, Aunty.'

He climbed to his feet again, rubbing the tears from his puffy eyes, smudging the grime wetly, looking at the backs of the two going down the street.

'F- - - youse,' he sobbed after them. 'Your mother! Your baskets. Your mothers, man.'

He backed along the pavement, crying and cursing the two faces in his high-pitched, seven-year-old voice, while the stout woman clucked around him.

'Don't cry, klonky.[10] Don't cry. The blerry skollies.'

In the gathering twilight he limped down a cobbled lane, past tumbled heaps of rubbish, into the narrow grey street lined with old grey tenements and overflowing dustbins. There were people lounging in the doorways and other children playing among the dustbins. He limped past the damp, decaying buildings, ignored by those in the street, another anonymous child—one of the hundreds of nondescript smudges on that district.

---

10 'Klonky' is a slang for a young man or boy.

Home was through a huge doorway and across a puddled hallway and into a courtyard, up a narrow, winding, rust-covered fire escape, and into a room that always smelt of boiled cabbage or burnt cooking oil. The lank-haired, young-old woman with the thickened body and the smell of sweat, who was his mother, would be up there, waiting. Slowly, with fluttering heart, he climbed the rusty iron stairs.

CHAPTER FIVE

Thang's Bicycle
(1976)

Set in Vietnam, and based on his trip there with the World Peace Council in January 1973, this short story marks an experimental departure in La Guma's work. It draws connections between French colonialism and the American war in Southeast Asia. It also recalls the Bicycle Messenger and the reimagined Sharpeville Massacre scene from his novel In the Fog of the Seasons' End *(1972). Along with 'Come Back to Tashkent', the story demonstrates La Guma's attempts at heralding a new era in Afro-Asian literature. It appeared in* Lotus: Afro-Asian Writings.

There were very few in the city who did not recognize the bicycle. Almost everybody rode a bicycle and the streets teemed with pedalling people, most of the heavy traffic consisting of army vehicles, so one would not have thought that another machine would turn a head, evoke some remark, even cause a smile or a chuckle. But this was a special bicycle.

It was first seen coming into the city over the pontoon bridge across the Red River. The original bridges, built a long time ago by the French, were down, distant steel girders sagging like broken toys into the slow-moving river. Now just before daylight the traffic edged cautiously over the beams of the pontoon, lurching along, a line of army trucks bumper to bumper with the drivers nursing the steering, their faces relaxed from long experience at this sort of thing, placid under the khaki sun helmets. The tyres boomed and rumbled across slats slung from steel float to steel float that spanned the dark water. Past the line of trucks and troop carriers streamed the civilians, country people coming into the city, baskets of farm produce in panniers slung from bamboo poles that bobbed across a shoulder, conical straw hats blurred in the half-light. Men, women, some pushing bicycles, workers who lived across the river heading towards their various stations. In the east the light was breaking across the countryside, and the traffic officers were anxious to get the convoy across before day came. The press of vehicles and people slowly moved across the floating bridge as the dawn spread across the sky.

And there in the growing light, in the line of the people by the trucks, was Thang and his bicycle. An intent young man in a blue cap, a haversack slung on his back, pushing the machine along, anxious to reach the other side.

The driver of the truck next to him looked down from the window, an arm resting on the door. 'Goodness, what kind of a bicycle is that, brother?'

Thang looked up at him frowning as they moved along side by side. 'What do you mean? It's a bicycle.'

The driver chuckled under his helmet. 'It looks more like a radar outfit on two wheels.'

True, in the half-light the bicycle did take on an unusual aspect. Its axles had been extended to support excess weight on the wheels, the handlebars were fitted with numerous hooks and the front fork hid several welded projections to which sacks or bundles could be lashed, apart from other odds and ends of struts and ribs to reinforce the frame.

'Brother, you would not scoff if you knew the history of my cycle,' Thang told the driver, scowling a little. 'This bicycle belonged to my father, and it was at Dien Bien Phu with him.'

'Hum,' replied the driver, looking polite. 'In that case it should be in a museum.'

'Museum?' Thang snapped crossly. 'A museum is for useless things. This bike still has a long time to live and a lot more service to give, old as it is. Not one of your new fancy Chinese or Soviet models.'

'I apologize for my disrespect for your wondrous machine,' said the driver, a little mockingly. 'I wish it a long life.'

'Thank you,' returned Thang primly. 'If there was time I would tell you about the days when my father transported supplies to the People's Army when they were preparing to attack the French. No, Comrade, do not judge a thing by its age only.'

'I stand corrected,' the driver said saluting and accelerated his truck as they reached the end of the bridge and bumped up the slope onto the bank.

The line of trucks and the crowd of people climbed the bank of the river in the morning light while the traffic officer there hurried them on. She was a young girl wearing a helmet, and a red band on one arm, and she too looked curiously at the bicycle, which the young man Thang was pushing.

Apart from the number of metal additions which had been made to the machine, it showed its age, too. Its original enamel had long been worn or gashed away. It had been painted several times and the paint was worn and scratched all over now, too. Its frame had been bent and straightened, bent and straightened, time and again, but somehow it had lasted over the years, indestructible. The girl in the helmet and the red band on her arm waved Thang on and he passed into the city for the first time.

He had come from a village to the north to work as a bricklayer in the city. 'You will take your father's bicycle, my son,' his mother had said the evening before they had parted. 'It will help you to get about the city. But care for it, for it served both your father and the people well.'

Thang recalled the stories his father had related to the family about how he had served in the transport section during the days when the People's Army had fought the French; how he and hundreds of others like him had carried valuable material for the Army up into the mountains during the great attack on the French fortress at Dien Bien Phu, way back in 1954.

The French colonialists had not thought that the Vietnamese, lacking vehicles, would manage to keep up the tons of supplies necessary for a major attack, but they had not reckoned on the people's stamina and on their cycles. The bicycles served as transport. It was calculated that a bicycle could carry between two and two-and-a-half times the weight of the man pushing it. In point of fact, the load of a bicycle could go up to as much as five hundred pounds, almost more than an elephant could carry. Struts to strengthen the frame and the front fork, and poles to extend handlebar and brake levers formed the basis of a new machine which each cyclist did his utmost to improve. Camouflaged and split up into several bundles, the load was more than ten times as big as that of a man, and there had been thousands of bicycles in service. With these bicycles it had no longer been a question of counting in pounds, but in tons.

Now here was Thang in Hanoi with his old bicycle. It took him to the sites where he worked at building or repairing air-raid shelters, and it took him to the anti-aircraft battery to which he had been attached, besides serving, as it had done before, as a means of transporting whatever was necessary for the life and defence of the bombarded city.

His workmates winked at each other and joked. 'What is this? A secret weapon for use against the enemy? Does it shoot off fireworks, play music? Surely, it is not a bicycle.'

They all rode the standard models, and circled Thang's bicycle, touching it, inspecting it. 'This machine has served our motherland,' Thang told them, frowning. 'There is no need to joke about it.'

'A thousand pardons,' they would say, bowing. 'We cannot help but stand in awe before such a marvel.'

Working and fighting. Manning his station at the anti-aircraft gun in a city square, Thang watched during a raid as the planes of the US Air Force swooped low over buildings, houses, pagodas, the silvery jets, bright predatory sharks in the clear blue sea of the sky; hearing the calm instructions of the gun captain, feeling the metal shake as the gun jolted in fire, the brass shells spilling out and the smell of cordite sharp in the air. Or there would be nights when the sky was full of the rumble and drone of the bombers high up and the shriek and whistle of bombs, and the dark would be crisscrossed with tracers, while the horizon glowed with fire, and all the time the familiar jolting of the gun and the brassy clatter of shells ejecting. A bright explosion as a bomber burst into flames.

Once an American bomb burst near the gun emplacement and the ground shook and shifted underfoot and the dust burst from the earth to fill eyes, mouth, throat, mingled with the harshness of explosive, but the crew never stopped loading the heavy clips of ammunition and the gun spat and jolted, its snout bouncing at the sky where the enemy droned and rumbled.

Later they discovered that the bomb had also smashed the bicycle park. The wreckage of cycles lay strewn around or tangled together like giant puzzles. But, miraculously, there was Thang's bicycle, the bicycle which had been at Dien Bien Phu, battered but still intact, flung aside by the blast, but its wheels spinning slowly and defiantly, alive.

Working and fighting. There were moments of peace too. Peace with the girl Lien, who was a saleswoman in a store. The first time he had met her, he noticed her as she came out of the shop where she worked, looking as if in a great hurry. He was at the kerbside and she had come over to him.

'Comrade, I have seen you in the district where I live. I know you live there too, so perhaps you are going there now. I must get home in a hurry to be in time for a meeting. Will you give me a lift on your bicycle?'

He said, 'I've seen you too, Miss. Well I am on my way to my lodgings. Very well, you can ride on the back.' She did not mind riding on such a strange-looking machine.

Afterwards when there was time they would go riding together. Content to sit sideways on the carrier behind him, holding on to his waist while she smiled under the conical straw hat, neat in her white blouse and black trousers, oblivious of the smiles and the stares the folk in the streets had for the bicycle.

The next time, after their meeting, Thang had offered to take her for a spin; he had said with embarrassed gruffness, 'I know the other day you were in a hurry, but I suppose you would not like to ride on such an old and ugly bicycle again.'

'I would like it very much,' she said, looking a little shy. 'It is a beautiful bicycle.'

'That's not what others say,' Thang said.

'They only joke because they are a little envious,' Lien told him. 'After all, none of their bicycles were ever at Dien Bien Phu.'

'Do you think so?'

'Certainly. Why the bicycles around here could be seen anywhere, everywhere. But who can claim that his bicycle served the people as well as yours? I would be very proud to ride with you on it.'

They would drive across to the lakes and walk along the banks or sit under the trees. They would stroll along the Lake of the Restored Sword, Thang pushing the bicycle with one hand and holding hers with the other. They would look at the Ngoc Son Pagoda on its island, or visit the red Huc Bridge arching over the water to where its pagoda stands among lotus blossoms under a great banyan tree. The girl, Lien, would show him the city. Sometimes she would take a turn at the pedals herself, with him sitting behind. They would coast along Ngoquyen Avenue and Tran Trien. The Dong Ba district had been severely hit, as well as the area under Kham Tien Street where Lien served as an air-raid warden in the local civil-defence unit. There was the Duong Dien Bien Phu, which excited him, for it was named after the battle where his father had fought.

Of course he would not hesitate to repeat, among other things he told her, the stories his father had imparted to him about the time of the great battle. His father had crossed the Fa Dinh Pass with the People's Army units. Some parts of the route were destroyed by French bombing, so that it was difficult to get by even on foot. As they approached the pass, a thrill of enthusiasm took hold of the soldiers and the waves of men, women and vehicles who were advancing towards Dien Bien Phu, and from Tuan Giao, the base at the foot of the pass, it had taken three consecutive nights on the march to cover fifty miles to their objective. Tree trunks used for bridge building had been carried on bicycles like Thang's or the backs of men, and the roads went up sheer cliffs, without handrails, camouflaged with wild banana trees and bamboos with long curved stalks, which had been transplanted there, roots and all. Hundreds of men, women and girls attacked the ground with pickaxes, taking the earth away in baskets and wheelbarrows, carefully shifting stones which were used for surfacing the road, or sometimes going for miles to fetch more. Step by step, day by day, night after night, the longed-for battle had come within their reach, until its success depended only on their courage. And Thang's bicycle had been there. It was something to be proud of.

Thang wrote home. 'I have met a girl, Lien.' He told the family all about her, but added, 'Also the bicycle is still in good order, and continues to function well.' Of course most of the letter would be about the girl Lien. How they went riding out together when they were off duty, she sitting happily on the rear carrier.

Now there was something greater than riding on the bicycle. They were engaged, preparing to be married. The gifts and the tea were exchanged between families; they would wait for some respite in the war, during which they would become man and wife.

The American bombers continued to come overhead, the earth shook under the explosives, the people fought back, went about their lives, wore their white bands of mourning for the dead, cleared away the rubble in the aftermath of destruction. Thang would always find the girl afterwards, working among the debris, lifting fallen beams and bricks, helping the wounded, and she would smile at him under her helmet, even though her eyes were sad in the presence of tragedy.

Always Thang's bicycle would be seen among the crowd of machines along streets, carrying him to work or to the anti-aircraft battery; or with Lien on the rear to her post on Kham Tien Street when she went on duty. Always the extraordinary-looking machine would receive a stare, a smile, an awed shake of the head. 'There goes Thang and his bicycle,' somebody would remark.

They were making their way from the lakes that evening, Thang pedalling leisurely, Lien behind him, clasping his waist, talking happily about the forthcoming marriage, until he started working harder at the pedals saying, 'It's growing dark and soon the alarms will be sounding, I'm sure. We'd better be on duty by then.' The bicycle carried them through the dusk. 'I'll hop off at the anti-aircraft site and you can use the bicycle to get to your post.'

They arrived at the battery position as the gun crews were coming on duty, and there was the usual cajolery. 'Ah, here is Thang and his bride-to-be. Tell us, Beautiful, will he drive you to the wedding ceremony on his famous bicycle?' The banter passed back and forth among them, while Lien, mounting the cycle, pedalled away with a wave amid the cheers of everybody.

Thang watched her go, smiling proudly, and as they took up their posts, asked, 'What's wrong with taking her to the ceremony on that bicycle? You know very well everybody uses a bicycle nowadays, and besides, what bride has ever been driven to her wedding on a cycle which actually was at Dien Bien Phu?'

That night the raids were exceptionally heavy. Along the skyline of the city, the red glow of fire hung like a devilish curtain, while the shriek of descending bombs and the thudding of the guns mingled with the shrilling of jets, pursued and pursuer, to compose an ear-shattering clamour. Again the night was lit up with multi-coloured tracers and the exploding stars of destroyed planes, while all the time the ground shook. Again and again the bombers screamed and droned over the city, coming in waves, and all the time the guns banged away and the fighter planes swooped like hawks. All night the firefighters fought the flames, and the medical teams braved danger to assist the wounded.

In the morning, smoke hung over the city, and the flames still licked here and there. The smoke-grimed gunners stood down from their places to make way for the relief crews, listening to the accounts of the night's events. The Bach Mai Hospital had been hit again, the Dong Ba district was burning, several American pilots had been captured, Kham Tien Street had been badly hit and the marketplace destroyed.

Kham Tien Street, Thang thought, as he headed into the city. The marketplace, Kham Tien Street—Lien, Lien, Lien, Kham Tien Street. He made his way past the hurrying Red Cross workers, civil defence personnel, soldiers, old people emerging from shelters, the piles of rubble, the drifting smoke. Kham Tien Street, the marketplace, the fallen beams and broken bricks, scattered tiles, the smell of smouldering fires.

Somebody said quietly, 'Comrade Thang.'

It was the Chairman of the street committee who knew him, an elderly man standing against a background of ruins and the bustle of anxious people. The Chairman looked at him but said nothing further, leading the way towards where the ambulance waited. Somehow his sandals dragged him after the Chairman while his heart thumped heavily in his chest. He did not have to ask the older man whether she was dead. She was there, laid out with the rest of the dead, waiting to be taken away. The red band of the civil defence was still on her arm, and he was glad somehow to see that that was the only sign of red about her, that she looked as if she slept, a slight figure in a jacket and black trousers, sandals.

The Chairman coughed awkwardly and said, 'She came on duty as usual, riding your bicycle. It was parked with the others in the marketplace.'

He did not want to see the ambulance worker draw the sheet over her and the stretcher-bearers lift her, to take her away. Later he would find her again, but now he preferred not to look any more. He turned and wandered blindly away through the ruins. He found himself in the devastated marketplace, stumbled over debris, brushed past people, and came upon the twisted metal of numerous bicycles.

He knew that among all the devastation he would find the old machine again, battered perhaps, scarred, but still intact, alive, defiant—the bicycle that had been at Dien Bien Phu.

CHAPTER SIX

Blankets
(1978)

Similar to 'Late Edition' (1972), this story echoes La Guma's earlier fiction regarding urban life in Cape Town, with attention to ordinary speech and the hardships faced on a day-to-day basis. 'Blankets' was first published in the Nigerian journal Black Orpheus *(1964) and was later reprinted in La Guma's story collection* A Walk in the Night and Other Stories *(1968). It was republished once more in* Lotus: Afro-Asian Writings *in 1978. I have included it in this volume as an example of how La Guma recirculated his past work for new audiences.*

Choker woke up. The woman's wiry hair got into his mouth and tasted of stale brilliantine. The old double bed sagged and wobbled when he shifted his weight, and there were dark stains made by heads on the crumpled grey-white pillows, and a rubbed smear of lipstick like a half-healed wound. His mouth felt parched from the drinking of the night before, and he had a headache.

The woman was saying, half asleep, 'No, man. No, man.' Her body was moist and sweaty under the blanket, and the bed smelt of a mixture of cheap perfume, spilt powder and human bodies mixed with infant urine. The faded curtain over the room window beckoned to him in the hot breeze. In the early, slum-coloured light, a torn undergarment hanging from a brass knob was a spectre in the room.

Choker felt ill and angry. The unwashed, worn blanket brushed his face and he smelt it with the other smells, and thought vaguely that he had slept under such blankets all his life. He wished he could sleep in a bed in some posh hotel, under fresh-laundered bedding. Then this thought was displaced by desire for a drink of cold beer, even water. He felt irritable, and thrust the bedding from him.

The woman turned beside him under the blanket, protesting in her half-sleep, and Choker sat up, cursing. The agonized sounds of the bedspring woke up the baby who lay in a bathtub on the floor, and it began to cry, its toothless voice rising in a high-pitched wail.

Choker sat on the edge of the bed and cursed the baby and the woman in his mind. He wondered why the hell he had crept in with somebody else's woman in the first place. And she with a bloody baby, too. The child in the tin tub kept on wailing.

'Ah,' he snapped angrily at the infant.

The woman woke up and looked at him, dishevelled, from the soiled pillow. 'You made such a noise. You woke the child,' she chided.

'Ah, hold your mouth,' Choker told her angrily. 'Get up and see to your damn kid.'

He stood up and walked around the bed to find his shirt and trousers. The woman asked, 'You going?'

'Of course, yes. You reckon I want to listen to this blerry noise?'

'Well,' the woman said crossly. 'Can I help it? You knew that I had the child.'

The baby kept on wailing. Choker looked at it as he pulled on his trousers and buttoned his shirt, 'Babies, dammit.'

She asked, in a humbler tone, 'You coming back?'

'Maybe, maybe not. I don't know.'

'Listen,' she said. 'Careful when you come, hey? I don't want my man to see you come here. He got an idea you been coming here. He'll maybe do something to you.'

Choker sneered: 'Him? Jesus, I'll break him in two with my bare hands.'

He laughed, standing hugely in the room. He was a big man, with muscles like bulges of steel wire, and great hands. He was brutal and vicious, and used the thick, ropy, grimed hands for hurting rather than for working.

She said, 'Awright, man. But even though he left me, he don't like 'nother man coming here. He may be watching out for you.'

'The hell with him,' Choker growled. 'His mother.'

The woman said nothing, and climbed out of the jangling bed to attend to the baby. She sat on the edge of the bed in her limp petticoat and suckled it.

She said, 'If you wait a little I'll make a little tea.'

'Forget it.'

Choker looked at her, sneered and shook his head, and then went out.

He walked along the corridor of the house, past the other rooms, frowning irritably against the nagging ache in his head, and the brittle feeling in his mouth and throat. There were holes in the boards of the floor, and he walked as carefully as his heavy body allowed.

In the morning sunlight, outside the smelly house, he headed for the tap in the dry, hollowed out area, which had once been a garden. He drank thirstily for a few moments, and then splashed his face, drying it on the sleeve of his shirt. He thought, To hell with her, I'll be boggered if I go back to that lot.

Around him were the rows of old, crammed houses and tumbledown box-board-and-tin shanties of the suburban slum. Chickens and dogs picked their way around among the weeds. He made his way idly through the broken streets and pathways. People avoided him, or gave him a casual greeting and passed on quickly, knowing his reputation. He was a drifting bulk, an accursed ship moving through a rotting Sargasso.

Choker was passing a walled-in yard when the three men stepped quickly from a gateway behind him. One of the cried, 'That's him,' and then, before he could turn, pain speared him with red-hot blades. He felt the pain in his head and the pain in his body almost simultaneously, and he fell, cursing. They didn't even wait to examine him, or to try again, but fled swiftly from the reach of the grappling-iron hands, leaving him to bleed in the roadway.

Choker lay in the road and felt the pain and the trickling of blood against his skin. He wanted to get up, but his legs were suddenly useless, and his arms would not lift his body. He lay there, his throbbing mind stubbornly cursing his attackers, while a crowd gathered, everybody talking excitedly.

Somebody said, 'Better carry him off the road.'

'I don't want nothing to do with it, hey.'

'Well, he can't most just lie about there.'

'Better go over to the shop and phone for the am'ulance.'

'OK, did you see them?'

'Look, pally, I didn't see nothing, man.'

'Well, pick him up. Look, Freddy, you take his feet. Sampie, you he'p him. Me and Points can take his arms.'

Lying there, bleeding and feeling ill, Choker thought, *you all . . .*, and then he felt himself being lifted roughly. He thought it was a hell of a thing to be so weak all of a sudden. They were bundling him about and he cursed them, and one of them laughed, 'Jesus, h's a real tough guy.'

Choker lay on the floor of the lean-to in the backyard where they had carried him. It was cooler under the sagging roof, with the pile of assorted junk in one corner: an ancient motor tyre, sundry split and warped boxes, and an old enamel display sign with patches like maps of continents on another planet, where the paintwork had worn away, and the dusty footboard of a bed. There was also the smell of dust and chicken droppings in the lean-to.

From outside, beyond a chrome-coloured rhomboid of sun, came a clatter of voices. In the yard they were discussing him. Choker opened his eyes, and peering down the length of his body, past the bare, grimy toes, he could see several pairs of legs, male and female, in tattered trousers and laddered stockings.

A man was saying, '... that was coward ... from behind, mos.'

'Ja. But look what he done to others, don't I say?'

Choker thought: To hell with those baskets. To hell with them all.

Somebody had thrown an old blanket over him. It smelt of sweat and dust and having-been-slept-in-unwashed, and it was torn and threadbare and stained. He touched the exhausted blanket with thick, grubby fingers. The texture was rough in parts and shiny, thin where it had worn away. He was used to blankets like this.

Choker had been stabbed three times, each from behind. Once in the head, then between the shoulder blades, and again in the right side. The bleeding had stopped and there was not much pain. He had been knifed before, admittedly not as badly as this, and he thought through the faraway pain. The baskets couldn't even do a decent job. He lay there and waited for the ambulance. Blood was drying slowly on the side of his hammered-copper face, and he also had a bad headache.

The voices, now and then raised in laughter, crackled outside, somewhere far away. Feet moved on the rough floor of the yard and a face not unlike that of a brown dog wearing an expired cloth cap, peered in.

'You still awright, Choker? Am'ulance is coming just now, hey.'

'—off,' Choker said. His voice croaked.

The voice withdrew, laughing: 'Ou Choker, Ou Choker.'

Another voice said: 'That burg was waiting for him a long time awready.'

'Ja. But Choker wasn't no good with a knife. Always used his hands, man.'

'That was bad enough, I reckon.'

The hell with them, Choker thought. He was feeling tired now. The hard grubby fingers, like corroded iron clamps, strayed over the parched field of the blanket... He was being taken down a wet, tarred yard with tough wire netting over the barred windows looking into it. The place smelt of carbolic disinfectant, and the bunch of heavy keys clink-clinked as it swung from the hooked finger of the guard.

They reached a room fitted with shelving which was stacked here and there with piled blankets. 'Take two, jong,' the guard said, and Choker began to rummage through the piles, searching for the thickest and warmest. But the guard, who somehow had a doggish face and wore a disintegrating cloth cap, laughed and jerked him aside, and seizing the nearest blankets, found two at random and flung them at Choker. They were filthy and smelly, and within their folds vermin waited like irregular troops in ambush.

'Come on. Come on. You think I got time to waste?'

'Is cold, mos, man,' Choker said.

But it was not the guard to whom he was talking. He was six years old and his brother, Willie, a year his senior, twisted and turned in the narrow, cramped, sagging bedstead which they shared, dragging the thin cotton blanket from Choker's body. Outside, the rain slapped against the cardboard-patched window, and the wind wheezed through the cracks and corners like an asthmatic old man.

'No, man, Willie, man. You got all the blanket, jong.'

'Well, I can't he'p it, mos, man. Is cold.'

'What about me?' Choker whined.

'What about me? I'm also cold, mos.'

Huddled under the blanket, fitted against each other like two pieces of a jigsaw puzzle . . . The woman's wiry hair got into his mouth and smelt of stale hair oil. There were dark stains made by heads on the grey-white pillow, and a rubbed smear of lipstick like a half-healed wound.

The woman was saying, half asleep, 'You see? You see? What did I tell you?' Her body was moist and sweaty under the blanket; and the blanket and bed smelt of cheap perfume, spilt powder, urine and chicken droppings. The faded curtain beckoned to him in the hot breeze. The woman turned from him under the blanket, muttering, and Choker sat up. The agonized sounds of the bedspring woke the baby in the tin bathtub on the floor, and it began to cry in a high-pitched metallic wail that grew louder and louder . . .

Choker woke up as the wail grew to a crescendo and then faded quickly as the siren was switched off. Voices still excitedly shattered the sunlight in the yard. Chocker saw the skirts of white coats and then the ambulance men were in the lean-to. His head was aching badly, and his wounds were throbbing. His face perspired like a squeezed-out washcloth.

Hands searched his body. One of the ambulance attendants asked: 'Do you feel any pain?'

Choker looked at the pink-white face above him, scowling. 'No, Sir.'

The layer of old newspapers on which he was lying was soaked with his blood. 'Knife wounds,' one of the attendants said. 'He isn't bleeding much outside,' the other said. 'Put on a couple of pressure pads.'

He was in mid-air, carried on a stretcher flanked by a procession of onlookers. Rubber sheeting was cool against his back. The stretcher rumbled into the ambulance and the doors slammed shut, sealing off the spectators. Then the siren whined and rose, clearing a path through the crowd.

Choker felt the vibration of the ambulance through his body as it sped away. His murderous fingers touched the folded edge of the bedding. The sheet over him was white as cocaine, and the blanket was thick and new and warm. He lay still, listening to the siren.

PART V

Interviews and Memoir

CHAPTER ONE

Alex La Guma,
South African Author Recently Settled in London
Interview with Robert Serumaga
(November 1966)

This interview with Ugandan playwright Robert Serumaga (1939–80), who was associated with the Transcription Centre in London, is likely the first that La Guma gave upon his arrival in exile at the end of September 1966. La Guma himself would later work at the Transcription Centre, writing plays and commentary for radio. This interview was published in the journal Cultural Events in Africa.

Robert Serumaga. Alex La Guma, would you tell me where you spent your early life in South Africa?

Alex La Guma. Well, I was born in Cape Town in the area known as District Six. That is the predominantly poor area, inhabited by people of the working class of the Cape Coloured community—that is the designation given by the government. It is the early part of my life there that inspired me to write, first a few short stories, and finally a novel, *A Walk in the Night*, which was based on some of my experiences and some of the experiences of friends and other people I met during those years.

Serumaga. This book, *A Walk in the Night*, for example, is concerned with the situation in South Africa as it affects the individual and what goes on, not only in the physical sense but also in the mind. You write about characters like the Afrikaans policeman. How difficult do you find it to project yourself into the character of an Afrikaner policeman whom you haven't lived and make him, as you do, really an individual?

La Guma. Well, I think that the Cape Coloured community is composed of people descended from a mixture of the Afrikaner people and the early aborigines. The background of the Coloured people is to a large extent Afrikaans—and English—and I might add that I don't see that the Afrikaner people—the white people in any case—are much different from the Coloured community so that there wasn't much difficulty from that point of view.

Serumaga. It has been said that many of the African writers from South Africa—I use the term 'African' to include the Coloured community—are preoccupied with the colour problem. Many of them do not create individuals but they create figures within a situation—they are more interested in the situation than in the individual. Would you think this true of many South African writers?

La Guma. Well, it's true and I think that it's inevitable—having to live in a society based upon racial discrimination, and where people are set virtually into compartments—black and white and Coloured and Indian. Whatever opinion they have to express inevitably becomes involved with the impact of this situation, the colour situation, on them. The difficulty, of course, is to try to project oneself across the colour line, and I think that is where most writers have failed or met with extreme difficulty. The problem is living in one set compartment and knowing only your own life and then trying to project yourself into the life and environment of another party.

Serumaga. You have said that, in fact, you have lived many of your characters. Now if we take a character like Michael Adonis, who is the main character in your novel, what experiences of his have you lived?

La Guma. I've forgotten what my own book is about. With Michael Adonis, I've tried to make a typical Coloured person. During the years I lived in District Six, I played with and met characters like him—young men who, because of their situation in life and because of the lack of opportunity and their colour, have been prevented from achieving any ambitions, have been forced into this situation. So that what Adonis experienced in the book, although I haven't personally experienced [it], I have seen around me. That made it easy for me to write and to create such a character.

Serumaga. The South African situation is clearly one that is very oppressive. How does this affect the creative writer? Here you have a lot of things that one could write about. But since the writer himself is involved in this situation, he might find himself unable to create a kind of aesthetic distance. Do you find this oppression inspires you, or does it inhibit you? Could you write better if you were completely out of this situation?

La Guma. Well, as far as the inspiration goes, I think what I found is that it has inspired me to expose the situation with a view to changing people's ideas about what is happening in South Africa—or their acceptance of ideas, so that they can move forward to take down the barriers which exist between different peoples. As I said earlier, the problem is the compartments in which people are divided that imbue them with set opinions about their positions—and the difficulty is getting people to rid themselves of these ideas. As a writer, I try to achieve a universality of opinion because I believe that writers are not confined to one set of ideas, but that a writer should try to spread out, extend his views, extend his opinions and get opinions from other sources so that he doesn't become confined to his little ivory tower! The danger in South Africa is that many writers have taken the easy way out, of writing only of what they know and not attempting to go beyond that. But even if one has to write within a particular environment, or portray a particular milieu, I believe that universal ideas can still be expressed within that milieu, so that your writing does not become confined. Although your stage may be set in a particular environment, your ideas and your writing are not confined.

Serumaga. Well, I think it might be fair to say that a great many of the South African writers at the moment have not succeeded in doing this particular thing you describe. It has been suggested by some critics of African literature that perhaps the best thing would be to suspend literature altogether in South Africa until the situation was solved, since so many writers cannot rise above it and become universal enough. What do you think?

La Guma. Well, I don't agree with that. I believe that there has been a lot said about South Africa but very little said about what the non-white people, in particular, are really experiencing. Writers have tried to describe the situation in South Africa in general, but very little has been said about the different national groups and the people who live in South Africa. For instance, I don't think a great deal has been said about the Coloured community or about the Indian community, and I think that even within a framework of racial separateness there is a task that writers have to perform. That is, to at least let the world know what is happening—even within their compartments.

Serumaga. Alex La Guma, thank you very much.

CHAPTER TWO

A Home Away from Home
(1969)

A satirical short piece, published in Sechaba, *that reflects on La Guma's experiences in South African prisons with a scathing sense of sarcasm. The title itself is ironic.*

When I was awaiting trial in the Cape Town prison for one of the numerous offences the South African government concocts in the name of 'the safety of the state', there were a number of long-term prisoners in the cell next door. They were waiting to appear in court for breaking the law right inside the jails where they had been serving.

They had committed these offences deliberately. The reason? They all wanted to get some respite from the hellholes where they had been doing time.

Some of them had attacked warders, others had destroyed prison property violently. They had made up their minds to do anything to get away to the relative ease of the awaiting-trial section of the city prison.

But, dear friends and readers, they must have been crazy. Crazy, that is, to want to get away from the salubrious atmosphere of such places as Belleville and Bien Donne or any of the calabooses that beautify the fair landscape of our Republic. They must have been bonkers because according to a report on 'Prison Administration in South Africa', published by the Ministry of Foreign Affairs, of all things, everything in South Africa's jails are as rosy as the blush of a wardress caught with the Kolonel's winter underwear.

Why, looking at this publication, one becomes more and more convinced that crime pays and all our clinks are really homes away from home.

There are lovely lawns around South Africa's prisons, and the sunlights, the suikerbossies and jacaranda with all the brilliance of a South African Airways handout.

There are polished floors that would outdo any state ballroom and lovely shining brass work, and sun and flowers and hillsides all the time.

But even a prostitute decorates and perfumes herself to disguise the fact that she can give a man the clap; and nail varnish only emphasizes the charm of dirty fingernails.

But there are those who have gone to see and wonder—or marvel, I should say.

For example, a Mr Manion from an American TV programme, purred: 'I am impressed, EDIFIED is a better word.' We admit that the capitals are ours. Somebody else, on viewing the beauties or our prisons: 'The dedication of the administration and the staff is most impressive.'

Perhaps where they come from the prison staff don't put soft cushions on the electric chair or Chanel No. 5 in the cyanide gas.

Those who come to inspect our prisons are of course told also of the self-inflicted wounds to escape the comfort of the quarries for the rigours of a hospital bed.

The Department of Foreign Affairs, acting as PRO to the Commissioner of Prisons, provides the prospective sojourner with glossy pictures of prisoners playing chess, table tennis and pouring over books in the libraries. All the facilities, and more perhaps, of the YMCA are thrown in to encourage the client to make up his or her mind. For the ladies there are concerts where they can do the cancan, if they wish. But the PRO slipped up, he forgot to include the pictures of elephants crossing the road and the surf breaking along the whites-only beach at Durban.

This regrettable omission is compensated for by colour pictures of the tomb of a Malay sheikh on Robben Island and panoramic views of the vegetable garden at Leeuwkap.

To add to the travel brochure effect, this 'monograph' by the Foreign Affairs-wallahs tells us that Robben Island is practically as good as Hawaii or Pago-Pago, and has all the idyllic atmosphere of the South Sea Island. 'Despite its falling into the category of maximum security institutions, DUE TO THE FAVOURABLE CLIMATE, ROBBEN ISLAND MAY BE DESCRIBED AS AN OPEN-AIR PRISON.' If you look carefully at the pictures, you might be able to make out the convicts dozing under the picturesque trees and even hear the throb of guitars.

There are guitars, of course. Pictures of convicts plucking away merrily at the strings in the homely atmosphere of their cells, and convict concert troupes serenading—to drown the screams of sodomy and the blows of buckle belts and truncheons, naturally.

'All members of the personnel shall at all times so conduct themselves and perform their duties as to influence the prisoners for good by their example and to command their respect.'

The personnel certainly conduct and perform.

I have seen blood fly from the nostrils of a prisoner who did not get into line quick enough for a warder's liking. No doubt the victim was influenced for good.

'The transport of prisoners in conveyances with inadequate ventilation or light, or in any way which would subject them to unnecessary physical hardship, shall be prohibited.'

Hmmm. As was the case recently of prisoners crammed into a van like paste into a tube, and the death of several of them through asphyxiation by carbon monoxide fumes. No isolated case. I seem to remember being transported back and forth several times with three other blokes sitting on my lap, my mouth full of shoulder blades, and my ribs nigh caved in from each side.

Item: 'Rules of general application 6 (1). The following rules shall be applied impartially. There shall be no discrimination on grounds of race, colour, sex, language, religion, political or other opinion, national or social origin, property, birth or other status.' Apartheid has been abolished!

Item: 'Corporal punishment, punishment by placing in a dark cell, and all cruel, inhuman or degrading punishment shall be completely prohibited as punishments for disciplinary offences.' Hallelujah! They have abolished 'the Hole', rice water is no more, and solitary confinement is all a dream.

Need we say more about the pleasures of prison life in South Africa? So ladies and gentlemen, as the sun goes down on the rolling hills, which provide—ouch—enchanting settings for the attractive resorts of Sonderwater, Witbank and Cinderella, and the sky fades from royal blue to gentle purple, we turn away with saddened hearts from the merry songs of convicts and the cooing farewells of jolly warders. We say a sad goodbye to these scenes of gentle friendship and enervating life, turn once more to the sorry prospect of the outside, knowing somehow, that, given another chance, we would return again outstretched arms to this our home away from home.

PRRRRRRT!

CHAPTER THREE

Why I Joined the Communist Party
(1971)

A short memoir, the first of two related essays published in The African Communist. *This version was published under the pseudonym Arnold Adams. These short reflection pieces offer valuable glimpses of La Guma's childhood and early family life.*

Many things pass through my mind when I try to pinpoint all the events and circumstances which brought me into the ranks of the world's communists, in particular into the party of our own country South Africa. Perhaps, I was influenced within the circle of our family—certainly that had something to do with it. On the other hand, there were independent experiences which made me as an individual more and more aware of the necessity to change the face of our country.

I was born in District Six, that area of Cape Town into which crammed thousands of families of the Coloured working class. Its slums stretched from the slopes of Table Mountain to the sea where the sewers belched their vomit into the Atlantic, and where we as children splashed in the foul water during the hot summer holidays. It was the cheapest outing for the poor, picnicking on Woodstock Beach, a stone's throw from the municipal dumping ground and the outlets of the sewerage system. Everybody came down out of the hot, grey streets, the blistering tenements, the foul alleyways.

My first recollection of life seems to have been an alleyway. It faced the front window of our house, and it was always piled with overflowing dustbins that left most of their contents behind in pools of stagnant water, so that we breathed a horrible odour of decay all the time.

My mother worked in a cigarette factory, and my father was a trade union organizer. I was cared for during the day by my grandmother who looked like a mahogany version of Queen Victoria. I seldom saw my father—he was always at what was described to me as 'meetings'. Most of the family income came from my mother. Then my father started organizing tobacco workers in Cape Town, and my mother was fired for being his wife. Those were hard times, I remember. There was an old grocer in the district who used to give us parcels of provisions because he sympathized with the working-class movement.

I was about six years old when my father went to prison for leading demonstrations of the unemployed. I remember going to meet him when he was released ten days later. I could not recognize him at first because he had grown a beard during that time.

One day my mother took me to the circus. It was an incredibly exciting prospect, seeing the animals in their cages as we made our way towards the big top, the coloured flags, the balloons, the gay, noisy music beating on eardrums. But once inside the vast tent I had a peculiar experience. I discovered that I had no idea what most of the performers in the ring were doing because they had their backs to me all the time. When I asked my mother why this was so, she had to explain to me that we were in the seats for 'Non-Europeans' and that the white people were given the best view of the performances.

I never went to a circus again in South Africa. The next time I ever attended a circus performance was when I was a man of forty-three and went to see a show in Moscow. I could see everything the performers did, and I recalled, a little sadly, a small boy in South Africa who had only seen the backs of the clowns.

At School

All my youth was spent in the slums of Cape Town. I went to school on the hillside above the city, and in the afternoon I and my friends would come down again into the smelly environs of District Six. I recall a few faces from the past. There was Daniel, a jolly black boy with a smile full of white teeth. We were great chums. Somewhere along the line we drifted apart. When I met him again years later he had turned into a gangster and was continually in and out of prison. I remember the girls we used to chase along the streets. There was Habiba, a beautiful member of the Moslem community. She was my favourite, with her great eyes and long, straight black hair framing her olive-skinned face.

Again, many years later, when I was canvassing for an election, I knocked on the door of a municipal voter, and when it was opened, there was something which had been a woman looking out at me. Matted greying hair was untidily wrapped in a kerchief, the face had fallen into loose wrinkles, prematurely aged, the rotten teeth smiled curiously at me above the body that had collapsed under greasy clothes. She smiled at me from a background like a dark cavern full of smells. It took me some time to recognize the eyes in the ravaged face. It was Habiba, but not the beautiful girl I had known when I had been a young boy chasing her on the streets. Grim life had destroyed that Habiba. Now there was just a hag whose eyes I recognized and who recognized me.

The grinding misery of the slums destroyed our people, blighted their lives before they had time to grow up. On the street corners, the children shot dice and the dagga cigarettes passed from mouth to mouth. In the lamplight the razor-edged knives flashed, and the blood mingled with the spittle and the rivulets of stagnant black water.

I read *The Iron Heel* and saw in Jack London's 'people of the abyss' my own community ground down under the weight of poverty, oppression, ignorance. Could it be that oppressed people all over were the same? In *The Ragged Trousered Philanthropists*, I saw our own working men. These books moved me more than the set books we were given to read in school. I wasn't interested in *The Adventures of Maurice Buckler* or *Micah Clarke*. At second-hand bookstalls, I found the *Trial and Execution of Sacco and Vanzetti* and *The State: Its Origin and Function* by William Paul, from the old Socialist Labour Press.

Threat of War

While I was in high school the Spanish Civil War was on. The news in the South African press was scanty, but some of us followed it. There was a period of restlessness. You wanted to get through school in order to enter a more dynamic world. After high school, I turned away from further education because it appeared that life held more serious things than more certificates based on knowledge that had little to do with reality.

Nazism was overrunning Europe. I knew about the stupid system that turned my own people into strangers in their country. We were continually reminded that we were 'Non-Europeans Only'; in Europe they were butchering Jews and gypsies, and Hitler called us 'subhumans'. We were all one, because we were all being persecuted, and they were fighting in Europe. I wanted to fight the Nazis, but when I left home to join the armed forces the recruiting officer found me underweight and too skinny. But one could still gain experience in struggle here at home.

At the local Labour Bureau, I asked for a job in a factory. I wanted to know what it was like to be a worker, so I went into this place that manufactured metal containers. All day long the conveyor belts clattered and roared, and the shiny tin cans marched past like regiments of soldiers. In front of the pounding machines, girls and women sat as if welded to them, while we Coloured and African boys and men brought the sheets of plate, which they turned into cans. There were women who had had their fingers pulped off under the crashing die-stampers. The boss generously gave them a job for life at about four pounds a week. Once our blood froze when a man screamed above the roar of machinery as his arm was caught in a machine. At the waxing tables, women perspired in the hellish heat. The highest paid workers got about five pounds a week.

At lunchtime, I found myself talking to the workers. I seemed to have become a great talker. I talked about lots of things, I remember. International news, South African politics, the colour bar. Some of the workers viewed me with curiosity. They asked me whether I was a communist. Certainly I was a member of the trade union. Was I a communist? I must have been telling them things, explaining situations, in the manner of a communist.

Given the Sack

Then one day the trade union made demands, which the bosses did not accept. There was talk of a strike. The trade union wasn't very strong and the bosses acted quickly. Certain workers were no longer needed. Men, women, Coloured, African found themselves without jobs. They were members of the trade union committee and other outspoken workers. Among them was myself.

I worked for a while in the drawing department of a commercial firm, reproducing blueprints on a copying machine. There were other Coloured men working there too, but they were messengers or served the tea to the white staff. The whites referred to them all the time as 'boys'. They were married and had families, but they were still 'boys' in the eyes of the whites. One of them had worked for that firm for twenty-five years, and the managing director presented him with a watch. The heads of department looked on condescendingly, and he was promoted to head messenger. But he was still referred to as a 'boy' thereafter. All the time my gorge rose. I used to encourage the 'boys' to attend meetings on the Grand Parade in Cape Town, where the Communist Party held lunchtime talks. The whites in the firm looked at me with suspicion. Somehow they carefully avoided coming face to face with me. Perhaps I wasn't quite like the other 'boys'.

One day I realized that while I had been encouraging my mates to take more interest in those things which were keeping them in that position of indignity as second-class people in this their own motherland, I could do more myself. I was twenty-two years old. Perhaps I remembered the little boy who could not see what the performers were doing that time at the circus; or Daniel and Habiba, or those factory girls with their fingers cut off, or the hard life of my parents.

Around the corner from where I worked was the office of the Communist Party. A little nervously I climbed the narrow stairs. What responsibilities confronted me? It wasn't as if you were going to join a football club or a benefit lodge. That was when I first joined the Young Communist League. The next year the Nationalist government came into power and started making dire threats against the communists. I transferred from the YCL into the ranks of the Communist Party.

CHAPTER FOUR

Answers to Our Questionnaire
(1977)

This piece consists of answers to a questionnaire given to several authors who were popular in the Soviet Union at the time. The other authors included C. P. Snow (Great Britain), Faiz Ahmad Faiz (Pakistan) and Gaoussou Diawara (Mali), among over two dozen total. It thus provides a sense of the popularity La Guma had achieved among Soviet readers. It also demonstrates his knowledge of Russian and Soviet literature, in addition to his political identification with the USSR as witnessed elsewhere in his exile writing. This interview appeared in the Moscow-based journal, Soviet Literature.

The editors of *Soviet Literature* asked a number of prominent foreign writers whose works are widely known in our country to reply to the following questions:

1. What works by Soviet authors have attracted your attention? In what way have they been of interest to you?

2. What form do you think literary contacts between our countries should take in order to develop the spirit of Helsinki?

1. I remember as a young lad spending my meagre pocket money on books at second-hand stalls. Among the books I acquired were works by Maxim Gorky, especially his short stories. I did not consider becoming a writer then, although I did make an attempt to produce romantic little stories of adventure. Gorky showed me that ordinary people could be heroes of books; that there was dignity

in the common man; that even 'the lower depths' could produce profound manifestations of humanity. *The Stormy Petrel* had some sort of magic symbolism. Altogether, I might say that Gorky introduced me to working-class literature and the spirit of socialist humanism that goes with it.

Later I read Sholokhov—the Don books. Here was the young Soviet Union going through the turmoil of Civil War; the peasants torn between the old times and the new era. Sholokhov's heroes were full of contradictions, which reflected the birth pangs and struggles for adjustment and readjustment in those times. In addition, the novels teemed with excitement and action that was concerned with creation of a new society, the creation of a socialist state.

All this inspired me to learn more than I knew about socialism. Of course that also meant I searched for other socialist writers. V. Yan was thrilling with his historical novels, and Simonov's *Days and Nights* was the war novel that surpassed many others of the same category.

The suppression of literature from the USSR by the extreme reactionary government that came to power in South Africa after the war, cut off our supply of books. When I was again able to read the writers of the Soviet Union I found a new generation of writers. As a writer myself, I found myself, somewhat humbly, in the company of an international fraternity that included Chinghiz Aitmatov (what a wonderful story *Goodbye, Gyulsary*!—thank you for the English edition!) and Georgi Markov, and writers from the Asian republics. Here I must thank *Soviet Literature* for their economy-size editions, which helped me and others to reach Soviet writers of past and present. Certainly not all writers appealed to me equally—one also searched for satisfactory techniques and styles, but all have certainly helped me to understand a lot about Soviet socialist literature, about socialist humanism in writing, about the relationship between literature and everyday life, about the task of literature in helping to create a new life for the masses of the people.

2. Writers have a serious responsibility to fulfil these days. If we are at all serious we cannot ignore the problems of maintaining a peaceful world in which we can carry on our work. After all, it is difficult to work surrounded by heaps of nuclear ash. Among the tasks of securing peace is that of exchanging knowledge about one another. This is where the writer comes in. Mutual understanding, if not through personal contact, comes through reading. A lot of hatred comes through false propaganda, and the genuinely progressive writer can dispel the putrid air of suspicion by producing true works about his people's desires, aspirations and hopes of living in freedom and in peace.

When the Helsinki accord was signed it not only committed governments to ensuring peace but also committed their peoples, including the writing community.

Irrespective of the subjects we write on, literature has always identified with all aspects of human life, so through this means we learn about each other. But this exchange of knowledge depends on the governments and their agencies, which should disseminate the works of progressive foreign writers in their countries. Unfortunately, many only pay lip service to détente, to the exchange of information as stipulated in the Final Act of the Helsinki Conference. This arises out of the hypocritical attitude of imperialism, which continues to pursue predatory policies. This puts us writers in the position of having to join in the anti-imperialist movement to aid those who are clearing the way for a peaceful and democratic and progressive world. So we are all the time involved in ensuring that détente becomes a reality. Détente, peace and literature are all one, complementing each other, and only a writer who has his head in the sand can ignore this.

CHAPTER FIVE

Why I Joined the Communist Party
Doing Something Useful
(1982)

The second of the two memoirs published in The African Communist. *This version was published under the pseudonym Gala.*

In the winter, the rain came down in sheets for days on end, and when it stopped for a while a stench hung over the District, rising from blocked drains and rotting piles of rubbish. On the roofs could be seen people moving about, plugging leaks and patching holes. The landlords generally made each tenant responsible for repairs. We lived in a small house with a tiny backyard where we had to take our baths, where my mother hung the washing, and which opened on to a narrow and smelly lane. The odours from there in summer hardly competed with those of winter. We seemed to live in a constant atmosphere of bad smells against which my parents waged a stubborn battle often diverted to the mouse and bedbug front. This seemed to be a regular feature of life in that area of Cape Town.

My parents were of the working class, but they were also class- and politically conscious people. My mother worked in a cigarette factory, while my father was actively engaged in trade union and political work. I do not remember my parents ever sermonizing me as child, but one was always being advised to devote oneself to 'something useful', or to 'lead a useful life'.

A picture of Lenin hung in our living room. Very often people came to visit, and I would hover on the outskirts of the conversations, listening to chats about politics, trade union work, or 'the Party'. I also had an Aunt Maggie who was a staunch member of the garment workers' union and a class-conscious woman. She was one of those hard-case workers who stood on the picket lines during the garment strike. She related these incidents to the family with a mixture of amusement and anger. Her husband, Uncle Bob, named their house 'Stalingrad' during the war. Apparently, all this was part of dedicating oneself to 'leading a useful life'. I remember too that, being somewhat of a schoolboy-artist, I was asked to help paint posters, decorate the banners or illustrate the leaflets, which my father's work demanded.

Perhaps this helped one to see a little more clearly than other children what really went on around oneself. Life went on in the slums, and many succumbed. As children we enjoyed the periodic spots of gaiety. There was the New Year Carnival, or the weekly procession of the Salvation Army: the thumping of the big drum and the clatter of tambourines while a horde of us, mainly ragged children, pranced behind towards the barracks to the music of 'Brother take the hand of brother, Marching to the promised land...' In this case, the 'Promised Land' seemed to be a hall where they served mugs of watery soup to the 'poor and needy' in exchange for more prayers and hymn singing. But nothing seemed to change in the slums: knife fights, gang warfare, gambling. My childhood friends disappeared into this teeming limbo of bad smells, dirty alleyways and cheap liquor.

Something Else

But of course there was something else, as time moved on. One attended the meetings eventually. We young ones were made to pass the hat around while the leaders held forth on the platform. I was always happy to find some missing school-chum in the audiences, in the marches and demonstrations. We were at last beginning to do 'something useful' with our lives.

At high school, I discovered that we were being taught by 'politically conscious' teachers. After classes we were invited to attend lectures of a 'political nature'. There I heard long and dull discourses about the 'permanent revolution' as well as dire criticisms of and outright attacks on the Soviet Union. This was offensive to me, for in our family we had always been taught to cherish and admire the Socialist Sixth of the World. I soon gave up attendance of these 'activities', which also went under the guise of 'cultural programmes'.

I went through my teens in the atmosphere of anti-fascism, anti-Nazism. There was the Spanish Civil War and then the Nazi invasion of Europe and the Soviet Union. In the factory where I worked we manufactured metal 'dixies' for the army. My fellow workers listened with a certain curiosity to my youthful talks relating the manufacture of metal containers for soldiers to the struggle against fascism, oppression, exploitation. I was described as 'a Communist' and they elected me to the factory committee. When later a strike was organized for better pay and conditions, the whole committee was fired. I recall a somewhat juvenile talk I gave on the meaning of the 'class struggle'.

The end of the war did not mean the end of fascism in South Africa. But certainly the anti-Nazi struggle had opened the eyes and given confidence to many. In our community there was a greater interest in politics, in the national liberation movement, in the Communist Party. Especially, the struggle of the black people for liberation was developing—one had to belong, somehow.

The Whites

But there was something else which one remembered.

Next door to our house had lived a white family. When their babies were sick, my mother was called in to help. They borrowed rice and sugar from her. They were as hard-pressed as we were.

True enough, they eventually disappeared from the District, probably to live in some 'white' area. But they had actually been living on our street.

After the 'dixie' factory, I worked for a big commercial firm. Apart from the usual clerks and managers, there was one who was the firm's printer, producing company stationery. He was an ordinary white worker, in a 'skilled trade' of course. He had been with the firm for more than twenty years and considered himself part of the Company. Yet when the Company reorganized itself, this man received a circular letter (possibly one of the forms he had himself printed) bluntly informing him that his services were no longer required. He was aghast. After all these years! I remember him staring at me, a black worker, recounting all the service he had given the Company. And to my horror, he burst into tears. Perhaps at that moment, at the back of his mind, he might have felt himself at one with US.

One was concerned with black liberation. But we had also demonstrated on behalf of people of Europe—of Spain, Germany—against the horrors of the concentration camps and the execution of revolutionaries afar. One had to be able to be both a patriot and an internationalist. So on that basis there was only one party to turn to. It had to be the Communist Party.

CHAPTER SIX

Two Letters from *Sechaba*
(1984)

These two letters, though brief, provide a sense of La Guma's engagement with others in the pages of Sechaba. *In this instance, he spars over 'Coloured' identity and political terminology, harking back to his time with the SACPO and the CPC during the 1950s and 1960s.*

Dear Comrade Editor:

I take up my pen to write you these few lines. I have been a reader of *Sechaba* for a long time. Now I would like you to explain me one thing.

I have noticed now in speeches, articles, interviews, etc. in *Sechaba*, that I am called 'so-called Coloured' (sometimes with a small 'c'). When did the Congress decide to call me this? In South Africa, I was active in the Congress Alliance and was a member of the Coloured People's Congress, not the 'so-called Coloured People's Congress'. When we worked for Congress of the People and the Freedom Charter we sang, 'We the Coloured people, we must struggle to exist . . .' I remember in those times some people of the so-called Unity Movement referred to so-called Coloured people, but not our Congress. The old copies of *Sechaba* do not show when it was decided to make this change, or why. Maybe governments, administrations, political and social dealings over centuries called me Coloured. But clever people, the ethnologists and professors of anthropology and so on, did not bother to worry about who I really am.

Comrade Editor, I am confused. I need clarification. It makes me feel like a 'so-called' human, like a humanoid, those things who have all the characteristics of human beings but are really artificial. Other minority people are not called 'so-called'. Why me? It must be the 'curse of Ham'.

In the meantime, I remain, respectfully,

Your,

Capie (Alex La Guma)

P.S. Was Paul Peterson a so-called Coloured?

(Paul Peterson was the *nom de guerre* of Basil February, an ANC cadre who died fighting in Zimbabwe in 1967–68.)

* * *

Dear Comrade Editor:

Once again I take up my pen to write, and to take the liberty of saying that I am happy to have been able to wake up somebody to a discussion through my previous remarks about *Ons Bruin Mense*. But the writer of the reply to my humble effort, PG, (*Sechaba*, August 1984) has raised certain points, which, however, confuse me even further.

He says that 'so-called Coloured' was used in popular expression of rejection of 'apartheid terminology'. Yet, later he says that 'most, in the spirit of a nation in the making, opt for "South African"'. But, Comrade Editor, he does not tell us who gave our country the official name of South Africa? On what or whose authority? There are some who, rejecting this 'terminology', call the country 'Azania' (again, on whose authority?) and maybe they would call the rest of the population 'so-called South Africans'. But it would seem that even though the Boer anthem refers to *Suid-Afrika*, the name South Africa is accepted. Yet for any minority (even so-called) to assume the right to call themselves South African for their own studied convenience seems to me to be somewhat undemocratic, if not downright presumptuous, since the right naturally belongs to the majority.

I regret to say that I did not know (as PG seems to say) that the term 'Coloured' emerged as a result of the definition laid down by the Population Registration Act or the Group Areas Act. I was born long before these Acts, so our people must be a little older than that. And we should not believe that all the awful experiences described by PG (divided families, rejection, etc.) are only suffered by us. Mixed race or marginal communities in other parts of the world suffer similar trials and tribulations.

Now PG even says 'so-called' is not good enough, but neither is 'Coloured', which adds to my confusion, Comrade Editor. But it is not being called Coloured that has been 'a scourge for years', but the way our people have been and are being treated, whatever they are called, just as the term 'Asiatic' or 'Indian' in itself does not mean being scourged.

May I add, while MK and the militant resistance might well be manned by militant cadres not acting as 'representatives of ethnic groups', freedom fighters taking part on the basis of militancy does not dismiss the presence of different 'national groups' (the Freedom Charter) from our South Africa.

I see from his letter that PG was with the students in 1976. I myself may have been in the docks or picking apples. So he should be more able to clarify things for me, but I am sorry, he has cleared up nothing for me. While I wait patiently for the outcome of PG's 'mass debate', I would still like to know what I am today. So, Comrade Editor, call me what the devil you like, but for God's sake don't call me 'so-called'.

In reply to your own comment, Comrade Editor: while critical observations in the course of a book review are one thing, official declarations and speeches by our ANC representatives are another, which is the reason for my original question.

In the meantime, I will not sign myself 'Observer' or 'Disappointed' or 'Baainaar', so I will remain your respectful,

Capie.
28 August 1984

CHAPTER SEVEN

'My Books Have Gone Back Home'
(1984)

This interview appeared in World Marxist Review. *The preface to the interview described La Guma as a 'revolutionary prose writer' who 'owes his popularity not only to the depth and emotional power of his books but also to his public activity'.*

Q. *What factors influenced your political views and sympathies and the formation of your outlook as a writer?*

A. I will begin with the family, which undoubtedly played a part in forming my views, my ideas, my sympathies. I come from a communist family of Cape Town, where I was born in 1925. My father was a trade union activist, a founding member of the Communist Party of South Africa. I grew up in the atmosphere of political discussions that took place in our home. I listened as a young person to my father's conversations with others and tried to understand clearly what I heard. So it is natural that as I grew up I took part in the struggle for freedom and social justice by working in the Communist Youth League and writing for the democratic press. In the end, I joined the Communist Party, which was legal at the time.

But besides the environment in my home, I largely owe my formation as a writer to my social surroundings. The fact is that after school, I went to work in a factory and found myself among working people. What I came across in real life struck me and helped me understand many things.

I could see how the workers were exploited, and how they suffered. I came to know the day-to-day problems they had, the hopeless condition of their families and other slum dwellers. Those outcasts of South African society were poor, they were backward, they were unconcerned. Many of them died inside, like trees eaten by worms beneath the bark. I was amazed at their tolerance, their resignation. I couldn't understand why they didn't want to do something about it, why they didn't change these conditions but drifted along without a murmur, year after year. Subsequently I realized that things were actually much more complicated, but what I saw and thought about in my youth played an important part in my creative work.

I suppose my first inspiration or stimulation to become a serious writer was when I worked as a journalist for a progressive weekly newspaper in South Africa, *New Age*. On that occasion I was compelled to write a great deal, to report facts and news, to comment on them. In the end, it occurred to me that the facts which I was reporting could lead to creative work.

Of course, there was also the influence of the many books of classical authors I read—Victor Hugo, Henri Barbusse, Maxim Gorky and others. Many of the writers whose books I read in my youth had a certain outlook on life, on humanity, on its past and future. I was interested in their approach to the reality they depicted, in their implied political attitudes, in their ability to express their views unobtrusively, by means of details of seemingly little importance. All this helped me become a creative writer.

Q. *What would you describe as the main themes of your creative work and why?*

A. I've said that the condition of the slum dwellers of Cape Town had an impression upon me. I also realized on getting to know the people of African ghettos better that their apparent apathy, their tolerance, their resignation were only one side of the coin and that the other was hatred for racial and national oppression and class exploitation, that these people were engaged in a struggle for a better future. In spite of bans and persecution, there were trade unions, there were social, civic and political organizations, there was the Communist Party, the African National Congress. The very existence of these organizations showed that the people's spirit wasn't broken, that there was an urge for change.

And so most of my books, articles and short stories are concerned with the struggle of the African people to change their lives, to change society. I have written books about the beginnings of the idea of national liberation. I've tried to show the growth of the resistance movement in South Africa in the face of incredible obstacles, telling blows and bitter setbacks. I have always wanted to watch the transformation of unassuming, seemingly ordinary people into staunch fighters against the racist regime, for the freedom and social equality of the Black population. And I suppose these are the main themes of my work.

Digression One. Alex La Guma has been faithful to his chosen themes all his life. His books expose with brutal truthfulness the ugly reality that is the apartheid regime, and tell about the hardships and suffering of the indigenous population of South Africa. When an African turns sixteen, La Guma writes in *In the Fog of the Seasons' End*, he is reborn, as it were, being initiated into the rites of a diabolical sabbat, into the bloody rituals of slavery, coarse and cruel as in the days of Caligula and Nero. He is shackled by innumerable laws, put into chains sealed with rubber stamps. The blunted pens of commissioners for native affairs leave lifelong scars like red-hot iron.

But what La Guma creates are not only scenes of sorrow or the images of Africans humiliated and affronted by racism. His books—an impassioned plea for active and militant struggle—portray people of indomitable spirit and high moral qualities.

Q. *What made you leave South Africa? Doesn't life in exile make it difficult for you to write about events in your country?*

A. While in South Africa, I not only wrote books but joined the political struggle. I had to work in the underground movement and went through the racist regime's prisons. In 1966, I left the country by decision of the African National Congress. All that experience has gone into my novels and stories.

I've been a political exile for years now, doing solidarity work for the liberation movement in various parts of the world. At the same time, I try to continue my creative work. I don't think that living outside of South Africa has affected my views very much or told on my vision of the world. Some of my colleagues are unable to create while they are away from the scene but I have not had this problem.

* * *

Digression Two. Alex La Guma mentions important chapters of his political biography reluctantly and only in passing. Yet the last years of his life in South Africa were very hard and left a visible imprint on all his work. He was repeatedly arrested and tried. He was under house arrest, incommunicado for five years. Altogether he spent eleven years in the prisons of the Pretoria regime. His books and his very name were banned.

There was a remarkable episode. When in prison in Cape Town, La Guma counted the days by marking them on the wall of his cell. One day he realized on looking at his calendar that it was the anniversary of the October Revolution. Thinking instantly of a way to celebrate the great holiday, he rushed to the window and struck up the 'Internationale'. A minute or two later, dozens of voices joined in singing the proletarian hymn.

Q. *What is the role of your books in the struggle of the indigenous population of South Africa for national and social liberation? Do your books reach your compatriots?*

A. I suppose I write in order to stir the conscience of the reader. My works are of course prohibited in my country, but I had an interesting experience. A short time ago, I met some students who had just come from South Africa. I had never met them before, but they knew me and my books. I asked how. They said, 'Well, some people smuggle your books into the country. Sometimes the customs people are stupid, and they allow your books to pass. Sometimes we make typewritten copies of the books. Yes, we know you, Mr La Guma, you are one of our favourites.'

Any writer appreciates this sort of thing, and a writer in exile does so all the more. Of course, the young men did me a special honour when we got to talking about South African literature. They said there are three kinds of writers in South Africa—there are purely observers, then there are cautious critics of the racist regime, and then there are revolutionary authors. And they said I was one of the revolutionary writers.

So, at least, I've achieved something. Even though I'm in exile, my books have gone back home, and young people are able to read them. This gives me encouragement. I think I've succeeded in reflecting the social and national liberation struggle in our country, and so made some contribution to the spirit of the people.

Q. *How would you define the social mission of a democratic writer?*

A. Writers, I believe, are concerned with human beings and so they must be concerned with people in their relation to society. And if a writer is progressive he must expose and condemn the negative aspects of both man and society and encourage the positive. I believe that man is essentially good, that his goodness will prevail, and that he will create a good society for himself. And literature can play a notable part in changing man's psychology and man's outlook. Therefore a democratic writer, a progressive writer should be against the people-hating ideology of the capitalist system, against imperialism, neocolonialism, racism. It is his duty to his own conscience, and it's his social mission.

CHAPTER EIGHT

Report of the Secretary General to the Seventh General (Twenty-Fifth Anniversary) Conference, Tashkent, Uzbekistan, September–October 1983
(1985)

This speech provides an unconventional ending to this section on interviews and personal memoir. Nonetheless, it summarizes La Guma's activities and beliefs, providing a panoramic view of the political and cultural world to which he belonged. A true internationalist, it captures his spirit towards the end of his life. Given its composition in 1983 and its publication in 1985, it can be surmised that it was published in Lotus: Afro-Asian Writings *as an epitaph for his commitment to the Afro-Asian cause.*

There is every reason for African and Asian writers and their friends and supporters to celebrate the Twenty-Fifth Anniversary of our Afro-Asian Writers Association. Over the past 25 years, the Association has created a fraternity of writers, both organized and individual, from Africa and Asia, from the Middle East and the East Indies. In addition, we have made friends and contacts on the other continents, Europe, North America and Latin America, and in the Socialist Community.

Initiated with a conference of Asian writers in Delhi in 1956 and then born in 1958 with the first Afro-Asian Writers Conference in Tashkent in 1958 [*sic*], our Association was without doubt stimulated by the great social and political changes which took place on our continents, particularly by the strides taken by the independence and national liberation movements especially after the Second World War and the defeat by the world progressive forces of Nazism and fascism in Europe, militarism in Asia, the most reactionary representatives of imperialism.

Since those times actions on the part of the peoples of the colonial countries have made their impressions far and wide. The Bandung Conference, the emergence of the Afro-Asian solidarity movement, the Non-Aligned Movement, the Organisation of African Unity, the entry of new states into the United Nations Organization, all were manifestations of the colonial peoples' will to strive for and consolidate independence.

The growth and strengthening of the socialist system, headed by the Soviet Union, in many countries of Europe, as well as in Asia and the Caribbean guaranteed formidable allies for the peoples struggling to throw off the shackles of colonialism.

The years of the Sixties saw the emergence of many independent states in our two continents. Great changes appeared on the African continent and the defeat of Portuguese colonialism in particular gave great impetus to the national liberation movements of Southern Africa, in Zimbabwe (then Rhodesia), Namibia and South Africa.

The struggles and successes of the peoples of Africa and Asia during this period simultaneously gave rise to widespread cultural advances. Art and literature became important elements in the cause of the national liberation struggle and for consolidating the identities of once suppressed peoples; in the cause of positive relationships between the old ways of life and the new advances made through liberation and by the acquirement of modern technology in production and means of communication. The problem besetting artists and writers presented challenges, which have resulted in wholesale exploration, debate and investigation on the part of cultural workers. In spite of great changes, which took place in the lives of the peoples of our continent, the 25 years of our existence has by no means been smooth sailing, neither for ourselves nor for our peoples generally.

In spite of our successes, our common enemy, international imperialism, has not yet been defeated. Determined to regain its lost influence and domination over our countries and peoples, imperialism and its agents have not only intensified their neocolonialist hold over independent states, but have engaged in wholesale aggression against countries. We can never forget the sufferings of the Vietnamese people during the war caused by the US aggression on behalf of its puppets and against the democratic advances of the peoples of South East Asia. The victory of the Vietnamese and Laotian people over US aggression and the emergence of the United Socialist Vietnam and Democratic Laos is an everlasting tribute to their heroism and sacrifice and the solidarity of the world progressive forces. The emergence of a new Kampuchea after the appalling atrocities of the Pol Pot holocaust manifested once more the determination of the human spirit to rise up like the Phoenix from the ashes left by tyranny and the abomination of a people's culture.

In the Middle East, Israel launched an aggression against Arab countries in 1967, in continuation of its war against the heroic Palestinian people led by the Palestine Liberation Organization—a war and resistance immortalized by the thousands of words and verses of Palestinian poetry and prose. Up to this moment, the Israeli Zionists continue to occupy Arab territories including that of Lebanon and arrogantly continue to implant their own reactionary and racist way of life over expropriated lands and dispossessed people.

Notwithstanding its earlier aggression, 1982 witnessed further arrogance on the part of Israel in collusion with US imperialism—this time against Beirut, the capital of Lebanon, and its citizens and the Palestinian people.

What has happened in Lebanon and Beirut has stirred the conscience of the world, and a cry has gone up for the punishment of those who have committed atrocious crimes against innocent Palestinian and Lebanese people.

Israel has embarked on a policy of eventually obliterating the Palestinian Arab cultural heritage. According to reports, in 1982 the Israeli government issued 28 official orders to suspend or close down Arab schools, colleges and universities; 261 Palestinian lecturers were dismissed, 24 Arab and foreign lecturers deported, numbers of professors expelled and 2,100 textbooks banned; apart from vandalizing mosques, shrines and historical relics, acts which have been severely condemned by UNESCO.

While the peoples of our continents clamour for literacy, education, cultural advancement, imperialism and its agents have written pages of blood at Sabra and Shatila, at Kassinga and Soweto, Matola and Maseru.

The aggressive nature of world imperialism still casts a dark shadow over the world today. The message of the Non-Aligned meeting held in New Delhi in March of this year stated in its concluding sentence: 'The earth belongs to us all—let us cherish it in peace and brotherhood, based on dignity and equality of man.' There can be no doubt that peace remains the most important consideration of mankind today. The New Delhi appeal emphasized that 'peace and peaceful coexistence, independence, disarmament and development are the central issues of our time'. With the exception of those imperialists headed by the present US administration and whose aggressive designs are represented by NATO and others, the entire peace-loving peoples of the world have hailed the declaration from the Seventh Non-Aligned Movement Summit in New Delhi.

The insane possibility of nuclear holocaust created by the Reagan administration is manifested in the frenzied stockpiling of weapons of mass destruction. In its paranoiac ambition to reconquer the world, destroy the socialist system, the national liberation movements and the independence of peoples, international imperialism does not mind risking the destruction of the entire planet and all mankind. Ignoring the reasonable approaches made by the Soviet Union in connection with détente and disarmament, the Reagan administration is blindly intent on military superiority thus provoking the unprecedented arms race of today.

To prevent the nuclear holocaust is the concern of all the world's people. In this age of nuclear weapons, the very existence of mankind depends on whether it will be possible to rid the world of the arms race and turn the world away from the abyss of extinction.

It has been calculated that in the past 5,500 years, the community of man has lived only 292 years of full peace. It is beyond argument that after a future war, waged with nuclear weapons, man shall have only the eternal peace of the grave.

On the other hand, it has been also estimated that the resources invested in armament over the past 50 years would in total be quite sufficient to enable all mankind to live in comfort for an entire decade.

The movement of the peoples for peace has reached unprecedented proportions. The peoples of the world are daily becoming more determined to demonstrate that war is not unavoidable, that wars are not a natural part of the development of mankind. To this end, greater concentrations of the peace-loving forces have taken place over the past 25 years, which has brought us to our jubilee celebrations, which might also become a demonstration of Afro-Asian writers for peace and disarmament.

We have participated as writers in this great struggle to ensure just and lasting peace. At the numerous assemblies of cultural workers and writers, we have vowed to use at least our pens for peace as a contribution to this struggle. In Prague this year, there took place the greatest assembly of representatives of the world's peace forces of diverse opinions hitherto held. The special meeting of over 200 writers and cultural workers included among more than 3,000 delegates made a report on their findings and said:

[W]e have decided in concert that we not only have to make a very firm decision to unite and deepen our cooperation for saving a very fragile peace, but we should leave this assembly with a bridge between us that does not end, like the Pont d'Avignon, in the middle of the river, but joins people to people and nation to nation and culture to culture in this life-and-death struggle to save humankind.

As writers of Africa and Asia, let us remind ourselves that if literature has any significance, this is the time for us to make it known. If art and culture is to respond to humanity's urge for knowledge, harmony and perfection, let us do everything to aid this urge. Let us as writers do all to persuade and alert our peoples in order to prevent the Earth from becoming a planet-wide Hiroshima.

On the local level, the fanning of tensions and the attempts by imperialist quarters to draw African and Asian countries into military and political blocs reduces expenditure on the real needs of our peoples.

UNESCO has pointed out that the map of illiteracy coincides almost exactly with that of poverty and that in the 25 least-developed countries the proportion of illiterates still exceeds 80 per cent. In spite of prodigious efforts made by so many countries of the so-called Third World, it is estimated that in 1980, there were still 322 million children in the world between the ages of 6 and 17 not attending school.

This must be a terrible fact for the Third World intellectual to live with. Over 80 per cent of people can neither read nor write. Under these circumstances our debates will possibly produce once more the old question: Is it a contradiction to write for a population of illiterates, or is there any sense in writing if you have no audience due to illiteracy? The Moroccan writer, Tahar Ben Jelloun, claims, 'A continent of illiterates has a greater need for writers than a continent sated with knowledge. Writing is a refusal to accept defeat.'

And, 'We have this gamble on liberty and on the future, for this continent will not always be afflicted by the inevitability of illiteracy. Those who come later, perhaps the children of this period, will be entitled to call us to account. The writer will have to declare his books or his silence.'

While illiteracy remains part of the heritage of colonialism, most developing countries remain in the grip of multinational corporations who pursue their neocolonial policy with so-called aid, which prevents these countries from developing their own basic economies and raising the standard of living and culture of their peoples. At the same time, imperialism has created a model of its civilization and is imposing it on the Third World. As a result millions of people, especially young people, are denied the opportunity to acquire their own culture or any critical abilities. This denial is meant to ensure that their countries may continue to be mere producers of raw materials, but the concept of national identity implies the concept of a people's cultural autonomy, free from alienating conditions from abroad.

The assertion of this identity can be considered to be an act of liberation, a weapon in the fight for genuine independence and the development of societies. It is essential for the entry of a new world order based upon the inalienable right of nations to choose their destinies and on the recognition of the absolute equality and dignity of all cultures.

So cultural enrichment for the great masses can come only through long political activity. Culture and politics nourish one another and constitute the kernel of cultural revolution. For this reason our Writers Association has never spurned politics or the struggle of the peoples against imperialism, colonialism, neocolonialism, racism in all its forms and man's inhumanity to man.

While celebrating the 25th anniversary of our Association, writers of Africa and Asia may look back with some satisfaction at the achievements of our peoples on both the political and cultural level, at the same time we cannot but view with awe and dismay the tasks which confront men of letters. We must shudder at the aberrations, which in spite of the efforts of cultural workers still afflict our peoples, bringing internecine strife in various parts of our continents whether it be in regions of Africa, in the Middle East, on the Indian subcontinent, Sri Lanka or elsewhere.

Culture involves not only world change but also a change in man, the development of his working as well as his spiritual power, the identification of his environment and the humanization of those things which enable him to create a humanized world. This change must also affect for the better, man's attitude towards his fellow man and the knowledge accumulated by mankind.

* *' *

The year 1983 in which our 25th anniversary falls is also one in which other important events are being celebrated. There is the Bicentennial of Simón Bolívar, the Liberator of South America. There was also the hundredth anniversary of the death of Karl Marx in March of this year. It is a most remarkable fact of our age that the geographical breadth of Marxism is literally worldwide, while at the same time it achieves an integration and unity of various spheres of human thought and activity unknown in any other worldview.

Karl Marx was not meant to emerge as an outstanding poet. In fact he admitted to his father that his literary ability was extremely limited. Yet we might still gain encouragement from the sentiments expressed through one of his verses during a poetic effort:

> Therefore let us always dare,
> Never stopping, never resting,
> Never made so dull with care
> That we've finished with protesting.

However, Karl Marx's observant and descriptive letters from Africa (namely, Algeria), which he wrote to his relations and to Frederick Engels in 1882, may be included in collections of Afro-

Asian writing as our recognition of this genius. Anti-Marxism and anti-communism in the guise of false concern for 'freedom of expression' and 'human rights' is today one of the main features of imperialist propaganda against the world progressive movement and of efforts to penetrate cultural life on all continents and confound creative intellectuals. Imperialist 'literature' is steeped in the glorification of war and violence, anti-Sovietism, even sympathy for Nazism, and the aggrandizement of a spurious 'individualism'. But we writers cannot be duped by this scheme. Now more than ever it is our task to uphold the deep humanism, which is the natural character of man. It is our task to divert man from regression into the dark past and to make him see the bright sunlight envisaged by true philosophers.

This is also the United Nations' 'World Communications Year'. Obviously no creative writer can ignore the value of the mass media, radio, television, cinema, magazines, publishing enterprises, etc.

In terms of the developing countries, we learn that the need to deliver these countries from the state of dependence they are still in as regards communications is widely recognized. Eighty per cent of the news distributed throughout the world comes from the industrialized countries. To this lack of balance must be added the unequal distribution of books or radio and television programmes. Continuation of such imbalances involves profound economic, political, social and cultural consequences for the poor nations, constituting a major obstacle in the way of peoples getting to know each other and to the advancement of international understanding. Those who have the major wherewithal of circulating information often tend to neglect other cultures, and even to the developing countries are projected simplified or distorted and inaccurate images of the developed or industrialized countries.

It would not be enough to provide equipment and material as well as to mobilize financial resources in order to resolve all the problems of communications, both within individual countries and in relations between countries.

The questions which present themselves also concern the nature of social relations and the quality of communication and have social and cultural implications at all levels, national and international.

The aforementioned report of the cultural workers at the World Assembly for Peace and Life Against Nuclear War held in Prague underlined concern for the media and struggle for peace. 'Wars do not begin with bombs, they begin with brainwashing, and art and culture are often [the] first victims.'

The awarding of our Lotus Prize to writers of Africa and Asia since the inception of the prize has brought to the fore in our movement the names of many well-known literary figures who have over the past 25 years expressed through their works concern over the ravages of colonialism, aggression, corruption and dishonesty, disillusionment and compassion.

In Africa, whether attached directly to our association or not, the novels of Chinua Achebe, Ngũgĩ wa Thiong'o, Mongo Beti, Diop, to name but a few are landmarks. The poetry of the late Agostinho Neto and other writers of the former Portuguese colonies who participated in the anti-colonialist struggle have all added to the literature of progress, democracy and peace.

In Southern Africa, the struggle against racism and apartheid has given rise of late to dynamic poetic expression so that the names of Mtshali, Serote, A. N. C. Kumalo have become well known at readings, in publications and on recordings. Such collections as *Poets for the People* and *Malibongwe* (*Let Them Be Praised*) and others about the South African people's struggle has brought to the international readership the passion of the black masses in revolt.

An important event in terms of Southern African art and literature was the great gathering of cultural workers from South

Africa in Botswana last year to dedicate their talents and their works to the revolutionary struggle. We learn, too, that a literary event took place in Zimbabwe around the first Zimbabwe International Book Fair and the presentation in Harare of the Noma Award for publishing in Africa.

These events manifest the literary awakening, which is taking place as a result of the struggle for independence and against racism and apartheid in the region.

Perhaps side by side with the popular peasant theatre in Africa, the literature of the film industry is also flourishing. The names of African filmmakers and writers have made a large contribution to world cinematography, having enriched it with new techniques, themes and plots. Making use of the continent's own national traits and imagery, African cinema depicts the most important problems of the continent. The names of Sembène Ousmane, Issa Traoré, Ruy Guerra, Suheil Ben Barka, are those of giants in the art of African cinema, making use, among others, of the latter-day movement, of ancient myths, tales and legends to bolster people's faith in the triumph of justice and the downfall of evil.

In the Middle East, the struggle of the Palestinian people for the right of self-determination and to set up their own independent state has continued to be the prerequisite for a just peace in the region. This struggle equally involves a battle for cultural freedom without which the Palestinian people will not be able to identify themselves. Thus a notable feature of the Palestinian struggle has been the flourishing of literature deeply immersed in the cry of the people for justice and for the end of Zionist persecution. The works of Palestinian poets in particular bear witness to this and their names are on the lips of all Palestinian fighters.

Can one survey the literature of the Arab and Middle East countries within a range of only 25 years? Clearly not. The rich heritage of the Arab peoples' writing goes back far into past centuries. Were we not in our childhood made to read the *Arabian Nights* or the verses of Omar Khayyam? Let us say that the humanistic traditions created by the literature of the Arab peoples are today being carried out by many writers, and we are proud to be able to boast of their presence in our Association.

In Asia, and in such regions as the Indian subcontinent, the question of ethnic and language differences is one of the features of literary discussion which has been going on for a long time. In fact it is clear that various groups in a number of different countries, and including Africa, are actively seeking the preservation of their own cultural identity. An affirmation of individuality exists.

As M. Amadou-Mahtar M'Bow, director of UNESCO, put it in an essay, 'The Human Dimension': 'Communities—ethnic, rural and urban, cultural and religious—are asserting their originality and endeavouring to take in hand and defend with vigour those features by reference to which their identity is defined.'

The use of languages spoken by the community appears as a cultural imperative. But associated with this important choice should be various reforms, which, through the promotion of popular arts and traditions and social values, should aim at implanting consciousness of the realities and history of the nation as a whole. 'In this way it is certainly possible to gain from peoples that consciousness and active participation without which there can be no profound sense of cultural identity nor any truly endogenous development.'

It is therefore regrettable that countries are wracked by communal and ethnic antagonism, and this places an added burden upon the shoulders of progressive writers and cultural workers.

While this discussion or debate over the use of language will probably go on in both Asia and Africa, other aspects of literary output still develop on those continents.

While richer countries like some Arab states and Japan may not face the same degree of difficulty as others, it is well known that while the developing countries represent some 70 per cent of the world's population, they produce scarcely a fifth of the books published in the world, the rest of the production being concentrated in about 30 industrialized countries. While having to import books, these importations are by no means always suited to the aspirations of the Third World peoples, yet on the other hand national authors who are often forced to have their works published abroad may well be in a position to meet most of the peoples' needs if their societies were able to provide the opportunity of publication.

We have witnessed valiant efforts on the part of publishers in Africa and Asia to bring out books by national authors. This difficult task also has its effect on efforts to reproduce the works of foreign authors who must generally be sacrificed in favour of the local writers.

Socialist countries, the Soviet Union in particular, have produced millions of copies of translations of books by foreign writers apart from those by their own authors. Perhaps this is once more an indication of the necessity for profound socio-economic changes needed for the true and free flowering of culture, art and literature.

* * *

Our twenty-fifth anniversary coincides with our Seventh General Conference. In 1979, our Sixth Conference was held in Luanda, capital of the Angolan People's Republic, and opened by the famous Angolan and African poet, Agostinho Neto. Soon after the Conference, to our profound sorrow, we heard of the passing of this great revolutionary leader and giant of the poetic world.

Perhaps this Conference might give consideration to granting a special recognition from time to time to writers, particularly young writers, of an 'Agostinho Neto Award', in honour of this distinguished member.

In accordance with our recognition of the times in which we live, the main theme of our present Seventh Conference is concerned with 'peace and détente' and 'the writer's role in the struggle for the triumph of human reason over imperialism's aggressive designs and against the threat of nuclear war'.

As writers concerned with the fate of our peoples, we cannot but be concerned also with the alternative: either our lively voices or our everlasting silence. The penetration of the imperialist war machine into Africa, the Indian Ocean, Asia and the Pacific cannot be ignored by writers of Africa and Asia, and must be opposed in the name of peace.

In connection with the other items on the agenda of discussion, we can do no better than to quote once again from the Prague Assembly for Peace: 'The bridge of friendship is the bridge of life, and we have to build our bridge across chasms and continents and prejudices and ignorance and lies and fears and hatreds.' This is the duty of our Association.

In spite of the prevailing atmosphere we have been able to maintain the continuity of our activities due to the solidarity and cooperation of member national bodies. Regarding the activities of the Secretariat of the Association, these were held in conformity with the Constitution and Charter of the Association, and the Secretariat has in turn been guests of the Writers' Unions of India (1980), Mongolia (1980), Syria (1981), Afghanistan (1981), the USSR (1982) and Algeria (1983).

Literary activities by national bodies in these countries also took place, in the main coinciding with Secretariat meetings. Events were celebrated such as poetry recitals in Calcutta, a literary symposium in Ulan Bator, a festival of drama in Damascus. In addition, delegations from the Association also met government and party leaders, representatives of public bodies, in the countries mentioned. We also visited Beirut in 1982, on the occasion of the General Conference of the Lebanese Writers and were invited to the poetry festival in Aden, Yemen Democratic Republic, in 1981, and Addis Ababa, Ethiopia, in 1982.

The anti-progressive policies carried out by the government of Turkey prevented the Turkish Writers Syndicate from hosting a hoped-for activity in that country. We have protested to the Turkish President against the arrest of writers of that country. Similarly, we opposed the persecution of writers in South Korea, Egypt and Kenya. These writers upheld the principles of our movement and warranted our protection and our protesting voice.

We must congratulate our Soviet members for arranging events for young Afro-Asian writers in Frunze, which appears to be becoming a regular feature.

The Afro-Asian Writers Association participated in international meetings of writers for peace in Bulgaria and the World Assembly for Peace and Life in Prague, Czechoslovakia, this year.

Since the Sixth Conference in Luanda, we have received applications for membership from the Bureau for Promotion of Cultural Action, Réunion; the Reconstituted Writers Union of Afghanistan; Union of Libyan Writers; the Writers Unions of Laos and Kampuchea. All these applications were endorsed by the Executive Council which held its constitutional meeting in Ho Chi Minh City, Socialist Vietnam, in October 1982, after which members of the Council visited Kampuchea.

Since it was decided to award three 'Lotus' prizes each year to outstanding writers of Africa and Asia, we have awarded prizes to a large number of outstanding writers. Apart from the literary merit of such writers, it would appear that awards of the Lotus Prize also included political and patriotic considerations. Be that as it may, the Lotus Prize jury will no doubt present its report separately together with recommendations for strengthening itself and the quality of the prize so that the Lotus Prize for Afro-Asian Literature might achieve the status conducive to the character of Afro-Asian literature as outlined in our terms of reference.

It is a matter of principle to move a vote of thanks to the government of Tunisia and the Writers Union of that country for the outstanding expression of solidarity in granting us editorial offices in Tunis for *Lotus* magazine. This demonstration of support for our association came after the destruction of the *Lotus* premises and home of the Editor-in-Chief by the Zionist-fascist barbarians of Begin and Sharon during their attack on Beirut. Once more we call upon members to strengthen our magazine with contributions and broader circulation. The editorial board of *Lotus* will present its report to this Conference and elaborate on the progress of our official organ.

For a long time our Association has dreamt of an Afro-Asian publishing house. Efforts were made in the past to launch this project but unfortunately little headway was made. While we have aspirations that such a publishing house will help in the task of stimulating literary exchanges between our continents and encourage writers, we have possibly been caught up in the commercial, financial and political problems which afflict so many projects of our continents.

We also look forward to the Russian edition of *Lotus*, which has been on our agenda for some time.

In connection with future activities of the Association, it is our opinion that more effort must be made to assist the writing community of both continents to enter the circle of Afro-Asian solidarity and anti-imperialist commitment. While we have stimulated activities in many regions, there are still gaps, which must be filled. The influence of neocolonialism still prevails; disillusionment with prevailing authority and the sense of 'individualism' among some writers still prevails. Equally, fratricidal strife and communal antagonism is still a blight on the scene in some areas which must be eradicated as the task of all cultural workers. It behoves our Association to agitate among writers to devote their efforts to bridging the gap between peoples.

The Association might take up the appeal of the cultural workers gathered at the most important World Assembly for Peace, in

Prague this year, as part of its activities: 'To confront the worst aspects of the corruption of art, we suggest the compilation of a vocabulary of peace and culture, in the form of a dictionary or an anthology in as many languages as possible.'

On the organizational level, we still have some obstacles to overcome. The question of the headquarters or centre of the Association must now be resolved. It is hoped that the Seventh Conference will decide this matter finally. However, while deciding this matter of a formal head office, it may be that a form of organization involving a greater division of labour should be considered. We hope that the Organizational Commission will go into this question. Equally, it is required that greater participation of the Deputy Secretaries General in particular, in the international activities of the Association, should be a characteristic of our Association. The DSGs can do much to initiate activities on a regional basis but must also be seen to represent the Association in the international arena. This of course applies also to ordinary members of the Secretariat.

Our Charter has provided a sound basis for the future of our Association. Any forthcoming amendments, if any, must strengthen the Association, its organization and work.

* * *

In conclusion, let us note that our Association has grown to include what we believe to be the representation of the majority of the writing fraternity of Africa and Asia. On the basis of affiliated national bodies and individual members, we embrace more than sixty countries of our two continents. This is no mean achievement over the 25 years of our existence, in spite of pitfalls and difficulties. Let us salute those who have gone before, the forerunners and builders of the Afro-Asian Writers Association. In addition, we are attracting writers' organizations from outside our continents to join us as associate members.

We extend our hands in greeting to the progressive writers of all continents. We share the agony and triumphs of our fellow writers in Latin America, and we endorse the sentiments of the writers and artists of Cuba and their Third Congress when they said, 'The poetry of words and music, the language of form and colour, light and shadow, space and time must come to the defence of life, which is ultimately the very reason for their existence, before it is too late.'

We wholly endorse the statement of the Sandino Association of Cultural Workers—writers, artists and intellectuals of Nicaragua, who were called upon to defend their homeland, which said: 'We are sure we can count on the active solidarity of honest artists and intellectuals who, motivated by deep sentiments of justice, will respond through pronouncements, expositions and every type of manifestation of support, to the heroic people of Sandino.'

The Afro-Asian Writers Association is part of the gigantic and ever-growing worldwide community of peoples for justice, social progress and peace. Every pronouncement of our Association, wherever we have gathered, has affirmed this. Together with our people, together with the rest of mankind, we shall devote our energies, wield our pens, in the pursuit of these objectives.

Afterword
BILL NASSON

Dear Reader,

As in the classic Victorian English novel, it is usually best to start at the beginning. Although I never ever met Alex La Guma, my mind was visited by him in his absence. The first occasion was when I was very young, around eight or nine years old, around 1960 or perhaps 1961, at any rate before the assassination of John F. Kennedy or the sound of The Beatles. Then, our small suburban Cape Town home sheltered a political activist who was on the run from South Africa's notorious security police. A man called Reg September, he was secreted away at the rear of the house for several weeks, and I was sworn not to reveal his presence, especially not to any plain-clothed white Afrikaner strangers who might knock enquiringly on the front door.

Like La Guma, September was an office-bearer of the South African Coloured People's Congress. He was given refuge because of a childhood friendship with my mother, and not because either of my studiously law-abiding parents had any sympathies for what they viewed as the dangerously incendiary anti-apartheid politics of the country's Congress Movement. During those nervous nights, Reg September would emerge with a torrent of adult talk about friends and enemies, and what to read and whom to read.

While still addicted to *The Hardy Boys* and *Nancy Drew*, I was drawn in—one of the benefits (or, perhaps, the burdens) of being a hanger-on only child was being included, precociously. Our fugitive came with left-wing literature, including copies of the *Guardian* and *New Age* for my parents to blink at before these were whipped away. And it was impossible not to catch some of the names of friends who were 'comrades'. Talked of in September's dignified, hushed tones, one figure was Alex La Guma, admired as one of *our writers*, who ought to be read by everyone, including me when I got older.

Although Alex La Guma went into political exile in the mid-1960s, in South Africa his trenchant voice was not exiled into silence. Instead, it grew more muffled and found an appropriately discreet throat in an increasingly authoritarian country. Following the apartheid state's banning in 1960 of the small Trotskyist and independent socialist Non-European Unity Movement, in their Western Cape heartland its local leadership sought out molecular ways of sustaining its radical political influence. Operating beneath the radar of the snooping security branch of the police, in Cape Town a scattering of wholesome-sounding educational and cultural bodies like the South Peninsula Educational Fellowship and the Cape Flats Educational Fellowship offered high-school and university students the light of evening readings, recitals and lectures through a shuttered 1960s and beyond.

At the same time, these bookish worlds were more than a refuge. They were also fringe enclaves of anti-nationalist, anti-Stalinist (and hence, anti-Communist Party) meditation. Rooted in a blanket rejection of race and racial difference as an insidious construction of bourgeois capitalism, the principle of non-racialism taught by these training grounds meant not only an uncompromising rejection of any political dealings with the racial structures of the apartheid order. It also signified, no less implacably, non-collaboration with other anti-apartheid bodies which accepted the country's racial categories, and enmeshed themselves in the multiracialism of an ethnically based Congress Alliance. Or, in other words, in the circles of the ANC and the Communist Party of South

Africa that La Guma more openly embraced after his departure into political exile in the mid-1960s.

Yet, within this claustrophobic and studious Cape Town subculture, which I inhabited in the later-1960s and early 1970s, Alex La Guma's writings were still revered as those of a man of the left and an inspirational internationalist. The hush-hush library of the South Peninsula Educational Fellowship, located in the private flat of a Unity Movement veteran and restricted to a trusted circle of mostly younger users, held copies of La Guma's short stories and his early novels. These, including a particularly well-thumbed edition of his 1962 novel, *A Walk in the Night*, nestled alongside other banned literature. Among these were books by Soviet bloc Marxist dissidents like Isaac Deutscher's *Leon Trotsky* biography; the *Selected Poems* of the anti-Stalinist poet, Anna Akhmatova; influential early African independence novels such as Chinua Achebe's *Things Fall Apart* and *A Grain of Wheat* by James Ngũgĩ (Ngũgĩ wa Thiong'o); and the classic British working-class fiction of Robert Tressell's *The Ragged-Trousered Philanthropists* and the Communist Welsh miner, Lewis Jones' *We Live*. Those of us who were favoured by admission to this ecumenical left-wing library sneaked in by individual evening appointment. There, one was invariably initiated into instructive reading by its nocturnal keeper of subversive literature, a day-time accountant called Dawood Parker who favoured starched white shirts.

While Alex La Guma was well up on the list, we were never exposed to his explosive journalism—the realm of *New Age* and *Fighting Talk* was, naturally enough, that of Congress propaganda. His significance, therefore, was that of a banned local writer of proletarian fiction—personally, I first encountered his non-fiction only many years later, having long thought of him as a novelist and short story writer. Then, La Guma was a creative authority on black urban hardship, racism and working-class oppression in Cape Town—represented by the searing potency of *A Walk in the Night*. The importance of appreciating Alex La Guma as a socialist beacon also carried a special, politically educative significance in this era. Ideologically, his craft embodied the sensibility of kindred artists not only nationally but also internationally. For La Guma's frank depiction of the tragic lives of the rank-and-file who made history linked his affinities to a wider world of socially progressive novelists overseas, who reflected and critiqued capitalist exploitation. It was no accident that he shared a shelf with the books of Americans such as Jack London, John Steinbeck and Upton Sinclair, and Britons like Walter Greenwood and Alan Sillitoe. In that way, for readers like us almost fifty years ago, a censored Alex La Guma intersected with foreign writers who were not censored in constructing a radical alternative worldview within the bowels of apartheid society.

He came to life again, almost by chance, during my scholarship years as a student in Britain. As an arts undergraduate at the small University of Hull in northeast England, in 1974, I chose an English option on 'The Literature of the British Commonwealth', partly because it offered not only the allure of unknown Indian, Caribbean and Canadian writers, but also the prospect of a wordy connection with a detested apartheid place that I had been wanting to see the back of for so long.

For a bleak winter term on the Yorkshire coast, studying South African writers somehow promised aversion therapy as a kind of consolation. The novels prescribed were Alan Paton's *Cry the Beloved Country* (1948), Nadine Gordimer's *The Late Bourgeois World* (1966) and—somewhat less predictable as a choice of emblematic apartheid-era fiction—Alex La Guma's *In the Fog of the Seasons' End* (1972), a recently published and characteristically gritty short book which evoked the strain and sacrifice of an underground struggle for freedom from racial subjugation. As with Gordimer's novel, banned back in South Africa, not merely openly purchasing *In the Fog of the Seasons' End*, but writing a clumsy third-year undergraduate essay on it—dealing with, as I recall, the theme of 'human realization through collective action'—brought on an extraordinarily warm sense of post-adolescent intoxication.

The arrival of La Guma's fictional writing on a benign Department of English reading list in Britain was not only to experience it in an uninhibited, uncensored, liberal educational environment. It was also to find it as a key to the field of Marxist literary criticism, studied through that lens after having lapped up the realist mother's milk provided by leading 'literature and society' materialist English scholars such as Arnold Kettle in *An Introduction to the English Novel* (1951) and David Craig's panoramic *Marxists on Literature* (1975).

As if it were not enough to be given Leon Trotsky and Friedrich Engels to be baffled by, there was more to complement an appreciation of La Guma. It included Georg Lukács and *The Theory of the Novel* (1974) to explain 'the social mission of literature' as the vantage point from which to interpret Alex La Guma's acute grasp of the class position of a character like Bennett in *In the Fog of the Seasons' End*, an attribute by which he was bound almost as much as he was swaddled by his racial identity.

During this northern university time of draughty university bars and stuffy lecture halls, I ran into another prominent Cape Town writer, Richard Rive. Through fellow pupils at a neighbouring high school, I had first met him at the end of the 1960s and had, like many, been dazzled and amused by his posturing and supercilious manner. One could not be allowed to forget his seminal place in the celebrated Heinemann African Writers Series, nor to turn a deaf ear to repeated accounts of how he had assembled the South African short story-tellers of his 1963 anthology, *Quartet*. Those contributors were, in addition to Rive himself, Alf Wannenburgh, James Matthews and Alex La Guma.

Accompanied by an old high-school friend who had been one of his former pupils, I visited Rive during his years as a mature PhD student at the University of Oxford in 1973. There, he showed us a collection of South African literature in his study, including signed first editions of *A Walk in the Night* and *The Stone Country* (1967) and treated us, pontificating in his delicious style, to a lengthy lament over how Alex La Guma's exile faith in the politics of the ANC had stifled his natural literary talents. Had only he had the benefit of a superior education, he might have been, as he put it inimitably, a more civilized literary man. As essentially a liberal individualist concerned with individual liberties and human rights, Richard Rive always wrinkled his nose at doctrinaire anti-imperialist and anti-colonial ideologies.

Rive then regaled us with an anecdote which he enjoyed springing on unwitting white South African listeners. It was, he chuckled, to inform them that he was 'only the second Coloured South African in history to have been admitted to Magdalen College, Oxford'. Allowing for a moment of puzzled silence, this revelation would be followed by, 'the first was, of course, Sir De Villiers Graaff', Graaff having been the rather dusky-complexioned white former leader of South Africa's United Party from the 1950s to the 1970s. Our beaming Oxford host rounded off by murmuring, *sotto voce*, that 'as life usually worked best in threes,' the third student from South Africa ought, ideally, to have been 'my fellow scribe, La Guma, born to be the most Coloured of all our country's well-read Coloureds'. That aside, which has lingered in memory over decades, struck another chord soon after South Africa's transition to majority rule in 1994. Two years later, when the rain of post-apartheid freedom was yet to turn acid, the University of Cape Town historian, Mohamed Adhikari, published a small school-level educational book, *James La Guma*, in a publisher's 'They Fought for Freedom' biographical series. Intended to honour the previously overlooked lives of historically significant Southern African leaders, Alex La Guma's trade unionist and communist father was depicted in this 1996 portrait as a conspicuous and 'respected' advocate of democracy, 'an independent thinker and tireless fighter for justice'.

For his bustling son, it is hard to imagine a more militant apprenticeship in anti-apartheid resistance than that furnished by this kind of kinship line. Equally, that was only part of the *James*

La Guma picture. As reflected in his 1940 poem in praise of the wartime sacrifice of Africa's 'Brown Sons', it was 'Jimmy' La Guma's comfortable embodiment of a Coloured racial identity that made him a natural subject for a writer such as Adhikari, who has nailed his colours to the mast through a lingering preoccupation with ethnic identity in South Africa's minority Coloured community. Its transmission to, and personal absorption by, Alex La Guma is something which has, of course, been noted by numerous literary critics and other writers who have commented on his dizzying range of artistic accomplishments and fervent political activism.

Today, the writings of Alex La Guma are an important part of the political and cultural patrimony of the twentieth-century South African experience. His sustained, militant and passionate explorations of human endurance and political assertions are a vital memory of the emancipatory dreams of a talented figure, trying to sustain an egalitarian cause through a hard and dominant phase of the apartheid system. Considering that world, what Alex La Guma's pen made of it and how he interacted with it, both early on and later, may help to show us something of how revolutionary dreaming comes to be made. And it is also to appreciate something tragic. That lies in awakening, years after his life ended, to the yawning gap between the dismal incompetence and kleptocracy that has come to mark the crisis-ridden ANC and its allies, the liberation movement to which La Guma was so committed and the emancipation of the downtrodden that it continues to trumpet as the ruling mission of its National Democratic Revolution. For Alex La Guma—and for many others—a free South Africa has not become the revolution that they intended or, let alone, would even have wanted.

Bibliography

[EDITOR'S NOTE: This bibliography is not exhaustive. It focuses on La Guma's writings included or referred to in this volume. Furthermore, it does not include the sources originally cited by the author in his articles.]

PRIMARY SOURCES
Works by Alex La Guma

'Address by Lotus Award Winner'. *Lotus: Afro-Asian Writings* 4(10) (1971): 195–7.

'Africa and the USSR: A Friendly Handshake'. *Moscow News* 15 (1977), n.p.

'African Culture and National Liberation'. *Journal of the New African Literature and the Arts* 7–8 (1969): 99–101.

[As Gala]. 'Against Literary Apartheid'. *The African Communist* 58 (Third Quarter 1974): 99–107.

Interviewed by Robert Serumaga. 'Alex La Guma, South African Author Recently Settled in London'. *Cultural Events in Africa* 24 (November 1966, Transcription Centre, London): *i–ii*.

'Alexander Solzhenitsyn: "Life Through a Crooked Eye"'. *The African Communist* 56 (First Quarter 1974): 69–79.

And a Threefold Cord. Berlin: Seven Seas Publishers, 1964.

'Answers to Our Questionnaire'. *Soviet Literature* 11(356) (1977): 116–17.

(Ed.). *Apartheid: A Collection of Writings on South African Racism by South Africans*. New York: International Publishers, 1971.

'Apartheid Coloured Council Flounders'. *Sechaba* 9(1) (1975): 10–12.

'Apartheid and the Coloured People of South Africa'. Notes and Documents No. 18/72. United Nations: Unit on Apartheid, Department of Political and Security Council Affairs, 1972.

'Apartheid, Imperialist Monster'. *Tricontinental* 26 (1971): 43–55.

'Apartheid Is Not Just a Regional Problem'. *Tricontinental* 64 (1979): 85–6.

'Blankets'. *Lotus: Afro-Asian Writings* 36–37 (1978): 80–4.

'Caribbean Against Apartheid'. *Sechaba* (September 1979): 22–4.

'Caribbean—Nobody's Backyard'. *Dawn* 6(4) (1982): 30–6.

'The Coloured Cadets Bill'. *Sechaba* 1(10) (1967): 10–11.

[As Willem Abram Malgas]. 'The Coloured People of South Africa'. *The African Communist* 34 (Third Quarter 1968): 51–9.

'Come Back to Tashkent'. *Lotus: Afro-Asian Writings* 4(4–6) (1970): 208–10.

'The Condition of Culture in South Africa'. *Présence Africaine* 80 (Fourth Quarter 1971): 113–22.

'Cuba and Africa'. *Sechaba* (March 1984): 20–3.

'Culture and Apartheid in South Africa'. *Tricontinental* 8 (1968): 131–6.

'Culture and Liberation'. *Sechaba* 10 (Fourth Quarter 1976): 50–8.

'Culture and Liberation'. *World Literature Written in English* 18(1) (1979): 27–36.

'Culture and Revolution'. *Sechaba* 3(10) (1969): 23.

'Dialogue "A Gross Betrayal"'. *Africa Report* 17 (1972): 24–5.

'The Exile'. *Lotus: Afro-Asian Writings* 11 (1972): 68–75.

'Final Speech, Secretary General of the Afro-Asian Writers Association'. *Lotus: Afro-Asian Writings* 42/43 (1979–1980): 111–12.

'GDR Opera Supports Liberation Struggle'. *Sechaba* 8(2) (1974): 12–13.

'*Great Power Conspiracy*: Review'. *Sechaba* 1(1) (1967): 15.

'Has Art Failed South Africa?' *The African Communist* 69 (Second Quarter 1977): 78–83.

'Hello or Goodbye, Athol Fugard?' *The African Communist* 57 (Second Quarter 1974): 100–105.

'A Home Away from Home'. *Sechaba* 3(11) (1969): 11–12.

'I Came Here to Sing: A Tribute to Pablo Neruda'. *Lotus: Afro-Asian Writings* 22 (1974): 145–7.

'The Immorality Act: South Africa's Sex Law'. Notes and Documents No. 21/70. United Nations: Unit on Apartheid, Department of Political and Security Council Affairs, 1970.

In the Fog of the Seasons' End. London: Heinemann, 1972.

'In Memory of Hutch: Alfred Hutchinson (South Africa)'. *Lotus: Afro-Asian Writings* 17(3) (1973): 135.

'Israel–South Africa: The Unholy Alliance'. *Tricontinental* 86 (1983): 86–91.

'Israel and South Africa—Where the Vultures Perch'. *Lotus: Afro-Asian Writings* 52 (1983): 84–7.

[As Gala]. 'Is There a South African National Culture?' *The African Communist* 100 (First Quarter 1985): 38–43.

'Late Edition'. *Lotus: Afro-Asian Writings* 12 (1972): 152–7.

[As Capie]. 'Letter to the Editor'. *Sechaba* (June 1984): 31.

[As Capie]. 'Letter to the Editor'. *Sechaba* (November 1984): 32.

'Literature and Life'. *Lotus: Afro-Asian Writings* 4(4–6) (1970): 237–9.

[As Gala]. 'Lust without Passion'. *The African Communist* 55 (Fourth Quarter 1973): 116–18.

'The Man in the Tree'. *The Literary Review* 15(1) (1971): 19–30.

'Message to the People and the Government of the Socialist Republic of Vietnam'. *Lotus: Afro-Asian Writings* 52 (1983): 148–9.

'My Books Have Gone Back Home'. *World Marxist Review* 27(5) (1984): 71–3.

[As Willem Abram Malgas]. 'On the Coloured People'. *The African Communist* 40 (First Quarter 1970): 108–10.

'On Short Stories'. *Lotus: Afro-Asian Writings* 17(3) (1973): 132–3.

'Paul Robeson and Africa'. *The African Communist* 46 (Third Quarter 1971): 113–19.

[As Gala]. 'A Poet Is Born: *Sounds of a Cowhide Drum* by Oswald Joseph Mtshali'. *The African Communist* 48 (1972): 114–17.

'Pumpkins and Dark Skins'. *Sechaba* 3(5) (May 1969): 19.

'Report of the Acting Secretary General'. *Lotus: Afro-Asian Writings* 42/43 (1979–1980): 72–80.

'Report of the Secretary General to the Seventh General (25th Anniversary) Conference, Tashkent, Uzbekistan, September–October 1983'. *Lotus: Afro-Asian Writings* 56 (1985): 181–92.

'*Sounds of a Cowhide Drum* by Oswald Joseph Mtshali'. *Lotus: Afro-Asian Writings* 21 (1974): 180–7.

'South African Freedom Poetry'. *The African Communist* 61 (Second Quarter 1975): 106–7.

'South African Writing under Apartheid'. *Lotus: Afro-Asian Writings* 23 (1975): 11–21.

A Soviet Journey: A Critical Annotated Edition (Christopher J. Lee ed.). Lanham, MD: Lexington Books, 2017[1978].

The Stone Country. London: Heinemann, 1967.

'Thang's Bicycle'. *Lotus: Afro-Asian Writings* 29 (1976): 42–7.

'The Third Afro-Asian Writers' Conference'. *Cultural Events in Africa* 29 (April 1967): 4–5.

'The Time Has Come'. *Sechaba* 1(5) (May 1967): 14–16.

'The Time Has Come: The Coloured People Must Prepare to Bear Arms for Liberation'. *Sechaba* 1(6) (June 1967): 15–16.

'The Time Has Come: New Forms of Struggle Face the South African Coloured Community'. *Sechaba* 1(3) (March 1967): 14–15.

'The Time Has Come: S. A. Coloured People's Social and Economic Deterioration'. *Sechaba* 1(4) (April 1967): 13–14.

Time of the Butcherbird. London: Heinemann, 1979.

'This Is Our Vanguard, a Vanguard of Communists'. *The African Communist* 85 (Second Quarter 1981): 64–75.

'To Alternate Member of the Politbureau, CPSU CC, First Secretary of the Communist Party of Uzbekistan, Comrade Sharaf R. Rashidov'. *Lotus: Afro-Asian Writings* 38/39 (1978–1979): 124.

'To Yuri Andropov, General Secretary of the CC CPSU, President of the USSR Supreme Soviet'. Seventh Conference of the Writers of Asia and

Africa, Tashkent, 26 September–2 October 1983. *Press Bulletin* 6 (1 October 1983), n.p.

'Tribute to Indira Gandhi'. *Lotus: Afro-Asian Writings* 56 (1985): n.p.

'Vietnam: A People's Victory'. *The African Communist* 53 (Second Quarter 1973): 29–35.

'Walk Among the Multitudes'. *Tricontinental* 75 (1981): 39–42.

A Walk in the Night and Other Stories. London: Heinemann, 1967[1962].

'What I Learned from Maxim Gorky'. *Lotus: Afro-Asian Writings* 34(4) (1977): 164–8.

'Whither South Africa?' *The Black Scholar* 5(10) (1974): 30–6.

[As Arnold Adams]. 'Why I Joined the Communist Party'. *The African Communist* 47 (Fourth Quarter 1971): 57–61.

[As Gala]. 'Why I Joined the Communist Party: Doing Something Useful'. *The African Communist* 89 (Second Quarter 1982): 49–52.

Spanish-Language Articles by Alex La Guma Published in *Tricontinental*

'*Apartheid*, Engendro Imperialista'. *Tricontinental* 26 (1971): 43–55.

'La Carta de la Libertad a un Vive'. *Tricontinental* 99 (1985): 44–52.

'El Movimiento de los No Alineados: un Aliado de la Lucha de Liberación Nacional'. *Tricontinental* 65 (1979): 65–9.

'Notas Históricas Sobre el Congreso Nacional Africano de Sudáfrica'. *Tricontinental* 67–68 (1980): 105–115.

'Particularidades de la Lucha de Liberación en Sudáfrica'. *Tricontinental* 69–70 (1980): 4–12.

SECONDARY SOURCES

ABRAHAMS, Cecil (ed.). *Memories of Home: The Writings of Alex La Guma*. Trenton, NJ: Africa World Press, 1991.

AHMAD, Aijaz. *In Theory: Classes, Nations, Literatures*. London: Verso, 1992.

ANDRADE, Susan Z. *The Nation Writ Small: African Fictions and Feminisms, 1958–1988*. Durham, NC: Duke University Press, 2011.

APPLEBAUM, Anne. *Gulag: A History*. New York: Anchor, 2004.

APTER, Emily. *Against World Literature: On the Politics of Untranslatability*. London: Verso, 2013.

ATTWELL, David. *Rewriting Modernity: Studies in Black South African Literary History*. Athens, OH: Ohio University Press, 2006.

BAKHTIN, Mikhail M. *The Dialogic Imagination* (Michael Holquist ed., Caryl Emerson and Michael Holquist trans). Austin: University of Texas Press, 1981.

BARNARD, Rita. *Apartheid and Beyond: South African Writers and the Politics of Place*. New York: Oxford, 2007.

BIKO, Steve. *I Write What I Like: Selected Writings* (Aelred Stubbs ed.). Chicago: University of Chicago Press, 2002.

BULSON, Eric. *Little Magazine, World Form*. New York: Columbia University Press, 2016.

CABRAL, Amílcar. *Unity and Struggle: Speeches and Writings* (Michael Wolfers trans.). New York: Monthly Review Press, 1979.

CHEAH, Pheng. *What Is a World?: On Postcolonial Literature as World Literature*. Durham, NC: Duke University Press, 2016.

CROSSMAN, Richard (ed.). *The God That Failed*. New York: Harper, 1949.

DERRIDA, Jacques. *Specters of Marx: The State of the Debt, the Work of Mourning and the New International*. London: Routledge, 2006[1993].

DICK, Archie L. *The Hidden History of South Africa's Book and Reading Cultures*. Toronto: University of Toronto Press, 2012.

DU BOIS, W. E. B. *Dark Princess*. Jackson: University Press of Mississippi, 1995[1928].

ELLIS, Stephen. *External Mission: The ANC in Exile, 1960–1990*. New York: Oxford University Press, 2013.

FANON, Frantz. *A Dying Colonialism* (Haakon Chevalier trans.). New York: Grove Press, 1965[1959].

———. *Toward the African Revolution* (Haakon Chevalier trans.). New York: Grove Press, 1988[1964].

———. *The Wretched of the Earth* (Richard Philcox trans.). New York: Grove Press, 2004[1963].

FIELD, Roger. *Alex La Guma: A Literary and Political Biography*. London: James Currey, 2010.

——— and André Odendaal (eds). *Liberation Chabalala: The World of Alex La Guma*. Bellville: Mayibuye Books, 1993.

FIRST, Ruth. *117 Days: An Account of Confinement and Interrogation under the South African 90-Day Detention Law*. London: Penguin, 2009[1965].

FORE, Devin. 'Introduction'. *October* 118 (2006): 3–10.

GLISSANT, Édouard. *Caribbean Discourse: Selected Essays* (J. Michael Dash trans.). Charlottesville, VA: University Press of Virginia, 1989[1981].

HALIM, Hala. '*Lotus*, the Afro-Asian Nexus, and Global South Comparatism'. *Comparative Studies of South Asia, Africa and the Middle East* 32(3) (2012): 563–83.

HARNEY, Stefano and Fred Moten. *The Undercommons: Fugitive Planning & Black Study*. New York: Minor Compositions, 2013.

HUNT, Lynn. *Inventing Human Rights: A History*. New York: W. W. Norton, 2007.

JAMESON, Fredric. 'Third-World Literature in the Era of Multinational Capitalism'. *Social Text* 15 (1986): 65–88.

KALLINEY, Peter. 'Modernism, African Literature, and the Cold War'. *Modern Language Quarterly* 76(3) (2015): 333–68.

LALU, Premesh. 'Incomplete Histories: Steve Biko, the Politics of Self-Writing and the Apparatus of Reading'. *Current Writing* 16(1) (2004): 107–26.

LEE, Christopher J. 'Introduction. Anti-Imperial Eyes' in Alex La Guma, *A Soviet Journey: A Critical Annotated Edition* (Christopher J. Lee ed.). Lanham, MD: Lexington Books, 2017, pp. 1–60.

———. *Frantz Fanon: Toward a Revolutionary Humanism*. Athens: Ohio University Press, 2015.

MACMILLAN, Hugh. *The Lusaka Years: The ANC in Exile in Zambia, 1963–1994*. Johannesburg: Jacana, 2013.

MANDELA, Nelson. *Long Walk to Freedom: The Autobiography of Nelson Mandela*. Boston, MA: Back Bay Books, 1995.

MORETTI, Franco. *Distant Reading*. London: Verso, 2013.

MPHAHLELE, Es'kia. *Afrika My Music: An Autobiography, 1957–1983*. Cape Town: Kwela Books, 2013[1984].

———. 'Exile, the Tyranny of Place and the Literary Compromise'. *UNISA English Studies* 17(1) (1979): 37–44.

———. 'The Tyranny of Place and Aesthetics: The South African Case' in Charles Malan (ed.), *Race and Literature/Ras en Literatuur*. Pinetown: Owen Burgess, 1987, pp. 48–59.

MUFTI, Aamir. *Forget English!: Orientalisms and World Literatures*. Cambridge, MA: Harvard University Press, 2016.

NDEBELE, Njabulo. *Rediscovery of the Ordinary: Essays on South African Literature and Culture*. Pietermaritzburg: University of KwaZulu-Natal Press, 2006.

NKOSI, Lewis. *Home and Exile, and Other Selections*. London: Longman, 1983[1965].

PADMORE, George. *Pan-Africanism or Communism? The Coming Struggle for Africa*. London: D. Dobson, 1956.

PALUMBO-LIU, David, Bruce Robbins, and Nirvana Tanoukhi (eds). *Immanuel Wallerstein and the Problem of the World: System, Scale, Culture*. Durham, NC: Duke University Press, 2011.

POPESCU, Monica. *South African Literature Beyond the Cold War*. New York: Palgrave Macmillan, 2010.

QUAYSON, Ato. 'Introduction: Postcolonial Literature in a Changing Historical Frame' in Ato Quayson (ed.), *The Cambridge History of*

Postcolonial Literature, VOL. 1. Cambridge: Cambridge University Press, 2012, pp. 1–29.

RASSOOL, Ciraj. 'Rethinking Documentary History and South African Political Biography'. *South African Review of Sociology* 41(1) (2010): 28–55.

SACHS, Albie. 'Preparing Ourselves for Freedom: Culture and the ANC Constitutional Guidelines'. *TDR* 35(1) (1991): 187–93.

SAID, Edward W. *Culture and Imperialism*. New York: Vintage, 1994.

———. *Representations of the Intellectual*. New York: Vintage, 1996.

———. *On Late Style: Music and Literature Against the Grain*. New York: Vintage, 2006.

SARTRE, Jean-Paul. *What Is Literature?* London: Routledge, 2001[1948].

SIMPSON, Thula. *Umkhonto we Sizwe: The ANC's Armed Struggle*. Johannesburg: Penguin Random House, 2016.

SPILLERS, Hortense J. *Black, White, and in Color: Essays on American Literature and Culture*. Chicago: University of Chicago Press, 2003.

TAMBO, Oliver. *Oliver Tambo Speaks: Preparing for Power* (Adelaide Tambo ed.). London: Heinemann, 1987.

VAN DER VLIES, Andrew. *South African Textual Cultures: White, Black, Read All Over*. Manchester: Manchester University Press, 2007.

——— (ed.). *Print, Text and Book Cultures in South Africa*. Johannesburg: Wits University Press, 2012.

VAN DER POST, Laurens. *Journey into Russia*. London: Hogarth, 1964.

WRIGHT, Richard. *The Color Curtain: A Report on the Bandung Conference*. Jackson: University Press of Mississippi, 1995[1956].

YOUNG, Kevin. *The Grey Album: On the Blackness of Blackness*. Minneapolis, MN: Graywolf Press, 2012.

Index

Abdurahman, A. (Abdullah) 60, 92, 145, 146

Abrahams, Cecil 13, 19, 347

Achebe, Chinua 19, 28, 46, 338, 339, 549, 560; in chapter overview 336

African Communist, The (journal) 6, 18, 41, 42, 48, 176n3; in chapter overviews 85, 102, 123, 165, 206, 273, 312, 343, 364, 374, 377, 389, 397, 408, 423, 517, 526

African National Congress (ANC) 5, 6, 17, 18, 20, 29, 33, 34, 41, 47, 48, 56, 57, 59, 75, 76, 122, 147, 154, 155, 164, 180–1, 183–4, 201, 202, 203, 204, 205, 207, 228–9, 234, 239, 249–50, 264, 266, 277, 300, 310, 363, 390, 425, 429, 533, 536, 537, 559, 563, 564; in chapter overviews 55, 64, 85, 238, 252

African Writers Series 19, 26, 562

Afro-Asian Writers Association (AAWA) 4, 6, 18, 27, 39, 41, 44, 49, 319, 327, 334, 540, 554, 556–7; in chapter overviews 230, 235, 252, 255, 419, 479

Asian-African Conference (1955) 45. *See also* Bandung Conference

Algeria 22, 32, 243, 368; Portuguese colonies of 340; Writers' Union of 553

Algerian Revolution 32

Allende, Salvador 419, 420

And a Threefold Cord (La Guma) 19, 20, 21

Anti-CAD movement 92, 151, 154, 156; National Anti-CAD Conference 150. *See also* Non-European United Front

Arafat, Yasser 326

Attwell, David 37

Bakhtin, Mikhail 23

Bandung Conference 541

Bantustans 118, 203, 205, 301, 348

Bantustan policy 177, 203, 204

Barnard, Rita 38

Beti, Mongo 338, 549

Biko, Steve 29, 32, 44

Bolívar, Simón 207, 547
Bolshevik Revolution 17, 34
Boumédiène, Houari 267
Black Atlantic 31, 33, 34, 36, 45
Black Consciousness 187
Black Scholar, The (journal) 171
Botha, P. W. (Pieter Willem) 142, 162, 232–3, 242; Botha–Smith regimes 204, 205
Brecht, Bertolt 24
Breytenbach, Breyten 436
Brezhnev, Leonid 195, 319
Brutus, Dennis 39, 374–6, 424, 438
Bukharin, Nikolai 34
Bunting, Brian 3

Cabral, Amílcar 29, 41, 47, 298, 301, 322, 337
Cape Liberal Tradition (Cape liberalism) 143
Carmichael, Stokely (Kwame Ture) 22
Carter, James (Jimmy) 199, 200, 217
Castro, Fidel 22, 40, 207–20, 246, 248, 250
China, People's Republic of 326–7, 420
Cleaver, Eldridge 22
Coetzee, J. M. 12, 38, 343
Coloured Advisory Council (CAC) 62, 63, 150, 161
Coloured Affairs Department (CAD) 62, 63, 71, 142, 150–7, 161

Coloured People's Congress (CPC) 71, 75, 76, 86, 96, 151, 154–6, 164, 186, 190, 530, 558; in chapter overview, 85
Coloured Representative Council (Coloured Persons Representative Council, CRC) 64, 74, 85, 86, 138, 151, 153, 158, 159, 161–2, 185–91
Comintern (Communist International) 34; League Against Imperialism 33
Communist Party of South Africa (CPSA) 20, 34, 534. *See also* South African Communist Party (SACP)
Congress Alliance 34–5, 530, 559; in chapter overview 85. *See also* Congress Movement
Congress of the People 155, 181, 530
Congress Movement 75, 96, 264, 558
Council of Coloured Affairs (CCA) 63, 73, 151, 152n45, 161
Cuba 5, 22, 31, 40, 206–8, 212–14, 216–17, 219–21, 223, 226, 227, 321, 324; people and government of 327; writers and artists of 557
Cuban Revolution 5, 213, 214

Davis, Angela 22, 274, 280; in chapter overview 273
Dawn (journal) 222

Derrida, Jacques 47, 47n41
Dien Bien Phu 165, 490, 492–6, 498
Distant reading (concept) 24
District Six (Cape Town) 20, 25, 27, 44, 65, 76, 148, 156, 442, 509, 511, 517, 519
Dreiser, Theodore 36
Duarte, Napoleón 224–5
Du Bois, W. E. B. 31, 33, 36, 280
Dube, John L. 33, 343, 428, 429

El Salvador 220, 224, 225, 226–7, 327
El Sebai, Youssef 255, 321, 329
Ellis, Stephen 16, 17n1
Engels, Friedrich 47, 206, 209, 273, 345n2, 349, 349n2, 548, 562
Ethiopian Revolution 324

Faiz, Faiz Ahmed 330, 523
Fascism 31, 32, 70, 78, 181, 215, 228, 274, 277, 278, 279, 528, 541
Fanon, Frantz 8, 29, 30, 31, 32, 44, 47, 336, 337
Farah, Nuruddin 28
February, Basil 32, 164, 531
Feinberg, Barry 313, 423, 424
Field, Roger 2, 19, 19n6, 20n9, 26n16
Fighting Talk (magazine) 19, 373, 389, 560
First Pan-African Cultural Festival 266, 270, 272

First, Ruth 4, 28, 29n17, 32, 255
Fischer, Bram 390
Freedom Charter 75, 96, 102, 155, 163, 181, 205, 264, 344, 530, 532,
FRELIMO (Frente de Libertação de Moçambique) 191, 196, 206, 266
Fugard, Athol 39, 42, 289, 308, 313, 343, 389–96
Fugitive cosmopolitanism 37

Garvey, Marcus 33
Gandhi, Indira 5, 252
Gandhi, Mahatma 201, 359
Genet, Jean 437
Gide, André 36
Glissant, Édouard 37
Global South 48
Gordimer, Nadine 7–8, 38, 39, 42, 289, 313, 343, 347, 398–9, 401–6, 434, 561; in chapter overviews 397, 426
Gorky, Maxim 9, 21, 26, 43, 362, 379, 386, 440–7, 523–4, 535; in chapter overview 353
Gramsci, Antonio 20, 46
Grenada 220, 223, 227, 244
Group Areas Act 4, 55, 65, 72, 89n4, 155, 259, 264, 289, 372, 432, 456, 532
Gumede, Josiah 34, 193, 277

Hani, Chris 3
Harney, Stefano 37

Havana 5, 10, 16, 17, 18, 22, 26, 41, 50, 207, 219, 244; in chapter overview 206
Head, Bessie 28
Helsinki Conference 525
Hughes, Langston 36
Hutchinson, Alfred 39, 42, 372–3, 434

Immorality Act 106–16, 187; in chapter overview 123
In the Fog of the Seasons' End (La Guma) 19, 21, 32, 536, 561, 562; in chapter overview 489
Israel 40, 230–4, 238–43, 325–6, 542–3

Jameson, Fredric 49

Kenyatta, Jomo 275, 276
Kgositsile, Keorapetse 438
King, Martin Luther, Jr, 50, 274, 280; in chapter overview 273
Kotane, Moses 3
Kumalo, A. N. C. (Ronald 'Ronnie' Kasrils) 424, 549
Kunene, Mazisi (Raymond) 4, 255, 268, 424, 437; in chapter overview 426

La Guma, Bartholomew (Barto) 17
La Guma, Blanche 1, 4, 5, 14, 17, 44
La Guma, Eugene 17
La Guma, James (Jimmy) 20, 33, 147

Labour Party (South Africa) 74, 152–3, 158, 162–3, 185, 186–9
Lebanon 255, 368, 542; Israel's invasion of 40, 234, 238, 243; in chapter overview 230
Land Act (Natives Land Act, 1913) 174, 284, 428, 429
Lenin, Vladimir 34, 36, 92n10, 93n11, 194, 207, 209, 349, 383, 444, 527. *See also* Marxism–Leninism
Lotus (journal) 6, 13, 18, 39, 43, 48, 330, 368, 370–1, 436, 555; in chapter overviews 230, 234, 252, 318, 321, 333, 353, 358, 373, 408, 419, 426, 440, 451, 469, 479, 489, 499, 540
Lotus Prize for Literature (Lotus Award) 5, 19, 42, 328, 330, 358, 362, 549, 554; in chapter overview 252
Lukács, Georg 405, 562
Lumumba, Patrice 50, 275; in chapter overview 273
Lusaka Manifesto 116
Luthuli, Albert (Chief) 291, 362, 375

Machel, Samora 249
Macmillan, Hugh 16, 17n1
Mandela, Nelson 32, 311
Manley, Michael 203; in chapter overview 202
Martí, José 206, 244, 338, 340
Marx, Karl 47, 273, 345n2, 349, 444, 547–8

Marxism 16, 47, 196, 206, 209, see also Karl Marx, Marxism-Leninism

Marxism–Leninism 32, 103, 170, 211, 215; politics 34, 211; writings 215; language 196; theory 345

Mbeki, Govan 436

Mda, Zakes 38

Ministry of Coloured Affairs 63, 151

Mixed Marriages Act 106, 107

Modisane, Bloke 26, 343, 437; in chapter overview 426

Mogadishu Declaration 117

Moretti, Franco 24

Moscow 10, 17, 18, 22, 34, 35, 193, 198, 385, 518; in chapter overview 451

Moten, Fred 37

Moscow News (journal) 18; in chapter overview 192

Mphahlele, Ezekiel (Es'kia) 6, 20, 26, 37, 38, 50, 230, 343, 348, 398, 400, 401, 404, 438

Mtshali, Oswald Joseph (Mbuyiseni) 39, 42, 343, 364–7, 375, 408–18, 424, 549

National Liberation League (NLL, South Africa) 147, 154

National Party (Nationalist Party, South Africa) 61, 73, 107, 124, 125, 132, 139, 141, 148, 150, 162, 188, 257, 223, 433

Native Republic thesis 34

Nazism 31, 70, 78, 150, 273, 520, 541, 548

Ndebele, Njabulo 50

Négritude 6, 7, 338–9, 398–9, 401

Neto, Agostinho 321, 322, 549, 552

Neruda, Pablo 42, 388, 419–22

New Age (newspaper) 2, 19, 93n12, 373, 535, 559, 560

New Jewel Movement (Grenada) 223

Newton, Huey 22

Ngũgĩ wa Thiong'o (James Ngũgĩ) 6, 28, 255, 297, 328, 338, 340, 346, 549, 560

Nixon, Richard 168, 169, 280

Nkosi, Lewis 26, 38, 51, 255, 437; in chapter overview 426

Nkrumah, Kwame 275, 338, 400; in chapter overview 171

Non-Aligned Movement (NAM) 45, 243, 252, 541, 543

Non-European United Front (NEUF, South Africa) 147

Non-European Unity Movement (NEUM, South Africa) 151, 154, 559

Nzo, Alfred 122, 207

Odendaal, André 2, 19

Okara, Gabriel 369

Organisation of African Unity (OAU) 45, 121, 266, 309, 541; in chapter overview 117

Padmore, George 29, 36, 338; in chapter overview 171

Palestine Liberation Organization (PLO) 234, 239, 326, 542

Pan Africanist Congress (PAC) 20; in chapter overview 85

Pasternak, Boris 387

Paton, Alan 4, 289, 435, 561; in chapter overview 426

Plaatje, Solomon (Sol) 33, 313, 343

Population Registration Act 4, 126, 155, 432, 532

Présence Africaine (journal) 18; in chapter overview 281

Progress Publishers (Moscow) 17

Quayson, Ato 39

Reagan, Ronald 217–9, 226–7, 243, 244; administration of 40, 223, 228, 244, 543–4

Reddy, E. S. (Enuga Sreenivasulu) 106

Rive, Richard 27, 343, 562–3

Rivonia Trial 311

Robben Island 374, 375, 437, 515

Robeson, Paul 41, 273–80

Roux, E. (Edward) 103

Sachs, Albie 50

Said, Edward 17, 25n14, 36

Sartre, Jean-Paul 29

Schreiner, Olive 38, 343, 348

Sechaba (journal) 6, 18, 32, 44, 48, 530–3; in chapter overviews 55, 58, 64, 69, 75, 80, 97, 185, 202, 244, 266, 293, 295, 513

Second World 45, 48; Second Worldism 35

Sembène Ousmane 338, 550

Seme, Pixley ka Isaka 33, 300, 428

Separate Representation of Voters Act 149

September, Reginald (Reggie) 3; in chapter overview 85

Sharpeville Massacre 20, 155, 372; in chapter overview 489

Sheikhzadeh, Maksud 358

Sholokhov, Mikhail 387, 524

Simpson, Thula 16, 17n1

Sixth Pan-African Congress 171

Skotnes, Cecil 312, 313, 314–15, 316, 318

Small, Adam 27, 159

Smith, Ian 183

Solzhenitsyn, Alexander 42, 377–88

South African Coloured People's Organisation (SACPO) 34; in chapter overviews 85, 530

South African Communist Party (SACP) 16, 102, 207, 249; Programme of 174n1, 180n7, 390. See also Communist Party of South Africa (CPSA)

South African Indian Congress (SAIC) 154

Soyinka, Wole 28, 46

Spanish Civil War 420, 520, 528
Special Committee Against Apartheid (United Nations) 106, 202, 305
Spillers, Hortense 37
Stone Country, The (La Guma) 3, 19, 20, 562
Suppression of Communism Act 4, 34, 156, 263, 289
SWAPO (South West Africa People's Organisation) 205, 234, 239, 249

Tambo, Oliver 29, 32, 183
Tangential literature (concept) 30
Tashkent 10, 22, 27, 41, 44, 328, 329, 341, 451–4, 540; in chapter overview 319
Themba, Can 26, 343
Third World 5, 18, 22, 25, 28, 31, 41, 45, 48, 197, 244, 296, 354, 377, 545, 546, 552; Third Worldism 33, 35
Time of the Butcherbird (La Guma) 19n8, 21; in chapter overview 469
Transcription Centre (London) in chapter overviews 255, 454, 510
Treason Trial 20, 155, 372, 392
Tricontinental (journal) 18; in chapter overviews 171, 199, 238, 257, 336
Tripartite Alliance 47
Trotsky, Leon 562
Turner, Richard (Rick) 32

Umkhonto we Sizwe (MK) 32, 58, 77, 164, 222; in chapter overview 222
Unit on Apartheid (United Nations) 135n11, 139n22, 140nn26–7, 140n30, 141n32, 142n34, 143n35, 175n2, 306, 307n4; in chapter overviews 106, 123
United Nations Special Committee on Apartheid 40, 202
United Nations (UN) 55, 121, 200, 229, 241, 309, 541, 548; Charter of 305
United Party (South Africa) 62, 63, 72–3, 116, 150, 154, 157, 158, 563

van der Ross, R. E. (Richard Ernest) 74, 77, 152
van der Vlies, Andrew 18n5, 25n15, 49
van Riebeeck, Jan 88, 172, 283, 297
Verwoerd, Hendrik, Dr, 64, 101, 260, 261, 285, 286, 302
Vietnam 40, 165–70, 218, 220, 234–7, 274, 354, 356, 360, 362, 424, 542, 554; in chapter overview 488; people of 57, 327, 363, 334, 357

Walk in the Night, A (La Guma) 2, 12, 19, 20, 21, 509, 560, 562; in chapter overview 499
Wankie Campaign 32

World Peace Council 167; in chapter overviews 165, 489
Wright, Richard 31, 346

Young, Kevin 44
Young Communist League 20, 522

Zimbabwe African People's Union (ZAPU) 183, 267, 268
Zionism 231, 234, 235, 239, 324, 332, 341